Legal Writing: Getting It Right and Getting It Written

Second Edition

By

Mary Barnard Ray
University of Wisconsin Law School

Jill J. Ramsfield
Georgetown University Law Center

AMERICAN CASEBOOK SERIES®

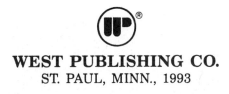

WEST PUBLISHING CO.
ST. PAUL, MINN., 1993

American Casebook Series, the key symbol appearing on the front
cover and the WP symbol are registered trademarks of West Publishing
Co. Registered in the U.S. Patent and Trademark Office.
COPYRIGHT © 1987 WEST PUBLISHING CO.

COPYRIGHT © 1993 By WEST PUBLISHING CO.
                        610 Opperman Drive
                        P.O. Box 64526
                        St. Paul, MN 55164–0526
                        1–800–328–9352

Library of Congress Cataloging-in-Publication Data

Ray, Mary Barnard.
    Legal writing—getting it right and getting it written / by Mary
Barnard Ray, Jill J. Ramsfield. — 2nd ed.
        p.   cm.
    ISBN 0–314–02255–4
    1. Legal composition.   2. Law—United States—Language.
I. Ramsfield, Jill J.   II. Title.
KF250.R39   1993
808' .06634—dc20   93–22762
                                                            CIP

ISBN 0–314–02255–4

 TEXT IS PRINTED ON 10% POST
CONSUMER RECYCLED PAPER

    R. & R.–Leg.Writing 2d Ed.
    2nd Reprint—1995

To William, Kathryn, and Mark;

———————

To Eugenio, mio caro;

———————

and to our students.

*

Introduction

This book addresses the full scope of questions that professional legal writers face, questions that arise from the nature of legal discourse itself. In legal writing, both lawyers and students must simultaneously interpret and translate archaic legal language. The interpretation requires facility in language that is hundreds of years old; the translation requires precise transfer of concepts into modern English. And the varied audience of experts, non-lawyers, clients, and judges makes that translation even more challenging. Often the legal writer is not sure what audience will read a given document, and must adjust accordingly. Moreover, the purpose of legal documents varies widely: a letter may be designed to inform, persuade, motivate, warn, cajole, or request. The scope of a document's content may range from a narrow question to the broader history and analysis of a legal concept. Even the role of the writer may vary, with the writer sometimes deferential, sometimes commanding.

To interpret and translate effectively in this complex world of multiple audiences, purposes, scope of content, and roles, legal writers must constantly adjust their approaches and analyses. Conceptually, it is a labor that requires Herculean intellect and fortitude.

But this Hercules needs the speed of Atatlanta, too. Lawyers are pressed to work harder and faster than they ever have, and their work requires more researching and more writing. Faced with these pressures, the writer is too often tempted to release a document with problems unresolved and questions unanswered because the next project is waiting impatiently. But projects should not be released prematurely, nor should they require more time. Instead, the answers should be available for ready reference.

This book is a desktop reference that provides quick, reliable answers to those questions, whether they arise from the writing process or the product itself. It addresses questions that occur to all legal writers, such as identifying the writing priorities for complaints or the proper uses of commas. It also addresses the individual writer's propensities with entries on such topics as writing blocks and perfectionism. It covers small particulars, such as whether to use *infer* or *imply*, and large issues, such as research strategies. This book helps the legal writer resolve incidental problems, review a document efficiently, and develop an overall writing process. It is designed to serve as a professional resource, handbook, and style manual.

This books answers the busy lawyer's questions on the job, the law student's questions at the word processor, and all legal writers' questions about process of writing well under pressure. The book also addresses the individual writer's quirks and habits. For example, some writers enjoy starting a project, but bog down in the middle and then rush at the end. Some are good at organizing information but have trouble translating that organization into smooth, coherent sentences. And some are perfectionists, stopping at every sentence, enjoying the perfecting, while the clock ticks away and other projects accumulate. This book helps the legal writer even out, refine, and develop his or her approach to researching and writing.

This book also helps the legal writer develop over time. What sufficed in undergraduate studies falters in law school and may fail in practice. Year by year, lawyers must achieve more, becoming more prolific, more productive, and perhaps more profound. Such development requires a conscious effort to release old habits that are no longer useful to gain new ones that are. This book allows legal writers to examine in detail the written product and the manner of writing it.

Use this book, then, to identify the places in your writing that need improvement. Make a list of entries that are useful, then return to those entries whenever the question reoccurs. When you no longer need to return to them, you can move on to other entries, thus creating a plan of long-term improvement for your writing. This book is yours to use as a reference, a text, or both. You can tailor its use to your writing, your process, and your personality. Mark it up, fold down page corners, and comment in the margins. Make it your own personal legal writing guide.

Acknowledgements

We thank the many contributors to this book: students, practitioners, and non-lawyers. They offered ideas for entries, corrections on the first edition, and reflections on overall content.

Thanks to our readers of the first edition, whose attention to detail and critical perspectives enlivened the second edition: Eleonora Di Liscia, Elizabeth Nork, Nancy E. Nunan, Kristin Oelstrom, and Jennifer Widmer. Special thanks to Noelle Adgerson, whose cheer and efficiency kept communications between us timely.

We also thank our family and friends, who cheered us on throughout the second edition; Kathy Soukup, who provided excellent child care; and Dennis and Gene, who always understand. We thank each other for the synergy that continues to develop as we work through the abstract toward the concrete with humor, openness, and good will.

*

How to Use This Book

All the entries are arranged alphabetically. The book, therefore, is one large index with text or cross-references under each entry, so that individual entries are easy to find. For example, to determine how to punctuate a list, you can look under LISTS, STRUCTURE OF or SEMI-COLONS or COMMAS. For ideas on how to design and structure issues, you can look under ISSUE STATEMENTS or BRIEFS. If you do not find the answers you need under the term you check first, think of an idea related to the entry and look there, or check the list of entries. Thus you should be able to find your answer easily. If, after finding the entry you were looking for, you want more information on related topics, you can find that information by referring to the other entries or outside sources cross-referenced within the entry.

To avoid a clutter of quotation marks, examples within the text are set off in italics. Longer examples are indented, good examples in bold type. In longer entries, subsections are numbered for easier and more precise reference. Citations used in examples are fictitious, but conform in format to *The Bluebook, A Uniform System of Citation* (15th ed. 1991). The one exception is book citations, which include the publisher so that readers can more easily find the book. Controversial grammatical points have been resolved in favor of the clearer choice for legal writing. When applicable, we have resolved these points according to the Blue-book, and the *U.S. Government Printing Office Style Manual* (1986), because these sources are the recognized authorities in legal writing.

Three common ways to use this book are as a textbook, a reference book, or a book for personal improvement. To help you with each of these uses, see the subsections below.

1.   USING THIS BOOK AS A TEXTBOOK

The book covers a number of topics that arise in legal writing. To teach a course or to fashion a personal course of action, read through the list of entries and group the entries that cover the subjects you wish to study. For example, if you are examining memo writing, you might want to assign or read all the entries under MEMOS in the topical index. Inherent in analysis is an approach to ORGANIZATION, so you might want also to assign entries listed under that topic. In addition, you might want to cover those entries under LEGAL ANALYSIS. Typical mistakes occur in memo writing, such as overuse of FLOWERY LANGUAGE and misuse of MODIFIERS, so you might want to add those entries as well. As you assign entries, you can list them in an order that makes sense to you. You may even create a quick reference, such as the one that follows.

QUICK GUIDE TO THE WRITING PROCESS
WRITING PROCESS

POLISHING

Individual legal writers encounter varied problems, depending on their writing backgrounds, and the Topical Index can also help identify groups of entries that address these individual problems. So, you can read a series of entries about common kinds of legal writing questions, such as the usage of *infer* and *imply* or *due to* and *because of*. You may also use this book to understand how legal writing differs from other kinds of writing in its demands for PRECISION, such as the using *that* for restrictive clauses and *which* for non-restrictive clauses.

You may also find this book especially helpful to you when you are commenting on another's writing. Teaching good legal writing through written responses requires precise and thorough comments, which are hard to create in the limited time available to most teachers. To make the most of your limited time, you can use the entry on the PRINCIPLES OF GOOD LEGAL WRITING or LEGAL WRITING CHECKLIST as a checklist of requirements for each paper. Refer writers to the list you choose, or adapt from that list a specific set of goals for each assignment, such as for COMPLAINTS or SCHOLARLY WRITING.

You may also use this book to provide more information that can assist writers in understanding your points, such as the specific examples of useful techniques and general approaches within entries. Choosing different individual entries for different writers allows you to fashion a course that emphasizes what you think your writers need; you can guide writers through the entries with your expertise.

Finally, use this book to save time by delegating to it the routine explanations. Rather than write a long description of a principle in the margins of a paper, refer writers to explanations in this book. This allows you to save your time for doing what only you can do, such as looking at the text as a whole, speaking to the individual writers behind that text, and commenting on how the general principles of writing are playing out in this particular piece of writing.

If you want to improve your students' comfort or efficiency at writing, pay particular attention to the process entries. Help students determine what their strongest and weakest areas, whether PREWRITING, REWRITING, or PROOFREADING, for example. Suggest that they search out the entries on that area, reread them, and put techniques into practice until they have broken any old habits. If a student PROCRASTINATES, suggest he read that entry and try to determine the cause. If another has WRITER'S BLOCK, suggest she read that entry and discover ways to break through that block. In general, students can read this book in the order that addresses their needs.

To help you if you are planning a course based on this book, we have attached the syllabus for a full-year course in legal research and writing, using this book as a text. Your course may differ, and you could rearrange the entries accordingly.

LEGAL RESEARCH & WRITING
SYLLABUS

UNIT 1: THE CLIENT LETTER

8/27/90   **Overview of the Legal Research and Writing Process; Client Interview**

Ray and Ramsfield (R&R): WRITING PROCESS, EXPOSITORY WRITING, GENERAL CORRESPONDENCE LETTERS, OPINION LETTER, PREWRITING

8/30/90   **Introduction to Legal Research and Citations: Locating and Using Constitutions and Statutes**

R&R: RESEARCH STRATEGY CHART; CITATIONS; CITATIONS, BASIC FORMATS

9/4/90   **Writing to Clients: the Opinion Letter; Reading and Interpreting Statutes—Introduction**

R&R: BAD NEWS, GIVING IT; BAD NEWS, SOFTENING IT; CLIENT LETTERS; CLOSINGS FOR LETTERS; OPENINGS FOR LETTERS; OPINION LETTERS; OPINION OR ADVICE?; TONE IN LETTERS; WRITING; WRITING BLOCK; PROCRASTINATION

9/6/90   **Interpreting Statutes**

R&R: LEGISLATION, RULES, LEGAL ANALYSIS, APPLICATION

9/10/90   **Introduction to Legal Research & Citation: Locating and Using Cases and Digests**

R&R: CITATIONS; CITATIONS, BASIC FORMATS; CITATIONS, PARALLEL; CITATIONS, STRING; PINPOINT CITES

2/22/91 **Appellate Advocacy: Writing the Summary of Argument and Conclusion; Putting the Pieces Together**

R&R: SUMMARY OF THE ARGUMENT, CONCLUSIONS

2/25/91 **NO CLASS—MENTAL HEALTH WEEK**

(Conferences begin later in the week)

3/4/91 **Introduction to Oral Advocacy Conferences on Appellate Brief (throughout the week)**

R&R: ORAL PRESENTATIONS

3/5/91 **Speaker on Oral Advocacy**

3/7/91 **Oral Argument Demonstrations**

3/8/91 **Videotape Demonstrations of Oral Argument**

3/9/91–3/17/91 **Oral Arguments, Round 1**

3/11/91 **Practicing Precision: Cutting the Brief in Half**

R&R: REWRITING, POSITIONS OF EMPHASIS, CONCISENESS, SENTENCE LENGTH, SENTENCE STRUCTURE, TOPIC SENTENCES, SUBJECT–VERB COMBINATIONS, PARAGRAPH BLOCKS, PARAGRAPH LENGTH, PASSIVE VOICE, TRANSITIONS, VOICE

3/14/91 **Fine-Tuning the Brief**

R&R: PRECISION

3/18/91 **TBA**

3/22/91 **APPELLATE BRIEFS DUE**

3/25/91–3/31/91 SPRING BREAK

4/1/91–4/14/91 **Oral Arguments—Round 2**

4/15/91 **Final Class: Notes on Practice; Evaluations**
CONGRATULATIONS!

2. USING THIS BOOK AS A REFERENCE

You may want to use this book in short spurts, building up categories of information and areas of improvement. For example, you may be writing a brief and be unsure about whether to use *affect* or *effect*. Rather than guessing which to use, you can look it up quickly, fix it, and move on. Or you might be puzzling too long over the POINT HEADINGS of your argument. To speed up the process, look up that entry, apply the techniques to your document, make the adjustments, and move to the next task. If you are having trouble getting started on a tough letter to a client, you can turn to the entries on BAD NEWS, GIVING IT or BAD NEWS, SOFTENING IT, and imitate the form to get started.

You can then refine to your own style and approach once you have begun.

To see the possibilities, consult the following list of entries.

LIST OF ENTRIES

AND
AND/OR
ANIMALS, ARE THEY HE, SHE, OR IT?
ANSWER TO COMPLAINTS
ANTECEDENTS
ANTE- OR ANTI-?
ANTI- OR ANTE-? (See ANTE- OR ANTI-?)
ANYBODY, SINGULAR OR PLURAL?
ANYONE, SINGULAR OR PLURAL?
A OR AN?
APOSTROPHES
APPEAL
APPELLATE BRIEF
APPENDIX
APPLICATION
APPOSITIVES
ARGUMENT HEADINGS (See POINT HEADINGS.)
ARGUMENT SECTION
ARTICLES, GRAMMAR
ARTICLES, PUBLISHED
AS
AS A MATTER OF FACT
AS IF OR AS THOUGH?
AS OR LIKE?
AS PER
ASSONANCE
ASTERISKS
AS THOUGH OR AS IF? (See AS IF OR AS THOUGH?)
AS TO
AT THE TIME THAT
AT THIS POINT IN TIME
ATTORNEY OR LAWYER?
AUDIENCE
AUXILIARY VERB (See VERBS, AUXILIARY.)

BACKGROUND FACTS
BAD NEWS, GIVING IT
BAD NEWS, SOFTENING IT
BAD OR BADLY?
BAR GRAPHS
BASED ON
BASICALLY
BECAUSE OR SINCE?
BEGINNING (See GETTING STARTED or OPENINGS FOR LET-
    TERS.)
BENDING THE RULES
BETWEEN OR AMONG? (See AMONG OR BETWEEN?)

3. USING THIS BOOK AS A PATHFINDER

A third way to use this book is to develop your own plan for improvement with a little less structure than a course, but a more systematic approach than just looking up questions as they arise. This is the pathfinder approach, and is particularly useful for improving process or working on one particular aspect of writing as it applies to many legal writing situations.

One way to do this is to start recording entries you consult as you are writing. Over time, note the entries that you look up the most. You might keep a separate file, or mark this book with your own code of tabs to remind yourself periodically of those trouble areas. You might keep a list.

Date	Reader	Main Problems	Entries

After you have identified these areas, you can begin collecting further feedback. For example, specifically request feedback about those areas from your colleagues or supervisor. You can also read cross-referenced entries, especially those that discuss the related, broader topics. Gradually, after you categorize these areas, read supplemental entries when you are beginning the writing process or when you get to those areas of concern. Consciously build techniques to combat the problems. This way, you may gradually remove weaknesses and develop strengths.

Another way to encourage and guide your own improvement is to set goals for yourself as a writer and work toward those goals over time. Rather than starting with your problem, begin with your interest and read entries that are related to that interest. You can move through the book gradually, in order of importance for you. To help you find related entries of interest to you, we have added a topical list of entries following this introduction.

Remember that many good writers have models. Add to the examples in this book the good examples of your colleagues, professors, supervisors, and so on. Keep a personal library of examples, methods, tricks for efficiency and effectiveness. Also collect models of processes. Observe how others solve writing problems, and ask how they arrived at those solutions.

If you think about your writing, keep trying new approaches, honestly evaluate the success of your efforts, and try again, you will see gradual, but certain, improvement over the course of your career. Rather than risking burnout or stagnation, you will periodically recreate your writing process. Over time, you will broaden your capabilities and deepen your capacity for sophisticated, straightforward legal prose.

TOPICAL LIST OF ENTRIES

WRITING PROCESS

General Concepts

VARIOUS LEGAL DOCUMENTS

CHECKLISTS

GRAMMAR CONCEPTS

Generally

Nouns

HOW TO USE THIS BOOK

ORGANIZATION

Large-Scale

Small-Scale

In Specific Kinds of Documents

Processes of Organization

*

Legal Writing: Getting It Right and Getting It Written

Second Edition

*

ABBREVIATIONS IN TEXT

Use abbreviations only in the following situations.

1. Abbreviate the name of a party if the initials are widely recognized, such as *NLRB* or *NBC*. See Bluebook rule 6.1.

2. Abbreviate words commonly used and abbreviated in company titles, such as *Co., Corp., Inc., Ltd., &,* and *No.* See Bluebook rule 10.2.1(c).

3. Abbreviate conventional personal titles, such as *Mr.* and *Ms.*

4. In CITATIONS, abbreviate according to the form your AUDIENCE uses.

For related information, see INITIALS.

ABHORRENCE OF OR ABHORRENCE FOR?

Use *abhorrence of; abhorrence for* is incorrect.

ABOVE

Above is equivalent to *supra*. Although you can use *above* to refer the reader to previous text, avoid sending the reader back farther than a few paragraphs. Legal readers like to keep moving. For details about *supra*, see Bluebook rules 3.6 and 4.2.

When using *above* as a preposition, use it to indicate spatial relationships.

The defendant then placed the insecticide in the cabinet above the sink.

Use *over*, rather than *above*, to indicate higher quantities.

The driver was over 21.

rather than

The driver was above the age of 21.

For related information, see LEGALESE.

ABSTRACT NOUNS

Abstract nouns describe ideas or general concepts, in contrast to concrete nouns, which describe tangible items. For example, *justice* and *transportation* are abstract; *courtroom* and *bicycle* are concrete. In general, choose concrete nouns because they are more readable and more effective. Use abstract nouns when you need them to describe ideas accurately or to de-emphasize an unfavorable fact, such as the details of an auto accident caused by your client. In that situation, you might use the abstract noun *vehicle* rather than the concrete noun

1

truck. For problems related to abstract nouns, see PRECISION, subsections 3 and 7, and ACCURACY, subsection 1(b). For uses of abstract nouns, see EMPHASIS, subsection 2.

ACCURACY

In legal writing, you must always be accurate. Even when you are revising for READABILITY and eloquence, do not sacrifice accuracy. The following rules should help you maintain accuracy while REVISING.

1. Accuracy in WORD CHOICE.

(a) Use only one term to identify each key person, thing, or idea.

Even though the defendant <u>admitted</u> while in custody that he had been using drugs, this <u>admission</u> of impropriety is not relevant to the present case.

rather than

Even though the defendant <u>commented</u> while in custody that he had been using drugs, this <u>admission</u> of impropriety is not relevant to the present case.

The latter version leaves the reader guessing but not knowing the exact relationship between *commented* and *admission of impropriety*. Using synonyms is particularly risky with legal readers because they will wonder if your changed terms mean you changed meaning, when you may have only been trying to add VARIETY. For more examples and discussion of this point, see REPETITION and AMBIGUITY, WAYS TO AVOID.

(b) Use the most specific word you can. Often inaccuracies occur because the writer chose an unnecessarily general term and as a result inadvertently broadened the term's reference. For example, do not say *vehicle* when you mean to refer only to *school bus*. For more on this, see PRECISION.

(c) Make the meaning of your words clear in context so you avoid unintended innuendo or humor.

She released him from employment as soon as she was no longer bedridden.

rather than,

She let him go as soon as she could get out of bed.

The first version is not as concise or as interesting, but it is accurate. Although you always need to be accurate in legal writing, you may sometimes need to be less specific, even somewhat vague. For discussions of times you may avoid specificity, see EMPHASIS, subsection 2 and EXPLANATIONS, WHEN AND HOW MUCH?

2

(d) Make sure each pronoun is unambiguous. For example, if only one woman is mentioned in your text, you need not worry about *she* causing inaccuracy. If, however, two or more appear, then *she* is likely to be ambiguous. In this situation, check each *she*.

> **Ms. Jones did not ask Ms. Wilson to double-check the amount, because Ms. Wilson [not she] routinely checked all the amounts listed.**

For more on this, see PRONOUNS and AMBIGUITY, WAYS TO AVOID.

(e) Make sure each *this* is unambiguous. *This* is the pronoun most likely to cause inaccuracies. *This* can refer to an idea or a thing, one word or a whole sentence; as a result, you must make sure that the reader always knows what *this* means. If there is any question, add the appropriate noun after *this*.

> **The court reasoned that the difference in the age of the fetuses was not the factor determining this issue. This reasoning** ....

For more examples, see THIS; PRONOUNS; and AMBIGUITY, WAYS TO AVOID.

2. Accuracy in sentence structure.

Place all modifiers and modifying phrases immediately next to the word modified.

> **Our client has arranged with other subcontractors to fill the ditches.**

rather than

> Our client has arranged to fill the ditches with other subcontractors.

For related general information, see MODIFIERS and SENTENCE STRUCTURE.

3. Accuracy in citations.

(a) Make sure all the volume and page numbers are correct. Incorrect cites irritate readers. The reader checking the cite gets the volume listed, flips to the page, and finds some case having nothing to do with the point. See CITATIONS and CITATIONS, BASIC FORMATS.

(b) Use a pinpoint cite to refer to a particular rule, holding, quotation, or proposition in a source. PINPOINT CITES pinpoint the exact page. These specific references are greatly appreciated by any reader whose job it is to evaluate the merits of the point being made. For a general discussion of citations, see CITATIONS; CITATIONS, BASIC FORMATS; and CITATIONS, PARALLEL.

(c) Use correct citation form. Especially watch the spacing, a frequent source of error. Judges in particular find citation errors distracting, so use letter-perfect citations to enhance your credibility. For details on proper citation form, see CITATIONS; CITATIONS, BASIC FORMAT; CITATIONS, PARALLEL; and CITATIONS, STRING.

For general accuracy concerns in the earlier stages of the WRITING PROCESS, see ORGANIZATION, LARGE–SCALE and ORGANIZATION, SMALL–SCALE. For accuracy concerns in some specific legal situations, see CONTRACTS, DRAFTING; GENERAL CORRESPONDENCE LETTERS; and BAD NEWS, SOFTENING IT. For related writing concerns, see PRECISION.

ACTIVE VERBS

See ACTIVE VOICE.

ACTIVE VOICE

Active voice is the term for the grammatical structure indicating that the subject of the sentence performs or causes the action expressed by the verb. Because the subject does the acting and the verb describes that action, active voice moves the reader's eye from the left to right.

The boy hit the ball.

Defendant argued that the court should suppress the evidence.

The court decided that freedom of association was not an issue.

This use of active voice prevents the legal reader from having to double back to understand the point.

The ball was hit by the boy.

It was argued by the defendant that the evidence should be suppressed by the court.

It was decided that freedom of association was not an issue.

The passive voice can also create a sentence that is less precise, as in the last example, which makes the reader wonder who decided.

Active voice also makes the sentence shorter in most cases.

The court held that the plaintiff could not collect punitive damages.

rather than

It was held by the court that punitive damages could not be collected by the plaintiff.

4

Therefore, if wordiness is a problem in your writing, read through the draft once when REVISING just for passive voice. Check each subject and verb and translate from passive to active whenever active is appropriate. For related information, see CONCISENESS.

Use active voice unless the writing requires the passive for effect. For examples of times when passive is useful, see PASSIVE VOICE.

Additionally, use active voice to eliminate any ambiguity caused by vague verbs, such as *consists of, concerns,* or *involves.*

> **The government's actions in this case violated the plaintiff's right to privacy.**

rather than

> This case involves the right to privacy.

Active voice also can eliminate ambiguity caused by linking verbs, such as *seems, feels,* or *were.*

> **The court has presented two inconsistent standards of review in jury misconduct cases.**

rather than

> The court seems unsure about the standard of review in these kinds of cases.

Use linking verbs only when they accurately state the situation.

> **Awarding custody to the mother is in the best interests of the children.**

For related information, see VERBS, LINKING.

ACTUALLY

Actually means *in fact.* It is an ADVERB used to communicate that the action stated did indeed happen and the writer is communicating literally, not figuratively.

> **The defendant actually hid the knife by sliding it under the cake.**

Because legal writers rarely use figurative speech, they also rarely use *actually.* Therefore, for ACCURACY, avoid using it casually. See also LITERAL MEANING and FIGURATIVE MEANING.

AD HOC

This Latin phrase means *for a particular, specific purpose.* Usually it applies either to committees that have been created to fulfill a certain function or to situations that are unusual and need particular attention.

> **The ad hoc committee on Zoning Enforcement will meet each Thursday for four weeks.**

or

> **The <u>ad hoc</u> solution is to pay the directors less and the workers more.**

In legal writing, ad hoc is neither capitalized nor italicized. As with all LATIN PHRASES, use it sparingly; substitute English where possible. For related information, see READABILITY, LATIN PHRASES, and JARGON. See also LITERAL MEANING and FIGURATIVE MEANING.

ADJECTIVES

Adjectives modify nouns or pronouns. Proper adjectives are adjectives derived from proper names. Capitalize most proper adjectives: *American banking system*, *the Atlantic seaboard*, *Vietnamese refugees*. Do not capitalize an adjective derived from a proper name when it has been used frequently and for a long time in the general language: *cesarean operation*, *india ink*, *italic type*, *murphy bed*, or *venetian blinds*.

For an extensive list of adjectives derived from proper names, see *U.S. Government Printing Office Style Manual* (1984).

Predicate adjectives are adjectives that follow linking verbs, such as *is* or *seems*, and describe the subject of those verbs.

> **The case is <u>relevant</u>.**

Use adjectives only when they are needed or, as Twain said, "As to the adjective: when in doubt, strike it out." If you find yourself writing several adjectives to modify one noun, stop and find the noun that more precisely states your meaning.

> **Mr. Barnes has frequently testified as an expert witness on bone disease.**

rather than

> Mr. Barnes is a known, respected, and often-used authority on bone diseases.

For related examples and explanation, see MODIFIERS.

ADJECTIVES AFTER A LINKING VERB

Adjectives after the verb do not require hyphens.

> **The youth was fear stricken and guilt ridden.**

rather than

> The youth was fear-stricken and guilt-ridden.

In contrast, adjectives placed before the subject may need HYPHENS.

> **The fear-stricken, guilt-ridden youth could not move from the street.**

6

ADVERBS

Adverbs modify verbs, adjectives, or other adverbs.

Mr. Smith justly cannot be penalized for acting very carefully.

Avoid overusing them; too many adverbs can bog down a sentence while adding a minimum of information. Three adverbs you can omit readily are *clearly, merely,* and *obviously.* Another adverb you can view with suspicion is *very,* because it usually weakens the point rather than strengthening it, as in the example above. For related information, see CLEARLY, OBVIOUSLY, VERY, CONCISENESS, and MODIFIERS.

AFFECT OR EFFECT?

In legal writing you usually want *effect* when using the noun and *affect* when using the verb.

This law had a sweeping effect.

but

This law affected police procedures.

This is because *effect* as a noun means *something that was the result of another action,* while *affect* as a noun means a *feeling.* *Affect* as a verb, however, means *to influence.* Occasionally you will need *effect* as a verb if you mean *to cause to come into being.*

Through persistent lobbying, the group effected a change in the inheritance laws.

AFORESAID

When writing to clients, substitute *mentioned earlier, named earlier,* or some other more explanatory phrase. One of the most virulent complaints coming from the general public is that lawyers use LEGALESE, and *aforesaid* is viewed as legalese.

In a legal document written to be read by other lawyers, such as a pleading, you may use *aforesaid,* but you must use it precisely because lawyers will interpret the term literally. Never toss it in carelessly, thinking that it will in itself add a patina of authenticity to the document. *Aforesaid* means you are referring to something mentioned earlier rather than something mentioned afterward. For example, you would say the *aforesaid defendant* only if another defendant is mentioned later and you mean to exclude that other defendant. Do not use *aforesaid defendant* if you have only one defendant or if you mean to include all defendants.

If you observe this rule, you will find that you have few occasions to use *aforesaid.*

AFRICAN AMERICAN OR AFRICAN–AMERICAN?

Write it without the hyphen, just as you would write *Swedish American* or *Chinese American*. *African American* is capitalized because it derives from the names of geographic areas. Many people prefer *African American* over *black;* be sensitive to the preferences of your AUDIENCE.

AGES

Use NUMERALS for ages, unless the age is the first word in a sentence.

The document is 75 years old.

but

Sixty-five year olds are eligible for Social Security.

Use HYPHENS when the age is expressed as a modifier before a noun.

She is a 6–year–old child.

But do not use hyphens when it comes after a linking verb.

She was 6 years old.

AGREEMENT, SUBJECTS AND VERBS

Agreement here means using plural verbs with plural subjects and singular verbs with singular subjects. Problems with agreement most frequently occur when the subject and verb are separated by a long phrase and the writer loses track of the subject along the way. As a result, the verb may agree with some noun in the long phrase rather than with the subject. You can usually avoid this problem by keeping the subject and verb close together. This will also improve the readability of your text.

Since 1979, <u>section 4</u> of the Export Administration Act has created much controversy. That section gives the President authority to impose foreign policy and national security controls on exports.

rather than

Since 1979, the <u>section</u> of the Export Administration Act giving the President authority to impose foreign policy and national security controls on exports *have created* much controversy.

For a general discussion of related concerns, see READABILITY and SENTENCE STRUCTURE.

AGREEMENTS, WRITTEN

See CONTRACTS, DRAFTING.

AGREE TO OR AGREE WITH?

The choice between *agree to* and *agree with* is based on IDIOM, which means there is a right or wrong choice in most cases. For example, you would always say, *I agree to help you*, but *I agree with your idea*.

In general, use *agree to* when the subject is concurring with something and will act accordingly. For example, *agree to* is frequently used in contracts.

We agree to represent you in this matter.

or

My client agrees to settle out of court with the following provisions.

Use *agree with* when the subject is voicing agreement but not making any actual commitments.

I agree with you that large settlements are increasing insurance premiums.

or

The State agrees with the court's concern for the preservation of fifth amendment rights, but ....

ALL AROUND OR ALL ROUND?

Use *all round*, because you mean *well rounded*, not *circling around*.

ALLITERATION

Alliteration is the repetition of similar consonant sounds, as the *f*'s in *fast and furious fighting*. Alliteration can occasionally be useful in legal writing because it can help the reader remember a phrase or can add drama, but it must be used sparingly and with care.

Having been terrified twice by the defendant's previous assaults, the plaintiff hesitated before she fled.

but not

Two times terrified, Theresa tarried before taking off down the alley.

When using alliteration, first be sure that the content of the phrase is indeed worth remembering. If it is not, the alliteration will be a distraction, no matter how graceful it sounds. Second, make sure that the repeated sound creates an appropriate feeling. For example, a repeated *t* sound can sound harsh, while a repeated *s* can sound soothing.

9

The attorney was known for the smoothness and simplicity of his writing style.

Finally, read the passage aloud to make sure it works, because *longer twisters torture tired readers*. For a discussion of related techniques, see ASSONANCE, EMPHASIS, and REPETITION.

ALL READY OR ALREADY?

All ready means a group is *prepared for some sort of action*. *Already* means *by this or a specified time or previously*.

ALL RIGHT OR ALRIGHT?

In legal writing, use the space. *Alright* is the informal, less accepted equivalent.

ALL ROUND OR ALL AROUND?

See ALL AROUND or ALL ROUND?

ALL, SINGULAR OR PLURAL?

All is singular when it means *the only thing*.

All that the new law can do is force the courts to resolve the conflict.

All is plural, however, when it means the *whole group*.

All the changes in the contract were made in writing.

ALL TOGETHER OR ALTOGETHER?

All together means that a group of people, things, or events are together. *Altogether* means *entirely and with all included or counted*, or *on the whole, with everything considered*.

The plaintiffs were all together as they left the courtroom.
but

Altogether, the medical costs for these victims exceeded $3 million.

ALREADY OR ALL READY?

See ALL READY OR ALREADY?

ALRIGHT OR ALL RIGHT?

See ALL RIGHT OR ALRIGHT?

ALTERNATIVE

Use *alternative* only when referring to two choices, not more. Commonly *alternative* is used when more than two choices exist; however, readers who enjoy the proper use of language will appreciate your precise use of *alternative*.

ALTHOUGH OR THOUGH?

In many situations you can use either word. *Although* is more elegant and therefore more appropriate for briefs, law review articles, and all but informal legal writings.

In two situations you can use *though* only.

1. Use *though* in such phrases as *even though* or *as though*.

2. Use *though* at the end of a sentence or at the end of a phrase.

She promised, though.

or

She promised, though, to come to the hearing.

Though at the end of a sentence is correct but rather informal for legal writing, so try substituting the following.

Nevertheless, she promised.

or

She promised, however, to come to the hearing.

ALTOGETHER OR ALL TOGETHER?

See ALL TOGETHER OR ALTOGETHER?

A.M.

It is written *a.m.* Use the phrase only after an hour.

We will meet at 9:00 a.m.

When *a.m.* appears at the end of a sentence, as in the previous example, use only one period.

AMBIGUITY, WAYS TO AVOID

In legal writing, a word or phrase is ambiguous if, in context, it permits more than one meaning. "Given a choice between a word that can carry the proper meaning and one that must carry it, choose the latter." William Rivers, *Writing: Craft and Art* 34 (Prentice-Hall 1975). The following rules should help you avoid ambiguity.

1. Avoid misplaced MODIFIERS.

11

Sometimes a modifying phrase, because of its position, could modify any of several words in a sentence.

The defendant refused to service the car belonging to the man who insulted him <u>with good reason</u>.

Here *with good reason* should modify *refused* instead of *insulted*. To avoid ambiguity, place the modifying phrase right next to the word modified.

The defendant, <u>with good reason</u>, refused to service the car belonging to the man who had insulted him.

For other problems associated with modifiers, see MODIFIERS, DANGLING and MODIFIERS, SQUINTING.

2. Avoid ambiguous PRONOUNS.

Sometimes pronouns cause ambiguity because they can logically refer to either of several nouns. The pronoun most likely to cause ambiguity is *this*, because *this* can refer to any idea or object.

You must ultimately make a judgment about the weight of the evidence. This will help you decide what the verdict should be.

Does *this* refer to *judgment* or *evidence*? To avoid the problem, add the appropriate noun after *this*.

You must ultimately make a judgment about the weight of the evidence. This judgment will help you decide what the verdict should be.

The pronoun second most likely to cause ambiguity is *it*, again because *it* can refer to any object or idea. Usually *it* becomes ambiguous when some other noun comes between *it* and the antecedent, which is the noun to which *it* refers.

The first will is less ambiguous than the second will because it omits the deceased's spouse.

To solve this problem, you may replace *it* with the noun.

The first will is less ambiguous than the second because the first will omits the decedent's spouse.

Or you may rephrase the sentence, so that no other noun comes between *it* and its antecedent.

The second will created some confusion by referring to the decedent's spouse; as a result, the first will is less ambiguous because it omits the decedent's spouse.

Although *this* and *it* are the most likely offenders, all pronouns should be watched for potential ambiguity. In general, check *he* or *she* whenever the content of your writing involves two people of the same sex. Check *they* to make sure there is no question about who is included in the group. *We* is a special problem in legal writing because you may, by using *we*, inadvertently speak for your whole law firm or organization. Never use *we* when you really mean *I*; use *we* only when you are speaking officially for the organization of which you are a part, as one judge may do when drafting an opinion for the whole bench. For related information, see PRONOUNS and ANTECEDENTS.

3. Avoid unnecessary vagueness.

   (a) Use only one term to identify each key person, thing, or idea.

> **Even though the defendant <u>admitted</u> while in custody that he had been using drugs, this <u>admission</u> of impropriety is not relevant to the present case.**

rather than

> Even though the defendant <u>commented</u> while in custody that he had been using drugs, this <u>admission</u> of impropriety is not relevant to the present case.

The latter version leaves the reader guessing but not knowing the exact relationship between commented and admission of impropriety. Using synonyms is particularly risky with legal readers because they will wonder if your changed terms mean you changed meaning, when you may have only been trying to add VARIETY. For more examples and discussion of this point, see REPETITION.

(b) Use the most specific word you can. Often inaccuracies occur because the writer chose an unnecessarily general term and as a result inadvertently broadened the term's reference. For example, do not say vehicle when you mean to refer only to school bus. For more on this, see PRECISION.

(c) Make the meaning of your words clear in context.

> **She released him from employment as soon as she was no longer bedridden.**

rather than

> She let him go as soon as she could get out of bed.

Although the first version is not as concise or as interesting, it is accurate. Although you usually need to be specific in legal writing, you may need to be vague on some occasions. For a discussion of these exceptions, see EMPHASIS, subsection 2.

4. Avoid unnecessary abstraction.

   Use concrete nouns and specific verbs rather than ABSTRACT NOUNS and general verbs. This will help focus the reader on your main points.

> **The defendant moves to dismiss the case under Fed. R. Civ. P. 12(b)(6).**

rather than

This concerns the defendant's motion to dismiss.

For related information, see PERSUASIVE WRITING and EMPHASIS.

AMENDMENT CAPITALIZED?

Capitalize *amendment* when you are using it in text, but do not capitalize it in citations.

The Fourth Amendment to the United States Constitution prevents warrantless searches except in extraordinary conditions.

but

U.S. Const. amend. IV, § 1.

AMONG OR BETWEEN?

Use *between* when discussing two options and *among* when discussing more than two.

Conferences were held between the plaintiff's and the defendant's attorneys, the plaintiff's attorney and estate's trustees, and the defendant's attorney and the estate's trustees.

rather than

Conferences were held between the plaintiff's attorney, the defendant's attorney, and the estate's trustees.

Although the former version is less concise, it leaves no question about who met with whom.

Use *among* to indicate that more than two parties are meeting.

A conference was held among the plaintiff's attorney, the defendant's attorney, and the estate's trustee.

ANALOGOUS CASES

An analogous case is a case whose facts are similar to the factual situation being analyzed; thus the details of the analogous case are essential to the analysis. When writing your analysis in MEMOS or BRIEFS, describe those essential details, which may include the rule, the rationale, the holding, the LEGALLY SIGNIFICANT FACTS, or DICTA central to understanding the case's significance. Make sure that, if the comparison is essential to the analysis, you include enough information to allow the reader to compare or distinguish the analogous case from the subject of the memo or brief. Avoid including unnecessary detail. For related information, see ARGUMENT SECTION, DISCUSSION SECTION, RULES, HOLDINGS, and PARALLEL STRUCTURE.

AND

There are three points to remember about this conjunction. First, although it is not wrong to start a sentence with *and*, doing so draws attention to the word. Therefore, before starting a sentence with *and* ask yourself if that word is really what you want to emphasize. Often it is not.

Second, use *and* to join sentences only when the sentence logically should be joined with the verbal equivalent of a plus sign.

Finally, avoid overusing *and* to join sentences, because it can lead to long, lackluster sentences.

For related general information, see CONJUNCTIONS.

AND/OR

Avoid this construction because it creates ambiguity. Decide whether the logical connection between the two phrases, words, or clauses is disjunctive, which requires *or*, or conjunctive, which requires *and*.

> **The court may, in its discretion, meet with the child <u>or</u> parents <u>or both</u> to determine <u>all of</u> the following factors affecting the best interests of the child: (1) the child's own preferences, (2) the parents' ability <u>and</u> willingness to provide consistent, adequate care, <u>and</u> (3) the parents' willingness to cooperate with each other if joint custody is awarded.**

rather than

> The court may, in its discretion meet with the child <u>and/or</u> parents to determine factors affecting the best interests of the child, such as (1) the child's own preferences <u>and/or</u> desires, (2) the parents' ability <u>and/or</u> willingness to provide consistent <u>and/or</u> adequate care, <u>and/or</u> (3) the parents' willingness to cooperate with each other if joint custody is awarded.

If the items can be disjunctive, conjunctive, or both, state that explicitly.

> **Either the Company or its agents, or both, may** . . . .

rather than

> The Company and/or its agents may . . . .

For related information, see OR and AND.

ANIMALS, ARE THEY HE, SHE, OR IT?

Use *it*.

15

ANSWERS TO COMPLAINTS

When drafting an answer, your first substantive task is to tell the court which paragraphs in the COMPLAINT your client denies. If the client is making a general denial, you may state that in one paragraph.

Defendant denies each allegation in Plaintiff's complaint.

Your client may deny some, but not all, of the allegations. Then you must also tell the court which paragraphs your client admits and which the client can neither deny nor admit. For example, it may be only sensible to admit paragraphs that correctly identify your client, but your client may have insufficient knowledge to determine if paragraphs identifying other parties are correct. Additionally, your client may admit that some of the facts stated in the complaint are true, although he or she will usually deny the legal conclusions based on those facts. You may then have several paragraphs in your answer, grouping the references to the complaint's paragraphs as follows:

1. **Defendant admits the allegations in paragraphs 1, 5, 7, and 8.**

2. **Defendant denies the allegations in paragraphs 4, 9, 10, 11, and 12.**

3. **Defendant does not have sufficient information to admit or deny allegations in paragraphs 2, 3, and 6.**

Think carefully about the decisions made when answering, for your client's responses begin to shape the course of the litigation. As with all documents for a court, learn and follow all rules and forms in your jurisdiction. For general information, see PLEADINGS. For related information, see COMPLAINTS.

ANTECEDENTS

An antecedent is the noun to which a pronoun refers.

Ms. Williams' <u>aunt</u> willed her estate to charity.

Here *aunt* is the antecedent of *her*. For problems related to this, see AMBIGUITY, WAYS TO AVOID, subsection 2. For related information, see NOUNS and PRONOUNS.

ANTE– OR ANTI–?

Ante- means *in front of* or *before*, as in *antebellum*.

Anti- means *against*, or *opposite*, as in *anti-intellectual* and *antibody*.

ANYBODY, SINGULAR OR PLURAL?

Anybody uses singular verbs.

Anybody who believes in justice believes in a fair trial.

Anybody is rather informal, so use *anyone* in formal legal writing, such as briefs or articles.

ANYONE, SINGULAR OR PLURAL?

Anyone uses singular verbs.

Anyone is entitled to a fair trial.

A OR AN?

Use *an* before all nouns beginning with a vowel or vowel sound; this includes nouns that begin with *h* where the *h* is not voiced, such as *an hour*. Use *a* before all nouns beginning with a voiced consonant, such as *a hearing*. For related information, see ARTICLES, GRAMMAR.

APOSTROPHES

Apostrophes, like decimal points, belong in specific places.

1. Use an apostrophe to create the possessive form of a noun.

plaintiff's = belonging to one plaintiff.
plaintiffs' = belonging to more than one plaintiff.
Pettuses' = belonging to the Pettuses.

Do not, however, use an apostrophe to form the plural of a name ending in *s*. Instead use *es:* the Joneses.

Also do not use an apostrophe to form possessives of PRONOUNS.

its = belonging to it.
yours = belonging to you.
theirs = belonging to them.
whose = belonging to whom.
ours = belonging to us.
hers = belonging to her.

For more explanation, see POSSESSIVES.

2. Whether you use an apostrophe expressing figures depends on your AUDIENCE. General style manuals have shifted to forming the plural of a letter, figure, or symbol by adding s without an apostrophe. But the Government Printing Office Style Manual still requires the apostrophe, so that is the correct Bluebook form.

general style manuals	Government manual
7s	**7's**
Cs	**C's**
s	**'s**

But in either style, use an apostrophe when it is needed to keep the text readable.

> **a's   has's**

rather than

> as   hass

3. Use an apostrophe as a substitution for a letter or letters.

it's	= it is.
you're	= you are.
don't	= do not.

In most legal writing, however, do not use contractions. For more explanation, see CONTRACTIONS.

APPEAL

Use *appeal* as a term of art only, referring to the appeal of a case. Avoid using *appeal* informally in legal writing.

> **The appeal will be decided next week.**

rather than

> The defendant's counsel appealed to the court to deny the motion.

For related information, see TERMS OF ART.

APPELLATE BRIEFS

Appellate courts have specific rules about the FORMAT and content of appellate briefs. Read your local rules carefully, because most appellate courts will reject briefs that do not conform to their rules. For example, most courts require certain colors for covers; certain typesets, margins, and page lengths; and certain organization and content. Be aware of these rules before you begin writing your appellate brief, so that you know the confines within which you must work. Similarly, check the number of days you have for writing the brief and know how your jurisdiction counts those days. Pay particular attention to how your jurisdiction counts weekends and holidays. Then mark the deadline on that calendar and count backwards to schedule your WRITING PROCESS.

In your schedule, make sure you allow a lot of time at the end for refining the format. Most jurisdictions require a table of contents that includes the POINT HEADINGS and a table of authorities that includes references to specific pages where each authority is used; these tables take time to assemble. Also make sure that the typist has plenty of time to finish this process before filing the brief, so that you will be sure to meet your deadline. For related information, see DEADLINES, MEETING THEM.

Generally, an appellate brief contains a STATEMENT OF THE CASE with specific references to the record, ISSUE STATEMENTS, an ARGUMENT SECTION, POINT HEADINGS and subheadings, and a conclusion. Use PERSUASIVE WRITING when writing your appellate brief. For more information on format, see BRIEFS.

APPENDIX

Appendices can be used in any kind of legal writing to assist the reader but not to replace important material that should be included in the text. Legal readers prefer appendices to refer to statutes, cases, excerpts from the record, and similar documents that are not needed in their entirety in the text but are helpful for reference. Therefore, use appendices in MEMOS to include applicable statutes; in PRETRIAL BRIEFS to include affidavits, references to any pretrial documents, or applicable statutes; in TRIAL BRIEFS to include references to the record or to applicable statutes; and in APPELLATE BRIEFS to include references to the pretrial record, trial record, JURY INSTRUCTIONS, or statutes.

Label each appendix as Appendix A, B, C, and so forth. Refer to each separately by surrounding this phrase with PARENTHESES. (*See Appendix A*).

Check your local appellate rules for any specific requirements for appendices to appellate briefs.

APPLICATION

In MEMOS or BRIEFS, *application* refers to the process by which the relevant RULES of law are applied to the factual situation being analyzed. In a memo, the application is part of the DISCUSSION SECTION. In a brief, it is part of the ARGUMENT SECTION. While a comprehensive approach to application is beyond the scope of this book, the following may get you started.

1. Apply the law according to its own structure. For example, if there are three subsections of a statute, apply all three in the statute's order or in the order used by courts in interpreting the statute. If your rule evokes a balancing test, apply the rule to the facts by showing one part of the test, then the other part, then how they balance against each other.

2.   Make sure your application reflects step-by-step logic. Do not jump to any conclusions. Show the reader how you reach your conclusions by explaining each step that moves from the general rule to the specific conclusion. To do so, you might use some devices from EXPOSITORY WRITING, such as definition, cause and effect, or enumeration. If you want to show that your client did not violate a restrictive covenant, for example, you must show the rules on restrictive covenants, define violations of that covenant by showing what actions the courts have held to be violations in previous cases, and then compare or contrast your client's situation with the situations in those cases. To support your conclusions, you must examine the reasoning used in those cases; the policy, equity, economic, or social questions those courts discussed; and the steps used to reach results. You must then explain why your client's case is similar enough that the court should reach a similar conclusion for your client. For some hints on reasoning, see SYLLO-GISMS. For a more detailed approach to reasoning see Pierre Schlag and David Skover, *Tactics of Legal Reasoning* (Carolina Academic Press 1986).

3.   Examine both the strengths and weaknesses of your client's case and balance them against each other. The reader should know how the RULES, POLICY, and EQUITY can be used to build or challenge your arguments. Then the reader should know how and why these factors tip the balance in one direction. For example, if others who signed the same restrictive covenant have violated it and not been punished, you must include in your application that information and an argument that your client should similarly not be punished.

Include the ideas listed above in your application, but do not limit your application to just these ideas or include them as a list of parts of an analysis. Instead, weave these parts together as dictated by the law and facts themselves. A mechanical listing will defeat the analytical purpose, while a careful consideration and building of the subparts will result in a thorough analysis. Give your readers the confidence that you have included all relevant law and facts, examined all arguments thoroughly, and constructed a logical progression for the reasoning. For related information, see LEGAL ANALYSIS and SYLLOGISM.

APPOSITIVE

An appositive is a noun or phrase that comes right after a noun and describes that noun.

The defendant, <u>Great West Power</u>, settled before the trial began.

It is useful for inserting extra information into a sentence. Keep the appositive short, however, to avoid creating sentences that are hard to read. For related problems, see READABILITY and AGREEMENT,

SUBJECTS AND VERBS. For a discussion of other uses of appositives, see UNOBTRUSIVE DEFINITIONS.

ARGUMENT HEADINGS

See POINT HEADINGS.

ARGUMENT SECTION

The Argument is that section in a pretrial, trial, or appellate brief presenting the legal argument from the client's point of view.

The Argument should contain the following information:

(1) all the RULES applicable to this fact situation, whether from statutory or common law;

(2) an APPLICATION of the rules to these facts, which argues the strengths of the client's position and rebuts the weaknesses; and

(3) an analysis of the POLICY and EQUITY questions, if useful to client's position or essential to complete analysis.

Write the Argument in a persuasive style and from the client's point of view. For more on how to do this, see PERSUASIVE WRITING and POINT OF VIEW. The Argument should include POINT HEADINGS and subheadings, which outline the argument's main legal points and give the reasons behind those points.

Organize the Argument either inductively or deductively. Deductive organization, which is usually best, begins with a rule, uses analogous cases where appropriate, and then applies the law to these facts to reach a specific conclusion based on that rule. Inductive organization begins with the particulars of the case being analyzed and works through each rule to reach a general conclusion. For more help with organization, see ORGANIZATION, LARGE–SCALE and ORGANIZATION, SMALL–SCALE.

The Argument should include LEGALLY SIGNIFICANT FACTS, or those facts of the case being analyzed that are necessary to the outcome. All facts used in the argument section should also appear in the STATEMENT OF THE CASE; no new facts should appear in the argument section.

ARTICLES, GRAMMAR

Articles is the grammatical term for *a*, *an*, and *the*. For a discussion of their use, see A OR AN? and THE. For law review articles, see ARTICLES, PUBLISHED.

ARTICLES, PUBLISHED

Articles differ from other forms of legal writing because their AUDIENCE is scholarly as well as practical and because they reflect the writer's opinion more openly than do other forms. Consider the following in writing an article.

1. Tell the reader your point at the beginning of the article rather than building up to it at the end. Most legal readers like to know what they are reading about and then see the explanation because they can then follow and evaluate the writer's reasoning that leads to that point. This point can be stated at the end of your introduction or in the very first sentence of the article. For related information, see ORGANIZATION; ORGANIZATION, LARGE–SCALE; ORGANIZATION, SMALL–SCALE; and PARAGRAPHS.

2. Make sure that your FORMAT reflects the substance of your piece. As in a brief, any HEADINGS or subheadings should be helpful signals, not merely a parroting of traditional format. Try using sentences or phrases that communicate your argument, rather than just depending on words like *Introduction*, or *Historical Background*.

3. Use FOOTNOTES to substantiate points and to provide valuable historical or background information. Avoid using footnotes just to use them; instead make sure they are sensible and useful to the reader.

4. Allow yourself more leverage in using FIGURATIVE MEANING, EMOTIONAL LANGUAGE, and your own PERSUASIVE STYLE than you would in briefs or memos. Because the article is your commentary on a given subject, also allow your STYLE and TONE wider range. Do not, however, range so far that you lessen your credibility.

5. In articles, honor the same fundamental of legal writing that you do in briefs; make every word count. It is tempting to say more than is necessary in articles, but giving into that temptation can lose readers. For related information, see SCHOLARLY WRITING, SCHOLARLY WRITING CHECKLIST, SCHOLARLY WRITING PROCESS, CONCISENESS, PRECISION, and READABILITY.

AS

To avoid ambiguity, avoid using *as* in place of *because* or *since*.

The trial was delayed because the plaintiff fell ill.

rather than

The trial was delayed as the plaintiff fell ill.

For related information, see TRANSITIONS and PRECISION.

AS A MATTER OF FACT

You probably do not need this phrase. Try marking it out and revising what is left into a more concise, forceful statement.

It was within her power to do so. She was the supervisor on duty.

rather than

It was within her power to do so. She was as a matter of fact the supervisor on duty.

See CONCISENESS.

AS IF OR AS THOUGH?

Either one means *in the same way that it would be if.*

They can be used interchangeably.

AS OR LIKE?

In a comparison, use *as* to connect CLAUSES.

She argues as a good lawyer should argue.

rather than

She argues like a good lawyer should.

Use *like* only to introduce a noun phrase.

She argues like Justice Cardozo.

AS PER

Substitute *under, according to,* or another appropriate term.

Under the terms of this contract,....

rather than

As per the terms of this contract,....

Or use

This number is inaccurate according to the most recent data.

rather than

This number is inaccurate as per the most recent data.

The number of words that substitute for *as per* indicate that the phrase is vague, as well as an example of JARGON.

ASSONANCE

Assonance is repeating vowel sounds within a series of words to create a mood. Because it requires a broader discretion in word choice, it is a more useful tool for poets than for legal writers. But it may occasionally be useful in a persuasive Statements of Facts. Use it sparingly, or you may engender humor. Also avoid sacrificing CLARITY for effect. For example, to create a staccato effect, you might repeat the short "i" sound.

The plaintiff's insistent clicking of his stick against the defendant's chair irritated the situation and provoked the assault.

But repeating an *oo* sound that much would invite readers to giggle, because the repetition is more obvious.

The crooning moonlight soothed the plaintiff's mood, and she signed the new contract.

For related information, see ALLITERATION.

ASTERISKS

Asterisks are sometimes used for acknowledgements in law review articles or for a single footnote. In typeset print, asterisks are also sometimes used interchangeably with ELLIPSES. In typewritten, formal legal writing, asterisks are distracting, so use periods for ellipses. In informal writing, asterisks are used to mark a single footnote; in legal writing, this is only likely to happen when adding a small point to an informal memo to a coworker.

For related information, see QUOTATIONS, HOW TO PUNCTUATE.

AS THOUGH OR AS IF?

See AS IF OR AS THOUGH?

AS TO

As to can be used as a preposition, in which case it takes an object.

As to the adjective: when in doubt strike it out.—Mark Twain

As to jury trials, our system compares with few others in the world.

Use *as to* rarely and with care to avoid two problems. First, do not use *as to* if it is stuffy in context. For example, in a letter to a client, write the following.

Regarding your request for ....

rather than

As to your request for ....

Second, avoid overusing *as to*. If you use it once a page, you are probably overusing it. To find a different but equally accurate connecting phrase, see TRANSITIONS.

AT THE TIME THAT

Try using *when* instead. See CONCISENESS.

AT THIS POINT IN TIME

Try using *now* or *currently* for a clearer, more concise sentence. See CONCISENESS.

ATTORNEY OR LAWYER?

Generally, *attorney* refers to the specific person representing a party to a suit.

Attorney Schwartz moved for a new trial.

or

The attorney for the defense objected to the question.

The term *lawyer* refers to the general category of people qualified to practice law.

Several hundred lawyers attended last year's ABA convention.

AUDIENCE

To maximize the effectiveness of your writing, define your audience, or readers, before your begin to write. This will help you organize and present your information to communicate more effectively. Then consider that audience throughout WRITING, REWRITING, REVISING, and POLISHING. The concept of audience is one of the four guiding stars that you must keep in sight throughout the WRITING PROCESS. (The other three are PURPOSE, SCOPE, and your PROFESSIONAL POSTURE.)

Most legal writing is read by more than one person, and those readers may each have different levels of expertise, experience, and patience. For example, a BRIEF will be reviewed by a judge, the judge's clerk, opposing counsel, clients, and sometimes the press or the public; an OPINION LETTER may be reviewed by a supervising attorney before being sent to the client and another attorney who pulls it from the file to read later. The legal writer must try to please each of these potential readers, all of whom should be able to understand the document in the first reading.

1. Identifying your audience.

When you begin a project, consider exactly who will be reading your document. Specifically, consider the following.

(a) Identify all possible readers.

(1) Who is the primary reader, the reader to whom you must direct your message? Find out as much as you can about that reader's preferences in scope, style, length, and overall approach. Consider whether the reader is hostile or open to your position. At a minimum, pause to remember whether your primary audience is a nonlawyer, a lawyer, or a judge, so you can adjust your content and organization for that reader.

(2) Who are the secondary readers, those who may read the document for other purposes? This group might include the judge's clerk, other partners who are deciding the course of the case, or the client who may read the memo you originally composed for the partner. Consider whether appendices, explanations, or summaries should be added for the reader.

(3) What are the readers' levels of expertise? You may have some readers who are experts in this subject and others who know very little, or you may not know whether or not your reader is an expert. If all of the document's audiences will be experts, you may use TERMS OF ART and briefer references to generally held legal assumptions or generally known information. If a non-expert may read the document, however, include enough background to make the document CONTEXT INDEPENDENT. To avoid losing the expert reader, do not resort to FOOTNOTES, which irritate many readers. Instead, consider the alternatives: set the background apart by using PARENTHESES, separate sections, HEADINGS, clearly defined paragraphs with strong TOPIC SENTENCES that are easy to skip, or an APPENDIX.

2. Organizing to coordinate audience and purpose.

Next consider the document's purpose. You might want to write out that purpose, such as *to inform the client of her tax liability* or *to suggest that the client settle the case.* When you have clarified your audience and purpose, structure the document so each reader will understand the purpose and message.

Ask yourself what ORGANIZATION will best track the audience's reasoning processes. For example, when explaining to a nonlawyer, (a) begin your explanation with the effect of the law on the reader, rather than with the legal language itself; (b) omit unneeded legal terms; and (c) define any remaining terms.

To transfer ownership of this land to your son, you will need to .... According to Illinois property law, all transfers of ownership must .... The reason the law requires you to do this is because some land has not been transferred according to the parents wishes when ....

rather than

> Parkinson v. Palmer outlined Illinois precedent for the proper transfer of property in fee simple absolute .... Accordingly, current property law requires all deed transfers to be .... Thus, deeding this property properly to your issue would require ....

This fine-tuning may require sketching several possible organizational schemes for the document during PREWRITING, especially when addressing hostile audiences or varied purposes.

Then choose the version that will suit the greatest number of readers, giving the primary reader highest priority. When you have determined your structure, communicate it clearly by using HEADINGS, TOPIC SENTENCES, and GRAPHICS to illustrate that structure. These will help your reader know at a glance where you are going and how you are getting there.

3. Writing to the audience.

Even though you have chosen and organized your content with the reader in mind, you still need to write to ensure immediate comprehension by the reader. To do this, consider the following questions when REWRITING.

(a) Are the PURPOSE and message clear to any reader? Usually the reader wants to know the reason for reading the document, as well as its thesis. Present both immediately: in an Introduction or in the QUESTION PRESENTED and BRIEF ANSWER of a MEMO; in the introductory paragraph of an OPINION LETTER; or in the opening of a BRIEF. Then, throughout the document, make sure each of the primary and secondary readers can continue to understand the questions, the answers, and the reasons for reaching the answers.

(b) What content may cause problems for either primary or secondary audiences? Review your audience to make sure that your analysis includes all essential authority and steps, nothing more and nothing less. Omit tangents; delete redundant or otherwise unneeded support and unnecessary detail. Check LARGE-SCALE ORGANIZATION and PARAGRAPH BLOCKS for COHERENCE. Omit unnecessarily long explanations; reorganize, if necessary, to serve your audiences' needs. Make sure you have responded to all requests, including those for practical information, remedies, actions, or advice.

(c) Does the ORGANIZATION suit the audience? If your audience is friendly, you may be able to use a more straightforward organization of the law. If they are hostile, you may need to organize for persuasiveness, to offer more definitions and detail, and to use more distinct markers for your arguments. See PERSUASIVE DEVICES, TERMS OF ART, and TONE.

4. REVISING with your audience in mind.

At this stage, look for smaller scale concerns that will affect your readers' understanding of your message. For example, consider the following.

(a) Will any words cause problems? Omit JARGON and FLOWERY LANGUAGE that will confuse or annoy your readers. Make sure that TERMS OF ART are used accurately and definitions are included wherever needed.

(b) Can the language be tailored to attorneys? When WRITING TO OTHER ATTORNEYS, focus on being concise and businesslike in TONE, rather than particularly formal or informal. Avoid extremes. Be concise but not unsupported, professional but not pretentious, advocating yet not biased, and caring yet not illogical. Resist any urge to impress the reader by driving him or her to the dictionary; you would annoy, not impress.

5. POLISHING with the audience in mind.

Are your readers particular about FORMAT or STYLE? If so, conform to their wishes. Even if you disagree with these requirements, it is wiser to follow them because your job as a writer is to communicate your point to these readers, not to change their preferences. If no common ground exists among your readers, choose the primary reader's preference. If you do not know what they prefer, use a conventional, comprehensive format familiar to all legal readers.

AUXILIARY VERB

See VERBS, AUXILIARY.

BACKGROUND FACTS

These facts fill in the gaps between LEGALLY SIGNIFICANT FACTS. Although they are not essential to the issues, they are essential to the reader's understanding of the general situation. Thus the STATEMENT OF FACTS contains enough background to complete the context. Background facts should be minimized, however, to avoid making the Statement of Facts too long. For related information, see ISSUE STATEMENTS and QUESTIONS PRESENTED.

BAD NEWS, GIVING IT

For any lawyer, being the bearer of bad news is as unavoidable as it is distasteful. Unlike a fortune teller, who can base predictions solely on the client's desires, the lawyer must base his or her prediction on sound analysis of law and fact.

A lawyer can, however, use an understanding of readers and of writing to make that bad news more palatable. The following techniques can be helpful for presenting bad news in a letter, memo, or brief.

1. In a letter.

When you must write a bad news letter, try organizing the letter into three parts that do the following: (a) set the TONE of the letter, (b) deliver the bad news, and (c) re-establish the tone. Think of this as a sandwich organization; place your meat between two slices of bread to make it more palatable.

(a) The first slice of bread: set the tone.

In the first paragraph, establish the TONE you want to take with the reader. For example, you might want to be kind.

> **Mr. Alexander has asked us to help straighten out some apparent confusion regarding your bill to him for equipment repairs made in June 1985. As I understand it,**
> . . . .

Or you might want to be tough.

> **You stated in your letter of March 14, that our client, Mr. Alexander, owes you $480 for equipment repairs you made in June 1985. This is incorrect. As Mr. Alexander has explained previously,** . . . .

You might choose to be warm and personal.

> **Thank you for inviting me to speak at the Society's annual awards banquet. Regrettably,** . . . .

You might choose to be distant.

> **This letter concerns a bill for $480 from Efficient Equipment Repair Service to Alexander Associates, which states that the charges are for equipment repairs completed in June 1985** . . . .

If answering a request, you may want to restate that request, so that the reader knows you paid attention to the request before saying no.

> **In your letter to Mr. Alexander dated March 14, you asked him to pay $480 for "equipment repairs made to three typewriters in June 1985." You stated that this payment was long overdue and you threatened to bring suit if you did not receive payment by May 1, 1986.**

(b) The meat: deliver the bad news.

At the beginning of paragraph two, state the bad news plainly so that the reader cannot misinterpret what you are saying.

> **In your letter to Mr. Alexander dated March 14, you asked Mr. Alexander to pay $480 for "equipment repairs**

29

made to three typewriters in June 1985." You stated that this payment was long overdue and you threatened to bring suit if you did not receive payment by May 1, 1986.

Mr. Alexander, however, does not believe he owes you this money because he has no record of these repairs being made . . . .

Follow this statement with your reasons, if appropriate. This paragraph will be unemotional and matter-of-fact, regardless of the tone of the other paragraphs.

Mr. Alexander, however, does not believe he owes you this money because he has no record of these repairs being made. Instead, his records show only that Efficient Equipment Repair Service repaired one typewriter on June 12, 1985. Alexander Associates received a statement charging $40 for this work from the repairman before he left. On July 1, 1985, Alexander Associates mailed a check for $40 to Efficient Equipment Repair Service . . . .

This section may also extend for several paragraphs if needed.

(c) The other piece of bread: re-establish the tone.

In the final paragraph, re-establish your tone while you state some closing technicalities. For example, you may suggest that the reader call if he or she has questions.

If you have any further questions concerning this matter, you may call me at (505) 555–1234.

If you are being kind, you may wish the reader some sort of relevant good fortune.

I enjoyed our conversation at the convention and look forward to reading your article on . . . .

If you are being tough, you may close with a final declarative statement.

I trust that this explains the matter to your satisfaction.

For related information see BAD NEWS, SOFTENING IT; GENERAL CORRESPONDENCE LETTERS; and TONE IN LETTERS.

2. In a memo.

Sometimes you must tell a senior partner that a client does not have a case. When this happens, state your conclusion in specific, matter-of-fact language.

Mr. Allen will probably not convince a jury to award damages under the theory of strict liability because he cannot show that . . . .

Then lay out your reasoning thoroughly. Answer all possible questions your reader will likely ask, one by one.

If at all possible, offer viable alternatives. Maybe some other theory is possible. Maybe some other approach, such as negotiation, is desirable. These alternatives greatly reduce the sting of a negative answer. For related information, see MEMOS; ORGANIZATION, LARGE–SCALE; SYNTHESIS; and SYLLOGISM.

3. In a brief.

Sometimes you must deal with precedent, policy, or facts that go against your client's position. For help here, see BAD NEWS, SOFTENING IT.

BAD NEWS, SOFTENING IT

Soften bad news when you do indeed have to communicate the bad news to the reader but you want to keep the reader from reacting to the news in some way undesirable to your position.

Be careful about softening bad news too much, however, because it is possible to state the bad news so abstractly that the reader misses the point altogether. For example, if in an opinion letter you needed to tell your client that he or she would lose a suit, you might state the following.

> **Although you may bring suit, your chance of recovering your investment is slim. The company at fault has declared bankruptcy, and thus** ....

rather than

> Although the results might not be exactly what you desire, you may nevertheless choose to bring suit.

With that caveat in mind, use the following techniques to soften the blow. For related information, see BAD NEWS, GIVING IT; GENERAL CORRESPONDENCE LETTERS; and TONE IN LETTERS.

1. Use a dependent clause.

You can put the bad news in a dependent clause (see PARTS OF A SENTENCE) and then put that clause in a sentence based on a more favorable fact.

> **Although he was exceeding the speed limit, Mr. Jones was driving no faster than other cars on that road at that time. Indeed he was passed by several cars just a few minutes before the accident.**

This technique is particularly useful in PERSUASIVE WRITING.

To determine what word to use at the first of your dependent clause, see TRANSITIONS. For a general discussion of the technique, see SENTENCE STRUCTURE, Subsection 3.

2. Use more abstract terms.

A second way to soften bad news is to state it in abstract, rather than concrete terms. This technique is most likely to be useful when you have an unfavorable fact that cannot be logically set in a more favorable context. Thus if your client hit a parked car, you might refer to the event this way.

Both cars were damaged in the collision.

If, however, the other party hit your client's parked car, you might refer to the same event this way.

When the defendant's car smashed into the rear left fender of the plaintiff's car, the impact crumpled the fender and shoved it into the back seat, so that the folded metal came within three inches of the driver's seat.

The limitations of this method are obvious in this example; even if you offer the court your abstract version, your adversary will probably offer the concrete one. It may be, however, that your adversary will overdo it, or underdo it, and you can take advantage of that mistake.

3. Use a less emphatic sentence structure.

You can use sentence structure to de-emphasize one point at the same time you are using it to emphasize another, more favorable point.

Although defendant violated his parole on one occasion three months ago, he has shown exemplary behavior ever since.

For a more detailed discussion of this technique, see SENTENCE STRUCTURE.

BAD OR BADLY?

Use *bad* when modifying a noun and *badly* when modifying a verb. The main problem writers have here is exemplified in the following sentence.

I feel bad about ....

rather than

I feel badly about ....

Use *bad* because you are describing your emotions, not your ability to physically feel things. Grammatically, *feel* is a LINKING VERB, so the ADJECTIVE is used. When the verb modified is an action, then the ADVERB *badly* is used. You will probably find few occasions to use this phrase in legal writing.

He performed badly in the game following the incident.

BAR GRAPHS

See GRAPHICS, WHICH FORMS TO USE, subsection 2.

BASED ON

Watch this phrase at the beginning of a sentence, because it can create a dangling modifier.

Based on the plain meaning of this word, this interpretation of the clause is valid.

rather than

Based on the plain meaning of this word, my client should not have to honor this contract.

The interpretation, not the client, is based on the plain meaning. For related general information, see AMBIGUITY, WAYS TO AVOID.

BASICALLY

This word often has no specific meaning in a sentence; if it does not, omit it. Use *basically* if you are in fact contrasting the basis of something to some other aspect of that same thing.

Basically, this is a good theory, but in practice ....

It would be better to state your point more precisely.

This theory is based on precedent, but its application of that precedent is flawed in three ways.

BECAUSE OR SINCE?

Use *because* if you mean *because*. *Because* is a precise term; it means only that one event or thing is the cause of something else. Use *since* if you mean to show a relationship in time.

Since the restraining order was issued, the defendant has approached the plaintiff four times.

If you are worried about overusing *because*, you can do three things. First, check to see how frequently *because* appears. As a general rule, you need not worry about overusing *because* until it appears once in every paragraph and more than once in many paragraphs. Second, even if you are using *because* frequently, consider whether that use is needed to make your text clear. For example, you may decide that using *because* more frequently is appropriate because you are explaining the reasoning for a particular conclusion. Finally, if you decide some *because's* must be omitted, you may restructure the sentence to use *as a result, therefore*, or some other accurate transition. For help here, see TRANSITIONS. For a discussion of general, related writing problems, see PARAGRAPHS; LOGICAL LINKS; and CON-NECTIONS, MAKING THEM.

BEGINNING

For help beginning the WRITING PROCESS, see GETTING STARTED. For help beginning letters, see OPENINGS FOR LET-TERS.

BENDING THE RULES

This can be done with law, with grammar, or with general writing principles. With the law, bend as far as POLICY, EQUITY, canons of construction, and custom will dictate.

With grammar, bend less. Bending grammatical rules often re-sults in ambiguity, which is costly in legal writing. (See AMBIGUITY, WAYS TO AVOID.) Further, many legal readers pride themselves on their knowledge of grammatical rules and are easily distracted by any bending. Your goal in writing is that any reader can understand your content; if readers have to pause to decipher grammatical variations as well as legal ones, they may get lost.

Undaunted, Attorney Jones proceeded with the cross-exami-nation, ignoring the defense's objections.

rather than

Attorney Jones proceeded undauntedly with the cross-examination, irregardless of the defense's objections.

With general writing principles, bend only with good reason. Al-though concrete rules are useful to help any writer make decisions quickly, at some time or another some rules just do not make sense. For example, you may need to split an infinitive to make your point clear.

The mayor agreed to only suggest the alternative.

rather than

The mayor agreed only to suggest the alternative.

Here, leaving the infinitive unsplit creates a SQUINTING MODIFIER.

The safer route, however, is to avoid bending the rule by REVISING.

The mayor agreed that she would only suggest the alterna-tive.

If you cannot revise to avoid the problem, ask yourself, "What will be clear to my reader?" "What most accurately states my point?" Then, using the answers to these questions and your own common sense, bend the rules if need be. For more detail on this point, see COMMON

SENSE. For some related concerns, see ACCURACY; PRECISION; READABILITY; and AMBIGUITY, WAYS TO AVOID.

BETWEEN OR AMONG?

See AMONG OR BETWEEN?

BETWEEN YOU AND ME OR BETWEEN YOU AND I?

Use *between you and me*, always; me, the objective case, is the object of the preposition *between.*

BILLS, WRITING THEM

See LEGISLATION or REQUESTS FOR PAYMENT.

BLACK

This term is not capitalized.

For blacks, the Act was particularly significant.

Also see AFRICAN AMERICAN.

BLUEBOOK

This term refers to *The Bluebook: A Uniform System of Citation* (Harvard Law Review Association 15th ed. 1991), the recognized authority for CITATIONS across the country. Most users of the book refer to it now as the Bluebook, as the authors do here. Become familiar with each section of the Bluebook, especially with the inside covers, where forms appear for BRIEFS and MEMOS, and FOOTNOTES. Another helpful section is Table T.1, which includes standard citations for U.S. jurisdictions.

Unless your state has rules to the contrary, Bluebook rules govern citation form. For details on citation forms derived from the Bluebook, see CITATIONS; CITATIONS, BASIC FORMATS; CITATIONS, PARALLEL; and CITATIONS, STRING.

BOLDFACE TYPE

Now that computers have made this technique available to most writers, boldface has become a popular substitute for underlining to create emphasis. But when used within a paragraph, boldface text can affect the reader like a sudden increase in the volume of a television: it draws attention, but to the medium rather than the message. For alternative ways to stress a point, see EMPHASIS.

BOLDFACE TYPE

A better use of boldface is for headings or other words that stand apart from the body of the text. But the words in bold will stand out on the page, so the reader may scan those words before reading the rest of the text. Therefore, make sure that each boldfaced phrase makes sense. For example, you might use bold for the following.

Do not answer any questions until you have talked to me.

rather than

Do **not** answer any questions until you have talked to me.

As with any graphic device, avoid overusing the technique. For more on the effective use of graphic aids, see GRAPHICS, HOW TO USE, subsection 3.

BOTH

Use *both* when you are joining two people or things logically in a sentence.

Both courts used this reasoning.

but

The cases are similar.

rather than

Both cases are similar.

In the latter example, the writer is not saying that both cases are similar to something else and therefore should not join the two logically in the sentence.

BOTH ... AND

Use *both* ... *and* to emphasize an upcoming pair of entities or concepts.

Both the mayor and the city council approved this action.

rather than

The mayor as well as the city council approved this action.

For related information, see CONJUNCTIONS and TRANSITIONS.

BRACKETS

In general, brackets indicate changes made in a quote. Use brackets around SIC to indicate any significant mistakes occurring in an original quote. See Bluebook rule 5.2.

"The court hold [sic] the evidence admissible."

Also use brackets to change a letter from upper case to lower case or vice versa and to substitute words or letters or other material into the text.

> "[E]xcellence in [administrative] procedures is indispensable to carrying out the statute's intent."

Brackets have a few other specialized uses, such as marking shortened forms of case names within footnote CITATIONS. See Bluebook rules 4.2, 19.2.3, 19.4.3, and 19.6.2.

For more specific information on how to use brackets in quotes, see QUOTATIONS, HOW TO PUNCTUATE.

BREAKING THE RULES

See BENDING THE RULES.

BRIEF ANSWERS

This may be the first section the reader looks at in a memo, so it should give the answer to the QUESTION PRESENTED as definitively as possible, such as *Yes*, *No*, or *Probably yes*. Then give the specific reason for that answer. This should be done in one concise sentence, if possible; in any case, it should be brief. Avoid simply restating the Question Presented in sentence form or leaving the terms too vague. These techniques defeat the purpose of the Brief Answer, which is to inform the reader at a glance whether the answer is *yes* or *no*, and why. Together with the Question Presented, the Brief Answer provides the concise thesis of your memo.

For example, if the Question Presented is *Under Fed. R. Civ. P. 4(d)(1), Summons: Personal Service, was notice effective when it was delivered to the defendant's wife at her home?* then the Brief Answer could be as follows.

> **Yes; notice was effective because the home of the defendant's wife is his "usual place of abode," that is, the defendant had lived there within the last year, he had moved back there one week after the summons was delivered, and he had received other mail there.**

BRIEFS

Briefs are persuasive documents filed with a court to support a client's case. Briefs use PERSUASIVE WRITING to predispose the reader to the client's point of view by informing the reader of the applicable law and persuading the reader to decide the issue in favor of the writer's client. They may take the form of PRETRIAL BRIEFS (sometimes called *Memorandum in Support of a Motion* or *in Opposition to a Motion* or MEMORANDUM OF POINTS AND AUTHORITIES), TRIAL BRIEFS, post-trial briefs, or APPELLATE BRIEFS.

The FORMAT of briefs varies with jurisdiction, so check your local rules for any variation from the following standard format.

[CAPTION]

Check your jurisdiction for the formalities of the caption. This should include (1) the name of the court in which the memorandum is filed; (2) the names of the parties; (3) their status, such as *plaintiff* or *defendant*; (4) the case file number; and (5) the title of the memorandum of points and authorities and a description of the motion the memo supports or opposes. For related information, see CAPTIONS.

ISSUE[S]

ISSUE STATEMENTS state the legal questions that, when answered, will determine the outcome of the case. An issue should include the rule of law applicable in this case, the legal question, and the legally significant facts. It differs from the QUESTION PRESENTED in POINT OF VIEW; the ISSUE is persuasive. It should be worded so that the subject and verb focus the judge on the precise question he or she should answer, and so that it suggests an outcome. For examples of this method, see ISSUE STATEMENTS. Many courts like to have the issue presented first, although some prefer this section to follow the Statement of the Case. For related information, see QUESTION PRESENTED.

STATEMENT OF THE CASE

The STATEMENT OF THE CASE should contain the LEGALLY SIGNIFICANT FACTS, the BACKGROUND FACTS, and the significant EMOTIONAL FACTS. It should also include all applicable procedural history. The facts should be organized logically: by chronology, by topic, or by a combination of both. Facts should be cited to the record or to the pretrial documents as they exist at the time of filing the brief. For related information, see PARENTHETICALS and PERSUASIVE WRITING.

ARGUMENT

The ARGUMENT SECTION, like the DISCUSSION SECTION of a memo, presents the general rules of law and any exceptions, and examples of previous applications of that law. The argument then applies that law to the facts of this case, usually using some form of a syllogism, and reaches a specific conclusion. The general ORGANIZATION should follow the structure of the law itself, using POINT HEADINGS and subheadings to outline salient legal points and reasoning. The ARGUMENT SECTION should present the law from the perspective most favorable to the client. For more help here, see SYLLOGISMS; ORGANIZATION, LARGE–SCALE and ORGANIZATION, SMALL–SCALE. For more suggestions on how to build reasoning, see Pierre Schlag and David Skover, *Tactics of Legal Reasoning* (Carolina Academic Press 1986).

CONCLUSION

The conclusion should summarize briefly the reasoning presented in the argument and should request specific relief. The court should know at a glance what result the writer asks for and why. Avoid the traditional *For the foregoing reasons*. This forces the reader to either reread the entire Argument Section or skip the point. Instead, use this last opportunity for a focused summary that delivers the final punch.

BULLET POINTS

A bullet point is a large, centered dot placed before a line of text. This graphic device can be useful to mark the division of points when numerals are unneeded.

This new will includes the three changes you requested, as we discussed at our last meeting.

> • **Provision for minor grandchildren's college education.**
>
> • **Designation of alternate personal representatives.**
>
> • **Special bequest to Middleton College.**

As with any graphic tool, however, avoid using this solely because it is in fashion; use it instead to clarify your meaning without distracting from it. Similarly, avoid overusing this or any particular graphic device. For more on the effective use of graphic aids, see GRAPHICS, HOW TO USE, subsection 3. For related information, see LISTS, STRUCTURE OF.

BUSINESS LETTERS

See GENERAL CORRESPONDENCE LETTERS.

BUT

But is a powerful conjunction that can mean any of the following: (1) *on the contrary*, (2) *however*, (3) *except that*, or (4) *other than*. Use it in legal writing to make a strong distinction between ideas. Because *but* is so strong, be careful not to overuse it.

He has a strong case for an appeal, but he failed to file the notice of appeal on time.

They should have objected, but neither they nor the court noticed the objectionable grounds in time.

But can also be effective at the first of a sentence, one of the POSITIONS OF EMPHASIS, if you want to emphasize the logical connection between two sentences.

No moral right as such exists in America. But Congress has made several attempts to add the moral right to Title 17.

For related general information, see CONJUNCTIONS; TRANSI-TIONS; and CONNECTIONS, MAKING THEM.

CAN

Use *can* as an auxiliary word when you want to suggest capacity.

The plaintiff can anticipate such misuses of their product; ample cases of misuse of similar cutting tools exist.

For more information, see CAN OR MAY?, MAY, and VERBS, AUXIL-IARY.

CAN HARDLY OR CAN'T HARDLY?

Can hardly is always correct. *Can't hardly* never is. In legal writing, it is often better to replace *can hardly* with some other phrase, like *can scarcely* or *can barely*. *Can hardly* is used loosely and frequently in speech, and as a result sounds rather informal.

CANNOT OR CAN NOT?

Cannot is the correct form in almost all cases.

I cannot represent you in this case.

Can not only appears when *not* is part of another phrase.

He can *not only* request a new hearing but also require a change of venue.

CAN OR COULD?

See VERBS, TENSES.

CAN OR MAY?

Use *can* when you mean that the subject is able to do something.

The plaintiff can still lift packages weighing up to thirty pounds.

Use *may* when you mean that the subject has the permission to do something.

The police may search the glove compartment without first obtaining a search warrant if . . . .

CAPITALIZATION

Legal writers have trouble with capitalization in five places: (1) with proper adjectives; (2) with titles of officials, courts, and organizations; (3) with the first word after a colon; (4) with common nouns used to refer to specific people or groups; and (5) with subheadings.

1. Proper adjectives.

Capitalize most proper adjectives, which are adjectives formed from proper nouns, such as *American banking system, the Atlantic seaboard,* or *Vietnamese refugees.* Do not capitalize an adjective when it has been used frequently and for a long time in the general language, such as *cesarean operation, india ink, italic type, murphy bed,* or *venetian blinds.* For an extensive list of adjectives derived from proper names, see the *U.S. Government Printing Office Style Manual* (1984.)

2. Titles of officials, courts, and organizations.

Capitalize a title, such as *judge* or *justice,* only when it precedes the judge's or justice's name or when it replaces the name.

Justice Brennan wrote the concurring opinion.

Thank you, Judge, for your advice.

but

The judge signed the search warrant at 3:00 a.m.

Also capitalize *court* when you are referring to the reader, to show respect for the court. Do not capitalize *court* when you are referring to a different court that decided another case.

This Court three times upheld this principle.

but

There, the trial court ruled in favor of the defendant.

For related information, see JUDGES, HOW TO ADDRESS.

3. The first word after a colon.

In general, do not capitalize the first word after the colon, because doing so usually makes the sentence self-consciously ornate, like a person wearing a tiara to a picnic. Capitalize the first word after the colon only to emphasize that word or phrase.

Plaintiff asks the court to invoke the most severe penalty: Child abuse must be stopped.

For an explanation of when to use colons, see COLONS.

4. Common nouns used to refer to specific people or groups.

Capitalize *Elk* in *He was an Elk,* because the word refers to a specific person and organization, rather than to generic elk grazing on the ranges of Montana. Similarly, write *The Representative spoke at length to us,* because the term *Representative* replaces the person's name, and thus refers to a specific person.

Capitalize *Constitution* only when naming any constitution in full, as in *Constitution of the State of Iowa,* or when referring to the *United*

States Constitution. Also capitalize parts of the U.S. Constitution when referring to them in text.

Fourth Amendment   Article I, Section 8   Preamble

But do not capitalize these terms in CITATIONS. See Bluebook rule 8.

5. Subheadings.

In subheadings, capitalize the initial word and all other substantive words; do not, however, capitalize CONJUNCTIONS or PREPOSITIONS of four or fewer letters. Also do not capitalize *a*, *an*, or *the*. One common exception to this is in POINT HEADINGS, where often a specific court will require you to capitalize every word, even conjunctions, prepositions, and articles. See Bluebook rule 8. See also *AMENDMENT* CAPITALIZED?

CAPTIONS

Captions appear at the beginning of interoffice memos and all legal documents filed with the court. Captions identify the parties to the dispute, the type of document, and the purpose of the document. Each document has its own specific format and requirements for the caption.

1. Interoffice memos.

In interoffice MEMOS, captions should identify to whom the memo is addressed, who wrote the memo, what the subject matter of the memo is, and what the date is. Check the specific requirements of your office for captions. A typical memo caption follows.

<u>MEMO</u>

To: Fred P. Jones

From: Emily Barnett

Re: Krugman, file no. 48–6709; possible motion to suppress identification evidence

Date: March 27, 1996

2. Pretrial and trial documents.

The caption for a pretrial or trial document filed with a court usually identifies the court; the parties; the status of the parties, such as *plaintiffs*, *defendants*, *respondents*, or *appellants*; the file number of the case; and the title of the brief. Check your jurisdiction for its conventions in doing a pretrial brief caption. Many courts will not accept document for filing if the caption does not conform to that court's rules. A typical caption follows.

IN THE SUPERIOR COURT OF THE STATE OF WASHINGTON
FOR KING COUNTY

STATE OF WASHINGTON,	)	NO. 93–3–11658–6
Plaintiffs,	)	BRIEF IN SUPPORT OF THE MO-
vs.	)	TION TO SUPPRESS IDENTIFICA-
	)	TION EVIDENCE
SIDNEY KRUGMAN,	)	
Defendant.	)	

3. Appellate briefs.

Check your jurisdiction for your specific requirements for the caption of an appellate brief. A typical one follows.

NO. 93–1–01248–5

COURT OF APPEALS, DIVISION II OF
THE STATE OF WASHINGTON

STATE OF WASHINGTON,

Appellant,

v.

MITCHELL WAYNE JOHNSON,

Respondent.

APPEAL FROM THE SUPERIOR COURT
FOR PIERCE COUNTY

The Honorable Robert H. Peterson, Judge

BRIEF OF APPELLANT STATE OF WASHINGTON

Marilyn F. Corning
Attorney for Respondent

222 Broadway Plaza
Suite 403
Tacoma, WA 98402
(222) 256–2222

CASE

To avoid confusion, use *case* only as a term of art, when literally referring to a case. For example, instead of *in case of*, use *if*; instead of *in many cases*, use *often*; instead of *that is not the case*, use *that is not so*. For related, general information, see TERMS OF ART.

43

CASE BRIEFS

When briefing cases, consider first the reason for which you are briefing, whether it is for class, for research, or for some other purpose. Then tailor your format to that purpose. A number of possibilities exist, ranging from full, formal briefs that find a place for every detail of the case to book briefing, where comments are made in the margins of your book. Whatever your system, make sure it works for you. From the following list and other sources, collect the suggestions that you like to create your own system. Using someone else's system, no matter how comprehensive, will not work unless it makes sense to you.

1. Case briefs for class.

Brief for classes according to the topic outlined by your professor or according to the relevant topic from your table of contents. Then make sure that the issue and HOLDINGS focus on that topic. For example, if the topic is intentional torts, make sure the issue considers the question of intent and the holding answers that question with a specific finding regarding the reason for intent or lack of intent. For related information, see QUESTION PRESENTED.

2. Case briefing for research.

Tailor your case briefs in research to the questions presented, outlined in Step 3 of the RESEARCH STRATEGY CHART. Then brief the case for its purpose in that context and ignore anything irrelevant to that purpose. For example, if you are researching the question of mistake in formation of the contract, brief the case for what it says about mistake; do not go into the details of any irrelevant procedural questions.

There is one exception to this. You may include some other details, such as reversal based on a procedural issue, when the result of the case being briefed differs from the result you want in your factual situation but you still want to use the case to support your client's position.

3. Format.

Whatever your format, make sure it is thorough enough to fulfill your purpose. Consider the following checklist in creating a case brief format that works for you.

SAMPLE FORMAT FOR CASE BRIEFS

CITATION: Make sure you put down the complete citation of the case in proper form here; this will save you time later.

PARTIES: Include all parties to the suit and their status, such as *plaintiff-respondent-victim* or *defendant-appellant-tortfeasor*.

PRIOR PROCEEDINGS: Include any relevant procedural history here, such as *trial court found for the defendant; defendant appealed, court of appeals reversed the trial court's decision; and now this appeal is before the supreme court.*

THEORIES OF THE PARTIES: Include here the theory under which the plaintiff or appellant is bringing the case, such as *false imprisonment* or *breach of contract*. Include here also any defenses the defendant might be raising, such as *consent* or *lack of consideration.*

OBJECTIVES: Consider here the objectives of the parties and write them in your own words, such as *getting specific performance—he wants the goods themselves* or *getting damages—all $55,000* or *getting acquitted.*

FACTS: List here all LEGALLY SIGNIFICANT FACTS and any BACKGROUND FACTS necessary to your own understanding of the case.

ISSUE: State the issue in terms of your purpose in reading the brief. Be as specific as you can with respect to that issue. See QUESTION PRESENTED and ISSUE STATEMENTS.

Did defendant Curtis falsely imprison plaintiff Butterworth when he drove around in the car for seven hours without stopping to let her out?

HOLDING: Answer the issue and give a reason here. See HOLDINGS.

Yes; Curtis falsely imprisoned Butterworth because he used words or acts intended to confine Butterworth, he actually confined her in the car, and Butterworth was aware that she was confined.

REASONING: This is probably the most important part of the case brief. It should include relevant RULES, the APPLICATION of those rules, and the conclusion the court reached. If possible, state this reasoning in terms of a syllogism: the rule is the major premise, the application is the minor premise, and the conclusion is the conclusion. For example, you might first state the entire rule of false imprisonment in your jurisdiction. Then you might show how the court applied that rule to the specific facts of this case; take it step by step so that any holes in the reasoning become clear. Finally, show how the court reached its conclusion. For related information, see SYLLOGISMS.

DICTA: In an opinion, *dicta*, which means *words*, is anything a court says that does not have a direct effect on the outcome of the case. Dicta differs from a holding in that dicta is not binding on courts in subsequent opinions. Dicta can be significant, however, in your use of a case in research or in class. Use dicta to predict a trend in the law, to illuminate the reasoning in this case, or to understand future cases.

COMMENTS: Write here any reaction you have to the case. This may become important when you continue your research or when you are asked in class to give your opinion of the case. Include your gut reaction and any other response you have that synthesizes this case with other cases in the chapter, with other cases in your research project, or with your own understanding of the trend of the law in this particular area. When briefing for class, ask yourself, "Why did the textbook author choose this case? Why is it here?" Answer those questions here.

For a detailed approach to case briefing, see William P. Statsky and R. John Wernet, *Case Analysis and Fundamentals of Legal Writing* (West 1989).

CASE NAMES

Check first with your AUDIENCE to learn their preferences in presenting case names, and then conform to those preferences when deciding what typeface or underlining is required. If nothing is specified, underline the case names. The Bluebook states that only ITALICS are used in law review FOOTNOTES, but either italics or underlining may be used in court documents or legal memoranda. When using underlining, include the "*v.*" and any procedural phrases, such as "*In re*" and "*Ex parte.*" The underlining includes the spaces between the underlined words, but not the comma that follows the case name.

Spann v. Goldberg et al., 999 U.S. 101 (1999).

CASUAL LANGUAGE

See COLLOQUIALISMS.

CERTAIN

Use *certain* only if your point is literally certain. Because few points you make in legal writing are indeed certain, beware frequent use of the word. For a discussion of related concerns, see MODIFIERS and LITERAL MEANING.

CERTAINLY

See CERTAIN.

CHARTS

Charts can be useful to summarize a mass of detailed data or to communicate its significance. But the points a chart supports should also be stated explicitly in the text; this helps you insure that your point is communicated to all your AUDIENCES, whether they study graphics or skip them. For more information, see GRAPHICS, WHICH FORM TO USE.

CHRONOLOGICAL ORGANIZATION

Use chronological organization in a STATEMENT OF FACTS or STATEMENT OF THE CASE to allow the reader to follow the events in order of occurrence.

Use this organizational scheme when the chronology itself is important to the analysis or when a chronological arrangement would be easiest for the reader to follow. Avoid using this scheme only if TOPICAL ORGANIZATION would be more beneficial to the analysis because the facts separate into categories for each issue. Sometimes combining both works best, such as separating the facts into substantive and procedural categories and then giving the chronological order of events under each category. For related concerns, see ORGANIZATION; ORGANIZATION, LARGE–SCALE; and TOPIC SENTENCES.

CIRCUMLOCUTION

See CONCISENESS, subsection 3.

CITATIONS

The most commonly used standard for citations is *The Bluebook: A Uniform System of Citation* (15th ed. 1991). Most jurisdictions, however, make some adjustments to these rules. If your jurisdiction has its own style manual or has otherwise established exceptions to Bluebook rules, follow those exceptions in all documents filed to courts in that jurisdiction.

Citations serve two functions: (1) to provide the reader with a specific authority within the text and (2) to replace long explanations of how that authority is used, for example as a quotation, as a rule, as a related authority, or as an authority that states the contrary of the proposition. Correct use of citations both establishes your credibility as a careful analyst and streamlines your legal writing STYLE. To make citations work for you in these capacities, consider the following.

1. Use citations and SIGNALS to make the reader aware of your precise use of authority. For example, using no signal automatically indicates that the cited authority clearly states the proposition, identi-

fies the source of a quotation, or identifies an authority referred to in the text. For further reference, see Bluebook rule 1.2.

2. Use citations as separate sentences following a proposition; avoid using a citation at the beginning of a sentence. A citation stops the reader's eye before the substance of the statement is clear. If it is necessary to cite support for the first proposition in a sentence, you may use a citation as a clause mid-sentence.

> **While contracts can provide some protection for an artist's moral rights, <u>Youngs v. Taylor,</u> 999 F.2d 999 (9th Cir. 1999), no single contract can cover the entire scope of those rights.**

This use does not stop the reader as much as a cite before the proposition being cited, but it is still less than ideal. For this reason, use this structure only when it would be inaccurate to place the citation at the end.

For related information, see INTRUSIVE PHRASES.

3. Eliminate text that repeats information given in the citation, such as *The court stated that* ... or *The court went on to say that* ... or *Another case stated the opposing view* ....

4. Use short citation forms when citing to immediately preceding authority. If the previous citation is a page or two back, use the full citation, so the reader does not have to backtrack too far. See CITATIONS, BASIC FORMATS. For further reference, see Bluebook rule 4.

5. Include the publisher and the date for all unofficial versions of statutes.

> **17 U.S.C.A. § 20 (West 1999).**

> **Wash. Rev. Code Ann. § 29.09.040 (West 1999).**

6. Give a PARALLEL CITE to all state cases that have them.

> **<u>Shaw v. Snyder,</u> 101 Wis. 2d 348, 345 N.W.2d 3 (1996).**

but

> **<u>Sandvold v. Twombly,</u> 345 P.2d 534 (Alaska 1996).**

7. Give PINPOINT CITES when referring to any rules, holdings, quotations, specific propositions, or particulars of a case.

> **<u>Reason v. Pearson,</u> 33 Wis. 2d 987, 989, 201 N.W.2d 73, 76 (1999).**

8. Put spaces after abbreviations that include more than a capital letter.

> **33 Wis. 2d 987.**

or

> **222 Wash. 2d 346.**

Do not insert spaces when the abbreviation is only a capital letter.

> **345 N.W.2d 31.**

or

486 P.2d 692.

9. Check your jurisdiction for its variations on Bluebook rules. For example, the following table shows how cases would be cited under the Bluebook rules and then how the same cases would be cited under Washington's variations as provided in the *Washington Style Manual*.

For related information, see CITATIONS, BASIC FORMATS; CITATIONS, PARALLEL; CITATIONS, PINPOINT; and CITATIONS, STRING. For comprehensive directions on citation form, see Elaine Maier, *How To Prepare a Legal Citation* (1986).

RULE	CATEGORY	BLUEBOOK CITE	WASHINGTON CITE (if different)
	FEDERAL STATUTES:	17 U.S.C. § 106 (1999) 17 U.S.C.A. § 106 (West 1999) 17 U.S.C.A. § 106 (Law. Co-op. 1999)	
	FEDERAL CASES: a. Supreme Court:	Powers v. Lloyd, 45 U.S. 238 (1999).	Powers v. Lloyd, 45 U.S. 238, 436 S. Ct. 733, 42 L. Ed. 2d 36 (1999).
	b. Circuit Court:	O'Sullivan v. Pernitz, 337 F.2d 498 (9th Cir. 1999).	
	c. District Court:	Orth v. Ostrander, 167 F. Supp 553 (W.D. Wash. 1999).	
	STATE STATUTES:	Wash. Rev. Code § 2.06.10 (1983). Wash. Rev. Code Ann. § 2.06.10 (West 1999).	RCW 2.06.10.
	STATE CASES: a. Supreme Court:	Fischer v. Mundt, 54 Wash. 2d 632, 45 P.2d 877 (1999).	Fischer v. Mundt, 54 Wn. 2d 632, 45 P.2d 877 (1999).
	b. Court of Appeals:	McDonald v. Noel, 237 Wash. App. 699, 473 P.2d 89 (1999).	McDonald v. Noel, 237 Wn. App. 699, 473 P.2d 89 (1999).
	TO CITE SPECIFIC PAGE: a. First time cited:	Keating v. Cutts, 233 Wash. 2d 56, 58, 77 P.2d 321, 324 (1995).	Keating v. Cutts, 233 Wn. 2d 56, 58, 77 P.2d 321, 324 (1995).
	b. Subsequently:	Keating, 233 Wash. 2d at 58, 77 P.2d at 324.	Keating v. Cutts, supra at 58. OR Keating, 233 Wn. 2d at 58. OR Keating, at 58.
	c. If no intervening cite or if there is not too much distance:	Id. at 58, 77 P.2d at 324.	

TO GIVE SUBSEQUENT HISTORY:
Koutnik v. Landon, 234 F. Supp. 583 (N.D. Pa. 1999), aff'd, 292 F.2d 37 (3d Cir. 1999), cert. denied, 458 U.S. 334 (1999).

CITATIONS, BASIC FORMATS

Case citations should include (1) the name of the case; (2) the volume, standard abbreviation for the book, and page number of the case; (3) the parallel citation, where appropriate; and (4) the year in which the decision was made. The reader should also be able to determine from the citation what court made the decision. Thus if the name of the court is not evident from the abbreviation of the book, as in *Wash. 2d* which indicates the Washington Supreme Court, then indicate (5) who the court is by putting its abbreviation before the date inside the parentheses.

Leraas v. Martin, 894 Wash. 2d 723, 468 P.2d 387 (1999).

but

Johnson v. Strus, 499 P.2d 387 (Alaska 1997).

Because the Alaska Supreme Court does not have an official reporter, the official reporter for that state's decisions is the Pacific Reporter. But the reader would not know what court had made the decision unless *Alaska* was put in the parentheses with the date. Similarly, for federal district court decisions and federal circuit court decisions, the court must be indicated in the parentheses with the date.

Knight v. Skover, 999 F. Supp. 287 (S.D. Iowa 1999).

What follows are examples of basic citation formats for the most-often-used jurisdictions.

1. State cases.

When citing state cases, give the name of the case; the volume of the official reporter, the abbreviation of the official reporter, and the page number on which the case begins; the volume of the parallel citation, the abbreviation for the book in which the parallel citation is found, the page on which the case starts in that book, and the year of the case in parentheses.

Birchler v. Polewski, 978 Wash. 2d 496, 901 P.2d 444 (1999).

Leraas v. Martin, 894 Wash. 2d 723, 468 P.2d 387 (1999).

If the state's official reporter is a regional reporter, include the state in parentheses with the date.

Hansen v. Wark, 946 P.2d 27 (Alaska 1999).

2. Federal district court cases.

When citing federal district court cases, include the name of the case, the volume of the *Federal Supplement* in which the case is found, the abbreviation *F. Supp.*, and the page on which the case begins. Then, in parentheses, put the abbreviation for the court making the decision and the year in which the decision was made. Federal district court decisions after 1932 are cited as follows. See the Bluebook Table T.1 for pre-1932 citation forms because the formats differ.

Knight v. Skover, 987 F. Supp. 287 (S.D. Iowa 1999).

Mahr v. Huston, 908 F. Supp. 486 (D.D.C. 1999).

For a list of the abbreviations of the district courts see *Bieber's Current American Legal Citations,* 354–62 (Mary M. Prince, ed., 2d ed. 1986).

3. Federal circuit court cases.

When citing federal circuit court decisions, include the name of the case; the volume of the *Federal Reporter* in which the case is found; the abbreviation *F.* or *F.2d* and the page on which the case begins. Then in parentheses include the name of the circuit and the year in which the decision was made. Federal circuit court decisions are cited as follows.

Armstrong v. Williams, 977 F.2d 124 (D.C. Cir. 1999).

For a list of citations of all the circuit courts, see *Bieber's Current American Legal Citations*, 350–53 (1986).

4. U.S. Supreme Court cases.

For U.S. Supreme Court cases, the Bluebook requires that only the *United States Reporter* be cited. Thus give the name of the case, the volume in the United States Reporter in which the case is found, the abbreviation U.S., the page on which the case begins, and, in parentheses, the year of the decision.

Weiner v. Koutnik, 959 U.S. 123 (1999).

Always check your jurisdiction for variations on this standard format; for example, some states require that all three reporters be cited, and prefer them in a certain order. The usual order is as follows.

Weiner v. Koutnik, 980 U.S. 123, 999 S. Ct. 234, 965 L. Ed. 325 (1999).

For examples of specialty courts, see *Bieber's Current American Legal Citations* (1986) and Elaine Maier, *How to Prepare A Legal Citation* (1986).

CITATIONS, PARALLEL

All United States Supreme Court cases, most state cases, and some federal cases appear in more than one book. Thus a case may have more than one citation, and those are called parallel citations.

The United States Supreme Court and most other courts have one official reporter, which is that jurisdiction's authoritative text. For example, the United States Supreme Court's official reporter is labeled U.S. The Bluebook requires the author to cite to that official text but does not require parellel citations for United States Supreme Court cases. For state cases, however, the Bluebook does require parallel citations to unofficial reporters; when including parallel citations list the official reporter first. Parallel citations are useful because they refer to sources accessible to most legal readers.

Fischer v. Doerr, 437 U.S. 893 (1999).

but

Lamb v. Laffon, 145 Ariz. 212, 700 P.2d 1312 (1999).

Check the tables of the Bluebook for specific directions regarding which reporters to cite in parallel citations for each state. When using PINPOINT CITES, include the specific page number for the parallel cite as well.

CITATIONS, STRING

String cites are citations of two or more cases for the same point. Semicolons separate the individual cites in a string cite, and cases are cited in reverse chronological order.

This rule has been applied uniformly in Arkansas. Lorey v. Jacobi, 99 Ark. 111, 222 S.W.2d 22 (1999); Zuckerman v. Kidwell, 100 Ark. 841, 224 S.W.2d 444 (1999); Arthur v. Christopoulos, 101 Ark. 502, 226 S.W.2d 321 (1999).

String cites can be used to convey the message to the reader that not just one authority stands for a point, but two, three, or four do. If that message is essential to your analysis, then use the string cite. Do not, however, use a string cite just to show that you found more than one case. If one case is sufficient to make the point, omit the other citations. Remember that the doubting legal reader will check most authorities and will be annoyed if each is not pertinent. For format and order of string cites, see Bluebook rules 1.1, 1.4, and P.2.

CLARITY

Clarity means writing so the reader can follow the writing step by step, without wondering what a phrase means or what the point of the paper is. When the writing is clear, the reader can forget about the writing itself and focus instead on the merit of the content. The main tools of clarity are (1) using straightforward and logical ORGANIZATION, (2) using precise and familiar words, and (3) using readable and effective SENTENCE STRUCTURE. For related information, see ORGANIZATION, LARGE–SCALE; ORGANIZATION, SMALL–SCALE; PRECISION; and READABILITY.

CLAUSES

A clause is a group of words that includes a subject and a predicate. Several clauses may be combined to form a compound or complex sentence.

Even if the court remands the case *[dependent clause]*, **the** *Plaintiff will not appreciably increase his reward* [independent clause].

An independent clause can stand alone as a logical sentence.

The plaintiff will not appreciably increase his reward.

A dependent clause cannot, because it begins with a word or phrase that makes the clause depend logically on another point.

Even if the court remands the case

Not knowing the difference between dependent and independent clauses can lead a writer to misuse COMMAS. This occurs most often with the word *however*.

The court remanded the case; however, the plaintiff did not receive an appreciably higher reward.

rather than

The court remanded the case, however, the plaintiff did not receive an appreciably higher reward.

Because *however* joins two independent clauses, those clauses must be separated with a semicolon. For a discussion of clauses in the context of sentences, see SENTENCE STRUCTURE.

CLEARLY

Is the point really clear? If not, omit *clearly*. Similarly, whenever you read the word *clearly* in a text, look for a hole in the writer's logic. In most situations, *clearly* will remind you of the orator who pounds on the podium in the hope that his ardor will obscure his argument's weakness. For a discussion of related concerns, see MODIFIERS, CONCISENESS, and LITERAL MEANING.

CLEAR WRITING

See READABILITY and CLARITY.

CLIENT LETTERS

Client letters may be formal or informal OPINION LETTERS or GENERAL CORRESPONDENCE LETTERS. See those entries or, if appropriate, BAD NEWS, GIVING IT or BAD NEWS, SOFTENING IT.

CLOSINGS FOR LETTERS

Choose the standard closing that suits your writing STYLE and the TONE of your letter. If the tone of your letter is businesslike yet friendly, try *Sincerely* or *Sincerely yours*. If your tone is more formal, try *Yours truly* or *Very truly yours*. Do not worry about seeming insincere; these closings are not taken literally.

Using innovative alternatives only creates undesirable responses, rather than underscoring your sincerity. If you were to use something more accurate, like *Don't bother me anymore*, you would only seem unprofessional or petulant. If you omit the closing, you create an abrupt, impersonal tone that is usually not appropriate, even in a tough collection letter. For more detail on related issues, see TONE IN LETTERS and GENERAL CORRESPONDENCE LETTERS.

COHERENCE

Coherence in writing means writing so that any reader can see easily how all the content fits together. Your first tool for achieving coherence is organization, your second is consistent and unambiguous wording, and your third is clear and adequate transitions. For detail on how to accomplish this, see ORGANIZATION, SMALL–SCALE; PARAGRAPHS; PRECISION; REPETITION; AMBIGUITY, WAYS TO AVOID; CONNECTIONS, MAKING THEM; and TRANSITIONS.

COLLABORATION

Collaborative writing is wonderful, when it works. It improves the product when it builds on individual strengths and compensates for weaknesses. It improves the process when it reduces the pressure to be perfect, provides more perspective as the process wears on, and provides someone with whom you can commiserate and celebrate.

But making collaboration work requires clear-headed planning; the collaborators need to have congruent expectations regarding the project, the process, and each other. The following process is one way to achieve this congruency.

1. Set parameters for the project.

Meet to decide on the project's PURPOSE and SCOPE. A little time spent determining the goals and limits of the document can help you find common ground and identify any areas where compromise is needed. Then discuss all possible ISSUES, theories, and strategy and decide which you will pursue. Even at this early stage, begin to develop a sense of your communal VOICE to the extent you can.

Determine concrete constraints such as page length, scope of research, and use of citations. Discuss such factors as the client's priorities, the AUDIENCE, and the balance you seek between thoroughness and conciseness. Include other important areas, such as PROFESSIONAL POSTURE, time commitments, and other personal goals regarding this piece of writing. Determine priorities together, identifying what qualities are not just desirable, but essential. This will help you allocate time most effectively and avoid long debates over minor wording or style points as the DEADLINE nears.

2. Establish your procedural structure.

Note the final deadline and set interim DEADLINES. You will be dependent on each other to finish this document, so be clear on who gets what to the others, and when. When using word processors, check such details as whether you are using compatible systems and whether you will be exchanging text on disks, on paper, or directly from computer to computer. For related information, see COMPUTERS, USE OF. If you are not in the same location, determine whether you will trade text by mail, electronic mail, or *FAX*. Resolving these questions can avoid costly delays as you near the project's deadline. For related information, see TIME MANAGEMENT.

3. Establish your technical roles.

Whenever possible, determine who is in charge of each technical area of writing. For example, choose one person to resolve grammar questions, another to plan persuasive strategy, another to monitor the document's tone, and another to resolve questions of citation location and form. Although these questions may not arise until much later, establish your roles early. This division of responsibilities will enable you to avoid time-consuming debates over small points; you can instead refer the question to one collaborator. Additionally, this structure will shift the focus of this part of the collaborative writing process from personal ego to personal responsibility.

4. Clarify tasks throughout the WRITING PROCESS.

Before the end of each meeting, decide together what each collaborator will accomplish before the next meeting. Preferably, put these lists in writing, so each collaborator has a copy. These lists encourage helpful communication and reduce the chance for duplication of effort or failure to complete some necessary task.

5. Keep in touch.

Since the main benefits of collaboration flow from an interchange of questions and suggestions, do whatever you can to make it easy for those exchanges to occur. Confer while WRITING. These conversations need not be long; you may just ask a collaborator a question or share a new idea you plan to bring up at the next meeting. As soon as you finish them, share drafts of essential guiding points, such as ISSUE STATEMENTS and POINT HEADINGS, or section headings and subheadings. Do not wait for several revisions before you share drafts.

Long periods of separate work invite writers to become personally invested in their own wording and approaches; that makes it harder to listen to suggestions or questions from collaborators. Effective collaboration requires sharing the whole process, not just the credit for authorship.

Frequent interchange during WRITING will also help you develop a consensus of thought that will allow you to fuse the parts into a seamless whole. Without this consensus, no amount of editing can create a cohesive presentation of each message.

6. Focus on the questions that are most important to your stage in the writing process.

During PREWRITING or WRITING, whenever you have organization roughed out, meet to combine your work and review the overall logic of the organization you have chosen; consider variations on the organization, so you can make sure your choice is the best one. Check your scope to make sure it still fits your purpose and adequately supports your reasoning. Also begin to discuss tone. Although you will revise for tone later, begin to think about the appropriate tone at this early stage in the process, especially in light of your AUDIENCE. If you wait until revision to address this aspect, you will find it harder to establish a unified tone.

During REWRITING, ask yourselves if the overall purpose has been sustained, if the theme is consistent, if the law is accurate and complete, and if the organization is coherent. See REWRITING, RHETORIC, and ORGANIZATION.

When REVISING, put all collaborators' work together, if you have not done so earlier in the process. Have each collaborator edit the text as a whole, so that individual voices begin to blend into one unified melody. For qualities to check at this stage, see REVISING CHECK-LIST.

When POLISHING, divide the responsibilities between collaborators, so you can be sure to check each item that needs checking. For example, you might check the complete text for consistent use of terms, accurate CITATION, CONCISENESS, correct spelling, correct use of COMMAS, and so on. For further information on what should be checked, see POLISHING CHECKLIST. Refer questionable passages to the appropriate collaborator whenever possible.

Discuss any remaining debatable points as a group. Move through these questions carefully, but quickly. Avoid the tendency to dwell with great emotion on the placement of a comma or a phrase. You want to get it right, but you must get it written.

7. Celebrate completion.

Congratulate yourselves when you are done. You have all worked hard, and you deserve the euphoria you will likely feel. For related information, see EDITING and MANAGING WRITERS.

COLLECTIVE NOUNS

A collective noun represents a collection of persons or things regarded as a unit. As such, a collective noun takes a singular verb when it refers to the collection as a whole.

The EPA is determined to press its [not their] claim.

The American Bar Association meets at least once a year.

A collective noun takes a plural verb, however, when it refers to the collection as separate persons or things.

The Student Bar Association have all gone home.

Make sure you do not treat a collective noun as both singular and plural in the same construction.

For a general discussion, see NOUNS.

COLLOQUIALISMS

Colloquialism refers to informal or regional phrases, or words or phrases used in conversation but not in formal writing, such as *ripped off* or *got into*. Rarely will you use colloquialisms in legal writing, not only because they are informal but also because they are usually not precise enough for legal writing. Colloquialisms may appear, however, as a part of a quote. Never resort to colloquialisms only because you cannot think of another word for the idea. There always is another word, so using the colloquialism would be admitting that your vocabulary is inadequate. For related information, see ACCURACY, LITERAL MEANING, and QUOTATION MARKS.

COLONS

The most common use of a colon in legal writing is to introduce a list.

In justifying the exclusion of expert psychiatric evidence, the court listed three concerns: maintaining the integrity of the bifurcated trial procedure, avoiding allowing the guilty to go free, and preserving the defendant's right against self-incrimination.

or

The Company's liability does not include any of the following: (1) any damage occurring in connection with the use of the equipment in any nuclear facility;

C

(2) any consequential or incidental damages, including but not limited to loss of profit, damage to associated equipment, cost of capital, and cost of substitute products;

(3) any costs beyond the price of the product and service that gives rise to the claim; or

(4) any claims arising from advice or assistance given by the Company without separate compensation for that advice.

Do not, however, use a colon if each item listed is punctuated as a complete sentence. In that situation, write the introduction to the list as a complete sentence and end it with a period, not a colon.

During the period of this maintenance agreement, if the Company determines that it cannot maintain the equipment in good working order, then the Company must replace the equipment with another unit in good working order. This requirement is subject to the following provisions.

1. If the Company replaces the equipment within two years of the warranty expiration date, then the replacement unit must be one that is newly manufactured, re-manufactured, or reconditioned.

2. If the Company replaces the equipment more than two years after the warranty expiration date, then the replacement unit will be one that is refurbished in accordance with the process used to refurbish rental units.

3. If the Company cannot replace the equipment with another unit of the same model, then the replacement unit will be substantially similar or will have greater capabilities.

4. . . . .

You may use a colon instead of a period between two sentences if one sentence sets up an expectation in the reader's mind that the next sentence fulfills.

The intent was clear: he pointed the gun directly at the victim's chest.

You may also use a colon, for emphasis, to introduce a phrase that is not a complete sentence.

The plaintiff has only one motive: recovery for his loss.

Avoid overusing the colon; it creates a dramatic sentence structure that will become too noticeable if overused. For related information, see EMPHASIS.

In general, do not capitalize the first word after the colon, because doing so usually makes the sentence self-consciously ornate. If you want, however, you may capitalize the first word after the colon to emphasize that word.

> **Plaintiff asks the court to invoke the most severe penalty: Child abuse must be stopped.**

COMBINING WORDS

See HYPHENS.

COMMAS

In general, commas coordinate one part of a sentence with another. A comma may (1) set off an introductory phrase, (2) set off an interrupting phrase, (3) indicate that more information follows in a phrase at the end of the sentence, or (4) signal that a new subject and verb follow a conjunction. Commas also (5) coordinate dates, (6) set off quotes, and (7) separate items in a list.

Do not use a comma to (8) separate a subject from its verb or (9) join two sentences.

1. Comma setting off an introductory phrase.

Use a comma when you place a phrase before the subject, unless that phrase is short and closely related to the subject.

> **In negligence actions, the theory is that the person being sued had a duty to act and failed to fulfill that duty.**

> **If the consumer disagrees with the information in the report, the agency must investigate again.**

> **First, it assumes that creditors have a definite criteria for creditworthiness.**

> **In contrast, a father who once attempted to retain physical possession of his son by the use of a gun was later determined by the supreme court to be a fit parent for custody. In Edwards v. Edwards, the father obtained a divorce from his wife ....**

2. Comma setting off an interrupting phrase.

Use commas before and after a phrase inserted in the middle of a sentence.

> **Most economists agree that, in terms of equity, this income should be taxed.**

> **The case is, however, a sample from that system.**

> **The plaintiff, despite warnings from his friends, jumped off the embankment.**

60

Willard Evans, Louise's father, testified at the hearing on the post-conviction motion.

Do not, however, put commas around a restrictive phrase, which comes after the subject but is necessary to describe the subject accurately.

The defendant's belief that the man was reaching for a gun supports instructions about both self-defense and manslaughter.

The standards adopted by the court reflect a prudent lawyer's conduct with his or her client.

For more explanation of restrictive phrases, see THAT OR WHICH?

3.   Comma indicating that more information follows.

Use a comma before extra information added to the end of a sentence.

The holding was poorly reasoned, filled with vague terms and illogical statements.

Privileges fall into the category of exceptions to a general rule, the rule of disclosure.

This court announced its decision in Sherman v. Freedman, which abolished the locality rule.

4.   Comma before a conjunction introducing a new subject and verb.

Use a comma before a conjunction that joins two independent CLAUSES.

The defendant expressed a desire to change his plea, but his attorney advised him not to do this.

Some proposals advocate continued use of the family as the basic unit of taxation, but others urge a return to the individual as the taxable unit.

5.   Commas coordinating dates.

Use a comma between a specific date and the year (*July 4, 1986*) but not between a month and the year (*July 1986*). Also do not use a comma when the date is written before the name of the month (*4 July 1986*).

6.   Commas setting off quotes.

Use a comma immediately after a phrase preceding a quote when the phrase introduces the quote.

She said, "I killed him."

Do not use a comma when the following quote is an integral part of the sentence.

He said "killed," not "stabbed."

Place the comma inside the quotation marks. One exception to this is legislation in some jurisdictions, where the comma goes inside the quotation marks only when it is part of the quote. Another exception is British English, which also puts commas and periods outside the quotation marks when they are not part of the quote. For related information, see QUOTATIONS, HOW TO PUNCTUATE and LEGISLATION.

7. Commas separating items in a list.

In legal writing, place a comma at the end of each item listed, including the item listed immediately before the *and*.

My estate is to be divided equally among my nephew, my son, my daughter, and my son-in-law.

Adding the comma before *and* avoids any possible confusion about how many items are listed. For more detail, see LISTS, STRUCTURE OF.

Also use a comma to separate modifiers listed before a noun. The comma is the grammatical equivalent of *and* in this situation.

The urgent, persistent messages were ignored by the defendant.

In contrast, if two words work together to state one modifying idea, do not use a comma. In this situation, one of the modifiers is an ADVERB.

The defendant ignored these <u>exceedingly</u> clear messages.

Sometimes, you may need a HYPHEN instead.

Age-old traditions do not necessarily create legal precedent.

8. Do not use a comma to separate a subject from its verb.

If two verbs share a common subject, do not put a comma before the conjunction between the verbs.

The driver lost control of his car while moving to the passing lane [ ] and slammed into the rear left fender of the defendant's truck.

Both the defendant and the plaintiff agree that the defendant had the obligation to post appropriate warnings [ ] and was within his rights when he posted the "no trespassing" signs.

The defendant had a duty to act [ ] and failed to fulfill that duty.

Do add a comma, however, if omitting it can cause a misreading of a sentence.

The defendant did see that an ambulance was called, and notified the proper authorities.

Also, do not use a comma between two subjects that share one verb.

> **Both custodial spouses seeking back payments of child support [ ] and divorcing parents seeking an order for child support will benefit from this rule.**

If two phrases are joined by a conjunction but both phrases are short, you may omit the comma if you wish.

> **The attorney recommended this action [ ] and the client did not object.**

9.   Finally, do not use a comma to separate a long subject from its verb.   Instead, reword the sentence so the subject is not so long.

> **A bystander does not have a duty to stop and render assistance solely because he or she passed by soon after an accident occurred.**

rather than

> Any bystander who sees an automobile accident but is in no way responsible for that accident, injured by the accident, or in any other way directly involved other than coming by soon after the accident occurred, does not have a duty to stop and render assistance.

COMMON NOUN

See NOUNS.

COMMON SENSE

You must use common sense in legal writing because few rules are absolute.   But proceed cautiously when common sense hints at breaking a rule; do so only if the answer to all of the following questions is *yes*.

1.   Can I break the rule without sacrificing one shred of ACCURACY?

2.   Can I break the rule without sacrificing CLARITY?

3.   Can I break the rule without sounding cute, trendy, or overly dramatic?

4.   Am I breaking this rule only to meet the requirements of some higher rule?   For example, you might choose a less concise phrase because it is more accurate and is easily read, or you might break a rule because the court has broken the rule in stating a proposition and you must for some reason quote the court directly, rather than using a PARAPHRASE.   For related information, see BENDING THE RULES.

COMPARE TO OR COMPARE WITH?

Use *compare to*   when you are introducing a similarity.

> **This harm, losing the ability to continue running competitively, can be compared to losing the ability to continue working.**

Use *compare with* when you are introducing two items you will subsequently compare or contrast.

> **This situation can be compared with the defendant's situation in Wheeler v. Bailey** ....

COMPARISON

Three factors can be used to clarify comparisons: parallel structure, clear transitions, and effective subjects and verbs.

1. Use PARALLEL STRUCTURE.

One of the best ways to write a graceful, effective comparison is to place the items compared in parallel structures. The framework of the parallel structure highlights the similarity or difference in the substance.

> **In Sampson, the landlord had been asked by tenants to replace burnt-out light bulbs in a stairwell, but had refused to do so. Similarly, Mr. Tyler had been asked to place higher wattage light bulbs in the stairwell, but had refused to do so.**

2. Use clear transitions.

Additionally, you can use TRANSITIONS to let the reader know that a comparison or contrast is coming.

In 1919, when the doctrine of the best interest of the child became the controlling consideration in custody disputes, the results of those disputes changed. Until then, custody usually was awarded to fathers. After 1919, *however*, custody usually was awarded to mothers.

3. Use effective subjects and verbs.

Another way to make a comparison shine is to make sure that you have placed the items compared in the main parts of the sentence, the subject and verb. For example, the following passage emphasizes the point that both fetuses were viable.

> **In *Kwaterski*, the court found that the unborn infant, in its eighth month of gestation, was viable before the car accident causing its death. Similarly, Dr. Bernhardt found that the Jones infant, in its seventh month of gestation, was viable before the accident causing its death.**

The main parts of the sentences are *the court found that the unborn infant was viable* and *Dr. Bernhardt found that the Jones infant was viable*. Making these points the main parts of the sentences emphasizes the similarity, while the difference (*eighth month of gestation* instead of *seventh month*) is stated but downplayed in PREPOSI-

TIONAL PHRASES. For a general discussion of this technique, see
SENTENCE STRUCTURE.

COMPLAINT

The complaint, the document that generally starts a lawsuit, has
six parts: the caption, the commencement, the body, the demand for
judgment, the signature, and the verification. Although your writing
concerns will differ for various parts, your overall priorities will be
identifying the content needed and ordering that content effectively.

1. General writing principles for different parts of the complaint.

When drafting the caption, signature, and verification, focus on
observing all pertinent court rules and avoiding unnecessary LE-
GALESE. You may find it helpful to look at samples of other complaints before writing your first one; see FORMS, USE OF for ways to
do this effectively. For related information, see POLISHING.

When writing the body and demand for judgment, focus on identifying all the needed content while omitting extraneous information.
The complaint must be precise enough to provide adequate notice to
your opponent and to survive a motion to dismiss, yet flexible enough to
allow you to include information you may want to introduce at trial.
For samples and discussion of strategies and concerns involved in
writing complaints, see Chapter 11, *Beyond the Basics: A Text for
Advanced Legal Writing,* Mary B. Ray and Barbara J. Cox, West, 1991.

2. Process for identifying the content.

To identify your content effectively, you need to research thoroughly so you can develop your theory and practical goals for the case,
including avoiding any appeals. To make certain that you do not miss
any needed points, try working backwards. Identify the relief you
want, including alternatives the trial court might provide. Also identify results you would want from an appeal court, if that were needed.
Then identify the causes of action that support the request and the
relevant law. Finally, identify the elements of each cause of action and
choose the facts that show those elements are met. This should provide
the content you need for your complaint.

3. Organizing the content.

You may find it most effective to organize the complaint inductively, alleging the specific facts, then the element those facts show, and
finally the legal conclusion supported by the facts and elements alleged.
Also observe your jurisdiction's format; many jurisdictions divide the
content into numbered paragraphs.

Usually, the first paragraphs identify the parties. The next paragraphs lay out the evidence establishing that the first element of the
first charge is met. After this evidence is stated, the following para-

graph asserts that the evidence shows the ultimate fact, or the logical conclusion stating that an element of the cause of action has been met.

For example, a complaint might be organized as follows.

1. [identity of plaintiff]
2. [identity of defendant]
3. [identity of additional defendant]
4–5. [evidence of standard sanitization practice used at hospital]
6–7. [evidence of actual practice used on a particular day when injury occurred]
8. [ultimate fact that hospital staff failed to exercise due care]
9–20. [other evidence, followed by ultimate facts establishing other elements of negligence]
21. [assertion that defendant's actions constituted negligence]
22. [allege damages plaintiff suffered as a result of the negligence]

WHEREFORE [demand for judgment]

COMPLETELY

If it is not really *complete*, do not use *completely*.

COMPLEX SENTENCES

A complex sentence has two or more CLAUSES, or groups of words that each has its own subject and verb; however, unlike in a compound sentence, a complex sentence contains a dependent clause.

Although John was in the room while his father was reading and discussing the will with the attorneys, John sat on the opposite side of the room and did not participate in the discussion.

A dependent clause cannot stand on its own as a sentence because it is attached to the other clause with a subordinating conjunction.

although John was in the room

while his father was reading and discussing the will

Complex sentences are useful for downplaying information because the reader views the independent clause as more important than the dependent clause. But use this structure with discretion; if complex sentences are overused, the text becomes hard to read.

If you wanted to read about complicated sentences, rather than about the grammatical category of complex sentences, see READABILITY or SENTENCE STRUCTURE.

COMPOUND SENTENCES

A compound sentence has two or more independent CLAUSES that are joined by a conjunction. Independent clauses are clauses that have a subject and verb and could stand on their own as complete sentences. Although compound sentences are not as frequently useful in legal writing as COMPLEX SENTENCES, they can be helpful for combining two points that are both logically and structurally parallel.

Other doctors in similar situations do disclose some risks to their patients, [independent clause] and [conjunction] thus you may argue that Dr. Walker did not meet the standard of disclosure set by his profession for cases such as yours [independent clause].

Occasionally compound sentences can also be helpful for avoiding undue emphasis of a minor point. Short sentences are emphatic, so putting a minor point in a short sentence confuses the reader by overemphasizing that point.

The supervisor told Mr. Sykes to remove the cartons from the loading dock before the end of the day, and Mr. Sykes did so.

rather than

The supervisor told Mr. Sykes to remove the cartons from the loading dock before the end of the day. Mr. Sykes did so.

For related information, see SENTENCE STRUCTURE.

COMPUTERS FOR RESEARCH

Using computers for research is fast and effective, but expensive. Therefore, use computers to supplement, not to replace, book research. When you decide to use a computer, go through the first five steps of the following Ten-Step Guide before going to the terminal. Additionally, know the vocabulary of the computer system you are using, whether it be Lexis or Westlaw. They do have differences, although the approach is essentially the same, and you need to be familiar with these differences before you start the following steps.

TEN–STEP GUIDE TO COMPUTER RESEARCH

At your desk.

1. Collect the facts. List the who, what, where, when, why, and how.

2. Analyze the facts according to your preferred system.

   (a) *Westlaw: parties, places, objects, basis, defense, relief.*

(b) *Lexis*: *things, acts, persons, places.*

Brainstorm at this stage; avoid editing. Give each category a page or a column, and then think of every possible synonym and antonym in order to get accurate search words.

3. Formulate the QUESTION PRESENTED. Brainstorm again, thinking of all the possible questions. Write out those questions following this three-step formula.

(a) *Under* [what you think the general law is]

(b) *did* [the legal question, such as, *did X assault Y*]

(c) *when* [LEGALLY SIGNIFICANT FACTS applicable to this legal question]?

Then organize Issues logically, putting threshold issues first, such as *standing*, and substantive issues later such as *whether X assaulted Y*.

4. Formulate your query.

(a) Choose terms from the list you made in step 2 and identify the search words most important to your issue, concentrating on terms a court might have used, such as *consideration*, rather than more general terms, such as *payment*.

(b) Formulate the query according to your specific computer language system, using *Westlaw* or *Lexis* root expanders or natural language.

(c) Carefully limit your query. Consider first the scope of the topic. If it is wide, use more restrictive connectors or specific terms. If the scope is narrow, use broader connectors or more general terms.

5. Choose your database, which is the computer equivalent of the set of books to which you would go to research your QUESTION PRESENTED. Each computer system has a list of databases, such as Northwest (*NW*), which corresponds to the *North Western Reporter*, or New York (*NY–CS*), which includes the *New York Reporter*. Make sure you know which jurisdiction's law will apply and therefore which database you wish to search. If the scope is narrow, put terms within the same case.

6. Map out your research strategy, depending on what sources you already have and what data bases you would like to search.

At the computer terminal.

Before beginning, be certain you know the basic mechanics of the computer system and the options that are available to you. For example, make sure you know how to save your research for a later time, how to move between the researching function and your word processing system, and how to print excerpts.

7. Sign on to the system according to its rules.

8. Enter your query according to the directions, and when you come up with a list of sources, make sure you have a usable amount; if not, edit your query.

9. Print out only the material essential to your work; take notes on the rest but be aware of your time, so that you can minimize the time actually signed on. One useful shortcut is to print a list of cases, sign off, and then locate the cases in the reporters.

10. Update the law on the computer only insofar as hardcover SHEP-ARD'S and other sources are incomplete. The computer's data base may not be as current as the most recent volume supplement. However you use the computer, remember that it is not a panacea; it cannot solve all research problems. Similarly, the computer is not error-proof. It is literal, so formulate your query carefully.

For related information, see WRITING PROCESS and GETTING STARTED.

COMPUTERS FOR WRITING

Computers can make your life as a writer much easier with their capacities for processing text, generating graphics, and managing files. But beware of their liabilities: computers can either devour your time and energy or save it, depending on how you use them. To maximize the usefulness of computers to you as a writer, remember these general principles.

1. When the task is the goal, focus on completing that task, not using the computer.

Use the computer whenever it helps, but consider whether it is more efficient to use simpler technologies such as the phone, the post-it note, or the pencil. For example, computers are wonderful for generating rough drafts for some writers, particularly those who touch-type. Yet they are not useful for writers who feel more comfortable and focused with a yellow pad in front of them or a dictation machine's microphone in hand.

2. Decide whether or not you need to learn to use a computer program.

Mastery of a computer or piece of software takes time; you must determine when that investment of time is worthwhile. For example, if you need a complex table or other graphic, it may be more efficient to delegate the job. Learning the program may be worthwhile only if you will be using graphics more in the near future. In contrast, learning to use a basic word processing program is more likely to be useful because you can rewrite your own drafts on the computer and see results immediately.

3. When you decide to learn a computer program, allocate time for that learning.

Do not plan to learn about the computer while you are working on an important project. Rather, choose a simpler project and allocate additional time to both learning the program and using it while completing the project. Or schedule a separate training time, which you can use as a break from other projects.

CONCISENESS

Conciseness is at a premium in legal writing. Achieve it whenever possible, although never at the expense of substance. Revise for conciseness by doing the following.

1. Eliminate facts or law that do not bear on this particular analysis. Concentrate on the scope of this problem, so the reader can concentrate on that too. For example, if the only legal issue being discussed in a memorandum is *whether or not there has been an intentional tort*, do not include facts in the analysis that do not bear on intentional tort. For related information, see LEGALLY SIGNIFICANT FACTS, BACK-GROUND FACTS, and EMOTIONAL FACTS.

2. Move important material to the beginning of paragraphs and sections; this will eliminate long explanations that reach a result. Instead, give the result and explain it. For more detail and related information, see PARAGRAPHS, TOPIC SENTENCES, and POSITIONS OF EMPHASIS.

3. Make sure that each paragraph advances one of the points in your reasoning. This should help you avoid circumlocution, or discussing again a point already established. Similarly, present only one main point in a paragraph. This will help you make sure you support and explain that point adequately, which will lessen the chance that you will repeat the point later to bring in further support. For related information, see PARAGRAPHS and ORGANIZATION, SMALL-SCALE.

4. Use the key words in a sentence for your subjects and verbs.

Exigent circumstances justify the police's failure to obtain a warrant.

rather than

The crucial fact here is that exigent circumstances existed justifying the police's failure to obtain a warrant.

5. Make CITATIONS speak for themselves, rather than using *the court held* or *the court went on to say*.

The doctrine of moral right is not expressly recognized in New York. Hesler v. Alley Book Division, 952 N.Y.S.2d 552, 555, 761 Misc. 2d 104, 105 (1999).

rather than

> The New York Court in <u>Hesler v. Alley Book Division</u>, 952 N.Y.S.2d 552, 555, 761 Misc. 2d 104, 105 (1999), has stated that the doctrine of moral right is not expressly recognized in New York.

6. Use ACTIVE VOICE, rather than passive, because passive voice often requires more words.

> **The defendant argued that the court should suppress the evidence.**

rather than

> It was argued by the defendant that the evidence should be suppressed by the court.

7. Omit unneeded ADJECTIVES and ADVERBS.

> **The court in <u>Thomas</u> does not establish a standard for viability that is any more specific than the fetus' ability to exist separately from its mother.**

rather than

> Obviously, the court in <u>Thomas</u> appears to fail to definitively establish an unambiguous and undebatable determining standard for when a fetus reaches the medical state of viability that seems to be any more clearly specific than ascertaining medically the fetus' ability to exist separately and apart from its biological mother.

8. Omit duplicate terms.

> **The donation's purpose was to provide assistance to the community's AIDS victims, not to expand the program's administration.**

rather than

> The donation's thrust and purpose was to provide aid and assistance to the community's AIDS sufferers or victims, not to augment or expand the program's administration and overhead.

9. Delete unneeded prepositional phrases. For example, substitute *legally* for *on a legal basis* or *defendant's* for *of the defendant.*

> **The defendant's obligation may have existed morally, but not legally.**

rather than

> The obligation of the defendant may have existed in a moral sense but not on a legal basis.

10. When possible delete *that* constructions, such as *there are . . . that, there is . . . that*, and *it is . . . that.*

> **You must go through this process to identify any opinion's key facts.**

rather than

> This is the process that you must go through to identify any opinion's key facts.

11. Delete long empty phrases that add words with no meaning. If sentences were twenty mule teams, these phrases would be weak mules dragging down the rest of the team. For example, remove *it is clear that*, and just state your point. Remove *it is important to state at the outset that* and just say *first*.

CONCLUSIONS

The Conclusion is the final section in a memo or brief. It is also part of an opinion letter. In all three, the Conclusion may be the first section to which the legal reader turns. In briefs, the Conclusion should summarize briefly the reasoning presented in the argument and should request specific relief. The court should know at a glance what result the writer asks for and why. Avoid the traditional *For the foregoing reasons*. This forces the reader to either reread the entire Argument Section or skip the point. Instead, use this last opportunity for a focused summary that delivers the final punch. For related information, see SUMMARY OF THE ARGUMENT.

In MEMOS, the Conclusion summarizes the main points made in the Discussion, giving a capsule of the reasoning that led to the Brief Answer. It may also contain recommendations to the reader. It does not, however, include any information or reasoning not covered in the Discussion.

In OPINION LETTERS, the Conclusion answers the client's question, often in one sentence. Usually place the Conclusion in the opening if the news is good, after the facts if you want to soften the news, or at the end if the conclusion would not make sense without a lengthy explanation.

In your WRITING PROCESS, write your Conclusion when it is most helpful to do so. For example, if you are having trouble seeing how all your points fit together, you may find it helpful to write the Conclusion before finishing the rest of your draft. Conversely, you may find it more helpful to write the conclusion only after you have written the rest of your draft and your REASONING is clarified.

CONCLUSORY

This term refers to a presentation of LEGAL ANALYSIS that jumps from the general principle or rule to the conclusion. A conclusory presentation omits the reasons for reaching the conclusion as well as the logical connections between the steps in the reasoning. In a SYLLOGISM, conclusory analysis jumps from the major premise to the conclusion, omitting the minor premise. Make sure your analysis is complete so no reader will apply the term *conclusory* to your writing.

CONCRETE NOUNS

See ABSTRACT NOUNS.

CONFORM TO, CONFORM WITH, OR CONFORM IN?

Conform to.

CONJUNCTIONS

Conjunctions join phrases, words, or sentences.

1. Classifying conjunctions.

Conjunctions can be coordinating, such as *and, but, for,* or *or.* They are correlating when they include two words working together, such as *both . . . and* or *either . . . or.* Finally, they are subordinating when they introduce DEPENDENT CLAUSES, such as *although, because, unless, despite, until.*

2. Using conjunctions effectively.

Conjunctions serve as clear and effective transitions only when used accurately, so choose the conjunction that most accurately communicates the logical connection between the two sentences.

> **Although the project was not finished by the date scheduled for completion, the contract was not breached because the delay was due to a hailstorm.**

rather than

> The project was not finished by the date scheduled for completion and the contract was not breached because the delay was due to a hailstorm.

For help in finding the most accurate conjunction, see TRANSITIONS. For related information, see CONNECTIONS, MAKING THEM.

Two problems to watch for when using conjunctions are (1) overusing one conjunction, such as *and,* and (2) using a conjunction to join two things not logically and grammatically parallel. For a discussion of the latter, see PARALLEL STRUCTURE. For advice on the use of specific conjunctions, see AND, AND/OR, BOTH . . . AND, BUT, OR, and NOT ONLY . . . BUT ALSO. For related information, see HOWEVER and SENTENCE STRUCTURE, subsection 2.

CONNECTING WORDS

See TRANSITIONS.

CONNECTIONS, MAKING THEM

Making the connection clear between phrases or sentences is like using your car's turn signals correctly when leading a convoy. By letting your readers know where you are going, you increase the chance that those readers will be able to follow your logical route. Consider the following techniques in constructing strong connections.

1. Use parallel structure. This structure can immediately underscore both the similarities and differences. For example, you can compare two items like this.

> **In <u>Sampson</u>, the landlord had been asked by tenants to replace burnt-out light bulbs in a stairwell, but had refused to do so. Similarly, Mr. Tyler had been asked to place higher wattage light bulbs in the stairwell, but had refused to do so.**

For more on this technique, see PARALLEL STRUCTURE.

2. Repeat key terms. Use repetition when it is needed for ACCURACY. For example, if you mean this *contract*, do not shift to this *document* or this *agreement*. Changing terms confuses legal readers, who will think that you must mean something else if you changed terms. For more on this technique, see REPETITION.

3. Use a transition, such as *furthermore, because, although*, or *even if*. Keep in mind, however, that this connection is only as good as the accuracy of the transition word.

> **The Act did not successfully treat the broader problem of marital status discrimination. Instead, it shifted inequitable tax burdens between taxpaying groups.**

rather than

> The Act did not successfully treat the broader problem of marital status discrimination; however, it shifted inequitable tax burdens between taxpaying groups.

Because using an inaccurate transition is more confusing than using none, never throw in a transition carelessly. For more help in choosing accurate transitions, see TRANSITIONS.

CONNECTORS

See TRANSITIONS and CONNECTIONS, MAKING THEM.

CONNOTATION

Connotation refers to the meaning implied by a word beyond that word's LITERAL MEANING. For example, a person holding the same position could be described as *stalwart, resolute, determined, unwavering, headstrong, stubborn, mulish*, or *pigheaded*. These words do not differ so much in literal meaning as they do in connotation.

As you can see from these examples, words do not just have a positive or negative connotation, but fall on a continuum stretching from extremely positive to extremely negative. The extremes of the continuum are effective only if the reader or listener already agrees with you. In legal writing, because you are not addressing such an AUDIENCE, you should avoid the extremes on either end of the continuum. For a discussion of this and related concerns, see WORD CHOICE and PERSUASIVE WRITING.

CONTACT

Contact is rather vague; before you use the word, make sure you want to be that vague. For example, *contact* is not as specific as *telephone, write*, or *meet with*. For related concerns, see PRECISION and WORD CHOICE.

CONTEND

Courts do not *contend*, only counsel does.

CONTEXT, CREATING

To keep your readers engaged, remind them often of the context within which you are explaining, comparing, arguing, or illustrating. Avoid the pitfall that engulfs many legal writers, who lose their readers by racing into an idea without connecting it logically to the previous section or paragraph. Remind your reader of your topic, answer, analysis, or direction in the following ways.

1. In MEMOS, create clear QUESTIONS PRESENTED that focus the reader on the precise question being resolved. Give the BRIEF ANSWERS as soon as possible, using details that orient the reader.

2. In BRIEFS, tell the court in the introduction specifically why the case is before it. Use the ISSUE STATEMENTS and POINT HEADINGS to remind the reader of the context throughout the document.

3. Use HEADINGS, in sentence form, to explain your message and to guide the reader through the document. To make sure that they present a complete and unified synopsis of your message, read your headings in order without the intervening text.

4. Use TOPIC SENTENCES as first sentences of paragraphs. These sentences can sometimes relate to the previous paragraph or to the overall message, as well as introduce the idea of this paragraph. To check the logical flow of your presentation, read through all your topic sentences, without the supporting text.

5. Use SENTENCE STRUCTURE that reflects the logical structure of the content.

6. Use REPETITION of key words to show how central concepts recur throughout the text.

7. Chain ideas together from sentence to sentence. For example, the idea at the end of one sentence often reappears early in the next.

> **The meaning of this statute is clear on its face. Because of this clarity, ...**

For more on this, see CONNECTIONS, MAKING THEM.

CONTEXT–INDEPENDENT WRITING

Most legal writing should be self-sufficient; that is, it should include all the information needed to understand the full meaning. Many legal documents have long lives and many readers, so include enough information or cross-references to enable a new reader to understand the document in one sitting.

In a MEMO, for example, include all the LEGALLY SIGNIFICANT FACTS needed to understand the memo without having to go to the pleadings, correspondence, or previous memos. This inclusion is needed because a memo written to a supervising attorney in June may be used in December by a new lawyer assigned to the case. Similarly, cite to the record in a BRIEF and include essential excerpts in an APPENDIX. These additions will avoid requiring the judge to leave the brief and search the record to understand the argument. Making the document context independent will build your CREDIBILITY, ease the reader's burden, and keep the document resilient through its potentially many uses.

CONTINUAL OR CONTINUOUS?

Continual means *intermittent* or *repeated at intervals*, such as *continual requests for advice*.

Continuous means *uninterrupted* or *unbroken*, such as *continuous vigil* or *continuous preoccupation with the law*.

CONTRACTIONS

Do not use contractions, such as *don't* or *isn't*, in legal writing. They are too informal for almost all legal situations. The only exceptions would be in a letter or memo where you want to sound casual.

CONTRACTS, DRAFTING

Keep these general writing principles in mind when drafting contracts.

1. Before writing, make sure you are clear about what parts the contract must include and what situations the contract must cover. Know what the parties in fact want. Precisely because this is an obvious point, it is often overlooked. Try outlining the contract to make sure that all the needed pieces are included and are organized logically. For ways to accomplish this, see OUTLINES and ORGANIZATION FOR THOSE WHO CAN'T OUTLINE.

2. Reconcile yourself to writing many DRAFTS of the contract to get it right. If you try to get all the details right in the first draft, you are likely to miss some important larger points. For help in organizing your drafts, see WRITING PROCESS.

3. Use clear, simple, businesslike language. Much progress has been made in this area, particularly in the areas of insurance and finance. Be on guard, however, for slipping back into the mire of LEGALESE. Use only the technical terms you need and define them if necessary. For ways to do this, see UNOBTRUSIVE DEFINITIONS.

4. Make each clause do one thing, not more. OUTLINES can help you here by breaking down the whole contract into a series of small points.

5. When REVISING, check for ambiguities.

(a) Check to make sure that you have used only one term for one item or person. Referring to the same person, item, or concept by two different terms creates an ambiguity that invites misunderstandings later. If needed, include a definition section to define all your KEY TERMS, so that the reader understands any unusual terms. For related information, see AMBIGUITY, WAYS TO AVOID.

(b) Check also to make sure that you have not used one term for several different items or persons. This can create unwanted ambiguities. For discussion of related ideas, see AMBIGUITY, WAYS TO AVOID; LISTS, STRUCTURE OF; and PUNCTUATING LISTS.

6. After POLISHING each clause in the contract, reread the document as a whole, looking for larger contradictions between parts of the contract, rather than wording problems within one clause. In your concern for the details, you may have overlooked some larger ambiguities.

7. Somewhere along the line, consult others. No one person can imagine all the pitfalls that the parties to any contract are hoping to avoid. No one person can imagine all the ways some reader can misconstrue a point.

CONTRAST

See COMPARISON.

CORPORATIONS, THEY OR IT?

The corporation is *it* because it functions as a single entity. For related information, see COLLECTIVE NOUNS.

CORRELATING CONJUNCTIONS

See CONJUNCTIONS and READABILITY.

CORRESPOND TO OR CORRESPOND WITH?

Use *correspond with* if you mean that you and another party are writing to each other. Use *correspond to* if you mean that one point is analogous to another.

COULD

Use *could* to suggest a capacity that has not been used.

The defendant could have prevented the misunderstanding simply by answering the plaintiff's question about the backhoe's maintenance requirements.

Thus *could* is useful to add a negative shading to an action by suggesting that it was possible for something else to have happened. For related information, see VERBS, AUXILIARY.

COULD CARE LESS OR COULDN'T CARE LESS?

Use neither in formal legal writing.

COULD OR CAN?

COUNTERARGUMENTS, HOW TO HANDLE

When defending against a counterargument, do so without losing the focus of your own argument. To do this, use the POSITIONS OF EMPHASIS to advance your position. Begin your PARAGRAPHS, PARAGRAPH BLOCKS, and sections with your affirmative position.

The proper standard here is the strict level of scrutiny; the category of persons suffering the discrimination is clearly defined.

Then, after you have established your reasoning in the reader's mind, address the alternative position. As you do this, you may refer to the

78

opponent's reasoning, but do so briefly, as an introduction to your counterargument. Rather than spending a sentence referring to the opposing position, merely imply that position as you state your own. Or relegate the opponent's position to a dependent clause; keep your SUBJECT–VERB COMBINATIONS focused on your own assertions.

> **When this court has allowed a lower standard, the category of persons being discriminated against was not clearly defined. In contrast, here the category is unquestionably women in their fifties and sixties.**

or

> **Although the defendant quoted reasoning from several cases that applied a lower standard of scrutiny, those cases did not address the precise issue of the age of the persons who were discriminated against. They dealt with factors such as personality traits and personal behavior. But the category in this case is women of a certain age. Thus ....**

rather than

> The defense argues that a lower standard of scrutiny should be applied to this case because the plaintiff is not part of a clearly defined group, as would be the case if discrimination were claimed to be based on race or gender. The defendant cites many cases to support this proposition. These cases include arguments of discrimination based on personality traits not directly related to the person's job or on the plaintiff's behavior in his or her personal life. Those cases did not address the precise issue of this case, which is the combination of the gender and age of the plaintiff.

By putting your argument first and subordinating your opponent's position, you clarify the surrounding reasons for your discussion while still maintaining your own position. It helps you avoid allocating too much space in your brief to your opponent's arguments and prevents the opponent's brief from dictating your organization.

When phrasing your counterargument, avoid wording that focuses on the opposition, such as *the opponent contends*. Similarly, avoid inserting personal attacks, such as *opposing counsel's claims are unreasonable and unwarranted* or *opposing counsel did not do her research;* these phrases detract from your CREDIBILITY and add no substance to your argument.

See VERBS, TENSES.

COURTS, HOW TO ADDRESS

See JUDGES, HOW TO ADDRESS. Also see Bluebook rule 9.

COURTS, THEY OR IT?

Even though several judges together make up the court, refer to the court as *it* when discussing the legal entity.

The court made its reasoning clear when it stated that it would not grant a new trial.

Use *they* only in the rare situation when you are referring to the individual judges serving within one court.

When preparing to hear oral arguments, the appellate court may ask their individual clerks to prepare bench briefs. They may also specifically ask their clerks to review the record when the briefs present disparate accounts of the facts.

CREDIBILITY

Your credibility as an attorney and a person can be affected by your writing. To make sure that the effect is positive, do the following.

1. Be accurate. Misstating facts, citing incorrect sources, and misrepresenting the situation would be remembered not only through this legal situation, but also in future dealings with this reader.

2. Keep to the point. Make sure your documents do not stray from the problem you are trying to solve. A clear focus will save your reader time and will help you earn a reputation as an incisive and clear-headed writer who takes time to understand thoroughly the problem he or she is addressing.

3. Check your citations. Make sure that each is impeccably presented, both in content and form. These are the proof that you have carefully researched the subject and that you are both familiar with the law and certain about its precise use for this case. Check statute numbers, case names, PINPOINT CITES, and SIGNALS.

4. Proofread. See that all documents leaving your office are proofread for correct spelling of names, correct dates and times, and correct spelling and grammar.

5. Meet your deadlines. This alone shows that you are in command of the case. If you know that you cannot meet the deadline, such as when it conflicts with other court dates, identify the problem at the outset and seek an extension immediately. Asking for extensions at the last minute would impair your credibility and the overall quality of your work. See DEADLINES, MEETING THEM and WRITING PROCESS.

6. Hold your temper. No matter how irate you are, avoid resorting to name calling. For alternatives, see TOUGH, SOUNDING THAT WAY.

DANGLING MODIFIERS

See MODIFIERS, DANGLING.

DASHES

The dash, the gigolo of the punctuation world, has its uses and its dangers. It intrigues the writer with its drama and its convenient ambiguity. Like a gigolo, however, its effectiveness is determined by the user's *savoir faire* and restraint. If you overuse the dash in legal writing, you run the risk of looking desperate.

1. Danger of the dash.

Beware the ambiguity of the dash. It can replace a colon, a pair of commas or parentheses, or a transition, so you might use it without thinking too much. As a result, the reader has to do the extra work of determining how the dash is functioning in this particular context. The reader may not appreciate doing this, may decide not to bother, or may come to the wrong conclusion.

Ms. Willard had decided not to pursue the action further because litigation would be too expensive.

rather than

Ms. Willard has decided not to pursue the action further—litigation would be too expensive.

2. Uses of the dash.

First, a dash will make a phrase stand out on the page. If you use dashes for drama, make sure the content within the dashes is indeed dramatic.

The defendant's action—both understandable and humane in this case—cannot be rightly condemned.

There are no spaces before or after the dash. COMMAS would be more formal here, but not as dramatic.

Second, a dash can show a sudden turn of thought with an undercurrent of humor. This is a pleasing and deft touch, but one for which legal writing provides few opportunities.

Mrs. Smith thought the intruder might be a burglar—or her husband.

Again, you must be very sure that the content can sustain the drama and wry humor the dash promises.

Finally, a dash can set off a mid-sentence phrase when commas would confuse the reader and parentheses would trivialize the content of the interruption.

81

> Julia was on a large and complex daily regimen of drugs. Daily she took three kinds of barbiturates—Tuinal, Fiornal, and Fiornal with Codeine—one of which included an opium derivative.

Here you are using it out of rude necessity, and you may prefer to revise the sentence.

> Julia was also on a large and complex daily regimen of drugs. Daily she took three kinds of barbiturates, one of which included an opium derivative. These barbiturates included Tuinal, Fiornal, and Fiornal with Codeine.

For alternative punctuation marks, see COMMAS, COLONS, and PARENTHESES. For related information, see EMPHASIS.

DATA

Data means *information* and is now commonly used in both the singular and the plural, as in *these data are fascinating* or *this data is inconclusive.*

DEADLINES, MEETING THEM

Meeting deadlines is a skill you must develop to succeed as a legal writer, because failure to meet them can be a source of malpractice suits. The secret to meeting deadlines successfully is becoming familiar with your overall WRITING PROCESS and adjusting it, so that you do not get behind at any stage in the process. Once you have developed your own process, break that process into subsections and set interim deadlines for each subsection. Mark those deadlines on your calendar, moving backwards from the deadline date and making a special effort to meet each of those interim deadlines. Sometimes it helps to tie the deadline to a person, such as to your secretary or a person who will do a read-through of the ideas. The potential embarrassment at missing the interim deadline may motivate you to meet it.

If you find yourself falling behind, examine your list of tasks to be done and determine which tasks are critical to that stage of the process. For example, you may not have updated your cases and are instead spending time reading law review articles. Or you are spending too much time revising and leaving no time for POLISHING or for absorbing unforeseen disasters. Force yourself to shift to completing the critical tasks before you spend time on nice-but-nonessential tasks.

Each writer usually feels uncomfortable or bogged down somewhere in the writing process; pinpointing which part of the process is uncomfortable and then overcoming this discomfort can also help you meet deadlines. For example, you may feel uncomfortable in (1) PREWRITING, when you are doing research, collecting facts, taking

NOTES, reading the law, outlining and organizing; (2) WRITING, when you are actually translating ideas to paper by dictating or typing or writing the first draft; (3) REWRITING, when you are checking large-scale organization and ideas, making sure that all parts of your analysis are present and in a logical order (see ORGANIZATION, LARGE–SCALE); (4) REVISING, when you are checking small-scale organization, PARAGRAPHS, SENTENCE STRUCTURE, WORD CHOICE, TRANSITIONS, and HEADINGS; or (5) POLISHING, when you are checking CITATIONS, spelling, punctuation, and typos.

One way to overcome this discomfort is to decide which stage is most uncomfortable for you, divide it into subparts, and attack those subparts directly. For example, if you are uncomfortable in PREWRITING, give yourself a time limit by which to have your prewriting done. Then divide your prewriting tasks by doing background research, briefing, and outlining separately. This can help you focus on each task so you do it more efficiently. Set a time to translate that prewriting to writing and force yourself to meet that deadline. Forcing yourself to meet these interim deadlines will help you avoid unnecessary procrastination and will allow you adequate time to fix any problems you find throughout the subsequent stages of writing.

Sometimes in prewriting you can let PROCRASTINATION work for you. As you delay writing, however, let the ideas flow by keeping a notebook handy for any new ideas that can occur any time, any place. Develop a system of taking NOTES that allows you to incubate on your ideas, even if you are not actually at your desk or in the library. Thus procrastination becomes creative incubation. For related concerns, see GETTING STARTED.

If you are uncomfortable about WRITING the first draft, clear your calendar and set aside a time just for that. Remember that the goal here is not to get it right, but to get it written. Do not revise as you write. It takes too much time, is too painful, and distracts you from your main task at this stage, which is to get all your ideas down on paper. Let the creative voice work here; let the ideas flow, no matter how strange they seem. Just get your ideas into words somehow and finish the draft within the time period you set. Then do something else. Let the draft sit. For related concerns, see WRITING BLOCK.

REWRITING is often ignored or subsumed within other writing stages, and this causes problems with meeting deadlines. Give rewriting its own time, again by clearing the calendar and setting aside one large block of time or several small blocks only for that. At this stage, do any major shifting of large sections. Check large-scale organization and make sure all the ideas you wish to include have been stated and are placed in a logical order. See also ORGANIZATION, LARGE–SCALE.

After rewriting, shift to the REVISING stage. Check small-scale organization, TOPIC SENTENCES, TRANSITIONS, SENTENCE STRUCTURE, and WORD CHOICE. Give particular attention to your ISSUE STATEMENTS or QUESTIONS PRESENTED and to the specific details of the Conclusion. See also CONCLUSIONS.

Finally, polish. Check cites, punctuation, spelling, grammar, typos, and any problems peculiar to your writing. Allow at least one day to proofread large documents. See POLISHING.

Thus, by focusing on specific goals at each stage of the writing process and by meeting your interim deadlines for each of these stages, you can successfully meet your final deadline. For related concerns, see WHEN TO STOP.

DEEM

Deem is LEGALESE for *is* or *held.* The court may deem something to be a conclusion, but this word is an imprecise assessment of the court's action.

The court held that a 22–week-old fetus is a minor child for the purposes of a wrongful death action.

rather than

The court deemed the 22–week-old fetus to be a minor child for the purposes of a wrongful death action.

Identify the action as a HOLDING or as DICTA, but avoid *deem,* which is ambiguous and archaic.

DEFINITELY

Definitely means *for certain* or *assuredly*, and therefore should be avoided in legal writing unless the point is literally definite.

DEFINITIONS, WHEN TO INCLUDE

Add a definition when you are using any technical term, legal or otherwise, that may be unfamiliar to your reader and that is central to your point. If you are worried about insulting the reader by defining a term, see UNOBTRUSIVE DEFINITIONS.

DEMAND FOR PAYMENT

See REQUESTS FOR PAYMENT.

DEPENDENT CLAUSES

A clause is a phrase that includes a subject and a verb; a dependent clause is a clause that is inserted into another sentence and cannot stand alone as a sentence. A dependent clause begins with a subordinating conjunction, such as *when*. For example, in the following sentence, *when it refused to submit a jury instruction on manslaughter* is a dependent clause.

The court abused its discretion when it refused to submit a jury instruction on manslaughter.

For more on how these dependent clauses work in sentences, see SENTENCES, PARTS OF and SENTENCE STRUCTURE. For related definitions, see CLAUSES.

DESPERATION

See HELP; GETTING STARTED; DEADLINES, MEETING THEM; WHEN TO STOP; or WRITING BLOCKS.

DICTA

In an opinion, *dicta*, which means *words*, includes anything a court says that does not have a significant effect on the outcome of the case. Dicta differs from a holding in that dicta is not binding on courts in subsequent opinions. Dicta can be significant, however, in your use of a case in research or in class. Use dicta to predict a trend in the law, to illuminate the reasoning in this case, or to understand future cases. For contrast and context, see HOLDINGS and CASE BRIEFS.

DICTATION

Speak to your secretary before you dictate anything. Ask about particular preferences in format, pronunciation, punctuation, and paragraphing. The more specific you are about the details of dictation, the fewer questions you will have to resolve later.

If you have never dictated, begin with small texts, such as a letter or NOTICE OF MOTION. Before dictating, make some notes for your reference; have your large-scale organization in mind and dictate accordingly; make rewriting corrections on the first draft you get back from the secretary.

If you are really uncomfortable about dictating, go ahead and write out what you are going to dictate and then just read it into the dictaphone to get used to the medium. Then, with each task, write less and talk more.

When you get the draft back from the secretary, delete any passages that are too conversational or otherwise inappropriate. In particular, check for wordiness, a common problem in dictated texts. For help here, see CONCISENESS. Also check for clear, coherent ORGANIZATION. For help here, see TRANSITIONS; ORGANIZA-

TION, LARGE–SCALE; ORGANIZATION, SMALL–SCALE; and CO-HERENCE. As you discover what your dictation habits are, you can work gradually to eliminate the bad habits, so that less rewriting will be necessary.

Eventually, with concentration, you can use dictation to close the gap between speaking, which can be too colloquial, and writing, which can be too long and arcane. As you revise works you have dictated, work to bring a readable quality to the text; note the changes and try to integrate them into your dictation so that you develop a versatile and eloquent dictating voice.

DICTION

Diction is your choice of words and vocabulary in speaking and writing. To keep your written diction clear, consider the following guidelines.

1. Avoid JARGON and LEGALESE; use PLAIN ENGLISH instead.

2. Use one sentence per legal point, and in that sentence use words that frame your meaning precisely. See SUBJECT–VERB COMBINATIONS.

3. Avoid unnecessary modifiers, which may muddle, rather than clarify, your meaning. Modifiers may also raise questions of subjectivity. Your reader may doubt your assessments and be unnecessarily lured away from your precise meaning.

4. When POLISHING, take time to check for the grammar problems that you know are most likely to occur in your writing. Especially check subject and verb agreement in complex sentences.

DIFFERENT FROM OR DIFFERENT THAN?

Different from is always correct. *Different than* is allowable sometimes, according to some sources, but the rule is unsettled here, so to be safe use *different from*.

DIGRESSION

Digression, or straying from the main point, usually occurs when you are not sure of the main line of the analysis. If you feel yourself digressing, stop and reread your QUESTION PRESENTED or ISSUE STATEMENTS and the RULES you are applying. Think about them. Then reanalyze your ORGANIZATION and decide whether or not the point is essential to the analysis.

If you are still uncertain, let the point sit and move to your Brief Answer or Conclusion. Try to see the larger picture and the result, both of which may illuminate the point's relevance. Alternatively, move to another part of the analysis and then come back. If you can sense that a point is digressing, fight the temptation to elaborate on it, or you will have to eliminate a great deal of your text when REVISING.

For related writing problems, see CONCISENESS. See also BRIEF ANSWERS.

DIRECT OBJECTS

See SENTENCE, PARTS OF.

DISCUSSION SECTION

The Discussion is the section in a memo that presents and analyzes the law. As such, it explains to the reader how the law applies to the facts under analysis and predicts the possible outcome of the problem. The Discussion then, should incorporate the following elements into a logical, unified whole:

(1) the RULES relevant to the analysis;

(2) ANALOGOUS CASES, where appropriate, describing cases that are analogous to the facts, issues, and reasoning being analyzed;

(3) an APPLICATION, which presents both sides' arguments about how the law applies to the facts being analyzed and balances those arguments; and

(4) POLICY and EQUITY, which interact with the rules to balance both sides' arguments and predict an outcome.

The Discussion should use an OBJECTIVE STYLE and should consider the specific requests of the AUDIENCE. Organize the Discussion according to the law being used, moving from the rule to be applied through the application to the specific outcome.

Avoid writing as if the law, application, and outcome are discrete subsections. Instead, let the logical organization of the law dictate your organization. For example, if you have a simple rule you might state the rule, give an example of it, apply it to your facts, and then reach a conclusion. If, however, you have a complicated rule with several subparts, you might state the point of law for each subpart and apply it to your facts before explaining the next subpart.

For related information, see MEMOS.

DISINTERESTED OR UNINTERESTED?

Use *disinterested* if you mean that the person is neutral on the point. Use *uninterested* if you mean that the person does not care about the point.

DO

As an auxiliary verb, *do* adds emphasis, especially when answering a question affirmatively when the reader is expecting a negative answer.

Our client does expect to have the building ready for occupancy by the agreed-upon date.

For related information, see VERBS, AUXILIARY.

DRAFTING

See the entry for the specific kind of drafting you are doing, such as CONTRACTS, DRAFTING; LEGISLATION; NOTICE OF MOTION; MOTIONS; or WILLS, DRAFTING. For general writing concerns particularly important in drafting, see ACCURACY; ORGANIZATION; LISTS, STRUCTURE OF; PRECISION; and WRITING PROCESS.

DRAFTS

Always try to write more than one draft of any given legal piece. Let the first draft be creative, thorough, and imperfect. Include everything you think necessary to the piece and all things that you think might be useful.

Then use second, third, fourth, and other drafts for REWRITING, REVISING, and POLISHING. For related information, see WRITING PROCESS, WRITING, and PERFECTIONISM.

DUE TO

Use *due to* only after a linking verb, such as *is* or *seemed*, and only where the phrase following *due to* modifies the subject of the sentence.

This omission was due to negligence, not unforeseeable circumstances.

Here *due to* modifies *omission* and *was* is a linking verb. See VERBS, LINKING.

In all other situations, use *because of*.

This omission occurred because of negligence, not unforeseeable circumstances.

Here *because of* modifies *occurred*, and *occurred* is a transitive verb. Using *due to* to modify a verb may become acceptable someday, but is not generally accepted yet. For related information, see MODIFIERS; TRANSITIONS; and VERBS.

DUNNING LETTERS

See REQUESTS FOR PAYMENT.

DURING THE TIME THAT

Try substituting *while* for CONCISENESS.

EACH

Each means *one of two or more persons, objects, or things considered individually.* As such, *each* takes a singular verb when used as a pronoun.

> **Each lawyer has his or her own manner of presenting an opening argument.**

> **Fourteen exhibits were presented at the trial; each is important to the outcome of the case.**

For related general information, see PRONOUNS.

EDITING

Whether you are editing your own writing or someone else's, you will find that editing involves adopting a role that is distinct from that of the writer. To adjust quickly and comfortably to this role, consider the following general principles, specific techniques, and overall process.

1. General Principles

(a) FOCUS on the task of getting this document to fulfill its PURPOSE and communicate to its AUDIENCE. Editing a document does not involve questions of personal style, nor does it involve evaluating the writing or the writer. Unlike teaching, editing focuses on the document itself.

2. Specific techniques.

(a) Speak in terms of the reader and the document, not the writer and editor.

> **Reader may need a definition or paraphrase to follow this point.**

rather than

> Your word choice is unclear to me.

This helps keep the focus on the task, reducing the sting of having one's work criticized.

(b) Avoid absolute judgments. Instead, describe the problem or revision within this specific context.

The logical link between these two paragraphs could be clearer—add a transition phrase? Repeat a key word?

rather than

Unclear logic.

Although this focused editing may require more words, it will save you time in the long run, because the clearer comment helps the writer revise successfully and willingly in the next draft; you will avoid volleying comments and building tensions.

(d) Add a few comments on strong passages as well as weak ones. This will help the writer see your goals more clearly, besides avoiding the purely negative context most writers have come to expect and dread.

3. Overall process

Even when time is limited, try the following three-step approach to editing. This approach helps you avoid the frustration of writing detailed comments that become moot later in the process.

(a) Step one: read through the document quickly from the AUDI-ENCE'S point of view. Ask yourself, *What does this reader want to know from this document? How will he or she use the document?* Flag any places where you were confused or had unanswered questions, but do not stop to determine the cause of the problem.

When you have finished this first reading, pause to consider whether REWRITING is needed. Note any of the following problems.

1. Content problems such as the following.
    - missing topic statements
    - missing support
    - missing logical links
    - inaccurate statements
    - inaccurate or incomplete CITATIONS
    - counterarguments unaddressed
    - unnecessary content
    - distracting or unhelpful tangents

2. Organization problems such as
    - missing logical steps
    - two steps blurred together
    - one step split unnecessarily
    - steps out of logical order

If these changes will fundamentally change the document, return it to the writer at this point. Avoid commenting at this stage on smaller points such as phrasing or punctuation. You want the writer to focus on large-scale concerns first, and you want to avoid editing text that will ultimately be deleted or totally reworked.

If your suggestions for REWRITING are minor, move on to REVISING concerns. But resolve any major organization or content problems before moving to step two.

(b) Step two: check the document for READABILITY and lack of AMBIGUITY. Reread the text quickly, marking any passages that force you to slow down or backtrack. Specifically, check the text for the following problems.

- words unfamiliar to the reader
- inconsistent terms
- vague phrases
- double entendres
- poorly worded transitions
- inaccurate or inadequate signals of structure
- long introductory phrases
- long sentences
- choppy sentences
- confusing lists

When improvements occur to you readily, note them. When you see a problem but a solution does not readily come to mind, describe the problem in your role as reader. Also read HEADINGS and TOPIC SENTENCES without the intervening text. If these two parts of the document outline the main points and organization, the chances are much greater that the message will be communicated to the AUDIENCE.

If the changes here are so significant that you cannot see how the text will look after they are made, return the document to the writer. If not, proceed with step three.

(c) Step three: focus on POLISHING. Check for the following.

- inconsistent TONE
- awkward WORD CHOICE
- distracting REPETITION
- unneeded PASSIVE VOICE
- inappropriate or inconsistent level of formality
- incorrect format

- PUNCTUATION
- GRAMMAR
- typographical errors
- anomalies caused by previous changes

When you see repeated PATTERNS of problems, note this objectively, so the writer can begin to check his or her future documents for these problems before they reach your desk.

EDITING QUOTES

Although some editing of quotes is desirable for effective focus and for READABILITY, too much can make the reader suspicious, as in the following example.

The court stated its reasoning explicitly when it said, "[w]e cannot ignore the plaintiff's complaint . . . . [because] [i]n this case, the issue of mutuality . . . requires . . . examin[ing] . . . the parol evidence . . . ."

When faced with this situation, PARAPHRASE or summarize the quote rather than overediting. For specific ways to edit quotes, see QUOTATIONS, HOW TO PUNCTUATE.

EFFECT OR AFFECT?

See AFFECT OR EFFECT?

E.G.

See SIGNALS.

ELEGANT VARIATION

Elegant variation means using different words for the same idea, solely for variety. Do not use this technique in legal writing.

This contract supersedes all previous contracts.

rather than

This document supersedes all previous contracts.

For discussions of related general points, see REPETITION, READABILITY, PRECISION, and WORD CHOICE.

ELLIPSES

An ellipsis is a series of three spaced dots (. . .) used to show omissions in quotes. See QUOTATIONS, HOW TO PUNCTUATE for the details of the use of ellipses.

EMOTIONAL FACTS

Used in persuasive writing, these facts are carefully chosen and included in a STATEMENT OF THE CASE to subtly persuade the reader. They have no bearing on the legal reasoning, nor are they chronological or informational facts necessary to complete a legal analysis. Rather, they play on the reader's emotions. For example, if Malcolm assaulted Alice one Saturday night with an unloaded gun, the writer may tell the reader that they had a sexual relationship in the past. This is an emotionally significant fact that has no bearing on the legal definition of assault. Because these facts are not legally significant, avoid inserting them carelessly or too often. For related information, see TONE, EMPHASIS, PERSUASIVE WRITING, and POINT OF VIEW.

EMOTIONAL LANGUAGE

Emotional language is appropriate only in PERSUASIVE WRITING, and then only if used sparingly. Use emotional language to describe significant EMOTIONAL FACTS, emotional arguments, or possibly POLICY arguments. Use emotional language only if it is necessary to convey the point and if it does not impair your TONE.

Emotional language can impair credibility if used inappropriately, personally, or excessively.

> **Admitting this evidence would rob the defendant of his due process rights.**

rather than

> The plaintiff's counsel foolishly suggests the court admit the evidence; such a move would be unjust and wrong.

For related problems, see CONNOTATION.

EMPHASIS

When emphasizing a point, you want to emphasize the content, not the writing itself. For this reason, avoid heavy-handed use of any emphasizing techniques. With that caveat in mind, try using one or more of the following techniques to emphasize your point.

1. Put the point to be emphasized at a position of emphasis: the beginning or end of a sentence or a paragraph. Conversely, bury phrases you want to de-emphasize in the middle, because the middle of sentences, paragraphs, and even whole sections gets less attention than the beginnings or ends.

In addition, in legal writing the beginning gets more attention than the end because the legal reader does not always finish reading.

93

Therefore, get your main points in early. This technique is particularly useful for introducing KEY TERMS and TERMS OF ART that will reappear throughout the text, because the terms can both gain emphasis and serve as TRANSITIONS. See ORGANIZATION, POSITIONS OF EMPHASIS, and PARAGRAPHS.

2. State the point to be emphasized in concrete, specific terms. Conversely, use more abstract terms to de-emphasize a point. When a point is stated in concrete or specific terms, the reader creates a mental picture of the point; this picture makes the point easier to remember. In contrast, something stated abstractly or generally does not leave a picture in the reader's mind and is less easy to remember.

> **When asked where he had been at 10:00 p.m. on the night of the assault, the alleged assailant looked away and mumbled, "Nowhere."**

rather than

> When asked where he had been, he seemed uneasy.

The concrete version also is more factual. For related information, see ABSTRACT NOUNS.

3. Put the point to be emphasized in a short sentence. Because SHORT SENTENCES are relatively rare in legal writing, they are particularly effective for emphasis. A short sentence will make a stronger statement and will also be easier to read. Both these facts work together to make the point easier to remember.

> **The defendant then fired three shots.**

Watch out, however, for using several short sentences in a row, because this can create an impatient, slightly angry tone. For occasions when you want to create this tone, see TOUGH, SOUNDING THAT WAY. For related information, see SENTENCE STRUCTURE, subsection 1.

4. Put the point to be emphasized in a one-sentence paragraph. Use this technique only when you have a sentence that can stand on its own logically. When you can use a one-sentence paragraph, however, it can make the point stand out from other paragraphs, just as a short sentence stands out from other longer sentences. For more information, see ONE–SENTENCE PARAGRAPHS.

5. Use strong SUBJECT–VERB COMBINATIONS that use terms central to your point, which may include TERMS OF ART or other words you want to emphasize.

> **The Family Car Doctrine holds parents liable for their children's accidents.**

rather than

> Under the Family Car Doctrine, liability exists for parents whose children have accidents.

Or use the following when representing the plaintiff.

Panicking, the defendant accelerated and struck the plaintiff's stalled vehicle at 40 miles per hour.

rather than

Seeing the plaintiff's stalled vehicle in the road, the defendant panicked, stepping on the wrong pedal and accelerating to 40 miles per hour.

Conversely, de-emphasize points by putting them in DEPENDENT CLAUSES. For example, the following sentence de-emphasizes *the defendant had not come to a full stop* by placing it after *although*.

Although the defendant had not come to a full stop at the official stop sign, he had slowed to less than five miles per hour and was not accelerating at the time of the accident.

For related information, see SUBJECT–VERB COMBINATIONS, KEY TERMS, and TERMS OF ART.

6. Put the point to be emphasized in an inverted sentence structure. In general, something unusual gets more attention just because it is unusual.

Imprudent it was, but not illegal.

But beware of overusing this technique. Inverted sentence structure draws attention to the writing itself as much as to the content; if you use it frequently, the reader will start to think about your writing style and may be distracted from your content. For more of this, see SENTENCE STRUCTURE, subsection 4.

7. Use CITATIONS at the ends of sentences, not as introductions to a sentence.

Only under exigent circumstances may police enter a person's home without a warrant or consent. Dayton v. New York, 945 U.S. 573, 590 (1999).

rather than

Dayton v. New York, 945 U.S. 573, 590 (1999) states that only under exigent circumstances may police enter a person's home without a warrant or consent.

EMPHASIS ADDED

See QUOTATIONS, HOW TO PUNCTUATE.

END RESULT

Result is adequate unless you are discussing complicated math formulas with both interim results and end results.

ENGLISH AS A SECOND LANGUAGE

If English is your second language, consider cultural and linguistic differences in PREWRITING. Because of these differences, you may need to add steps to your WRITING PROCESS to double-check ACCURACY and PRECISION. You might want to begin a project by studying several examples of the type of writing you are doing, such as BRIEFS, MEMOS, LETTERS, or PLEADINGS. Then, as you begin your project, ask yourself the following questions.

1. What are the expectations of this AUDIENCE? The American legal audience often expects more ANALYSIS than seems necessary to others. For example, because the American system is based on *stare decisis,* you need to include more information about cases than would be expected in a civil code context. For more on how to do this, see SUPPORT.

2. What is the proper approach? American legal REASONING is direct, and often follows the SYLLOGISM in presentation. Thus you need to begin with a SYNTHESIS of the law. State it directly, without overly general information or unnecessary preamble. This approach is considered rude in some countries, but is expected in American legal writing.

3. What writing conventions are appropriate for American legal writing? American legal writing is direct. Generally, American legal readers expect the writer to state the point in plain language and to guide the reader through every step in the analysis. To meet this expectation, state the main point at the outset of the document, and use the first sentence of each paragraph to introduce the main idea in that paragraph. Then use TRANSITIONS and CONNECTIONS to explain how each part of your analysis is related to the next part. Generally confine each sentence to one legal point, each paragraph to one idea. Concentrate on concrete subjects, verbs, and objects; omit all unnecessary modifiers. Avoid unnecessary language that opens a sentence by warming up to the main point, such as *it is my considered opinion that.* Finally, whenever possible, use the ACTIVE VOICE rather than PASSIVE VOICE.

4. Does the language conform to American English usage? Because American legal decisions are influenced directly by written documents and are themselves issued in writing, American lawyers rely on precise, correct expression. To bring your written English closer to that standard and to sound more idiomatic, evaluate the patterns in your writing. When crossing over to English from another language, you may bring writing patterns that are either closer to your language or to British English. With the help of a native speaker, try to identify successful and unsuccessful PATTERNS in format, content, STYLE, and approach.

After you have identified any patterns that are unusual in American English, read through your paper, checking exclusively for these non-native patterns. For example, if your native language uses complex SENTENCE STRUCTURE separated by commas, adjust throughout for the shorter and more direct English structure; separate the thoughts into complete sentences separated with periods. If your language does not use ARTICLES, read your final product specifically for those and insert them. Check also for proper use of PREPOSITIONS.

ENSURE, INSURE, OR ASSURE?

Ensure, insure, and *assure* can all mean to make certain of something. However, only *insure* means to guarantee against loss, and only *assure* has the sense of setting a person's mind at rest. To avoid ambiguity, you may want to use *ensure* for making certain of something.

Taking that approach ensures that our client will be vindicated.

Use *insure* for guaranteeing against loss.

Our client, State Farm Mutual, insured the plaintiff against hurricane damage.

Use *assure* for removing doubt.

The judge assured us that she would give the maximum penalty if the defendant were found guilty.

ENUMERATION

Enumeration, or inserting numbers into a list, can add clarity to a potentially overwhelming amount of information. Generally, add enumeration if each item in the list is more than a few words long or if the list includes more than four items. For more detail on how and when enumeration is useful, see LISTS, STRUCTURE OF.

If enumeration is used too much in a document, however, it becomes distracting rather than helpful. Scan the pages of your documents to see if the frequency of enumeration draws the eye from the content. For related information, see BULLET POINTS; GRAPHICS, WHEN TO USE; GRAPHICS, HOW TO USE; and LISTS, PUNCTUATION OF.

EQUITY

Equity refers to justice and fairness. If, for example, legal procedures and existing laws give inadequate or no redress for a grievance, then *equity* would require creating some redress.

Equity has several shades of meaning, which are beyond the scope of this book, but be sure to consider equity in making a complete analysis in your DISCUSSION SECTION, ARGUMENT SECTION, or explanation in an opinion letter. See also POLICY.

ETC.

Use *etc.* only in informal writing, because it looks rather informal and can be vague in some circumstances. Instead, use *and so forth*, *and others*, or another appropriate phrase. Better yet, complete the phrase with specific terms.

EVERYBODY

Everybody takes a singular verb.

Everybody has the right to his or her own fair trial.

Everybody is rather informal; consider substituting *everyone*.

EVERYONE

Everyone takes a singular verb.

Everyone is writing an outline for the course.

Do not confuse *everyone* with *every one*; *every one* refers to each person or thing of a specific group, and is usually followed by *of*.

Every one of the defendants is at fault.

EVIDENCE

Evidence always takes a singular verb.

The evidence points to this conclusion.

This is true even if there are many bits of evidence, because *evidence* is a collective noun. If you want to use a plural verb, you will need to make some other word the subject.

All the pieces of evidence point to this conclusion.

For related information, see COLLECTIVE NOUNS.

EX–

As a prefix, use *ex* with a hyphen.

ex-wife, ex-Governor Smith

As a part of a Latin phrase, write it as a separate word.

ex post facto

EXACTNESS

See ACCURACY.

EXCLAMATION

Exclamations are used in legal writing only as part of a quote. For related information, see also INTERJECTIONS.

EXCLAMATION POINT

An exclamation point is rather like shouting and thus is not used in legal writing, except as part of a quote. Let someone else do the shouting. For better ways to emphasize a point, see EMPHASIS and POSITIONS OF EMPHASIS.

EXPLANATIONS, WHEN AND HOW MUCH?

Explanations, like a good motor oil, can reduce friction and increase efficiency. But also like oil, too much can create a sticky situation.

Explain a point when it is your professional responsibility to do so. For example, explain why you recommend a specific way of structuring a bequest in a client's will, even if the client is inclined to trust you and does not seem to require the explanation. Similarly, explain your reasoning in an OPINION LETTER so the client has enough information to determine whether or not he or she agrees with you.

Explain the reason for an action or a request whenever your reader would want an explanation and when it is the reader's right or business to know. So, for example, explain to a client why you are requesting a piece of information whenever that reason is not readily apparent.

In PERSUASIVE WRITING, explain the reason for a request or action when you think that the explanation will increase the likelihood of a favorable response. Thus you might explain to an opposing attorney why you think a negotiation meeting between your two clients would be beneficial.

In contrast, do not explain reflexively, solely out of habit. Sometimes silence is wiser. It might be inappropriate or unwise to explain the motivations behind your client's request for a negotiation meeting. It would also be ineffective to explain to your superior why the memo you are submitting is longer than expected; in that situation, the context needs to communicate your reason. For related information, see CONTEXT–INDEPENDENT WRITING.

EXPLANATORY PHRASES

If you want to explain a term that some readers may not understand, you may choose to add a short phrase within the sentence stating your point.

The gaffer, or stage electrician, was responsible for setting up the band's equipment.

For ways to include these gracefully, see APPOSITIVES and UNOBSTRUSIVE DEFINITIONS.

EXPOSITORY WRITING

Much legal writing is expository writing. Traditionally, the primary function of expository writing is to inform a reader, rather than to narrate or convince. Expository writing explains factual information, supports a subject, or presents an idea. You often do one or all three when writing a MEMO, OPINION LETTER, or scholarly article: you describe the legal foundation of the analysis, support your reasoning, or present a new theory of law. As a reference, you can use the seven traditional devices for expository writing listed here.

1. Enumeration.

Enumeration explains a topic by identifying its divisions. For example, a MEMO might be structured by listing a statute's elements, the subissues that might be raised when considering a larger issue, or a series of provisions in a contract.

2. Definition.

Definition explains a topic by setting the limits of the topic or locating the topic within a larger structure or explanation. For example, an article might define a legal issue by placing it within a larger legal context, or by classifying the issue and then distinguishing it from other issues within that class. This technique is useful for isolating and distinguishing an issue from related issues or for defining subissues.

3. Process.

Process explains a topic by listing the steps that lead to the completion of an action. This expository device is often used to address a topic, event, or idea that involves some sort of change or development; the device identifies the steps in that change and their order. You might use process to identify the steps in filing a suit, in completing a settlement negotiation, or in gathering information for a will.

4. Analysis.

In the expository sense, analysis explains a topic by dividing it into its separate component parts by division, classification, or a combination of the two. Analysis by division is used when a subject is analyzed as a singular item, and its component parts are used to explain it. In contrast to enumeration, which simply lists the parts in the whole, division analyzes how the parts together create the whole. For example, several causes of action may make up an entire case, several errors by the trial court may comprise an abuse of discretion, and legal secretaries, paralegals, associates, and partners may make up a law firm.

Analysis by classification is used when a subject is analyzed as a plural; that is, the subject is viewed as a set of items bearing common characteristics. This method focuses on the whole more than the part; the whole is then analyzed in relation to a larger subject, rather than the parts of the topic in relation to itself, as in division. In a MEMO, for example, the law applicable to your client's case may be divided into statutes, cases, and regulations; all of these are then applied to your client's factual situation. Or, in a scholarly article, several cases may have developed a trend in a legal doctrine; that doctrine is then used to create a new legal theory.

5. Cause and effect.

This device explains why an event occurred. This technique is used to develop reasoning, to create proof, or to establish an explanation. For example, if a defendant watched a violent movie and then subsequently committed a similar crime, you might argue that the crime was caused by the first event.

To determine a cause-and-effect relationship, first sift through facts, law, practical circumstances, and your own point of view; then determine how to present these in a logical and objective written form. Beware of several traps, including hasty generalization, *non sequitur,* and the *post hoc* fallacy. In a hasty generalization, only one reason is used to create a cause-and-effect generalization, when in fact many other reasons could contribute. In the *non sequitur,* there is no connection between the first and the second events, so there can be no cause and effect. In the *post hoc* fallacy, there is a false assumption about the causal situation.

6. Comparison and contrast.

This device explains the subject by measuring it against something else. This is often used in legal writing when analogizing and distinguishing cases. To predict an outcome in a MEMO, for example, you may analyze your client's case by noting the similarities and differences between it and previous cases.

7. Illustration.

Use illustration to explain a topic by using an example or analogy to give concrete meaning to abstract ideas, to clarify or refine definitions, or to provide precise instances and meanings for generalizations. An example illustrates a point by giving a concrete illustration; an analogy compares the situation to something that is more familiar to the reader.

In legal writing, you are concerned with effectiveness rather than pure literary form. So, if it is effective to do so, you may combine expository writing with narration or persuasion. For example, in a BRIEF's Argument, you may want to narrate the facts of a case that is dramatically similar to yours and then use the expository device of comparison to show the court it must rule in your favor because of the similarity. Or you may want to enumerate several constitutional violations at the outset of an Argument to persuade the court that so many violations require reversal. Whatever your choices, make them carefully and deliberately so that the document's structure fulfills its purpose.

For more detailed information on expository writing, see Louis A. Arena, *Linguistics and Composition: A Method to Improve Expository Writing Skills* (Georgetown University Press, 1975) at 94–120; Thomas S. Kane, *The New Oxford Guide to Writing* (Oxford University Press 1988).

EXTENDED QUOTES

Resist the urge, please, to use quotes that extend for whole pages. No matter how good the quote is, many readers will skip over it, so use quotes of more than one long paragraph only when paraphrasing or EDITING QUOTES are not viable alternatives. If you must quote an extended passage, such as the full text of a statute, do so, but make sure the explanation surrounding it is adequate to make the reader see the essential use. If possible, append the full text and then refer to that APPENDIX, unless flipping too often to the appendix will distract the reader. See also PARAPHRASE; QUOTATIONS, HOW TO PUNCTUATE; and ACCURACY.

FACT OF THE MATTER, THE

This phrase can almost always be omitted with no loss of meaning.

The plaintiff did not raise this claim until she learned of the defendant's affluence.

rather than

The fact of the matter is that the plaintiff did not raise this claim until she learned of the defendant's affluence.

For a discussion of related problems, see CONCISENESS and SUBJECT–VERB COMBINATIONS.

FACTS

See EMOTIONAL FACTS, BACKGROUND FACTS, and LEGALLY SIGNIFICANT FACTS.

FACT THAT, THE

Avoid this phrase. Usually it adds extra words without adding extra meaning.

This failure was caused by the machine's inadequate design.

rather than

This failure was caused by the fact that the machine was inadequately designed.

For related information, see CONCISENESS.

FARTHER OR FURTHER?

Farther refers to literal distance.

She moved farther away from me than I had wanted.

Further refers to all other senses, such as additional degree, time, or quantity.

The attorney stretched the argument further than anyone could have imagined.

Further also denotes figurative distance.

That line of reasoning is further from the truth than would be acceptable.

FEEL

Use this word when you mean to talk about emotions, rather than thoughts or beliefs. Often in legal writing *think* or *believe* is the more accurate choice.

The defendant felt remorseful about his actions.

but not

The defendant felt that he did the wrong thing.

FEWER OR LESS?

Fewer refers to things that are being viewed as individual units, and would be counted as such. It takes a plural verb.

Fewer students are enrolling than the university would have liked.

Less refers to things that cannot be counted.

Plaintiffs believed there was less likelihood of success if they waited too long to file.

We need less talk, more action.

Less also refers to things that could be counted, but are being referred to as a group rather than as individual units. Examples of this include periods of time, sums of money, measures of distance, and weights.

Plaintiff must file in less than sixty days.

The prayer asked for less than one million dollars.

The engine lasted for less than 45,000 miles.

While the plaintiff weighed almost 200 pounds, the defendant weighed less than 130 pounds.

FIGURATIVE MEANING

In legal writing do not use a word figuratively, rather than literally, if there is any chance that the legal reader could take you literally.

When he tried to drive his car out of the marsh, he actually drove it farther into the mud.

rather than

When he tried to drive his car out of the marsh, he foundered in a swamp he himself created.

You may use a word figuratively when (1) you are writing for legal readers and (2) the figurative term is commonly used by those readers.

The plaintiff's own word bars his suit.

In this example, nothing is *barred* in the sense of *barred from entering the room*, but any legal reader will know what you mean.

For related concerns, see AMBIGUITY, LITERAL MEANING, and JARGON.

FIND

Courts *find*; counsel does not.

FLOWERY LANGUAGE

Avoid flowery language, or the use of unnecessarily ornate words in legal writing. Usually the ideas in legal writing are so complicated that flowery language will only serve to make them more complicated. The only time that flowery language might be appropriate would be if requested by an AUDIENCE, such as a client requesting it in a will.

In law review articles you may bend this rule a little; a few *arcane* words are allowable if they do not hide crucial meaning. Do not, however, *surfeit your reader with a multifarious array of sententious phrases.* Too quickly that becomes obnoxious and loses the reader.

See also JARGON, LEGALESE, ELEGANT VARIATION, and READABILITY.

FOCUS

Focusing on the essentials in both WRITING PROCESS and product helps you avoid wasting your energy on unnecessary chores. More important, it avoids wasting the reader's time on unnecessary tangents. For example, when writing a BRIEF, focus on the precise questions the court must answer to resolve each issue; this focus will help you resolve such varied questions about the final product as what research to include, what argumentation to use, and what tone to create. Similarly, when writing a MEMO, focus on the questions the senior partner wants answered to guide both your research and your writing. When writing a letter to a client, focus on what information the client needs to make a decision or take action, and let that focus dictate what points are emphasized in your letter.

In your WRITING PROCESS, focus on what parts of the process are most difficult or uncomfortable for you, and let that knowledge of your weaknesses help you choose what parts of your process to change or to give more time.

Together, your focus on the audience, purpose, and scope and your focus on the process will keep your product useful and your process efficient. For related information, see TIME MANAGEMENT, COLLABORATION, and EDITING.

FOOTNOTES

1. Using Footnotes.

Use footnotes in articles, treatises, and opinions but avoid them in LETTERS, MEMOS, pretrial documents, or BRIEFS. For example, when an explanation would distract from the presentation's flow in the main part of the text, put the explanation in a footnote. Or use footnotes to expand a point beyond the information essential to the purpose of the presentation. For example, a footnote in an opinion might give the text of a statute or case that is better read on that page than appended to the main text. Thus footnotes in law review articles and treatises are helpful to document authority, but footnotes in a memo or brief generally distract the reader. For more information see SCHOLARLY WRITING CHECKLIST, subsection 3(f).

2. Citing Footnotes.

Refer to footnotes when they contain pertinent text, just as a PINPOINT CITE would refer to a specific page.

FOOTNOTES

(a) Cite a footnote from a case as follows.

Brown v. Smith, 469 U.S. 27, 34 n.3 (1999).

(b) Cite a footnote from an article as follows.

1988 Wis. L. Rev. 349, 358 n.89.

For further reference, see Bluebook rule 3.3.

FOR

Sometimes *for* is used as a subordinating conjunction.

She had no patience with imprecise language, for she had a background in legal drafting.

Although this use of *for* is not grammatically wrong, it suggests a rather fuzzy logical relationship. *For* is not as precise as *because*. If you mean to show a causal connection, use *because*.

The operator cannot be considered negligent because he was not told that it was his job to check the hoses before starting the motor.

If you mean something less precise, try to revise to state exactly what you mean. For related information, see TRANSITIONS and CONJUNCTIONS.

FORCEFUL WRITING

See EMPHASIS and POSITIONS OF EMPHASIS.

FORMAT

Legal readers are particular about format because they want the structure to be transparent enough to make the substance clearly visible. For example, know and follow the requirements of the format peculiar to your jurisdiction when writing BRIEFS. Similarly, know and follow also the demands of your employer for format in memos and opinion letters. For specific formats, see MEMOS, BRIEFS, and OPINION LETTERS.

FORM BOOKS, USE OF

Referring to forms can save time and avoid the problem of missing a needed element in a routine task. Using forms, however, can also cause problems, such as including contradictory clauses in a contract or nonsensical phrases in a letter. Therefore, do not use forms as a substitute for your own thinking about the writing task you face. With this caveat in mind, when you do refer to forms, you can make good use of them if you remember to do the following three things.

1. Compare forms.

Compare different forms before you settle on one form to follow. Comparing different forms, whether from form books or from samples you have collected, helps you see which content and formats are common and which are unique to certain forms. This comparison in turn helps you get a clearer sense of the options you have and of the standard content and FORMAT used for this kind of legal document.

2. Prepare your form.

Prepare by identifying all the elements needed to complete your document, omitting any unneeded elements found in the forms but inappropriate to your document, and checking for logical inconsistencies between these elements. Check carefully for those logical inconsistencies, so that your document is not the next in the line of cases that outlines the problems of ambiguous and inconsistent clauses. Resist the temptation to include even one word you do not understand.

3. Repair your form.

Finally, repair the elements you have chosen from various forms. Draft original sections as needed to cover all of your situation. Then organize all sections and check for completeness and consistency. When all content is in place, edit the whole document. Most of the forms have unneeded FLOWERY LANGUAGE, obtuse SENTENCE STRUCTURE, and unnecessary words. You have used the forms to get a sense of content, structure, and format; you can retain those elements and still revise to gain increased READABILITY. For help in omitting unnecessary words, see CONCISENESS. For related information, see CONTRACTS, DRAFTING.

FORM CONTRACTS, USE OF

Form contracts can be useful as long as they are used as a resource rather than a substitute for your own thinking about the agreement. To use forms effectively, follow the three steps listed under FORM BOOKS, USE OF. For a checklist for drafting contracts, see CONTRACTS, DRAFTING.

FORMER

If the reference of *former* is more than a few words back, repeat the word to which you are referring rather than using *former*. To understand what *former* means, the reader must remember the items listed, remember which was first, and then insert that information into the sentence. As a result, *former* is inconvenient for the reader. The reader should never be inconvenienced for the convenience of the writer.

Also remember that *former* and *latter* can be ambiguous when they refer to a list of more than two items.

FOR THE PERIOD OF

For CONCISENESS, leave out the last three words.

FURTHER OR FARTHER?

See FARTHER OR FURTHER?

FUTURE PERFECT TENSE

See VERBS, TENSES.

FUTURE PROGRESSIVE TENSE

See VERBS, TENSES.

FUTURE TENSES

See VERBS, TENSES.

GENDER–FREE PROSE

See SEXIST LANGUAGE, WAYS TO AVOID.

GENERAL CORRESPONDENCE LETTERS

One common problem legal writers have with letters is time; letters take too long to write. Often this happens because writers spend a long time deciding how to begin and how to organize each letter.

Only four kinds of general correspondence letters are commonly written: (1) letters delivering information the reader requested or making routine requests for information, (2) letters delivering information the writer needs the reader to have (for-your-information, or FYI letters), (3) letters delivering bad news, and (4) letters trying to persuade the reader to do something. You can use a standard organization for each of these kinds of letters, which means you no longer have to decide how to begin or how to organize. All you have to decide is what kind of letter you are writing. Then you need only choose the appropriate TONE for your letter and the appropriate SALUTATION and CLOSING.

To decide what kind of letter you are writing, first jot down in one sentence the point of your letter. Be blunt; this is for your private use, not necessarily for inclusion in the letter. For example, your point might be (1) *Here, for your review, is your revised will*; (2) *You may need to change your method of keeping tax records*; (3) *After meeting you, I know that there is no way I would hire you to work for our company*; or (4) *I want to get you to pay even though I can't sue you because suit would cost more than it is worth.* Then decide which of the four kinds of letters this point requires.

1. Letters delivering requested information or making routine requests.

If the letter is delivering requested information (as in the first example: *Here for your review, is your revised will.*), refer to the request and then respond to that request.

At our conference on January 23, you asked me to help you make several changes in your will. I have subsequently drafted a new will incorporating these changes and am including a copy of this draft with this letter.

Elaborate or explain as needed in the second paragraph.

Please review this draft carefully. Specifically, consider the following questions:

(1) . . . .

Then close politely in the last paragraph.

If you have any questions or wish to make any further changes in the will, do not hesitate to call. I will have the final will prepared and you may come to the office to execute it on February 12, as we have scheduled.

When making a routine request, one which the reader will not think twice about answering, determine whether the context of the request needs to be explained. If not, simply begin with a polite request.

Please send me . . . .

If some context is needed, summarize that briefly with the request.

A few technical points need to be clarified to enable us to begin your lawsuit. Please provide answers to the following technical questions.

If there is any chance the reader will feel uncomfortable about fulfilling your request, or if the reader will hesitate at all, follow the approach for a persuasive letter, outlined in subsection 4.

2. Letters delivering information the writer needs the reader to have (for-your-information, or FYI Letters).

If it is an FYI letter (as in the second example: *You may need to change your methods of keeping tax records.*), start with a statement of the point of the letter.

As your attorney, I want to notify you of some recent changes in the tax law that may require a change in your record-keeping practices.

If needed, include this opening in a brief description of who you are or an explanation of why you are writing. In subsequent paragraphs, elaborate as needed.

Specifically, the new law requires you to keep a log of your use of the computer, so that you can document the percentage of time .... Additionally, the law requires ....

In the final paragraph, close politely.

Please feel free to call to set up an appointment if you have any questions about this or other tax matters.

3. Bad News Letters.

If the letter is delivering bad news (as in the third example: *After meeting you, I know that there is no way I would hire you to work in our company.*), try organizing the letter in three parts that do the following: (1) set the TONE of the letter; (2) deliver the bad news; and (3) re-establish the tone. Think of this as the sandwich organization, because in effect you place your meat between two slices of bread to make it more palatable.

(a) The first slice of bread: set the tone.

In the first paragraph, establish the tone you want to take with the reader. For example, you might want to be kind.

It was a pleasure to have the opportunity to interview you last week ....

Or you may be tough.

Mr. William Marshfield has asked me as his attorney to answer your demands that he pay for computer software he neither ordered nor received ....

You may choose to be warm and personal.

Thank you for inviting me to speak at the Society's annual awards banquet. Regrettably, ...

You may prefer to be distant.

Your request for a reduction in your child support payments has been received by ....

If answering a request, you may want to restate that request, so that the reader knows you paid attention to the request before saying no.

In your letter dated March 3, 1986, you requested a restructuring of your payment schedule for the land contract on .... Your reasons were that ....

(b) The meat: deliver the bad news.

At the beginning of the second paragraph, state the bad news plainly so that the reader cannot misinterpret what you are saying. Follow this statement with your reasons, if appropriate. This paragraph will be unemotional and matter of fact, no matter what the tone of the other paragraphs. This section may also extend for several paragraphs if needed.

In your letter to Mr. Alexander dated March 14, you asked Mr. Alexander to pay $480 for "equipment repairs made to three typewriters in June 1985." You stated that this payment was long overdue and you threatened to bring suit if you did not receive payment by May 1, 1986.

Mr. Alexander, however, does not believe he owes you this money because he has no record of these repairs being made. Instead, his records show only that Efficient Equipment Repair Service repaired one typewriter on June 12, 1985. Alexander Associates received a statement charging $40 for this work from the repairman before he left. On July 1, 1985, Alexander Associates mailed a check for $40 to Efficient Equipment Repair Service . . . .

(c) The second piece of bread: re-establish the tone.

In the final paragraph, re-establish your tone while you state closing technicalities. For example, you may suggest that the reader call if he or she has questions.

If you have any further questions concerning this matter, you may call me at (505) 555–1234.

If you are being kind, you may wish the reader some sort of relevant good fortune.

I enjoyed our conversation at the convention, and look forward to reading your article on . . . .

If you are being tough, you may close with a declarative statement.

I trust that this settles the matter.

For related information, see BAD NEWS, SOFTENING IT; LETTERS REQUESTING PAYMENT; and TOUGH, SOUNDING THAT WAY.

4. Persuasive Letters.

If the letter is being written to persuade the reader (as in the third example: *I want to get you to pay even though I can't sue you because suit would cost more than it's worth.*), you may use the same organization used for bad news letters.

Start with a paragraph that sets the TONE of the letter, such as a kind tone.

Throughout the years, Everly Auto Parts has valued Morgan Auto as a customer. Because Everly hopes to maintain this solid working relationship, Bob Everly has asked me to write to you concerning the rather large outstanding balance in your account.

You may set a tough tone.

Despite receiving three statements from my client, Everly Auto Parts, your company has not yet paid the balance of $2,015 owed for parts purchased four months ago.

Or you may choose something in between.

My client, Everly Auto Parts, has asked me to write to you concerning the outstanding balance on your company's account.

Do not go on too long, however, because a lengthy introduction can make the writer look rather timid or can make the reader impatient.

At the end of the first paragraph or the beginning of the second, state your point. Write this sentence with care; it must be unambiguous and yet inoffensive, if possible.

Everly will not be able to extend further credit to your company until this balance has been paid.

Then launch into your reasons, which may go on for several PARAGRAPHS. Make one point at a time, rather than rambling back and forth between several points.

Everly Auto Parts, as a general policy, limits credit to any company to .... Additionally, ...

In the last paragraph close politely, or at least civilly.

Everly Auto Parts will appreciate your prompt payment of this outstanding balance and looks forward to your continued patronage.

In general, persuasive letters will take more time and care than the other three kinds because you must tailor your argument and tone to suit the individual circumstances. Choose not what persuades you, but what will persuade your reader. If you are trying to persuade a party to settle out of court, for example, do not use threats if you think the party would view that threat as a challenge and submission as a weakness. In that situation, you might instead explain that the suit is not worth the expense of trial. For related suggestions, see SETTLEMENT LETTERS; LETTERS REQUESTING PAYMENT; and TOUGH, SOUNDING THAT WAY.

Similarly, if you think the reader is someone motivated by certain values, try to explain how the action you recommend is consistent with those values. For example, you might argue that paying a bill is essentially the same as keeping a promise. In short, try to explain how the action you recommend is consistent with some goal the reader has. Try to help the reader feel good, or at least not defeated, about taking the action you recommend.

In general, use an unemotional, polite tone. In most legal writing situations, the emotions you would arouse would work against you rather than for you. There are some exceptions to this, such as fundraising letters to sympathetic constituents or letters advising clients to do what they want to do already. Even here, however, you will usually want to present yourself as a logical, reasonable person who, although impassioned about a cause, is still capable of making a coherent and logical argument. For a discussion of related points, see TONE, EMPHASIS, PERSUASIVE WRITING, and COHERENCE.

5. Tone in Letters.

TONE is especially important in letters. As your general demeanor in an interview creates an impression in the mind of the interviewer, the tone of your letter creates an impression in the reader's mind. Thus, although your tone in various letters may range from friendly to tough, it should always be within the limits of temperate, businesslike communication. A chatty tone will seem slightly unprofessional in all but personal letters. An intemperate tirade will also seem unprofessional, even in the toughest collection letter.

Within these limits, however, you must make your own choices, based on what is appropriate to the situation and what suits your personal communication style.

Using tone effectively in letters involves three tasks: (a) choosing the appropriate tone, (b) creating that tone through word choice and sentence structure, and (c) keeping the tone consistent.

(a) Choosing the appropriate tone.

Before you begin writing the letter, consider what your relationship is to the reader. For example, if your reader is a judge or your supervisor at work, you will probably want to use a tone that is both businesslike and respectful. This means that you will state your points as concisely as possible but will not omit appropriate opening and closing amenities, such as the following closing to a letter requesting a favor.

Thank you for your help in this matter.

If your reader is a client, you may choose to be polite and businesslike, or you may choose an appropriately friendly tone.

Please call if you have any further questions.

or

I am looking forward to our next tennis match.

If your reader is your client's opponent or a client who has not paid you for one year, you may choose a tough, businesslike tone.

I trust this settles the matter.

or

Please pay this bill promptly.

(b) Creating the appropriate tone through WORD CHOICE and SENTENCE STRUCTURE.

Choosing your words carefully is one effective way to establish your tone. For example, if you want to create an informal, friendly tone, use less formal words, such as *talk* and *meeting*. If you want to create a more formal tone, use more formal words, such as *confer* and *discussion*.

Avoid, however, using formal words to the point that your letter becomes stuffy or hard to read.

Regarding this question, I have conferred with Ms. Jamison's attorney, who explained that ....

rather than

In pursuit of this query, I have held consultations with counsel for Ms. Jamison, who elucidated the point by stating that ....

Another way to avoid a stuffy tone is to avoid inappropriately using the third person, such as *this attorney*, when the first person, *I*, is accurate. In general, letters are addressed from one person to another, and so the use of I is appropriate, or *we* if you are speaking officially for a group of people, such as a whole law firm.

You may also establish your tone by using appropriate sentence structures. For example, if you want to create a friendly, informal tone, use longer sentences rather than terse ones.

Thank you for your kind invitation to speak at your annual banquet honoring outstanding alumni from the law school.

rather than

Thank you for the invitation to speak at the alumni banquet.

Conversely, if you want to create a tough, no nonsense tone, use short, rather choppy sentences.

My client, Ms. Ambrose, does not intend to pay this bill. She has no reason to pay this bill. She did not receive any software from your company. She did not order any software from your company. Until receiving your bill, she did not know your company existed.

rather than

114

GENERAL CORRESPONDENCE LETTERS

My client, Ms. Ambrose, does not intend to pay this bill because she has no reason to do so. She did not receive or order any software from your company, and in fact did not know your company existed until receiving your bill.

(c) Keeping the tone consistent.

Inconsistent tone occurs when a letter includes words that are noticeably more formal or informal than the rest of a letter. For example, a writer may use a formal phrase, such as *please be advised that,* in an otherwise informal letter. Or a writer may use a colloquialism, such as *ripped off,* in an otherwise businesslike letter. This inconsistency can make the writer seem insincere or not fully resolved about the situation. Or the writer may simply seem less skilled with language. To avoid any of these impressions, avoid the inconsistency.

Also, for tone, avoid using any unnecessary legal terms, or LEGALESE. Dexterity with legal terms does not impress all readers. What does impress readers is correspondence that gives them the information they need without making them work hard to get it, so try to be concise and organized. For related information, see CONCISENESS, FLOWERY LANGUAGE, and ORGANIZATION.

6. Opening and Closing Letters.

(a) Including or omitting SALUTATIONS.

In general, include a salutation. Some writers omit the salutation in business letters, substituting instead a subject line, and this is not technically wrong. Omitting the line, however, makes the letter seem rather abrupt and impersonal, which is not usually the tone you want in a letter.

(b) Writing non-sexist openings.

If you do not know the sex of the person to whom you are writing, substitute the name without a title.

Dear D.A. Young:

Dear Terry Holmes:

If you do not know a name, use the person's title, or some appropriate generic term.

Dear Administrator:

Dear Client:

If you cannot come up with even a generic term, you may use the following.

Dear Sir or Madam:

Use *Dear Sir* only when you are sure the reader is male.

115

(c) Choosing commas or colons for salutations.

Use colons in business writing. If you are writing something that is a social courtesy, such as a thank you note or an expression of congratulations, you may use a comma. A colon would also be appropriate, except in a note that is much more personal than businesslike in tone.

(d) Choosing an appropriate closing.

Choose the standard closing that suits your writing STYLE and the tone of your letter. If the tone of your letter is businesslike and yet friendly, use *Sincerely* or *Sincerely yours*. If your tone is more formal, use *Yours truly* or *Very truly yours*. Do not worry about seeming insincere; these closings are not taken literally.

Using innovative alternatives, rather than underscoring your sincerity, would only create undesirable responses. If you used something more accurate, like *Don't bother me anymore*, you would seem unprofessional or petulant. If you omitted the closing, you would create a distant, impersonal tone, which is not usually what you want.

For related information, see TONE.

GENERALLY

Generally is an adverb that means *for the most part* or *usually*. Be careful to use it in its exact meaning, rather than as a meaningless introduction.

Generally, states do not consider a non-viable fetus a "minor child."

rather than

Generally, the defendant would like a pardon.

GERUNDS

Gerunds are NOUNS formed from the *-ing* form of a verb.

Seeing is believing.

Using gerunds can often make a sentence more concise.

Imagining alone does not constitute intent.

rather than

The act of imagination alone does not constitute intent.

GETTING ORGANIZED

For help here, choose the entry most closely related to your concern: GETTING STARTED, OUTLINES, ORGANIZATION, WRIT-

ING BLOCKS, WRITING PROCESS, or ORGANIZATION FOR THOSE WHO CAN'T OUTLINE.

GETTING STARTED

You may have trouble getting started for any of several reasons. You may dread the job because it is boring, difficult, or crucial to your career. You may not know where to start. Or you may be stuck in the first step. Do not despair; all of these problems are fixable. But to solve these problems you may have to change your approach to the problem. For related information, see WRITING BLOCKS and HABITS, WRITING.

1. When you dread it.

Try listing what needs to be done and then dividing the tasks on the list into subtasks. Keep dividing them until you get down to small tasks that each seem manageable. Even if the list seems very long, just start completing the tasks one by one. If time is short, do first those tasks essential to the job, such as clear organization, and then those tasks desirable but not necessary, such as emphatic sentence structure. For more ideas, see DEADLINES, MEETING THEM.

2. When you do not know where to start.

Start anywhere. Many people think that they have to start with an outline, but in reality you can start in any of several places. For example, you might start drafting one subpoint of the Discussion of a memo because you understand that particular point best. Or you might start by trying to get your QUESTIONS PRESENTED exactly right. In a law review article, you might start with one sentence that sums up the point of your whole article, not worrying about whether that sentence will appear in the final draft. Then you could list the points needed to back up that statement and develop that list into an OUTLINE. For more ideas, see PREWRITING.

3. When you are stuck.

Try starting somewhere else. For example, if you cannot get the Question Presented right, try writing the Discussion or the Argument. If the Discussion or Argument is rambling, try writing your Conclusion; that may help you see how to organize the Discussion. You may discover that starting with any one of these always helps you get the job done more efficiently. The best starting place for one person is not the best for another, so experiment to discover what works for you. Remember, good writing does not depend on whether you start in the right place; it depends on whether you do all you need to before you stop.

GOOD OR WELL?

Use *good* to modify a noun.

She had good reason to doubt his word.

Use *well* to modify a verb or an adjective.

She could hear well enough to understand the general topic of the defendants' conversation.

Use *good* after *feel*, because *good* here modifies the subject, not the verb.

I feel good about this decision.

Well would be correct only if you were talking about your ability to feel physically, which almost never comes up in writing. For related information, see BAD OR BADLY?

GRAMMAR

Grammar refers to the rules for constructing communications in a language. An error in grammar usually makes the communication inaccurate or unclear. In contrast, *usage* refers to how words are used by native speakers and *style* is a more amorphous concept that usually implies a set of additional conventions adopted by a particular set of writers, such as journalists, scientists, or scholars. Differing from the reader's expectations in any of these areas may make the meaning awkward, ambiguous, or hard to understand, but grammar errors make it incorrect.

As in other kinds of professional writing, grammar counts in legal writing. Grammatical mistakes are potholes in the superhighway of a presentation. Therefore, use grammar carefully to convey your legal ideas clearly, and revise specifically for its proper use.

For specific grammar questions, see PARTS OF SPEECH, SENTENCE STRUCTURE, VERBS, TENSES, MODIFIERS, PARALLEL STRUCTURE, and PUNCTUATION. Also see BENDING THE RULES.

GRAPHICS, HOW TO USE

Graphics aids may be as elaborate as flow charts and three-dimensional graphs, or as simple as subheadings and tabulation. But in all situations, the graphics should support and clarify the information in the document's text. To make sure your graphic is effective, first make sure it is needed (for more on this, see GRAPHICS, WHEN TO USE). Then, when preparing the graphic, try to achieve the following qualities.

1. Keep it as simple as possible.

The reader sees a graphic presentation as a whole first; then the eye scans around the graphic for details. To make the most of that first impression, omit any information that distracts from the main point. For example, if you wanted to communicate that the chance of a drowning occurring increases as the depth of a pool approaches 15 feet, and that this correlation is more significant than other factors, you would first present a graph establishing the correlation with depth.

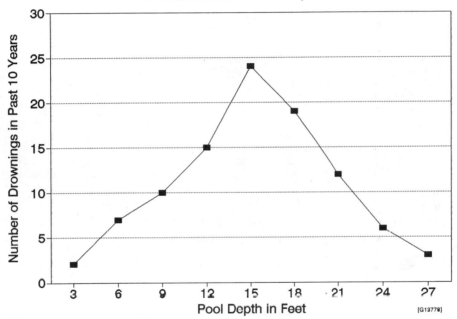

Number of Drownings
at Different Pool Depths

Then you would explain that this correlation was stronger than other factors, perhaps representing each other factor in a separate graph, like the one below, that could be compared with the first.

119

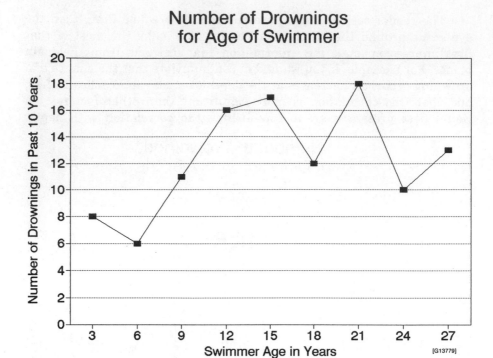

Avoid trying to present all the information in one graph; so much information together is likely to confuse the point rather than underscore it.

comparison of variables
related to drownings

[G13780]

Separating the information makes each point clearer.

2. Make sure that the graphic and the text both communicate the message.

Some readers will skip the text and go directly to the graphics. For that reason, word your titles and legends to communicate the same message as your text. Other readers will skip the graphics, so summarize in the text any message illustrated in the graphics.

Checking the correlation of graphics and text will also help you as a writer. Because graphics are generated separately from the text, they can become isolated from the text in the writer's mind. To keep this from happening, compare the text and graphics when REVISING, looking specifically for any differences that could confuse the reader.

3. Avoid overusing graphic aids in a document.

For example, the following text is visually clear and appealing.

When using boldface, check each page by reading the boldface words only. Check for the following qualities.
- The meaning of the words in boldface is clear without reading other text.
- The number of phrases in boldface is enough that the point of using bold is intuitively clear.

121

- The number of phrases in boldface is not so great that the effect of emphasis is lost.

In contrast, the following version is too busy to be clear or appealing.

> **When using boldface,** *check each page* by reading the boldface words only. *Check for* the following qualities.
>
> * The **meaning** of the words in boldface **is clear without reading** other text.
>
> ** The **number** of phrases in boldface **is enough that the point** of using bold **is** intuitively **clear.**
>
> *** The **number** of phrases in boldface **is not so great that the effect** of emphasis **is lost.**

Similarly, avoid using too many graphs or tables within one document. Just as with writing techniques for EMPHASIS, graphics, if overused, can distract more than clarify.

4. Make each graphic an accurate visual representation of the content.

The format of a graphic presentation communicates something about the content, even before the reader sees the numbers and other specific data involved. Because of this, choose the graphic form that most clearly communicates your point. For an overview of possible forms graphs can take, see GRAPHICS, WHICH FORM TO USE.

GRAPHICS, WHEN TO USE

Graphs, tables, and other such illustrations can be useful in legal writing. They can, for example, help illustrate the location of vehicles in an accident, show the significance of complex statistics on damage awards, summarize a company's financial situation, and explain complicated technological processes. Smaller graphic devices, such as TABULATION or BULLET POINTS, can help a reader to find his or her way through a formidable list of necessary details. But do not use a graphic aid without good reason, or you risk distracting your reader. Think through the reason for using the graph before you create it. The purposes of graphic aids vary depending on whether the aid will be used within the text or added as an appendix.

1. Graphics used within the text.

When deciding whether to use graphics within the text of a document, consider the following guidelines.

Use graphics only when all of the following are true:

(1) the information you are communicating in graphic form is central to your overall message,

(2) the graphic form communicates your information more clearly than words, and

(3) your reader will understand the information more readily in graphic form than in words.

If you have answered all of these questions affirmatively, then create the graphic aid and insert it immediately after the written explanation.

2. Graphics appended to a text.

For auxiliary or supporting information that does not need to be inserted into the text, consider the following guidelines when deciding whether to use a graphic aid.

Use graphic form when that form does any of the following:

(1) it makes a better reference because it allows the reader to retrieve a particular piece of information more easily,

(2) it creates a more efficient document because it allows the writer to present the information more concisely while maintaining clarity, or

(3) it makes a more pleasing document because it either makes the information more visually pleasing to the reader or makes the information seem less overwhelming to the reader.

If you answer any of these questions affirmatively, create the graph and append it to the document, with references to it inserted in text.

GRAPHICS, WHICH FORM TO USE

The form of a graph communicates immediately, before the reader studies the content it includes. As a result, you must use the graphic form that accurately conveys your meaning. Some common graphics and their uses are outlined below.

1. Pie charts.

Pie charts usually show how a whole unit is apportioned between subcategories. For example, they can show how much of your work day is devoted to various legal tasks or what portions of a company's income come from different sources.

Jayco revenue sources
by subsidiary

XLR Video (8.3%)
Quadrophon (11.1%)
Karascon (34.7%)
Certel (18.1%)
IntElect (27.8%)

[G13781]

Pie charts are the natural choice for showing how a whole is divided, especially because most AUDIENCES are familiar with this use. But avoid using them for other purposes, because most would be confused by that non-standard use.

2. Bar graphs

These graphs usually show how the quantity of something changes across the items compared. They suggest a pile of something, such as money, and so are particularly useful for this kind of information. For example, they can show how many complaints a company received over time regarding an item it continued to produce or how much income a company generated in different quarters or years.

Jayco Gross Revenues
for Each Quarter of 1990

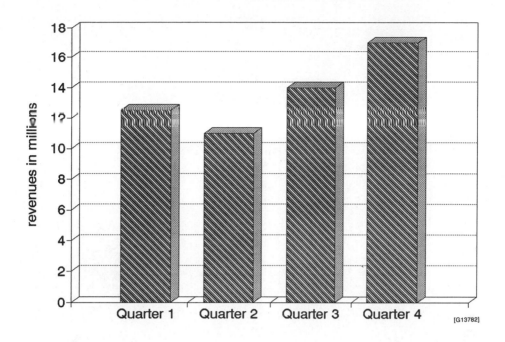

[G13782]

Watch the arrangement of bar graphs to make sure that you do not communicate an upward or downward trend if you do not intend to do so. For example, the following graph suggests bad news where none was intended, solely because of the order in which the categories are placed.

Jayco revenue sources divided by subsidiary

3. Stacked bar graphs or side by side bar graphs.

These formats enable bar graphs to compare two quantities to each other while also showing how both change across the items compared. For example, a side-by-side bar graph could show how one neighborhood's real estate taxes have risen in comparison to the taxes of the larger community.

COMPARISON OF PROPERTY TAXES
Linnwood neighborhood and rest of city

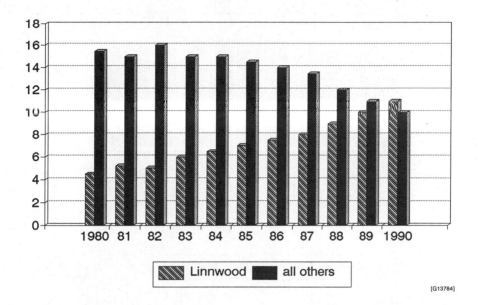

[G13784]

A stacked bar graph could show how the neighborhood's taxes have risen even while the overall community's tax rate remained relatively unchanged.

COMPARISON OF PROPERTY TAXES
Linnwood neighborhood and rest of city

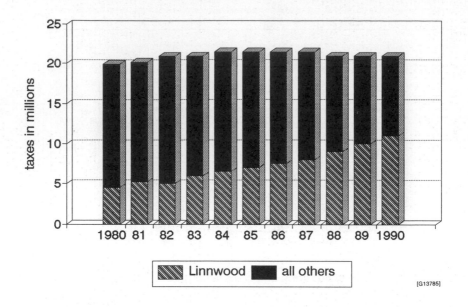

4. Line graphs.

Line graphs often show change across time or compare two varia-
bles that interact. These graphs suggest numbers and change, more
than the discrete quantities that bar graphs suggest. For example, line
graphs can illustrate the variability in a fire station's response time, or
the rise in accident rates at a particular intersection over several years.

128

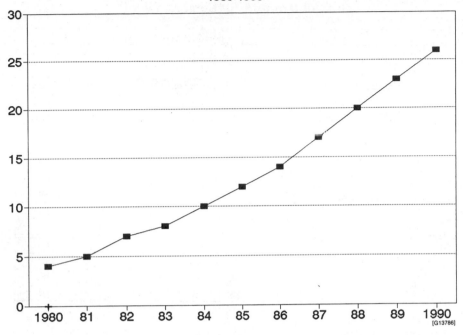

NUMBER OF ACCIDENTS AT 12TH AND VINE
1980-1990

5. Tables.

These divide data into discrete categories and coordinate those categories so any reader in your audience can find a particular category quickly. A table also organizes and unifies data, so the detail does not overwhelm any reader. For example, a table could chart how many clients came to a firm with each particular legal problem a firm handles, how many problems were subsequently settled out of court, and how many went to trial. (See next page).

To design useful tables determine (1) what information your audience needs and (2) what kind of category is most likely to be meaningful to that audience. Then divide the information about those categories into groups that answer questions the audience will have. This step is important, because often the categories that are meaningful to the audience differ from those that occur first to the writer. For example, when categorizing patients denied health coverage, you might first think of grouping them by the reason coverage was denied. Your reader, however, might be more concerned about the nature of the coverage denied, the effect of different state regulations on denial, or the cost that providing that coverage would have entailed. As always, be governed by what will be convenient and effective for the reader, rather than for the writer. For related information, see GRAPHICS, WHEN TO USE and GRAPHICS, HOW TO USE.

Summary of 1991 Cases

by Problem and Settlement Level

	Level at Which Settled					
Client Problem	Prelim. Corres-pondence	Pre-Trial	Trial	Pre-Appeal	Post-Appeal	Total
Family						
Custody	2	3	2	40	23	70
Child Support	3	3	21	45	9	81
Alimony	5	9	12	23	9	55
Other	15	20	4	3	0	42
Business						
Contr. Litigation	2	7	2	0	1	12
Debtor	36	35	15	5	0	91
Other	8	8	14	0	0	3
Injury						
Workman's Comp.	0	2	13	0	2	17
Tort	10	36	34	4	2	86
Other	3	15	7	2	0	27

HABITS, WRITING

Habits form in writing just as they do everywhere else. Because legal writing often requires high efficiency in short periods of time, keeping bad writing habits can cost both you and your client. But old habits die hard; you must consciously kill them. Therefore, in moving from the PREWRITING stage through WRITING, REWRITING, REVISING, and POLISHING, consider which habits work for you and which habits do not. Then start with the most troublesome habit and eradicate it by replacing it with a better habit. For example, if you habitually try to revise each sentence as you write, you will probably find that the writing process has become very time-consuming and agonizing. Instead, try giving yourself a time limit and forcing yourself to write without any revision until you finish your first draft. Then go back and rewrite. Similarly, if you spend too much time doing research and as a result do not have enough time for the actual writing, set a deadline by which the first draft has to be written and force yourself to meet that deadline by finding someone to give it to, whether a secretary or a coworker who is willing to read it at that point.

For suggestions for breaking habits in each stage of the WRITING PROCESS, see PREWRITING, WRITING, REWRITING, REVISING, and POLISHING. For help in facing the writing process itself, see GETTING STARTED and WRITING BLOCKS.

HANGED OR HUNG?

If you are talking about a person being *hanged by the neck until dead*, use *hanged*. If you are talking about *hung* in any other sense, such as a thing *hung on the wall*, use *hung*. Informally, you may refer to a *hung jury*.

HARDLY

Hardly is more informal than its synonyms *scarcely* or *nearly*, so use it sparingly in formal writing, such as MEMOS and BRIEFS. See also CAN HARDLY OR CAN'T HARDLY?

HEADINGS

In most legal writing, headings identify the subsections of memo, brief, letter, or article. Headings should ease the eye and the mind of the reader, so that the legal analysis is easier to follow. In BRIEFS, headings take the specific form of POINT HEADINGS, subheadings, and sub-subheadings, which outline the specific legal points of the argument and the reasoning behind those points. In MEMOS, headings distinguish each part of the memo, such as Questions Presented, BRIEF ANSWERS, Discussion, and Conclusion. Subheadings may be used to divide the DISCUSSION SECTION, so that the reader can see at a glance which legal issues are being discussed where. Usually these subheadings take the form of a label, such as *False Imprisonment* or *Jurisdiction*, although a sentence can be even more helpful.

This District Court Has Jurisdiction.

In long OPINION LETTERS, subheadings similarly subdivide the explanation. The same is true with articles.

In your headings and subheadings, try to convey a definite message to the reader. Use complete sentences rather than single words or abstract phrases. When appropriate, use PARALLEL STRUCTURE to convey your theme from one heading to the next. Include law, facts, and other information specific to your analysis, so the reader can understand the overall logic and content just by reading the headings. For related information, see ARTICLES, PUBLISHED; POINT HEADINGS; and TOPIC SENTENCES.

HEADNOTES

Headnotes are numbered paragraphs that summarize the legal points of a court's opinion. These summaries are written by the editors of the reporter in which the case appears, and they appear before the actual text of the case begins.

Headnotes are designed as research tools to aid the reader in using the case. For example, if you are researching intentional torts and a case contains, among others, a procedural headnote on jurisdiction and a substantive headnote on intentional torts, then you can use the headnote number to find the section of the case discussing intentional torts where that number reappears. Similarly, that headnote is Shepardized so that you can update just that section of the case on intentional torts. See SHEPARD'S.

Because headnotes are research tools and are not written by judges, never cite to a headnote. Also, never depend on the headnote to supply your understanding of the case. Read the text and check to see that you believe the case indeed covers this point.

HELP

If you have turned to this, you are probably in the midst of your writing process and under pressure. Consult the most relevant of the following entries: GETTING STARTED; OUTLINES; ORGANIZATION FOR THOSE WHO CAN'T OUTLINE; WRITING BLOCKS; WRITING PROCESS; or DEADLINES, MEETING THEM. Also look for an entry under the particular kind of writing that concerns you, such as ARTICLES, PUBLISHED; BRIEFS; CASE BRIEFS; CONTRACTS, DRAFTING; GENERAL CORRESPONDENCE LETTERS; MEMOS; and so forth. If none of these entries seems right, consult the master list of entries in the front of the book. Do not panic. Divide the tasks and conquer.

HELPING VERBS

See VERBS, TENSES.

HE OR SHE?

When the sex of the person referred to is unknown, *he or she* is preferable to *s/he* or *he*. For a general discussion of this question, see SEXIST LANGUAGE, WAYS TO AVOID.

HE/SHE, WHEN TO USE?

Use this construction only in a form document when the signer is meant to strike out the inappropriate form. Otherwise, use *he or she* or *she or he*. The slash version saves the writer's energy at the cost of the reader's. Do not ask the reader to make a decision you should have made. For related information, see S/HE, HE OR SHE?, or SEXIST LANGUAGE, WAYS TO AVOID.

HOLD

Courts *hold*; counsel does not.

HOLDINGS

The holding is the decision a court reaches in a case. A holding thus disposes an issue raised in the case, whether procedural or substantive and as such binds that court and those under it in making subsequent holdings based on similar facts. Therefore, holdings often provide the focal point for research constructing arguments, and measuring the strength of a client's case. Consider the following in using case holdings.

1. In CASE BRIEFS, use the holding to state the answer to the issue and give a reason for that answer

> **Yes; Curtis falsely imprisoned Butterworth because he used words or acts that intended to confine Butterworth, he actually confined her in the car, and Butterworth was aware that she was confined.**

For related information, see ISSUES, DICTA, and CASE BRIEFS.

2. In MEMOS, use holdings to explain RULES.

> **Hospitalization for alcohol abuse does not preclude being awarded custody of a child. Nagle v. Nagle, 999 Utah 2d 84, 101, 941 P.2d 1, 3 (1999).**

Or use holdings to describe ANALOGOUS CASES.

> **There, the mother was awarded custody of the daughter despite her previous hospitalization for alcohol abuse. Nagle v. Nagle, 999 Utah 2d 84, 101, 941 P.2d 1, 3 (1999).**

3. In BRIEFS, use holdings to argue.

> **Even a mother who has been hospitalized for alcohol abuse can win custody of her daughter. Nagle v. Nagle, 999 Utah 2d 84, 101, 941 P.2d 1, 3 (1999).**

4. In PARENTHETICALS, state the holdings as they relate to the use of the cases.

> **Artists must look outside the moral rights doctrine for protection. See Peabody v. Percival, 999 F.2d 17 (9th Cir. 1999) (holding that moral right is limited in the U.S., so breach of contract must be used to compensate artists whose work is mutilated).**

HOPEFULLY

Use *it is hoped* or *I hope*. Use *hopefully* only when you mean that something was done in a hopeful way.

> **The pilgrims sailed hopefully for America.**

It is rare that you will mean this. While *hopefully* is used widely in speaking, it is not yet accepted as meaning *it is hoped* in formal writing.

HOWEVER

However has two different uses, each of which can cause problems for the legal writer.

1. Use *however* as a transition. As such, it is a concise way of saying something roughly equivalent to *on the other hand*; it signals a shift to the other side or a contrasting subpoint. One way this may be done is to place *however* right after a semicolon joining two sentences.

> **The defendant has testified that he was not present at the scene of the crime; however, two witnesses have contradicted this.**

When using *however* this way, do not use it with only a comma. You must put a semicolon before *however* and a comma after. The semicolon is necessary because however is not a conjunction, like *and* or *but*.

> **The court remanded the case; however, the plaintiff did not receive an appreciably higher reward.**

rather than

> The court remanded the case, however, the plaintiff did not receive an appreciably higher reward.

Another way *however* may be used as a transition is to place it a few words into a sentence.

> **The defendant has testified that he was not present at the scene of the crime. Two witnesses, however, have contradicted this.**

2. Use *however* as an adverb. As such, it modifies a part of the sentence rather than serving as a transition between sentences.

> **However it happened, the fact remains that the defendant lost use of his arm as a result of this accident.**

Often this use of *however* sounds awkward in formal writing. In this situation, you may substitute another phrase.

> **No matter how it happened,** ....

or

> **Regardless of the cause of the accident,** ....

Avoid overusing the word. If, for example, you see *however* appearing in every paragraph you write, you are probably overusing it. To correct the problem, first check your organization: Are you trying to cover two points that would be better presented in two separate paragraphs? Are you wavering between two views, avoiding taking a stand when it is your job to take a stand? If so, see ORGANIZATION and PARAGRAPHS for possible solutions. Second, check the accuracy of your word choice: Are you using *however* when you really mean *nevertheless, additionally*, or something else? See TRANSITIONS for a list of transition words that may communicate your point more accurately. Usually the answers to these questions will show you how you must revise. If not, consider using synonyms for *however* to avoid overusing it. For related information, see REPETITION.

HUMOR

Effective humor is a deft and welcome stroke in legal writing, but it requires a precise choice of location and time. Some judges may find humor a relief in working on a case, so it may be effective to file a complaint in the form of poetry or to make light of a minor point in a brief. Be particularly sensitive, however, to all AUDIENCES; the client may not be amused. Also do not use humor with a serious topic, as with any behavior causing serious harm to someone. When legal writing is reaching a more varied audience, such as in scholarly writing, you may use humor to underscore your point or perk up interest. Many readers would find it a relief. Do not, however, insert humor that does not assist in your PURPOSE. For related information, see VOICE.

HUNG OR HANGED?

See HANGED OR HUNG?

HYPERBOLE

Hyperbole is an excessive exaggeration used as a figure of speech; avoid it generally, because its excesses often reduce the writer's credibility, as in the following examples.

Defendant was dying to get out of the courtroom.

The judge hung the defendant out to dry.

HYPHENS

Hyphens have three uses: (1) dividing words at the end of a line, (2) joining MODIFIERS that work together, and (3) connecting some prefixes to words.

1. You may use a hyphen to divide a long word coming at the end of a line. Check the dictionary if you are not sure where the hyphen should go. Do not hyphenate proper names and avoid hyphenating at the end of a page, as a favor to your reader.

2. Use a hyphen to signal that the words hyphenated work together to modify a subsequent word in the sentence: *bone-jarring blow, high-pitched voice, work-related expenses, owner-occupied housing, thirty-seven-year-old male,* or *three- to five-year sentence.* There are two

135

exceptions to this rule. Proper names are not hyphenated: *Southeast Asian conflict, Supreme Court opinion, West Coast phenomenon*. Also, modifying words are not hyphenated when they follow a linking verb, rather than preceding the word they modify.

The blow was bone jarring.

rather than

The blow was bone-jarring.

For more examples, see ADJECTIVES AFTER A LINKING VERB.

3. Also use a hyphen to connect some prefixes to words.

(a) You may use a hyphen when adding a prefix to a proper name: *un-American, ex-President Carter*.

(b) Use a hyphen when the prefix ends with the same vowel that begins the main word: *re-examine, semi-independent*.

(c) Use a hyphen with *self-*: *self-employed, self-sufficient*.

(d) Use a hyphen with *ex-* when it means *former*: *ex-wife*.

(e) Use a hyphen whenever omitting it will confuse readers.

He wanted to re-lease the apartment.

Or reword the sentence to avoid the problem.

He wanted to lease the apartment again.

I

Use this PRONOUN when referring to yourself doing your job. Thus in a letter to a client, write the following, rather than resorting to PASSIVE VOICE.

I have forwarded the forms to the IRS.

But do not use *I* in other circumstances. Keep the focus on the content, not the writer. So in a brief you might conclude as follows:

The defendant was fairly treated.

But you would not write this sentence.

I therefore conclude that the defendant was fairly treated.

For a general discussion of the reasons behind this use of *I*, see TONE.

IDIOM

An *idiom* is an expression or phrase that is acceptable English even though it cannot be understood by interpreting the literal meaning of its elements.

We gave them up.

or

I dropped off the package.

Idioms are often metaphors that have become so common that the original metaphorical image is lost: *to catch a cold, to strike a bargain* or *How do you do?* Avoid idioms that are ambiguous in context or that sound too informal.

I.E.

The abbreviation *i.e.* stands for *id est*, or *that is*. As an abbreviation, you may use *i.e.* in place of those two words, particularly in the context of further explanation, as in an explanatory footnote.

The 12(b)(6) motion succeeded, i.e., the case was dismissed.

Avoid using *i.e.* in text, such as a business letter or formal documents, such as wills. Use *that is* or another appropriate phrase instead, surrounded by commas.

On June 4, 1982, she initiated the action, that is, filed the motion.

rather than

On June 4, 1982, she initiated the action, i.e., filed the motion.

He agreed to the condition when he signed the waiver.

rather than

He agreed to the condition, i.e., he signed the waiver.

Avoid confusing *i.e.* with *e.g.; i.e.* introduces a phrase that explains in other words, but *e.g.* introduces an example.

IF

If is useful in legal writing because *if* has only one meaning, and therefore provides a precise transition between CLAUSES. Because *if* is precise and because you will often be writing about points that logically are *if ... then* situations, do not worry too much about overusing *if*. Worry only when several sentences in a paragraph contain *if* and when those *if*'s are not logically parallel. For related information, see SENTENCE STRUCTURE, PARALLEL STRUCTURE, REPETITION, and TRANSITIONS.

If the *if* phrase is quite long, use a *then* after the comma at the end of the *if* phrase.

If the court extends this reasoning to include all victims of industrial accidents, then Harris can establish a cause of action.

137

IF AND WHEN

Delete the *and when*; *if* says it all.

IF OR WHEN?

Use *if* when you are suggesting that something may or may not happen.

If the bill is not paid within 60 days, the refrigerator will be repossessed.

Use *when* when you are discussing something that will happen.

When the electricians complete their work, the inspector will set up an appointment to see the house.

Thus, on some occasions, you may choose between *if* and *when* to suggest pessimism or optimism about the likelihood of something happening.

When our candidate is elected, the convention center will be built.

or

If the campaign were to fail, the convention center would remain on the drafting board.

When using *if* to suggest that something will not happen, also shift the verb to the subjunctive mood. For more explanation, see VERBS, MOODS.

IMPACT

Use *impact* as a noun.

The impact caused extensive damages to defendant's vehicle.

The impact of such a decision would be far reaching.

Although *impact* is sometimes used as a verb, as in *to impact a decision*, this use is not yet acceptable English. As a verb, *impact* should refer only to such things as teeth.

His wisdom tooth was impacted.

IMPERATIVE MOOD

See MOODS.

IMPLY OR INFER?

These words are not interchangeable. *Imply* means *to suggest* or *to express indirectly.* *Infer* means *to surmise* or *to derive a conclusion*

138

from the information. As a result, use *imply* when the subject is a piece of writing, a thing, a speaker, or a writer.

This reasoning implies that . . . .

Use *infer* when the subject is a reader or a listener.

The court inferred from this phrase that . . . .

IN ADVANCE OF

Use *before* for a cleaner, more concise sentence. For a discussion of the general principles behind this, see CONCISENESS

INDENTED QUOTES OR QUOTATION MARKS?

Use quotation marks around direct quotes of forty-nine words or less and around titles of articles. When a direct quote is longer than forty-nine words, indent it, single-space it, and omit quotation marks. The only time you will use quotation marks in an indented, single-spaced quote is when there is a quote within the indented quote.

For related information, see QUOTATIONS, WHEN TO USE; EXTENDED QUOTES; and QUOTATIONS, HOW TO PUNCTUATE.

INDENTING

See QUOTATIONS, WHEN TO USE.

INDEPENDENT CLAUSE

See CLAUSES or SENTENCE, PARTS OF.

INDICATIVE MOOD

See MOODS.

INDIRECT OBJECTS

See SENTENCE, PARTS OF and CLAUSES.

INFER OR IMPLY?

See IMPLY OR INFER?

INFINITIVE VERBS

See VERBS, TENSES.

INFORMAL LANGUAGE

See COLLOQUIALISMS.

–ING WORDS

See MODIFIERS, DANGLING; GERUNDS; and VERBS, TENSES.

IN, INTO, OR IN TO?

In means *inside of, during* or *as part of the act or process of,* or *among other things.*

He is in the room.

Into means *to the inside of,* or *to the action or occupation of.*

She will go into law.

In to is used only informally.

My friend is in to body building.

For related information, see PREPOSITIONS.

INITIALS

When initials are used in a person's name, put a period after the initial.

Helen C. Walrich

When several initials are used in place of a person's first name, use periods after each initial, with no spaces between initials.

D.H. Lawrence

When initials are used in place of a name, use periods with no spaces between initials.

J.F.K.

The name United States is abbreviated when it precedes the word *Government* or when it precedes the name of a government organization. Use periods after the letters, but no spaces.

U.S. Navy

Initials are often used when they are more familiar to the readers than the full written title. When initials are used in place of the full name of a company, organization, or government agency, use no periods and no spaces between the initials.

IBM NLRB MIT NAACP TVA

But remember the reader. If the reader cannot readily decipher the initials, avoid using them, or place the written name in parenthesis after the first use of the initials. See Bluebook rule 6.1.

IN QUESTION

This phrase is often used to describe issues under consideration in the present memo, brief, or opinion. If used frequently, this phrase robs the text of CONCISENESS. Therefore, when possible, avoid this phrase by using *these* or *this*: *these facts*, rather than *the facts in question*; *these parties* rather than *the parties in question*, or *this issue* rather than *the issue in question*.

INSERTED PHRASES

See INTRUSIVE PHRASES and SENTENCE STRUCTURE, subsection 7.

INSTRUCTIONS TO THE JURY

See JURY INSTRUCTIONS.

INTERJECTIONS

Interjections are just that, interjections of exclamation.

Hurray!

Because they are emotional and informal, do not use them in legal writing, except as part of a quote.

IN TERMS OF

Reword to avoid this phrase, because it often invites imprecision.

This court has previously addressed the issue of when adult invitees are responsible for their actions, but not whether minor invitees have equivalent responsibility.

rather than

The issue is resolved in terms of the responsibilities of adult invitees, but not of minors.

INTRUSIVE PHRASES

Intrusive phrases are phrases inserted into a sentence.

Anorexics, <u>by failing to eat</u>, passively expose themselves to harm.

You may use short intrusive phrases to emphasize a legal or argumentative point because they will force the reader to stop and think about the content of the intrusive phrase.

These facts, which are outside the knowledge of most people, illustrate the kind of information expert witnesses can provide.

> **These issues, controversial and crucial, must nevertheless be resolved.**

> **Dr. Janssen, who attended the defendant in the emergency room, testified that her injuries were caused by the faulty design of the steering wheel.**

Do not use phrases longer than approximately seven words, however, because phrases that long will cause the reader to lose track of the point the rest of the sentence was making.

> **Without realizing she would be punished by this court for her action, the defendant committed perjury.**

rather than

> The defendant, without realizing she would be punished by this court for her actions, committed perjury.

Avoid using intrusive phrases if you do not want the reader to stop; also avoid overusing intrusive phrases if they make your style too cumbersome.

For more information, see SENTENCE STRUCTURE, subsection 7.

INVERTED ORDER

See SENTENCE STRUCTURE and EMPHASIS.

IRREGARDLESS OR REGARDLESS?

Use *regardless*, always.

ISSUE STATEMENTS

An issue is that question to be decided in a legal argument; it is the question that, when answered, determines the outcome of the case. The issue is the lens of the legal analyst's camera, so focusing it in legal writing is of utmost importance.

The issue or issues are part of CASE BRIEFS, memoranda of points and authorities, PRETRIAL BRIEFS, TRIAL BRIEFS, or APPELLATE BRIEFS. The issue is often the first part the reader consults to focus on the law, the facts, and the question their combination raises.

In OBJECTIVE WRITING, the issue focuses the reader without persuading. For related information, see QUESTION PRESENTED AND MEMORANDUM OF POINTS AND AUTHORITIES.

In PERSUASIVE WRITING, the issue must not only focus, but also persuade the reader. To do this, it should contain (1) a reference to the general law under which the question is being asked; (2) the legal question, which combines the law and the facts of this case; and (3) the

LEGALLY SIGNIFICANT FACTS. Sometimes the reference to the general statement of the law is omitted. Many jurisdictions require the issue to be fair and neutral, although most legal writers make the issue fair but persuasive. The following are examples of issue statements from appellate briefs.

Petitioner's Issue:

> **Is a large law firm exempt from Title VII of the Civil Rights Act of 1964, and therefore free (1) to discriminate on the basis of sex, race, or religion and (2) to discharge those associates whom they did not admit to partnership based on reasons of sex, race, or religion merely because the firm is organized as a partnership and has an established "up-or-out" policy?**

Respondent's Issue:

> **1. Are law partners organized for advocacy entitled to constitutionally protected freedom of association?**
>
> **2. Through Title VII of the Civil Rights Act of 1964, did Congress intend to give the Equal Employment Opportunity Commission, a politically appointed advocacy agency engaged in litigation, jurisdiction over invitations to join law firm partnerships?**

From a pretrial motion:

> **Under Iowa Code Section 99.99.99, <u>Custody of children</u>, is it in the best interests of two young children to award custody to their mother when she has a history of alcohol abuse, has shown no signs of abstention from alcohol, and is given to emotional outbursts?**

IT

Minimize the use of this pronoun because too often its ANTECEDENT is unclear. See PRONOUNS; IT IS SAID THAT; IT IS ... THAT; and AMBIGUITY, WAYS TO AVOID, section 2.

ITALICS

Italics are the typesetting equivalent of UNDERLINING. Like underlining, they should not be used to add emphasis in the general text of formal legal writing. Italics should, however, be used to indicate emphasis added to quotes. Italics are also used conventionally for some words in some legal documents, such as *resolved* in a bill and *ordered* in a court order. They may be used to indicate defined terms, as in a contract or for signals and cases in footnotes. Italics are also used to mark words from a foreign language, like *savoir faire*. Finally, italics are used for book titles. For more detail, see Bluebook rules 1 and 7.

Italic typeface is a commonly used graphic device, used for either emphasis or convention. Avoid using it for EMPHASIS, because italic typeface is actually less strong in appearance than many other typefaces. Use SENTENCE STRUCTURE, POSITIONS OF EMPHASIS, or WORD CHOICE instead. Conventionally, law review footnotes use italics for case names, rather than underlining. You may also use italics instead of underlining for case names in briefs, if your printer offers you this capability. For related information, see BOLDFACE TYPE.

IT IS SAID THAT, IT WOULD SEEM THAT, IT MIGHT BE SAID THAT

If you have reservations about the point you are making, state them. Do not rely on these phrases, because they make you seem uncertain without indicating the sound reasons for your lack of certainty.

IT IS ... THAT

Often this phrase can be omitted for a stronger, more concise sentence.

The attorney must prepare a thorough and accurate statement of fact.

rather than

It is important that the attorney prepare a thorough and accurate statement of fact.

For related information, see CONCISENESS.

IT OR THEY?

For COLLECTIVE NOUNS, which treat a group as one functional entity, use *it*.

As the crowd grew in size, it inched toward the cordoned-off area.

For a group of many individuals, use *they*.

As people crowded into the area, they moved closer to the cordoned-off area.

For related, specific questions, see COURTS, IT OR THEY?, COLLECTIVE NOUNS, and CORPORATIONS, IT OR THEY?

ITS OR IT'S?

It's = it is. *Its* = belonging to it. Legal readers are highly annoyed if one is confused with the other. See also APOSTROPHES and POSSESSIVES.

JARGON

Jargon is a pejorative term for technical language that the reader does not understand, such as *price/cost elasticity*, although the writer and others in the writer's field of expertise would understand it. LEGALESE is jargon used by lawyers. Legalese includes both special ized words unfamiliar to nonlegal readers, such as *estopped*, and flowery words that (1) are unfamiliar to the reader, such as *abovementioned* and *heretofore*, and (2) could be avoided by using a more familiar word, such as *this* or *previously*.

Because you as a writer are trying to communicate to the reader, you want to avoid using jargon. Remember that nonlawyers are not the only ones who will resent jargon; judges are just as likely to resent an unfamiliar or unnecessary technical term.

Therefore, if you must use the technical word to make your point, add a definition in text so the reader does not have to look it up elsewhere. See UNOBTRUSIVE DEFINITIONS for ways to do this.

JUDGES, HOW TO ADDRESS

Use *your honor* in person and *the honorable Judge [name]* for lower court judges, or *the honorable Justice [name]* for higher court justices in third person writing. Always precede the judge's name with *Judge* or *Justice*. This is what the *J.* following a court's name in an opinion represents. For more details on terms of court, see Bluebook rule 9.

JUDGMENT

A judgment is a court's final determination of the parties' rights in a legal controversy. In America, judgment has only one e.

JUDICIAL OR JUDICIOUS?

Use *judicial* when you want to refer to the courts; use *judicious* when you mean using sound judgment.

Determining the length of the sentence was properly left to judicial discretion.

but

The court appreciates a more judicious use of objections during a trial.

145

JUMP CITES

See PINPOINT CITES.

JURY INSTRUCTIONS

Jury instructions are submitted to the court by the attorneys for each side. The following techniques can help you in drafting your instructions and in making them an effective part of your advocacy. Whatever your method, make sure you check your jurisdiction for any specific requirements.

1. Drafting jury instructions.

When drafting jury instructions, you must reconcile conflicting matters in two different areas. First, you must strike a workable balance between two audiences. Jury instructions explain the law to jurors, yet they have to be accepted by the judge. As a result, you need to use some legal terms but also explain them in everyday language.

Second, you must conform patterned jury instructions to the specifics of your case. Most states provide patterned jury instructions that are established general statements of the law. Although these are good places to start, they need editing to be relevant to the particular facts involved in your case. For example, you may have to delete statements addressing issues settled before trial or you may have to combine several instructions to address the multiple issues in your case.

The following checklist can help you balance these factors when writing jury instructions.

(a) Use elements of the standard jury instructions. For example, you might retain the legal terminology in the instructions, but increase understandability by adding definitions if you think they are needed. Similarly, you might keep the wording of the standard instruction but break it into several shorter sentences to make it more readable. For help here, see UNOBTRUSIVE DEFINITIONS and READABILITY, subsection 1.

(b) When appropriate, include supporting CITATIONS or explanations with your submitted instructions, so that the judge knows there are legitimate reasons for your changes.

(c) When choosing instructions, list all the legal questions the jury must resolve to decide in your client's favor. Then lay out the specific law they need to know to resolve those questions. This can help you avoid gaps and present a logical overall package.

(d) Additionally, the jury often hears but does not read the instructions. As a result, you must reorder your priorities to meet the needs of the listener: you must worry more about CLARITY and less about CONCISENESS. The following checklist can help you achieve clarity.

(i) Use understandable words.

Use words that will be familiar to the jury. For example, use *automobile* rather than *motorized vehicle*.

Use verbs instead of nouns whenever possible.

You should <u>consider</u> all the evidence as a whole.

rather than

You should give <u>consideration</u> to all the evidence as a whole.

Avoid using several negative words in one sentence.

Mr. Allen should have come to a complete stop at the crosswalk.

rather than

Mr. Allen must <u>not</u> have <u>failed</u> to come to a complete stop at the crosswalk.

Use TRANSITIONS or phrases that precisely communicate the logical relationship between two points.

<u>Even if</u> Mr. Allen did stop at the crosswalk, he should have also stopped again at a point where his view was not obstructed.

rather than

Mr. Allen should have also stopped at a point where his view was not obstructed.

(ii) Use understandable SENTENCE STRUCTURE.

Keep sentences simple by making only one legal point per sentence.

You may decide that the testimony of one witness is entitled to greater weight than that of another witness, or even of several witnesses. In weighing the evidence, you may consider your own knowledge, observations, and life experiences.

rather than

In weighing the evidence, you may consider the testimony of one witness as entitled to greater weight than that of another or several others, your own knowledge, what you have observed, and the experiences you have had in life.

Use only one word for one idea. For example, use *capable* rather than *capable and able*.

Place lists at the end of a sentence.

> **In weighing the evidence, you may consider your own knowledge, observations, and life experiences.**

rather than

> You may consider your own knowledge, observations, and life experiences in weighing the evidence.

(iii) Personalize the instructions if permissible in your jurisdiction. You can still remain objective by using only objective, factual terms.

> **If Mr. Ellis had a gun concealed** ....

rather than

> If the defendant had a weapon concealed ....

2. Making jury instructions part of your advocacy.

To help make your instructions an extension of your advocacy, consider framing the instructions early in the litigation process, when you are drafting your brief, or at least before the start of the trial. Then you can word your arguments so that they lead to the conclusions you want to reach, based on the law laid out in the instructions.

JURY, PLURAL OR SINGULAR?

Use a singular verb with *jury* when it is a collective noun, which it usually is.

> **The jury receives instructions at the end of the trial.**

Use a plural verb only when you refer to the jury as a collection of individuals.

> *The jury appear nervous.*

Better yet, avoid this awkward-sounding phrase by using *members of the jury* or another similar phrase.

> **The members of the jury appear nervous.**

or

> **Each jury member appears nervous.**

KEY TERMS

Key terms are words describing facts crucial to an issue. As such, key terms work in tandem with TERMS OF ART to define and discuss legal issues. As terms of art are derived from the law, key terms are derived from BACKGROUND FACTS, EMOTIONAL FACTS and LEGALLY SIGNIFICANT FACTS. Thus, key terms may be definitions, facts, or descriptions of desired results, among other things.

For example, in a custody dispute where *best interests of the children* are the TERMS OF ART from the statute, the key terms in the

148

discussion or argument might be *custody dispute*, *father-son relationship*, or *son's wishes*. For related information, see ISSUE STATEMENTS and QUESTION PRESENTED.

LARGE–SCALE ORGANIZATION

See ORGANIZATION, LARGE–SCALE.

LATIN PHRASES

In general, limit your use of Latin to those phrases that enjoy widespread usage. Some of these phrases are more concise and are easily understood when WRITING TO OTHER LAWYERS. For example, you may need to use *res ipsa loquitur, habeas corpus, prima facie, stare decisis, res judicata,* and *sui generis*. But in almost all other cases, rewrite using the English equivalent; Latin phrases are jarring to the modern reader, even when that reader is a lawyer.

The defendant pleaded no contest.

rather than

The defendant pleaded nolo contendere.

No one would be impressed by this use of Latin; it would risk losing nonlawyer readers and irritating legal ones.

LATTER

See FORMER.

LAW REVIEW ARTICLES

See ARTICLES, PUBLISHED and SCHOLARLY WRITING.

LAWYER OR ATTORNEY?

See ATTORNEY OR LAWYER?

LAY OR LIE?

Lay is a transitive verb that always takes a direct object. It means *to place or set down* or *to produce or deposit*, among other things. The conjugation of this verb is *today I lay out my plan for the new Civic Center, yesterday I laid out an alternate plan,* and *I have laid out several plans over the last three months.*

The attorney laid the exhibit carefully on the bench before the bailiff.

She laid her briefs down before she left the office.

Lie is an intransitive verb that never takes a direct object. It means *to recline* or *to remain in a specific condition*, among other things. It is conjugated, *today the plaintiff lies resting in the hospital, yesterday he lay unconscious for three hours*, and *he has lain there for a week*.

The site of the crime lies between Fargo and Grand Forks.

When I lay down yesterday, the phone rang.

LEGAL ANALYSIS

Make sure that your legal analysis satisfies your readers' expectations for thoroughness, logic, and CLARITY. Most legal analysis still proceeds on the basis of the SYLLOGISM, although there are infinite variations on that theme. To construct the basic syllogism, develop a foundation that functions as the major premise. Then illustrate how that premise applies to your client's facts; explore all possible arguments, outcomes, contingencies, alternatives, and practical ramifications. To frame these aspects of analysis, determine the SCOPE of your analysis as directed by your supervisor, defined by your AUDIENCE, or dictated by your PURPOSE. When checking your analysis, you might want to ask yourself the following.

1. Is the analysis thorough?

    (a) Is all the relevant law included?

    (b) Are all possible arguments clearly articulated? See COUNTERARGUMENTS.

    (c) Are all policy and equity questions considered where appropriate?

2. Is the analysis logical?

    (a) Is the law synthesized properly? See SYNTHESIS.

    (b) Are the sub-topics well-defined?

    (c) Is the paper free of any unwritten assumptions?

3. Is the analysis clear?

    (a) Are the limits or definition of the sub-topics properly set forth? See EXPOSITORY WRITING.

    (b) Are the reasons for all conclusions stated explicitly?

    (c) Is each step in the reasoning connected to the next, so that any legal reader can see how the analysis reaches its conclusions?

Although legal analysis takes different forms in different documents, the principles behind the analysis are the same. Use exposition, narration, and persuasion to adjust your analysis for the subtle differences in purpose, audience, scope, and professional posture. As the following chart demonstrates, many forms of legal analysis include the following common elements: framing issues, answering questions, explaining authority and often challenging it, applying authority to the facts, reaching conclusions, and looking to the future. These forms may order the elements differently, as the arrows on the chart show, and they may treat the elements differently in TONE, VOICE, and level of PERSUASIVENESS, but each form includes the elements.

CASE BRIEF/OPINION	CLIENT LETTER	OFFICE MEMO	APPELLATE BRIEF
Citation	Letterhead, date, salutation, etc.	TO: FROM: DATE: RE:	Table of Contents Table of Authorities
	Introduction: In response to your.....	[INTRODUCTION]	[INTRODUCTION]
ISSUE	ISSUE/QUESTION	QUESTION(S) **PRESENTED**	QUESTION(S) **PRESENTED**
HOLDING	ANSWER	BRIEF ANSWER	STATEMENT OF FACTS
FACTS	REVIEW OF FACTS	STATEMENT OF FACTS	SUMMARY OF ARGUMENT
REASONING:	EXPLANATION OF LAW	DISCUSSION	ARGUMENT (by issue & remedy)
For each issue:	For each issue:	For each issue:	POINT HEADINGS
Rule	Rule	Issue & Rule	For each issue:
Application	Application	Application	Supporting rule or authority
Conclusion	Conclusion	Conclusion	Application
DISSENT			Conclusion
DICTA/Significance for future cases.	Potential Problems	Weaknesses in case considered	Counter-arguments acknowledged, rebutted.
	ADVICE (what next?)	CONCLUSION (summary + recommendation)	CONCLUSION: short request for remedy

[G13787]

152

LEGALESE

Legalese is a pejorative term for technical legal words or phrases, and it implies that the legal words are unneeded. To avoid the problem, avoid legal terms whenever common language terms can convey the meaning.

The testator, William James (James) then signed the will, which was witnessed by Ellen Brady, Katrina Birchler, and Mella White.

rather than

The *said* testator, *one* William James, (*hereinafter referred to as* James) then *duly* signed the *aforementioned said* will, *in witness whereof* were Ellen Brady, Katrina Birchler, and Mella White.

Similarly, although you will find that you do need to use many technical legal terms, you do not need to overuse them. You will be able to keep your writing style more direct and concise if you avoid the terms whenever possible.

If you must use a technical term and you are not sure the reader will know the meaning, add a definition.

The tortfeasor, who is the person committing the tort, ...

For ways to do this, see UNOBTRUSIVE DEFINITIONS.

For a discussion of a related problem, see JARGON.

LEGALLY SIGNIFICANT FACTS

Legally significant facts are facts that, if they were changed or deleted, would affect the outcome of the case. To determine what facts are legally significant, you therefore need to read the law. Then, by comparison, certain facts will emerge as significant, just as white emerges under a black light.

For example, a case may state that the waving of a loaded gun in someone's face is an assault. In the fact situation being analyzed, Michael waved a gun that was not loaded. The fact that it was unloaded is legally significant because it may mean Michael is not guilty of assault.

In a MEMO, legally significant facts should appear in the STATEMENT OF FACTS, in the QUESTION PRESENTED, in the BRIEF ANSWER, in the application during the DISCUSSION SECTION and in the CONCLUSION. Any legally significant facts used in the application should appear in the Statement of Facts first, in detail. No surprises.

Similarly, in BRIEFS, legally significant facts should appear in the STATEMENT OF THE CASE, the ISSUE STATEMENTS, the POINT

HEADINGS, the application during the ARGUMENT SECTION and in abbreviated form in the CONCLUSIONS.

In an OPINION LETTER, include legally significant facts in the separate section on facts, in the application during the explanation, and in the recommendation.

For an explanation of other kinds of facts, see BACKGROUND FACTS and EMOTIONAL FACTS. For related information, see ISSUE STATEMENTS and BRIEF ANSWERS.

LEGAL WRITING CHECKLIST

The following checklist is designed to give you a point of departure in checking your document. Not all letters or memos will require each of the elements suggested below. Edit the list according to your readers' preferences and your project's purpose. You might want to use some of these questions as a guideline for asking questions of the assigning attorney when the project is first given to you. For more detailed questions to ask at each stage in the WRITING PROCESS, see WRITING PROCESS CHECKLIST.

1. PURPOSE
   (a) Is the document's purpose clear?
   (b) Is it stated within the first two paragraphs?
   (c) Is the Issue stated?
   (d) Is the Answer stated?

2. CONTENT
   (a) Is the law itself stated? or accurately paraphrased?
   (b) Are the elements clearly delineated by the writer? consistent with the law?
   (c) Are the principles of statutory interpretation accounted for?
      (1) Plain meaning?
      (2) Legislative intent?
      (3) Purpose?
      (4) Previous interpretations?
      (5) Policy?
   (d) Are your client's arguments included?
   (e) The other side's arguments?
   (f) Are the arguments balanced, using principles of interpretation?
   (g) Is a "mini-conclusion" reached on each element?
   (h) Are elements connected to each other, where appropriate?
   (i) Are all conclusions synthesized in the last paragraph?
   (j) Is a recommendation made?

3. ORGANIZATION
   (a) Is the organization consistent with law and appropriate to these readers and this purpose?
   (b) Does the organization lead logically to the recommendation?
   (c) Can any legal reader not misunderstand the scheme?

(d) Do the first sentences of each paragraph guide the reader through the document?

4. READABILITY AND CLARITY
    (a) Is the tone appropriate to this audience? Are terms of address appropriate?
    (b) Is sentence length varied to create a readable rhythm?
    (c) Is the document free of legalese?
    (d) Are terms of art used accurately?

5. MECHANICS
    (a) Are the citations accurate in form and substance?
    (b) Is the grammar correct?
    (c) Is all technical material accurate?
    (d) Are all typographical mistakes corrected?

LEGISLATION

Drafting legislation requires particular skill, for legislation must bear up under generations of scrutiny. Consider those generations of audiences, as well as the current AUDIENCE of legislators. The following guidelines can help you do this when drafting legislation.

1. Draft the original idea you have in mind as clearly as you can, in your own words.

2. Consider all the legal problems raised by the legislation, both the original problem and any previously unanticipated corollaries. Run the draft past several readers from different audiences if possible.

3. Check the draft against other sections within that part of the statute to catch any possible ambiguities or other problems that may arise in this larger context.

4. Similarly, see if any terms used in your legislation are defined elsewhere in the statutes and make sure your use is consistent with those definitions.

5. Adjust the language to accommodate any ancillary problems created in the process of revising the legislation.

    (a) Avoid extra phrases that raise, rather than answer, problems. For related information, see PRECISION.

    (b) Use PLAIN ENGLISH.

    (c) Eliminate any JARGON or LEGALESE.

    (d) Define all terms that might lead to ambiguity. For help here, see AMBIGUITY, WAYS TO AVOID.

6. Unify STYLE when the legislation has been drafted by more than one person. For ways to do this, see EDITING.

7. When using quotation marks in legislation, put other punctuation marks, such as periods or semicolons, outside the quotation marks unless that punctuation mark is part of the quote.

"Dwelling", when used in this section, means ....

This differs from the use of quotation marks in general writing, where commas and periods always are placed inside the quotation marks.

Because there are so many audiences to please and so many things to consider in drafting legislation, do your best under the circumstances to create the clearest results.

LENGTHY QUOTES

See EXTENDED QUOTES.

LESS OR FEWER?

See FEWER OR LESS?

LETTERS

In letters, your information is not the only thing you communicate to the reader. Just as the clothes you wear to an interview communicate something about your general personality, the way you put together a letter communicates your attitude. Fortunately, you can use three basic writing tools to establish the appropriate impression by establishing the appropriate tone: WORD CHOICE, SENTENCE STRUCTURE, and overall structure.

For details about how to structure your letters, see specific kinds of letters: GENERAL CORRESPONDENCE LETTERS; OPINION LETTERS; BAD NEWS, GIVING IT; BAD NEWS, SOFTENING IT; and REQUESTS FOR PAYMENT. Further, for help in choosing and creating the appropriate tone, see TONE IN LETTERS. And if you are taking too long to get the letters written, see GENERAL CORRESPONDENCE LETTERS, PERSUASIVE LETTERS, OPINION LETTERS, and WRITING BLOCKS.

LIE OR LAY?

See LAY OR LIE?

LIKE OR AS?

See AS OR LIKE?

LINKING VERBS

See VERBS, LINKING.

LISTS, STRUCTURE OF

The following rules can help you use lists effectively and correctly.

1. Make sure the items in the list are both logically and grammatically parallel.

> **You may decide that the testimony of one witness is entitled to greater weight than that of another witness, or even of several witnesses. In weighing the evidence, you may consider your own knowledge, observations, and life experiences.**

rather than

> In weighing the evidence, you may consider the testimony of one witness as entitled to greater weight than that of another witness or several others, your own knowledge, what you have observed, and the experiences you have had in life.

In the first example, two ideas (*weighing evidence* and *using personal experience to weigh the evidence*) are divided into two sentences. Additionally, the list of kinds of personal experience in the second sentence is revised to be grammatically parallel. For related information, see PARALLEL STRUCTURE.

2. Use commas to separate items in the list.

> **The defendant moved his car into the left lane to pass, lost control on the snow-packed pavement, slid back into the right lane, and collided with the plaintiff's truck.**

When writing a list in legal writing, put a comma before the *and* or *or* that introduces the final item in the list. For example, in the following sentence, the comma before the *and* makes it clear that there are four shares, not three.

> **My estate is to be divided equally among my nephew, my son, my daughter, and my son-in-law.**

3. Use commas even if the list is set off from the text. Do not use semicolons just because the list is set off from the text. See subsection 4.

> **"Remanufacturing equipment" includes the following processes:**
>
> **(1) disassembly to a predetermined standard established by the manufacturer for each model,**
>
> **(2) cleaning,**
>
> **(3) refinishing,**

157

> (4) inspecting and testing to new machine test standards,
>
> (5) installation of all retrofits, and
>
> (6) operational testing.

4. Use semicolons only if there is a comma within one of the items on the list; otherwise use commas, no matter how long each item in the list is. See subsection 3 for an example of the correct use of commas. The following examples show the correct use of semicolons with commas.

> **The Company warrants for one year that its compressors (1) are free from defects in material and workmanship; (2) have the capacities and rating set forth in the Company's catalogs, provided that no warranty is made against corrosion, erosion, or deterioration; and (3) meet all relevant federal safety standards.**

> **The Company is not liable for any delay in performance due to any of the following:**

> **(1) any act of God, including but not limited to floods, epidemics, fires, storms, or earthquakes;**

> **(2) any acts of others beyond the reasonable control of the Company, including but not limited to strikes or other labor disturbances, riots, wars, acts of civil or military authority, or acts of the Customer; and**

> **(3) any cause beyond its reasonable control, including but not limited to delays in transportation, inability to obtain necessary materials or components, or labor shortages.**

5. Whenever possible, put the list at the end of the sentence. It is much easier to read there.

> **In justifying the exclusion of expert psychiatric evidence, the court listed three concerns: maintaining the integrity of the bifurcated trial procedure, avoiding allowing the guilty to go free, and preserving the defendant's right against self-incrimination.**

rather than

> The court listed the concerns of maintaining the integrity of the bifurcated trial procedure, avoiding allowing the guilty to go free, and preserving the defendant's right against self-incrimination in justifying the exclusion of expert psychiatric evidence.

For related information, see READABILITY.

6. Choose the format for your list by considering the complexity of the list. In general, the more complex the items on the list or the longer the list, the more graphically you should set off the list. You may use

your COMMON SENSE here, and also consider the following guidelines.

(a) Run the list in text if (1) each item is one to three words long and (2) there are three to five items in the list.

The plaintiff paid the defendant $2,550 in installments of $510, $700, $850, and $490.

(b) As this sentence illustrates, run the list in text and insert parenthetical numbers before each item if (1) each item in the list is several words long and (2) the list includes three or fewer items. This can be useful in those awkward situations when you need to include a list within a list.

The defendant agreed to provide the roofing materials needed and (1) construct the new roof or (2) subcontract the job to a bonded roofer.

(c) Introduce the list with a colon and insert parenthetical numbers if the list does not occur in a highly formal rhetoric situation and if (1) most items are more than three words long or (2) there are more than five items in the list.

Before drafting this warning letter, I will need the following information: (1) copies of all previous written correspondence you have had with Mr. Jones regarding this matter, (2) any information you may have forgotten during our interview regarding your conversations with Mr. Jones, and (3) copies of the relevant pages of your bookkeeper's records on accounts receivable.

(d) Introduce each item on the list with the same word (1) if you want to remain more formal, (2) if the items on the list are more than three words long, or (3) if the repeated word contains an idea you want to emphasize.

A doctor may forego disclosure to his adult patient if any of the following situations occur: if the patient is unconscious, incompetent, or otherwise incapable of understanding the information; if in the doctor's opinion the information would have a disproportionately adverse reaction on the patient's ability to make a rational decision; or if an emergency exists which allows no time to safely consult with the patient.

(e) Use a colon and parenthetical numbers and also set the list off from the text if (1) most of the items on the list are more than ten words long, (2) the items are phrases but not complete sentences, and (3) there are more than three items in the list.

The Company's liability does not include any of the following:

(1) any damage occurring in connection with the use of the equipment in any nuclear facility;

(2) any consequential or incidental damages, including but not limited to loss of profit, damage to associated equipment, cost of capital, and cost of substitute products;

(3) any costs beyond the price of the product and service that gives rise to the claim; or

(4) any claims arising from advice or assistance given by the Company without separate compensation for that advice.

(f) Set off complete sentences in a list, each introduced with a number, if (1) each item is a complete sentence of more than ten words, (2) there are more than two items, and (3) that format is appropriate in this writing situation.

During the period of this maintenance agreement, if the Company determines that it cannot maintain the equipment in good working order, then the Company must replace the equipment with another unit in good working order. This requirement is subject to the following provisions.

1. If the Company replaces the equipment within two years of the warranty expiration date, then the replacement unit must be one that is newly manufactured, remanufactured, or reconditioned.

2. If the Company replaces the equipment more than two years after the warranty expiration date, then the replacement unit will be one that is refurbished in accordance with the process used to refurbish rental units.

3. If the Company cannot replace the equipment with another unit of the same model, then the replacement unit will be substantially similar or will have greater capabilities.

4. ....

7. Set off complete sentences with *first*, *second*, and so on, if the items in the list introduce points that will be discussed at length or if you are writing in a situation where a set-off list seems inappropriate.

The appellate process has two major objectives, and it must meet both of them to be considered successful. First, the appellate process must give litigants a fair opportunity to have legitimate claims resolved by a court of law. Second, the appellate process must provide a framework within which the common law can develop in an orderly manner.

For related information, see PARALLEL STRUCTURE and LISTS, WHEN TO USE.

LISTS, WHEN TO USE

Use a list whenever you have three or more items that are logically parallel. Also use a list when you have a lot of information that the reader needs to remember, because grouping items into a list makes both reading and remembering easier. For help doing this, see LISTS, STRUCTURE OF. Two particular problems with lists are handling multiple lists and long lists.

1. Handling multiple lists.

Avoid using too many lists at once. For example, avoid using more than one list in a sentence.

If you need to include several lists, try to put each lengthy list in a separate sentence. Also try to separate clearly any small lists of two or three items.

> **Seller is to comply with all requirements of laws and regulations, whether federal, state, or local. For example, these requirements include but are not limited to compliance with laws and regulations relating to labor, worker's compensation, wages and hours, unemployment compensation or insurance, old age benefits, other social security and welfare laws, and payment of payroll taxes.**

rather than

> Seller is to comply with all requirements of federal, state, and local laws and regulations, including, for example, but not limited to, compliance with laws and regulations relating to labor, worker's compensation, wages and hours, unemployment compensation or insurance, old age benefits, any other social security and welfare laws and all requirements concerning the payment of payroll taxes.

2. Handling long lists.

If you can reduce the number of items listed, do so, because lists are hard to read if they run long, such as more than five items. The reader has difficulty remembering that many items at once. But, because often you cannot shorten the list in legal writing, you may have to try some other techniques. Try grouping the listed items into logical subgroups. For example, four lists of four items each is much easier to read than one list of sixteen items. If subdividing is not possible, use graphic devices to make the list easier to follow. For samples of these see LISTS, STRUCTURE OF, subsection 6.

LITERAL LANGUAGE

Literal language is used almost exclusively in legal writing because it is precise and accurately defines things exactly as they are. For a definition, see LITERAL MEANING. For some uses of figurative language, rather than literal, see FIGURATIVE LANGUAGE.

LITERALLY

Literally in a strict sense means *really* or *actually*. *Literally* is often misused to mean *figuratively*. The following sentence uses *literally* correctly.

There were literally three hundred people in the courtroom.

This means that there were actually three hundred people there. The following example uses *literally* incorrectly.

I am literally dying of boredom.

I am dying of boredom is sufficient to communicate the HYPERBOLE; boredom does not literally cause death. For related information, see LITERAL MEANING.

LITERAL MEANING

A word's literal meaning is its actual or exact meaning. Literal meaning avoids exaggeration, metaphor, or embellishment; it therefore conveys the explicit meaning of the word or words.

Four witnesses gave statements after the accident.

rather than

A handful of witnesses painted a vivid picture of the tragedy.

Legal writers expect literal language, particularly in drafting and OBJECTIVE WRITING. Save precise figurative language for persuasive or scholarly style.

LOGICAL LINKS

Logical links are those clues that show the reader how your sentences and paragraphs fit together logically. For ways to show the logical links in your argument, see CONNECTIONS, MAKING THEM; TRANSITIONS; ORGANIZATION, SMALL–SCALE; and PARAGRAPHS.

LONG QUOTES

See EXTENDED QUOTES.

LOOSELEAFS

See UPDATING THE LAW.

LUCIDITY

See ACCURACY, PRECISION, and READABILITY.

–LY OR NOT?

The suffix *-ly* is used to make ADVERBS out of ADJECTIVES, such as *carefully* from *careful* or *generously* from *generous*. When using *-ly*, make sure that the word is being used as an adverb, that is, it modifies a verb, an adjective or another adverb. If the word is modifying a noun or pronoun, there should be no *-ly*.

MAIN SENTENCES

See TOPIC SENTENCES.

MANAGING WRITERS

Good management creates active, engaged, continually improving writers; bad management creates passive, hostile, unresponsive ones. As a manager, you can increase your efficiency, increase the quality of the writing, and at the same time reduce stress for both you and the writers. Managing writers effectively requires a focused vision of the final goal, clear directions at the start, effective and timely feedback, and attention to writers' needs. Without that attention, writers may be unable either to meet your needs or to improve over time. Most writers do not respond well to vague directions and little feedback during the process. They are mystified by unexplained changes or cuts, and cannot improve when they see excessive red-lining that obliterates their work and does not relate to clearly defined goals. Good management can meet both your needs and theirs. In addition, good management saves you time.

To increase both your writers' effectiveness and your efficiency, evaluate how you distribute your projects and follow through on their progress. To do this, consider the following ideas.

1. Give written directions at the start of the project. Most writers respond well to clear directions, so give the writer a clear idea of the document's PURPOSE, AUDIENCE, SCOPE, ISSUES, PROFESSIONAL POSTURE, and VOICE.

2. Set realistic DEADLINES together, and include interim deadlines to check issues, organization, and overall structure so you and the writer do not find yourself panicking as the final deadline nears.

3.   After the writer's initial research has made the written issues more specific, have the writer return them for your review.   Make sure that the list includes the correct legal issues, that their focus is specific enough yet not too narrow, and that they are substantively accurate. Use these written issues to ascertain whether the writer is following directions and remaining within the scope of the project.   Many writers respond well to periodic checks on their progress, so if you have thought of new ideas since you gave directions, use the issues to help the writer incorporate those ideas.

4.   At the organizational stage, meet to discuss approaches to planning the overall document, especially if it is a big one.   Together, choose the best approach or organizational scheme.   This helps keep the writer invested in the project and helps the writer understand your reasons for suggesting specific structural approaches.   To unify the organization and help the writer build the structure, tie your suggestions to the overall purpose and audience.

5.   When you receive the first draft, assist the writer by addressing REWRITING concerns rather than REVISING ones.   Avoid EDITING for tone, wordiness, or other small-scale concerns, which lead you to appropriate the text and alienate the writer.   Editing extensively at this stage would be inefficient, in any event, because some of the sentences you edit will disappear in later drafts.   Rather, describe the objective the rewrite should meet, and then evaluate the structure and content against that objective.   Help the writer see what rewrites are necessary, rather than doing the rewrites yourself.   Give comments that foster their continued progress, encourage excellent analysis, and increase the product's usefulness.   Thus your comments will focus on substantive changes and their reasons.   This process will minimize editing time, reduce frustration, and maximize benefits to the writer and the document.   For specifics, see WRITING PROCESS CHECK-LISTS, subsection 3.

6.   Include your reasons for making any changes.   These can be brief, just *to clarify* or *for conciseness, try this version.*   Reasons are important; the writer will respond better if he or she knows why you have changed something.

7.   If you need to edit in detail, edit only one page or paragraph.   Then identify the PATTERNS in the writer's expression.   For example, you may notice unusually long sentences, LEGALESE, or weak TOPIC SENTENCES; identify these and ask the writer to edit the document throughout for similar examples.

8.   Return the drafts at the agreed-upon time so your writers get a strong sense of the importance of meeting deadlines.

9.   In later drafts, give unambiguous, consistent comments that help the writer more swiftly to the desired results.   Continue to tie comments to the document's purpose and audience, not your personal

preferences. Avoid changing words just to change them; if the writer has captured the concept so that any reader would find it unambiguous, leave it. Try to be as precise, organized, and specific as you expect the writer to be. For specific commenting techniques, see EDITING.

10. To create long-term improvement, help your writers determine their respective strengths and weaknesses overall. You might want to discuss those at the start of their tenure with you by having each writer self-evaluate. Then, together, you can design a long-range program that develops their writing and evens out their abilities. As each project closes, or at the end of a group of projects, relate the writer's development to the long-range plan.

Similarly, determine your strengths and weaknesses as a manager. Periodically, you may want to ask for feedback on your management techniques so that you can increase your effectiveness. Receiving feedback openly and implementing good ideas will give a strong message to your writers that you can help each other.

MAROON BOOK

The Maroon Book is another name for the *University of Chicago Manual of Legal Citation* (Law Co-op 1989). This book offers simplified citation forms as an alternative to the BLUEBOOK, whose entries are sometimes more complex or detailed than many legal writers need. Before you start note-taking, check with your AUDIENCE and your jurisdiction to see which version to use. Then you can record your initial citations in the form you will use for the document's final version.

MATTER OF FACT, AS A

See AS A MATTER OF FACT.

MAY

Use *may* to communicate permission from an authority.

Under this statute, the corporation may defer payment of income taxes for one year if three criteria have been met.

You can also use *may* to communicate possibility.

The outcome of the trial may depend on the credibility of the two attorneys.

In contrast, *can* suggests capacity or ability.

The corporation can file its return on either of two dates.

Might suggests a chance or possibility.

Your client might qualify as a holder in due course under three conditions.

For related information, see VERBS, AUXILIARY.

MAY OR CAN?

See CAN OR MAY?

MEANING OF WORDS

For topics in this area, see LITERAL MEANING, FIGURATIVE MEANING, CONNOTATION, PRECISION, and WORD CHOICE.

MEMORANDUM OF POINTS AND AUTHORITIES

A memorandum of points and authorities is a PRETRIAL BRIEF that outlines the legal arguments to be made on a pretrial issue. In some jurisdictions, this terminology is used because the format requires the writer to make each legal point separately and give authority for it. Check your jurisdiction for the appropriate terminology and FORMAT. For an example of one kind of format, see BRIEFS. For related information, see AUDIENCE, PURPOSE, and PERSUASIVE WRITING.

MEMOS

Memos are intraoffice communications that convey information from researchers to decision-makers before, during, and after litigation. Memos use OBJECTIVE STYLE to inform the reader of how the law measures the strengths and weaknesses of the client's position, to predict the court's decision, and to advise the reader on what decision to make. For related information, see OBJECTIVITY. The usual format for a memo follows.

MEMO

To: [This caption contains information
From: that gets the memo filed accurately and
Re: makes it useful for future reference.
Date: For more information see CAPTIONS.]

INTRODUCTION

An Introduction may be included to remind the reader of the assignment and summarize the memo's purpose and scope. As such, it should be a short paragraph.

Some readers prefer including this section in place of the Statement of Facts, Questions Presented, and Brief Answers. In this variation, the Introduction will be longer, and will include the information that is otherwise included in the three sections below. Also include a transition to the Discussion.

STATEMENT OF FACTS

The STATEMENT OF FACTS summarizes the procedural facts, LEGALLY SIGNIFICANT FACTS, and needed BACKGROUND FACTS. If the memo is written in the context of a dispute, it might note the facts in dispute and what each side claims. The Statement may also note what information must still be obtained. Alternatively, this information may be noted in the CONCLUSION. The Statement of Facts may precede or follow the Questions Presented and Brief Answers, so check with your primary reader to determine the order.

QUESTION PRESENTED

This section includes the final version of the preliminary QUESTION PRESENTED as it was formulated in Step 3 of the RESEARCH STRATEGY. It should contain the following three elements.

> **Under [general rule of law],**
>
> **did (or was) [legal question]**
>
> **when [legally significant facts of this case]?**

> **Under Wyoming law on false imprisonment, did Cornbloom falsely imprison Abernathy when he drove Abernathy around in the car for seven hours without letting him out?**

Check with your reader to see if the particular facts of your case should be included in the Questions Presented, which will focus the issue on one client's situation. Your reader may prefer that the facts be stated in general terms so the memo is easier to use as a reference in future cases, such as in the following example.

> **Under Wyoming law on false imprisonment, does the driver of a car falsely imprison a passenger when he drives the passenger around for seven hours without stopping and letting him out of the car?**

BRIEF ANSWER

The BRIEF ANSWER gives the writer's predicted answer to the question and gives the reason for this answer, usually in one sentence.

> **Yes; Cornbloom falsely imprisoned Abernathy because he intended to confine Abernathy in the car, because Abernathy was actually confined in the car, and because Abernathy was aware of his confinement.**

DISCUSSION

This section discusses the application of the law to the facts; generally, it will be organized around the structure of the law being used. For example, a discussion of a statute with several elements will progress element by element; a discussion of a balancing test will weigh the two sides. For each element, the DISCUSSION SECTION begins with the general RULES of law, describes useful ANALOGOUS CASES, and then applies that information to the facts of this situation. For related information, see APPLICATION.

Thus you will not necessarily have all the law in one place and all the application in another, but rather for each point of the analysis, you might state the law and then apply it. For more help, see ORGANIZATION, LARGE–SCALE and ORGANIZATION, SMALL–SCALE.

CONCLUSION

This section summarizes the main points made in the Discussion, giving a capsule of the reasoning that led to the Brief Answer. It may also contain recommendations to the reader. It does not, however, include any information or reasoning not covered in the Discussion.

MERELY

Avoid this word, especially in PERSUASIVE WRITING. Most legal matters would not be *mere* or you would not be writing about them. Additionally, this word is often substituted for LEGAL ANALYSIS: rather than proving the proposition, the writer relies on a label. Avoid this shortcut and make your point directly.

Defendant was not at the scene of the crime.

rather than

Plaintiff merely guesses where defendant was at the time of the crime.

MIGHT

Might is used to suggest that there is a possibility of the action occurring, often if a condition is met.

If we drop this third cause of action, the court might grant a summary judgment on the first two.

It is also sometimes used with suggestions to help create a tone of deference.

When deciding whether to accept this settlement, you might want to consider the legal cost you will incur by proceeding with the lawsuit.

For related information, see VERBS, AUXILIARY; MAY; and SHALL.

MISSPELLINGS, HOW TO AVOID

Fortunately, spelling problems can often be best cured by relatively painless measures. Here are two ideas.

1. Take a 3 × 5 index card and write on it three words you need to use frequently but have trouble spelling, such as *defendant* or *conceive*, and underline the part that gives you trouble. Then put the index card somewhere where you will see it frequently, such as on your bathroom mirror or inside your brief case. Do nothing more for two or three weeks. By that time, you will probably find that you can close your eyes and see the card in your mind, thus seeing how to spell the problem words. As you gain confidence with these three words, substitute new ones on the list.

2. Make an alphabetized list of words that commonly give you trouble, but keep the list to one page. Then carry this list with you and look up the problem word any time you need to write it. With this technique, you are not trying to learn to spell the words; you are finding a way around the problem, which is a practical alternative.

MODELS, USE OF

See FORMS, USE OF.

MODIFIERS

A modifier adds information about a noun or verb and can be either a single word or a group of words. Avoid using too many modifiers because they weaken the sentence. Particularly avoid using two modifiers that mean the same thing, such as *first and foremost* or *separate and apart*. Also avoid modifiers that have little substantive meaning, such as *in this manner*, *very*, or *obviously*.

> **These are the specific words of Minnesota lawmakers; consequently, the words must be given special significance.**

rather than

> Clearly these are the specific and precise words of Minnesota lawmakers regarding the issue; consequently, the words must be given special significance and appropriate attention.

> **The court in <u>Higgins</u> does not establish a standard for viability any more specific than the fetus' ability to exist separately from its mother.**

rather than

> Obviously, the court in <u>Higgins</u> appears to fail to definitively establish an unambiguous and undebatable determining standard for when a fetus reaches the medical state of viability that seems to

be any more clearly specific than ascertaining medically the fetus' ability to exist separately and apart from its biological mother.

For more general information on modifiers, see ADJECTIVES, ADVERBS, and PREPOSITIONS. For more on problems associated with the use of modifiers, see MODIFIERS, DANGLING; MODIFIERS, MISPLACED; and MODIFIERS, SQUINTING.

MODIFIERS, DANGLING

A dangling modifier is a modifying phrase that does not modify any word in the sentence. This situation invites ambiguity. Usually these dangling modifiers occur at the beginning of a sentence.

To argue contributory negligence, all elements of negligence must be shown.

It is not clear here who will be doing the arguing. In contrast, see the following revision.

To argue contributory negligence, the defense must show all elements of negligence.

You can avoid this problem by doing the following: when you start a sentence with an introductory phrase beginning with a verb, such as *to argue*, make sure that the subject of that verb is also the subject of the sentence following the introductory phrase. For related information, see AMBIGUITY, WAYS TO AVOID.

MODIFIERS, MISPLACED

Sometimes a modifying phrase, because of its position, modifies the wrong phrase in a sentence.

The defendant refused to service the car belonging to the man who insulted him with good reason.

Here *with good reason* should modify *refused* rather than *insulted*. To avoid ambiguity, place the modifying phrase right next to the word modified, such as *refused* in this example.

The defendant, with good reason, refused to service the car belonging to the man who had insulted him.

For other problems associated with modifiers, see MODIFIERS, DANGLING and MODIFIERS, SQUINTING.

MODIFIERS, SQUINTING

Squinting modifiers create ambiguity because they can modify terms either before or after the modifier. To correct this problem, move the modifier to an unambiguous location in the sentence.

Only Ms. Sparks suggested filing a suit for adverse possession.

or

Ms. Sparks suggested but did not recommend filing a suit for adverse possession.

rather than

Ms. Sparks only suggested filing a suit for adverse possession.

For a discussion of related problems, see ONLY and AMBIGUITY, WAYS TO AVOID.

MOODS

Mood refers to changes made in the form of the verb to indicate whether or not the action described by the verb happened in fact. These changes in the form of the verb are called inflections, and create three moods. These moods are important conveyors of meaning in legal writing.

1. Indicative

The indicative mood refers to actions that have in fact happened or will in fact happen. This mood is used most often in legal writing.

The defendant filed a motion for failure to state a claim upon which relief can be granted.

or

The plaintiff invited the defendant to dinner on the night of the robbery.

2. Subjunctive

The subjunctive mood refers to actions that will not necessarily happen, but are being discussed hypothetically.

If I were you, I would not use that argument with Judge Carwell.

or

If the defendant were younger, such an assault might have been possible.

3. Imperative

The imperative mood states commands. The subject of the sentence is *you*, which is understood.

Return the bottom portion.

Meet me at the hearing at 10:30.

Use it when explaining how to do something. Do not use the imperative mood when talking to courts. For further detail, see VERBS, MOODS.

MOST IMPORTANTLY

Avoid it. This phrase both diminishes the importance of the rest of the document and gratuitously points a finger at this part of the document. Instead use POSITIONS OF EMPHASIS, effective TOPIC SENTENCES and apt WORD CHOICE, precise TERMS OF ART, and clear ORGANIZATION to show your point's inherent importance. If you must, use the phrase *most important.*

MOTIONS

A motion is an application to a court for a rule or order in the moving party's favor. In most jurisdictions, the motion must be filed with the court as a separate document. In some jurisdictions, it is combined with a NOTICE OF MOTION, which tells the opposition when the court will hear the motion. Check your jurisdiction for specific FORMAT and filing requirements.

Often you will file a brief in support of the motion. This brief is designed to persuade the court to rule in your client's favor. When the opposition responds to the motion, it will usually file a brief in opposition to the motion. For a basic format, see BRIEFS. For related information, see PERSUASIVE WRITING.

MS., MRS., OR MISS?

If possible, find out from the person addressed what she prefers. If this is not possible, use *Ms.*

MUST

Must communicates a requirement.

Whenever a pedestrian is in a school crosswalk, all drivers approaching that crosswalk must stop ....

Must is a clearer indication of requirement than *should,* which in general speech can mean either must or ought. *Shall* is sometimes used instead of *must* in LEGISLATION, but is not more precise grammatically. For related information, see VERBS, AUXILIARY.

MUST OR SHOULD?

Use *must* to indicate requirement, inevitability, or legal obligation. *Must* has a more absolute connotation than *should.* Use *should* to indicate moral or ethical obligation, probable occurrence, or uncertainty about a future event.

You must register in order to vote.

but

You **should** vote in the coming election.

NAMES OR GENERIC DESCRIPTION?

There are two schools of thought on whether or not to use clients' names in any piece of legal writing. The first school holds that names are appropriate because they focus the reader on the specific outcome of the case being analyzed. The second school prefers using more general terms because the reader can get a concept of the legal question being analyzed, which in a memo will also be of use in future cases. Consider your AUDIENCE, and write accordingly.

> **Under Washington Law on false imprisonment, did Cornbloom falsely imprison Abernathy when he drove Abernathy around in the car for seven hours without letting him out?**

or

> **Under Washington Law on false imprisonment, does the driver of a car falsely imprison a passenger when he drives the passenger around for seven hours without stopping and letting him out of the car?**

Whichever format you use, remain consistent throughout any piece of legal writing. If you choose to use names in OBJECTIVE WRITING, use them in each subsection of the memo or opinion letter. Choose the form of name most appropriate to the setting, such as *Mr. Jones*, *Theodore Jones*, or *Ted*, depending upon your familiarity with the party and the formality of the document you are writing. Similarly, if you choose to use names in PERSUASIVE WRITING, use them in each part of the brief or opinion letter. Choose the form of name most favorable to your client. For example, use *Mr.*, *Ms.*, *Miss*, or *Mrs. Smith* if you wish to dignify the party by using a formal tone. In briefs, use first names only if needed for clarity or if referring to a juvenile. For example, if two brothers were contesting a will, you might use first and last names, such as *Allen Anderson* and *Andrew Anderson*, to distinguish the two. If one party was an eight-year-old girl, you might use the first name only, such as *Betty*, to underscore the sympathy the court might feel for the child.

Avoid using names of anyone other than the parties, such as the names of opposing counsel. Such references detract from the purpose of your argument.

NARRATIVE WRITING

In contrast to EXPOSITORY WRITING, narrative writing tells a story. When well-constructed, it can also make a point or support an argument. In legal writing, narratives appear in Statements of Facts, illustrative anecdotes, and longer hypothetical examples.

Narrative writing is not equivalent to CHRONOLOGICAL ORGANIZATION, although that organization may be used. A STATEMENT OF FACTS might start with the first event of significance to the issues in the case. Thus in a divorce case, the facts might begin as follows.

> **Edgar and Mary Plantagenet were married on June 9, 1963.**

But often another organization is more effective for EMPHASIS or CLARITY. For example, you might begin with a statement of the problem so the AUDIENCE will read the subsequent details in light of the legal question involved.

> **This case arises from an unlawful arrest of Defendant after the warrantless search of her house.**

This is particularly useful when you need to minimize the effect of some facts that occur early in the chronology but are not sympathetic to your client.

If the narration will be extensive or complex, you may begin with a summary of the situation.

> **Veldmar, Inc. and Thanco Corporation both agreed to a merger plan in July 1990. Since that time, however, a complex series of events has made this merger economically impossible for Veldmar.**

This overview provides a framework so the reader understands why he or she is reading the subsequent details.

For PERSUASION, you may begin with a fact that deserves emphasis and that can make sense to the reader even out of the larger context of the other facts. Then move into your chronological narration after that dramatic statement.

> **Alexander Oliaka, who used to run three miles each morning, will never run again. He will spend the rest of his life in a wheelchair as a result of spinal injuries he suffered in an automobile collision. The collision occurred on August 17, 1992.**

This opening allows the reader to focus fully on one dramatic, sympathetic fact. The impression made, the rest of the narration then adds the other facts needed to fill in the rest of the picture. For ways to emphasize key facts through WORD CHOICE or SENTENCE STRUCTURE within a narration, see EMPHASIS.

NEGATIVES

Negative statements are harder to understand than positive ones, so state things positively whenever possible.

> **Come to the meeting at 3:00 p.m. or later.**

rather than

> Do not come to the meeting before 3:00 p.m.

The negative statements that are hardest to read are those including *unless*, *neglect to*, *not unlike*, *hardly*, *scarcely*, and other such words. These negative words can be easily misread and so should be avoided when possible.

Multiple negatives are also hard to read, so try to avoid them.

Come to the meeting only if you are required to do so.

rather than

> Do not come to the meeting unless you are told not to neglect to come.

NEITHER

Use *neither* only when listing two items. Like *either*, *neither* is a helpful signal for the reader when it is followed by two listed items; it is much less helpful when it is followed by a list of more than two items, because *neither* leads the reader to expect only two. Therefore, if you are introducing a list of more than two items, try using *none of the following*, which will prepare the reader for a longer list.

Further, make sure that the terms after *neither* and *nor* are logically and grammatically parallel.

Neither the defendant's own testimony nor her written records support this assertion.

rather than

> Neither the testimony offered by the defendant nor the defendant's own written records support this assertion.

For related information, see PARALLEL STRUCTURE.

NOBODY

Nobody takes a singular verb.

Nobody has shown up on time for the hearing yet.

Nobody knows the trouble I've seen.

Nobody sounds slightly informal, so you may prefer *no one* in most legal writing.

NOMINALIZATION

Nominalization refers to the process of turning ADJECTIVES, ADVERBS, and VERBS into NOUNS. Nominalizations are grammatically correct, but their overuse can make the writing stodgy or hard to read. Whenever possible and appropriate, replace a nominalization with the verb, adjective or adverb form.

Use the following phrases	rather than these.
stated	made the statement that
Machines operated by inserting a coin	Machines operated by means of insertion of a coin
Counsel objected to the expert's testimony.	Counsel made an objection to the expert's testimony.
He was devoted to his father.	He showed great devotion to his father.

But use nominalizations where they make more sense, such as when the noun forms are TERMS OF ART.

He is accused of alienation of affection.

rather than

He alienated her affections toward her husband.

NONE, SINGULAR OR PLURAL?

None means no one of, and so is singular.

None of the reasons given is valid.

NO ONE

No one takes a singular verb; related personal pronouns and adjectives must also be singular.

No one has testified to plaintiff's innocence.

No one has all of his or her [not their] pretrial discovery ready.

NONRESTRICTIVE PHRASES

Nonrestrictive phrases are those phrases that describe but do not limit the words preceding them. They are surrounded by commas, which act as a kind of parentheses, because if the nonrestrictive phrases were taken out of the sentence the sentence would still be accurate. Nonrestrictive phrases often begin with *which* or *who*.

The defendant, who thinks he is innocent, looks terrified.

The fourth amendment, which protects citizens against unlawful searches and seizures, provides the foundation for this suit.

For related information, see THAT OR WHICH?

NOR

Nor is a conjunction that continues the negative force of *neither*, *never*, or *not*, and therefore can be used effectively in PERSUASIVE WRITING.

> **The defendant was never read his rights, nor was he allowed to make a phone call, nor was he allowed to talk with an attorney within the first twenty-four hours of his internment.**

> **Respondent objected neither to cross-examination nor to introduction of the evidence at trial.**

> **The statute has never been construed to have such a result, nor is such a result possible under the Constitution.**

NOT

Not is a small word that changes the meaning of a whole sentence. Therefore, proofread your text to make sure *not* is placed accurately. Additionally, whenever possible, try to write so the point will not be lost if the reader overlooks *not*.

NOTES

Develop an effective system of note taking so that PREWRITING is comfortable for you. Your system is personal, of course, but taking effective notes throughout RESEARCH and PREWRITING will make WRITING and REWRITING much faster. In developing your own system, consider the following.

1. Whatever form you use, such as note cards, legal size paper, or cut-and-pasted scraps of paper, write on only one side of the paper so that information can be moved easily.

2. If an authority looks at all usable, write down the entire correct citation right at the beginning. This will save you time when you use that authority later; you will not have to spend time in the library looking up citations. The time you save will outweigh any extra time you take to record citations at the beginning.

3. When using quotes, RULES, propositions, REASONING, or HOLDINGS from any case, note the exact page number so that you can incorporate PINPOINT CITES in the final draft without returning to the original source.

4. Try to develop a system, such as one using headings, using colors, or using tabs, one that organizes notes by topic, so that the notes can be easily organized according to issue.

5. Write legibly so you will not waste time later deciphering your notes.

6. Focus on the legal issue you are researching by translating your notes into relevant TERMS OF ART. Once you have formulated the QUESTION PRESENTED in step 3 of the research process described in RESEARCH STRATEGY, begin reading your cases with that issue in mind; then record holdings, propositions, rules with the terms of art important to that issue. For example, if you are researching whether or not your client committed an intentional tort, use *intend* as your main verb when stating the holding.

A five year old could not intend to injure an elderly woman because five-year-olds are not capable of forming intent.

7. Leave space for adding notes, which may include either cross-references or your own thoughts as the research and writing process progresses.

8. Take notes with your own thoughts in mind; work those thoughts into your theory of the case, whether writing a memo, a letter, or a brief. This will help you begin to organize and understand the significance of your research and will help you build your case.

NOTICE OF MOTION

A Notice of Motion accompanies a motion to a court. It notifies the other party of the time and place the motion will be heard. The Notice of Motion is accompanied by the motion itself and often a brief in support of or in opposition to the motion. In some jurisdictions, you may incorporate the notice into the motion's preamble, as shown in the following example. Combining the two, however, may create an awkwardly long sentence. For related information, see MOTIONS and BRIEFS.

STATE OF WISCONSIN CIRCUIT COURT DANE COUNTY

OLAF PETERSON, HENRY PETERSON and DOROTHY PETERSON,
 	
                    Plaintiffs,
        vs.
 	
BUDGET INSURANCE COMPANY, et al.,
                    Defendants.
	)
	)
	)
	)
	)
	)
	)
	)
	)
	)
		NOTICE OF MOTION AND MOTIONS AFTER VERDICT
		Case No: 000–999

TO: Attorney David A. Salverson
     Salverson & Johnson, S.C.
     Suite 6032
     9101 West Wisconsin Avenue
     Milwaukee, Wisconsin 53203

PLEASE TAKE NOTICE that on September 29, 1989, at 10:30 A.M., at the Courthouse in the City of Madison, Circuit Court, Branch

IX, the Honorable Albert Purdy, presiding, the Defendants, by their attorneys, will move the Court on Motions After Verdict as follows:

1. For judgment notwithstanding the verdict, dismissing the Complaint of the Plaintiffs, for reasons evident in the record and stated in these Motions;

2. In the alternative, to change the answers to Questions No. 1 and 2 from "Yes" to "No", dismissing the Complaint of the Plaintiffs on the ground of insufficiency of the evidence to sustain the answers;

    . . .

8. In the alternative, to set the judgment aside and order judgment in favor of the Defendants, dismissing the Plaintiffs' Complaint on the ground that the Plaintiff's negligence was a superseding cause of his injuries.

Dated August 15, 1981.

POTTERS, PEARSON, PEEPLES, & PRINCE

BY: _____

JOSEPH E. POTTERS,
Attorney for Defendants,
Budget Insurance Company
and Far Horizons
Foundation, Inc.

P.O. Box 6666
Madison, Wisconsin   53701

NOT ONLY ... BUT ALSO

These two phrases belong in partnership as conjunctions. In PERSUASIVE WRITING, use the pair to foreshadow and emphasize the logical parallels of two arguments.

Not only has the plaintiff failed to show that the father gave the son implied consent, but the plaintiff has also failed to show that the father provided the car for the son's use.

In OBJECTIVE WRITING, use the pair to connect legal concepts clearly.

The plaintiff must show not only that the father gave implied consent, but also that the father provided the car to the son.

In using this pair of conjunctions, remember to use *but also* after *not only*. Do not use *not only ... but*. The mismatched *not only ... but* is particularly confusing to readers because *not ... but* means almost the opposite of *not only ... but also*.

Also make sure that the term following *not only* is structurally and logically parallel to the term following *but also*. See PARALLEL STRUCTURE.

The defendant abused not only the privileges offered him, but also the procedure designed to protect him.

NOT SO MUCH ... AS

Like NOT ONLY ... BUT ALSO, these words work together as conjunctions and should be used together.

The key is not so much the existence of central authority as the frequency with which that authority is exercised.

rather than

The key is not so much the existence of central authority but the frequency with which that authority is exercised.

NOUNS

To lawyers, nouns are probably second only to verbs as the most important part of speech because nouns name clients, theories, causes, damages, results, and rights. Thus legal writers must choose nouns with care and use them with precision. In order to do so, first understand the uses of the various noun classifications. Second, avoid the common problems associated with the use of nouns in legal writing.

1. Classifications of nouns and their uses.

(a) Proper nouns name specific persons, places, or things, and are capitalized.

San Francisco, Sandstrom, Bill of Rights

(b) Common nouns do not refer to specific persons, places, or things, and thus are not capitalized.

lawyer, courtroom, fairness, alienation

(c) ABSTRACT NOUNS name concepts or ideas, rather than tangible things.

fairness, right, protection, weapon

Abstract nouns are necessary and useful in legal writing, but if misused or overused they make the content less memorable for the reader.

Equity dictates that the plaintiff be reimbursed for this loss.

rather than

Fairness dictates that plaintiff's rights should be protected.

(d) In contrast, concrete nouns name tangible things.

lawyer, courtroom, Doberman, knife

These concrete nouns are easier to remember and are thus more helpful to the legal reader. Therefore, use concrete nouns often, especially to emphasize a point.

The testimony of four witnesses proves Mr. Noble was mentally incompetent, and should therefore be spared the death penalty.

rather than

Fairness dictates that my client's mental state should absolve him of guilt.

For more examples of the uses of concrete nouns, see EMPHASIS, subsection 2.

(e) Collective nouns name groups that are to be treated logically and grammatically as a single unit.

The Supreme Court holds . . . .

With collective nouns, use the singular form of the verb, such as *holds*, even though the noun refers to a group, such as a court made up of several justices.

(f) GERUNDS are nouns formed from the *-ing* form of a verb. Often using gerunds makes a sentence more concise.

Imagining alone does not constitute intent.

rather than

The act of imagination alone does not constitute intent.

2. Common problems with nouns in legal writing.

Two common problems occur with nouns in legal writing: they are used imprecisely and inconsistently. Therefore, consider your choices carefully. First, choose the noun that most precisely states your meaning. To paraphrase Mark Twain, "the difference between the right word and the almost right word is the difference between *internment* and *interment*." Second, do not change a noun solely for VARIETY. The legal reader will assume a different noun represents a different idea. For more explanation and examples, see WORD CHOICE and REPETITION.

NOUN STRING

This phrase describes three or more nouns placed together without any connecting words between them to signal their interrelationship. Noun strings are concise, but often hard to understand.

Operations Reduction Contingency Plan Agreement

The reader has to fill in the connecting words to understand the meaning. When the noun string is unfamiliar to even one of your readers, revise the phrase to include prepositions and other helpful structural signals.

Agreement to a Contingency Plan for a Reduction in Operations

or

They agreed to use a contingency plan to reduce operations.

Noun strings are often a form of JARGON, and as such may be familiar to some readers. But use these noun strings only when they will be easily understood by all of your readers, as when all the words in the string are familiar

unemployment benefits claim

or when the string is a TERM OF ART.

work product privilege

Confrontation Clause issue

Do not use noun strings out of habit, but rather when they are the most readable way to present the idea. For related information, see CONCISENESS and CLARITY.

NUMBERS

See NUMERALS.

NUMERALS

The common question here is whether a number should be spelled out in words or written as a numeral.

1. Spell out a number that begins a sentence.

One hundred twenty-five pieces of evidence were admitted at trial.

The one exception to this rule is years.

1984 was not what we expected.

2. Spell out zero to ninety-nine in text and zero to nine in footnotes in law review articles. Different sources list different upper limits on spelling out numbers, but Bluebook rule 6.2(a) lists ninety-nine as the limit. According to the *Government Printing Office Style Manual*, however, units of measurement are an exception. See subsection 9 below.

3. Spell out *million, billion,* and so on, rather than using zeroes, because it is easier to read.

27 million

Also spell out numbers in indefinite expressions.

The plaintiff is in his seventies.

Spell out round numbers larger than ninety-nine, if you choose, as long as you are consistent throughout the text.

4. Spell out numbers and then insert numerals in parentheses only in drafting legal documents, and then only when the duplication is needed to avoid the possibility of a critical inaccuracy.

In consideration for these agreements, Howard Industries agrees to pay Liveson Construction the sum of four thousand dollars ($4,000).

5. Use numerals for numbers larger than ninety-nine.

The prosecution introduced 173 separate documents to support this claim.

6. Use numerals if, in one series, you have numbers both over ninety-nine and under.

The numbers of computers taken in these four robberies were 7, 25, 102, and 130.

7. Use numerals when you are referring to a section of a document and that section itself is identified by a numeral.

This exception is covered in subsection 5.

8. Use numerals for fractions and decimals.

The total purchase price was $10.4 million.

The production cost is now 2½ times greater than it was when the contract was signed.

9. Use numerals for units of measurement, such as for age, weight, money, and time.

6 years old, 95 pounds, 2700 yen, 4:30 p.m., 1.3 liters

Be sure to proofread all numerals to make sure they are accurate and equivalent to the written version.

OBJECT

See SENTENCE, PARTS OF, subsections 3, 4, and 5.

OBJECTIVE WRITING

Objective writing informs and predicts, using a neutral POINT OF VIEW. For example, use objective writing in MEMOS to inform the reader of the current status of the law, or in OPINION LETTERS to inform the reader of the current status of a case. In either situation, the reader is looking for an unbiased assessment of the circumstances.

The reader may also expect a prediction of the outcome of the case. This prediction should be based on objective analysis of the law that measures the strengths and weaknesses of the client's position and balances them. In doing so, objective writing does not minimize the weaknesses of the argument, as PERSUASIVE WRITING does.

> **The majority of states draws the viability line at around six months; only two states have drawn the line earlier.**

rather than

> Even though a majority of states has drawn the viability line at six months, two states have carefully considered the valid arguments for drawing the line earlier and have done so.

Consider the following in preparing objective writing, such as a memo or an opinion letter.

1. Keep an objective point of view, as a reporter would.

2. Report what the law or the status of the case is by giving an objective summary of the law.

3. Make sure both the strengths and weaknesses of the client's arguments are clear.

4. Make sure the reader sees the balance of those arguments, that is, what weight law, POLICY, and EQUITY give to each.

5. Avoid overuse of MODIFIERS, because objective writing informs but does not persuade. Concentrate instead on precise use of nouns and verbs.

> **The majority of states draws the viability line at around six months; only two states have drawn the line earlier.**

rather than

> The vast majority of states have clearly decided to draw the viability line at approximately six months, although two dissenting states have deviated somewhat from that popular course.

When using modifiers, also avoid those that argue, such as *unjust* or *unmistakably*; use only those modifiers that clarify the presentation, such as *unsettled* or *previously*.

6. Make sure the information in the memo is complete, despite your personal bias; do not omit unfavorable points the other side may raise.

For related information, see OBJECTIVITY and POINT OF VIEW, OBJECTIVE OR PERSUASIVE?

OBJECTIVITY

Objectivity is essential to all forms of legal writing at some stage. An attorney must remain particularly objective when planning the client's case so that the attorney can correctly anticipate all possible arguments on both sides of the issue. Equally important, an attorney must remain objective in any oral presentations designed to inform the court or another attorney of the law, such as in pretrial or intraoffice conferences.

Objectivity is paramount in pretrial work because the attorney must accurately assess the strength of the arguments. This objectivity paves the way for accurate use of law and POLICY to persuade the court in BRIEFS and oral arguments. Therefore, in intraoffice documents, such as MEMOS, present information objectively. For related information, see OBJECTIVE WRITING and ORAL PRESENTA-TIONS.

OBJECT OF A PREPOSITION

See PREPOSITIONS and SENTENCE, PARTS OF, subsection 6.

OBLIVIOUS OF OR OBLIVIOUS TO?

If you mean *unaware*, use *oblivious of*. If you mean *forgetful*, use *oblivious to*. Of the two, *oblivious of* is the narrower meaning. To avoid confusion, consider using another word, such as *unaware* or *unmindful*.

The defendant was unaware of the significance of this waiver.

rather than

The defendant was oblivious of the significance of this waiver.

The defendant was unmindful of her duty to see that all the children's seat belts were properly fastened.

rather than

The defendant was oblivious to her duty to see that all the children's seat belts were properly fastened.

OBVIOUSLY

Use *obviously* only when the point is indeed obvious. Use *obviously* sparingly in legal writing, because you seldom state an obvious point, and even when you do state it you seldom want to underscore its obviousness. If the point is not obvious, labelling it as such insults your reader and impairs your credibility. For related concerns, see MODIFI-ERS and LITERAL MEANING.

OF COURSE

This phrase is best avoided in legal writing; *of course* implies that the point is obvious, but the legal reader may not see your point as being this clear cut. Do not use *of course* to gloss over assumptions that need to be supported. For related problems, see IT IS SAID THAT, OBVIOUSLY, and MODIFIERS.

OK, O.K., OR OKAY?

Probably use none of the above in formal writing. If you need to use one of the three, *OK* is the most widely used form.

OMITTING WORDS FROM QUOTES

For when and how to do this, see QUOTATIONS, HOW TO PUNCTUATE, subsections 7, 8, and 9. Also see EDITING QUOTES.

ONE

One as a pronoun indicates a single person, a single unit, a single thing. It takes a singular verb.

One of the defendants is moving to have the case dismissed.

One of the problems with teaching legal analysis is that not all professors agree on the best way to teach it.

ONE–SENTENCE PARAGRAPHS

Occasionally you may use one-sentence paragraphs for EMPHASIS, but only occasionally. If you have several in one brief or memo, you are probably overusing them. The following one-sentence paragraph, coming after a detailed explanation of a Congressional policy statement, effectively emphasizes a point.

While this statement of Congressional policy has no direct effect on the commerce regulations, it may be such a strong policy statement that future Presidents will think twice about restricting scientific or scholarly transnational communications.

For problems one-sentence paragraphs may signal, see PARAGRAPHS and ORGANIZATION. For related information, see ORGANIZATION, SMALL–SCALE.

ONLY, WHERE TO PLACE

Each time you use *only*, check its placement; in general, place it immediately before the word it modifies. A misplaced *only* can create ambiguity, and often in legal writing that ambiguity is serious. For example, what does the following sentence mean?

Shares are sold to the public only by the parent corporation.

Are shares sold only to the public, or only by the parent corporation? Although the reader might be able to reason out the meaning in context, the sentence should be written so the meaning is unmistakable. See MODIFIERS, SQUINTING.

Often ambiguity occurs because *only* comes too early in the sentence.

> You should only introduce this evidence if the defendant chooses to testify.

The writer did not mean to say that the reader should *only introduce* this evidence and do nothing else with it. To avoid this ambiguity, try placing *only* as late in the sentence as possible without creating an inaccuracy.

> **You should introduce this evidence only if the defendant chooses to testify.**

For related information, see also ACCURACY, subsection 6.

ON THE CONDITION THAT OR WITH THE CONDITION THAT?

The most likely option here is a shorter, clearer phrase that avoids the question. Try replacing the phrase with the most accurate choice from the following list.

if	**when**
only if	**only when**
but only if	**but only when**

For example, you might write the following
> **The seller agrees to replace any defective widgets, but only if the buyer notifies the seller of the defect within forty-eight hours of delivery.**

rather than either
> The seller agrees to replace any defective widgets on the condition that the buyer notifies the seller of the defect within forty-eight hours of delivery.

or
> The seller agrees to replace any defective widgets with the condition that the buyer notifies the seller of the defect within forty-eight hours of delivery.

For related information, see IF OR WHEN?

OPENINGS FOR LETTERS

In general, open with a sentence or two explaining the point of your letter or why you are writing.

> **In response to your inquiry, I am enclosing** ....

or

> **Last Monday, we met to discuss ....   This letter formalizes our agreement that I would act as your attorney concerning** ....

This is preferable to starting with a sentence explaining who you are; that opening tempts the reader to say, "Who cares?" You can, however, explain who you are in the second or third sentence, after the reader has some reason to care, or you can add an explanatory reference as part of another sentence.

> **As your attorney, I want to notify you of some recent changes in the tax law that may require a change in your record-keeping practices.**

In some cases, you may want to be slightly less direct, including a brief explanatory paragraph before your point. See BAD NEWS, GIVING IT; BAD NEWS, SOFTENING IT; and PERSUASIVE LETTERS for ways to handle these situations. For more detail on ways to structure other letters, see GENERAL CORRESPONDENCE LETTERS.

Have stock phrases for opening routine letters, so that you avoid reinventing the wheel. But take care in selecting these stock phrases, because these opening phrases give the reader an impression of your personality, just as your demeanor creates an impression when you meet someone for the first time. In general, avoid stuffy openings, like *Pursuant to your request*, and long-winded ones, like *In regard to the matter of your request* ....   When you receive a letter that appeals to you, notice the opening. If you like it, modify it as needed and add it to your own collection of stock openings. For related information, see SALUTATIONS and GENERAL CORRESPONDENCE LETTERS.

OPINION LETTERS

Opinion letters serve the client in two ways: (1) they inform the client of the writer's legal analysis of the situation and any updating information and (2) they predict a possible outcome or recommend a certain path. In order to do both well, consider carefully your POINT OF VIEW, TONE, and AUDIENCE.

For example, choose OBJECTIVE WRITING if you are merely informing the client of the situation. Choose PERSUASIVE WRITING if you are trying to convince the client to do something, such as settle out of court or pay a bill. For more information on handling bad news, see BAD NEWS, GIVING IT and BAD NEWS, SOFTENING IT.

Likewise, choose the TONE appropriate to your AUDIENCE. If you know the client well and it seems appropriate, use a friendly tone; if you do not know the client well, be formal but not stuffy. Choose a style that considers the client's experience in law and the client's needs.

Additionally, because an opinion letter advises the client about a legal question, do make sure you answer the question. Do not write an abstract essay or a law review article on the general topic, but instead answer the specific question as best you can.

Finally, write in clear and understandable language unless you know the client prefers you do otherwise. Clients who want legalese may exist, but they are rare. See LEGALESE, READABILITY, and CLARITY.

Opinion letters should contain any or all of the following, depending upon the status of the case.

1. A heading, including the date.

2. A salutation.

Dear Dr. Brand:

For more information, see SALUTATIONS.

3. An opening or introduction that states the question the letter will answer and refers to the request you received.

If the news is good, you may want to include the conclusion and recommendation to the client here. If the news is bad, you may state the conclusion later. (See subsection 5.) Either way, include a caveat stating that the validity of the answer depends on the accuracy of the facts you were given. This caveat can serve as a transition into the next section. For related information, see OPENINGS FOR LETTERS.

4. A summary of the LEGALLY SIGNIFICANT FACTS, the BACK-GROUND FACTS, and any other facts you think the client should know that you know.

If the letter is long, set this section off with a subheading, such as the following.

FACTS OF THE CASE

or

RELEVANT FACTS

or just

FACTS

Clients may omit facts unfavorable to their position, so before writing you may want to probe to get those unfavorable facts that might influence your opinion. If appropriate, you may even draft the facts section and get the client to review it for accuracy before drafting the opinion itself. Ask the client to advise you of any additions or corrections needed in the letter, because your analysis depends on the accuracy of these facts.

5. Your conclusion, if this was not included earlier.

Make sure you answer the client's question. If the conclusion is long, you may set if off by using another subheading. See CONCLUSIONS.

6. An explanation of your conclusion, including a summary of the law and the application of the law to the facts.

If you are using subheadings, include one for this section. In the explanation section, lay out your reasoning step by step (see ORGANIZATION). Also take care to avoid using unneeded legal terms (see LEGALESE) and to define those legal terms that are needed (see UNOBTRUSIVE DEFINITIONS). Whether and when you include CITATIONS is a matter of judgment, depending on the sophistication of your reader, the extent to which your opinion rests on the case cited, and the possibility of the client misunderstanding the significance of the cites. Including citations, however, does not greatly affect READABILITY; readers can skip over citations easily if they so choose.

7. A prediction of the outcome of the case, based on the balance of the strengths against the weaknesses in the application of the law to the facts.

8. A recommendation of a course of action.

You will be balancing here your professional responsibility to inform the client fully and your need to protect yourself against potential malpractice problems. Do cover yourself, but do it by explaining the caveats and reasons behind your opinion, not by using spineless phrases that only create ambiguities. Avoid phrases like *in effect*, *it is said that*, and *of course*. For example, the following paragraph hedges by explaining the writer's position rather than by inserting spineless phrases.

> **It is my opinion that you should try to settle this claim because litigation would not be economically worthwhile. My research indicates that New York law may favor Mr. Polewski's position, and that your legal position is therefore unclear. As a result, although the outcome of a trial is not certain, you would be running a substantial risk of losing this claim even after investing the substantial amount required to litigate the case.**

Sometimes you will have to say that the client cannot do what he or she wants. When possible, make this bad news more palatable by offering alternatives that lead to the same objective or to similar ones. For example, you may have to state that a lawsuit would probably be financially unfeasible, but may be able to add that negotiation might bring about some of the desired result. When your answer is no, also include in your conclusion a brief outline of your strong reasons for the no, in case an unhappy or angry client skips reading the reasons section. For related information, see BAD NEWS, GIVING IT and BAD NEWS, SOFTENING IT.

9. A specific directive to the client to call or come in to discuss the matter further.

Unless the letter is meant to do so, add a sentence explaining to your reader that your letter does not create any legal rights. For related information, see OPINION OR ADVICE?

10. A closing.

Sincerely yours,

or

Yours truly,

For related information, see CLOSINGS FOR LETTERS.

For a discussion of letters in general, see GENERAL CORRESPON-DENCE LETTERS. For related information, see TONE IN LETTERS.

OPINION OR ADVICE?

When writing an opinion letter or conferring with a client, an attorney may give a client a legal opinion on a matter as long as that opinion is based on the law and the reasonable boundaries of the law. An attorney may also advise a client to pursue a certain legal course. Be careful, however, of personal, as opposed to legal, advice that could cross the line from professional opinion to coercion. Such advice could violate the *Model Code of Professional Responsibility*, a question beyond the scope of this book. For related information, see OPINION LET-TERS.

OPINIONS

When reading an opinion, consider the steps listed below to increase both your effectiveness and your efficiency.

1. Keep in mind the purpose for which you are using that opinion. For example, if you are reading an opinion to learn about a particular subject for class, such as personal jurisdiction, read the opinion for what it offers to enhance the analysis of personal jurisdiction. If you are reading the opinion for research, read with the thesis or issue of your memo, brief, or paper in mind.

2. Read through the opinion once to get the gist of it, without marking the text or taking extensive notes. This aids your understanding by helping you see the overall framework of the case before you begin dealing with the details.

3. While reading, focus on the holding, or the result of the case, and relate that holding to your topic or issue. For example, if a new trial

was granted because evidence was not properly suppressed, then study the case to find some definition of when evidence should be suppressed.

4. If you are working on an appellate brief, also note the STANDARD OF REVIEW, because this may affect your use of the case.

5. Then reread the case, briefing it according to your preference. For suggestions on how to do this, see CASE BRIEFS.

OPTIMAL OR OPTIMUM?

Most legal readers prefer *optimum,* although either is correct.

This is the <u>optimum</u> situation for the plaintiff, who would prefer to settle rather than file suit.

or

This is the <u>optimal</u> situation for the plaintiff because we settled for more than she had asked.

Optimum refers to the best condition, amount or degree for a particular situation. For PRECISION, do not use it to mean *best* in an absolute sense.

OR

Or is a conjunction that signals to the reader that you mean *any one of the listed items,* rather than *all of them.* Thus *or* is disjunctive. In legal writing, misuse of *or* can create AMBIGUITY in two situations.

1. *Or* alone is not always enough to communicate your meaning. If you mean to signal something else besides *any one of the listed items,* you must add other explanatory phrases, such as

by any of the following means

or

any of the following subsections.

2. *Or* alone is not always enough to signal that a long list is disjunctive. When you rely solely on *or* to show the structure of the list, the reader has to read through most of the list before finding out whether this is an *and* or an *or* situation. Therefore, if your list is very long, let the reader know before the list that this is an *or* situation.

Either party may notify the other of a delay <u>by any of the following means</u>: telephoning the other party, sending an agent with a written message, sending an agent with an oral message, sending a telegram addressed to the other party personally, sending a certified letter, or meeting with the other party in person.

rather than

Either party may notify the other of a delay by telephoning the other party, sending an agent with the message, sending a telegram, sending a certified letter, or any combination of these.

For related information, see CONJUNCTIONS and LISTS, STRUCTURE OF.

ORAL OR VERBAL?

Verbal refers to any communication using words, whether spoken or written; *nonverbal* refers to gestures, actions, and other unspoken communication.

A successful lawyer is usually a master of verbal communication.

Oral refers to any communication that is spoken, rather than written. Do not use *verbal* when you mean *oral*.

The contract was based on an oral agreement made July 6, 1991.

rather than

The contract was based on a verbal agreement made July 6, 1991.

ORAL PRESENTATIONS

Oral presentations must convey the essence of written presentations, but in less time and more simply. Whether it is an objective presentation to a senior partner or a persuasive argument before a court, the presentation should focus first on the issue to be resolved. It should focus second on the answer and, third, on a clear explanation.

1. In an objective oral presentation, consider the following.

(a) State the issue to which the listener wants an answer. Incorporate the same three parts used in ISSUE STATEMENTS or Questions Presented: the general law under which the question is being asked, the legal question, and the legally significant facts pertinent to that question.

(b) Give the answer. Do not make the listener wait for this.

(c) Make sure your listener is familiar with the facts of the case; if not, give a succinct presentation of the LEGALLY SIGNIFICANT FACTS, the BACKGROUND FACTS, and any significant EMOTIONAL FACTS, as they relate to the issue and answer.

(d) Explain the answer as succinctly as possible, stating the applicable rule or RULES, any pertinent ANALOGOUS CASES, an APPLICATION of the rule or rules that connects this case to those analogous cases, and a conclusion.

(e) Be extremely flexible in answering questions. It is likely you will get interrupted by any legal listener, so use the questions to explain to the listener what the answer is and to move gracefully through the pre-planned parts of your presentation. For example, if you are asked a question about the third issue you wanted to discuss while you are discussing the first, answer the question about the third issue and move gracefully back into the first by saying something like *which is why we are arguing under the first issue that* ....

2. In persuasive oral presentations, consider the following.

(a) State the issue to be resolved and the answer to that issue. State it first, so you can get this information out before you are interrupted.

(b) Explain the plan of your argument to defer questions about later issues.

(c) Make sure the listener knows the facts. If you are the moving party, you must give the listener the facts of the case. But if they so choose, let the listeners waive that presentation of facts.

(d) State the conclusions the court should reach, including a brief statement explaining that a decision in your client's favor is consistent with principles of law and fair under these facts.

(e) Know the record and the law thoroughly. There is no substitute for this. If you are comfortable with the record and the law, there will be no hesitation or weakness in your argument. Your confidence should then come automatically.

(f) Address the case's impact on the law in general, especially if addressing an appellate court. The listener wants to know how the decision in this case will affect subsequent cases.

(g) Be candid and flexible; deal with weak points directly and welcome questions as an opportunity to explain the answers to the listener.

(h) Be respectful, showing good manners and good humor and keeping personalities out of the argument.

ORGANIZATION

Effective organization guides the reader through the text, just as a map guides a traveler through the country. This organization is not easy to achieve, but it is worth the effort. More than any other single aspect of legal writing, clear and logical organization distinguishes excellent writing from mediocre.

1. When to organize.

You must organize any piece of writing, but you need not do it at one particular point in the WRITING PROCESS. Instead, you may develop your organization at any of several stages. For example, you may organize by outlining during PREWRITING. Alternatively, you may first collect your thoughts or even write a loose rough draft before you develop your organization. For further help, see OUTLINES and ORGANIZATION FOR THOSE WHO CAN'T OUTLINE.

2. How to organize.

Clear organization is easier if you think carefully about the information you want to convey. If you have expressed your message clearly to yourself, you are likely to communicate it more clearly to your reader

Plan for and take the time you need to include all the parts and develop a good sense of the overall pattern. Then consider several ways of expressing it. There are usually several logical ways to organize, each of which can still please your audience and conform to your purpose. Sketch many versions, at least three, even if some of them seem absurd. By comparing them all, you will get a stronger sense of which one is best. Consult with your reader, if possible, or with others at this stage. Then choose the organization that best fits your PURPOSE, AUDIENCE, and SCOPE.

Start at the micro-, middle or macro-levels of the project and work through to the rest. Depending on your preferred writing process, your thinking may be facilitated by starting with any of the following approaches to organization.

(a) You may find that you work best by starting at the macro-level with one overall statement of your thesis. This is often useful when the scope seems too broad or you need a sense of specific direction. Use PARALLEL STRUCTURE, clear WORD CHOICE, and whatever other devices are appropriate in your thesis statement. Then ask yourself what is needed to support that statement. Answering this question will help you identify content, organization, needed sources, and even some details. From these you can see what must be included in the organization. To complete your organization, connect these points logically, determining which points are subordinate to others and identifying all the support needed for each point.

(b) Or you may find that the middle level of your document appears first to you: you know what three or five points you have to cover. From those points, you can work to figure out what your thesis is, what broader CONTEXT your points fit into, as well as what support is needed to fill in the details.

You may list all the points that you think you need to include in your paper and then group each individual point with others that seem related. Experiment with different groupings until you find the scheme that seems logical and provides a place for each point you have listed. Ask yourself why those groups make sense, and write down your reasons. This process should help you determine the logical connections among the various points you will be including, so the points knit together in ways that help you to choose the best organization for the readers.

(c) If you prefer to start at the micro-level, get everything you want on paper or disk, and then start to look for ways it groups logically. You might write out your purpose or your issues, answers, and remedies. Then relate all sections of the document to the purpose and the substantive message. Extract the main points and list those subpoints that support each main point. See what organization works: try three or more plans, thinking how well each would work to suit your purpose. Let all of them rest and later choose one.

For further help, see HABITS, WRITING and WRITING PROCESS. For various ways to organize, see OUTLINING, ORGANIZATION FOR THOSE WHO CAN'T OUTLINE, GETTING STARTED, and PREWRITING.

3. How to present your organization to the reader.

In legal writing, worry more about making your organization clear to the reader, less about being too obvious. For example, use enumeration, such as *first, second, third*, or *(1), (2), (3)*. Use TRANSITIONS, such as *additionally* or *in contrast*. Use HEADINGS and subheadings.

Use focused PARAGRAPHS that include TOPIC SENTENCES, usually at the first of the paragraph, and that include support for that point only.

For more information, see CONNECTIONS, MAKING THEM; ORGANIZATION, LARGE–SCALE; ORGANIZATION, SMALL–SCALE; TOPICAL ORGANIZATION; and CHRONOLOGICAL ORGANIZATION.

ORGANIZATION FOR THOSE WHO CAN'T OUTLINE

The following steps can help you organize successfully, even if you have never been able to master the more traditional method of organization, OUTLINES.

1. Brainstorm.

Try listing all the points you want to make or might want to make, or just list everything you can think of. Do not worry about order, quality, or anything else at this stage except coming up with ideas. Allow enough time for this stage, so you do not cut it short.

2. Group your ideas.

Read through all your listed points and see if they fall into any logical groups. Try grouping the points several different ways before you settle on one way that makes the most sense to you. Often the organization that occurs to you first will be adequate, but not optimal. Alternatively, if your list of points includes six or fewer items, you may already have your logical groups. If so, fill in more supporting points on those items and then check to see if you are still satisfied with those groups.

3. Organize the groups.

Look at each group and decide which point is the major one and which are subordinate, or supporting, points. At this stage you may still find some errors in your grouping, but you can revise those groups as needed. You may also find that you have stated the same thing in two different ways, so that you can strike out redundant points.

4. Subdivide further, if needed.

Divide your arguments, and divide the subpoints made in those arguments. Check each item to make sure that it should not be subdivided further. Remember that you need to make only one point at a time. Even though all your points are inextricably interrelated, you must divide them into manageable portions, or PARAGRAPHS, for the reader.

5. Order the groups, points, and subpoints.

After the points are divided, decide how to order them. To determine this order, think about what will be logical to your reader, rather than what seems important to you. To help determine what is logical to the reader, ask yourself the following three questions.

(a) Is there some point that logically comes first? For example, if your case involved a jurisdiction question, that question would logically come first because the court will not look to any other issues until they have determined that it is the court's job to decide those issues.

(b) Is one point more significant than the others? For example, if your case involves clear-cut violations of freedom of speech and also involves some technical violations of proper notice, you may want to start with the violation of the freedom of speech. This point may convince your reader that justice favors your side, and will probably make more compelling reading. The technical point may then provide a convenient peg upon which to hang the hat of justice.

(c) Is one point stronger than the others? For example, if your case involves a clear-cut violation of proper notice but also involves a potential-but-debatable violation of freedom of speech, you may start with the violation of proper notice. This way you can establish some justification for your client's position before you present more questionable justifications.

6. Write.

At this point you will have all the information provided by a traditional outline, and you can rewrite it in outline format, if you wish, or go directly to writing your rough draft. If you had started trying to outline by writing a Roman numeral at the top of the page, you would have been expecting yourself to do all of these previous steps in your head, which is why trying to write a traditional outline is futile for many people.

7. Check the organization.

Once you have written your rough draft, recheck your organization. In fact, many successful writers write a rough draft first and then outline or go through the organization steps listed above. One way to check your organization is to read the first sentence of each paragraph throughout the document. This should give you a summary of the points of the paper, although it will not document the proof of those points.

For related information, see GETTING STARTED and OUTLINES. See also PARAGRAPHS; ORGANIZATION, LARGE–SCALE; ORGANIZATION, SMALL–SCALE; and WRITING PROCESS.

ORGANIZATION, IT OR THEY?

See CORPORATIONS, THEY OR IT?

ORGANIZATION, LARGE–SCALE

Large-scale organization conveys the overall logic of any piece of writing. Large-scale organization is communicated in HEADINGS, TOPIC SENTENCES, introductions, and CONCLUSIONS. The logic of this organization should grow from the logic of the content. For example, if one of the issues in a memo is whether or not the district court has jurisdiction over the issue, that procedural question should be discussed before any substantive question, because if the answer is no, the substantive questions will not matter. See MEMOS and PROCEDURAL OR SUBSTANTIVE?

Look at the overall picture in deciding what your large-scale organization should be, so that your choice of organization communicates to the reader how each subpart fits in the whole. For example, if there is a question of governmental immunity and two subissues must be raised to answer the larger issue of immunity, organize both the QUESTION PRESENTED and the DISCUSSION SECTION so that the reader sees how the subissues fit into the larger question of immunity.

Work on the large-scale organization early in the WRITING PROCESS, and keep working on it until it is clear to you. Most issues can be organized in several ways, and your paper must be organized in a way that makes sense to you. Consider your possible large-scale organization as you gather research in PREWRITING, as you outline, and as you rewrite. If the large-scale organization is not working at any of these three points, try rearranging. If you wait until REVISING or POLISHING, it may be too late and too frustrating to change. For related information, see OUTLINING and REWRITING. For more extensive discussion of different ways to organize, see Chapter 9 of Mary B. Ray & Barbara J. Cox, *Beyond the Basics: A Text for Advanced Legal Writers* (West 1991).

ORGANIZATION, SMALL-SCALE

Small-scale organization refers to the organization between and within PARAGRAPHS and sentences; it communicates the LOGICAL LINKS between those paragraphs and sentences. In contrast, large-scale organization refers to the overall format of the analysis or explanation.

Small-scale organization involves six skills, each of which is explained in detail in a separate entry. These skills include (1) using effective TOPIC SENTENCES, (2) putting sentences in logical order, (3) clarifying logical connections (see CONNECTIONS, MAKING THEM), (4) choosing the most effective SENTENCE STRUCTURE, (5) choosing accurate TRANSITIONS, and (6) making lists readable (see LISTS, STRUCTURE OF).

The revision for small-scale organization should take place after WRITING and REWRITING, so that you are not struggling with fundamental ideas at the same time you are straightening out the expression of those ideas. For related information, see WRITING PROCESS and REVISING.

ORNATE LANGUAGE

See FLOWERY LANGUAGE.

OTHERWISE

Otherwise means *in another way* or *apart from that.*

We cannot locate our expert witness, but otherwise the case is in good shape.

Avoid overusing *otherwise* or using it loosely.

If they accept this offer, we will settle. If they refuse, we will sue.

rather than

If they accept this offer, we will settle. Otherwise, we will sue.

OUTLINES

Outlines can help writers before or after writing a draft. Outlines can take any form, whether lists, barely legible scratching, flow charts, or Venn diagrams. Whatever the form, outlines help the writer make sure any reader can follow the document's logic.

Make an outline, either before or after writing, by sketching a general portrait of the large-scale ideas, such as the following.

Custody disputes

    Was "tender years"

    not any more

    ERA contributed

    changed in 1973

Now statutory—five factors + 1 = "best interests"

Apply here—probably mother

Conclusion

Then fill in the details as you reread authority and rethink your ideas.

Custody disputes

    Was "tender years"

        "best interests of child" paramount then Jones at 48, 50.

        Mother used to be thought best Id.

        ERA, general social changes say father or mother can "mother" Smith at 97

        Led to partial codification, some changes in 1973

    Statute R.C.W. 29.09.999 (quote)

        Court must show they looked at factors Smith at 85, all five + anything else relevant

        Broad discretion, but must be more structured now. Id.

Apply here

    Factor 1—wishes of parents

        both want, but both will give visitation rights

    Factor 2—wishes of child

        nothing expressed

    Factor 3—Interrelationship of children w/ parents

        mother drinks (Johnson mom drank too—distinguish)

father strict (<u>Pines</u>—father got son—same?)

mother stable? (see <u>Schwartz</u>—not as crazy as this
woman: distinguish)

Factor 4—Child's adjustment to home & community

with mom now, no adjustment

father will live in same city, but move required

Factor 5—Mental and physical health

mother stable? (see <u>Schwartz</u>; distinguish this mother, not that crazy)

father unemotional

Other factors—adultery, moral character

father having an affair, missed meeting with kids

cf. <u>Hildebrand</u>—doesn't mean he can't "mother"

Conclusion

Mom probably gets them because she is more respon-
sive to their needs, has them now, hasn't missed
any time with them.

If you outline before writing the first draft, then at the writing
stage you can just fill in the blanks left in the outline. Therefore, if
writing is uncomfortable for you, try doing a detailed outline first.
Make lots of notes in the margin if necessary; this will make WRITING
easier.

If you outline after writing, you can use the outline to check logic
and details. Any reader should be able to write your outline after
reading your writing, so you might make sure your writing is clear by
outlining it yourself.

If ORGANIZATION is a problem for you, outlining may offer a
solution. For other aids to organization and related problems, see
WRITING PROCESS; WRITING BLOCKS; ORGANIZATION,
LARGE–SCALE; and ORGANIZATION FOR THOSE WHO CAN'T
OUTLINE.

OVERDONE

See FLOWERY LANGUAGE, MODIFIERS, and EMOTIONAL
LANGUAGE.

OVERREFINEMENT

This term refers to the kind of errors writers commit when they
are trying hard to be correct but do not quite understand the rules.
For example, a writer might use *I feel badly* even though *I feel bad* is

correct. For other common overrefinement problems, see GOOD OR WELL?, BETWEEN YOU AND ME OR BETWEEN YOU AND I?, CAN OR MAY?, PRIOR TO, IN ADVANCE OF, and WHO OR WHOM?

In a broader sense, *overrefinement* refers to the tendency some writers have to revise their writing too much. For example, a writer might remove important TRANSITIONS in the name of CONCISE-NESS, or create FIGURATIVE LANGUAGE when LITERAL LAN-GUAGE conveys the point better. Fight the temptation to overrefine, which can rob your STYLE of its spontaneity and READABILITY. Overrefinement can also add unnecessary time to your schedule. For ways to refine effectively, see REVISING and POLISHING.

PADDING

In legal writing, avoid padding, or adding content not because it is needed but solely to increase length. Legal readers prize CONCISE-NESS; padding will not impress them.

PARAGRAPH BLOCKS

A paragraph block is a group of PARAGRAPHS that fit together as a visual and substantive unit, just as sentences fit into the unit of a single paragraph.

1. When to use.

Paragraph blocks are most likely to be useful when your analysis requires a sub-subsection of explanation in the text; in this situation, you often will not want to add another level of heading because you already have headings and subheadings, and a third level might frag-ment the ORGANIZATION too much. The visual separation of a paragraph block is not as strong as that created by a subheading, and thus it is useful without distracting from the headings already in place. The paragraph block is most likely to be useful in documents that run thirty or more pages. In shorter documents, HEADINGS, SUBHEAD-INGS, and PARAGRAPHS should provide sufficient organizational tools.

2. How to use.

To create a paragraph block visually, put an extra blank line between the previous text and the first paragraph of the block. At the end of the paragraph block, again add an extra blank line. Paragraph blocks work best if they are limited to three to six paragraphs; if the blocks are longer, the reader forgets about the paragraph block and its organizing value is lost. If the block consists of only two paragraphs, the reader may think that the blank lines are typographical errors.

Remember that substance dictates the form of your writing. Therefore, avoid creating a paragraph block solely for looks. Create one only when your analysis requires the sub-subsection.

PARAGRAPH LENGTH

In a brief, memo, or longer opinion letter, you should average about three paragraph breaks per page. In business letters, you will have more paragraphs per page. Whatever the setting, however, you should divide paragraphs logically rather than periodically. Therefore, first divide paragraphs logically and then change this paragraph division, if needed, using the following guidelines.

1. Long Paragraphs.

If you find one paragraph that runs two-thirds of a page, leave it undivided if it is logically one unit. If you have one paragraph that runs for more than two-thirds of a page, try to divide it, because the reader needs a visual break. If you have many paragraphs that run two-thirds of a page, check for general organization problems.

2. Short Paragraphs.

If you have written a one-sentence paragraph or many short paragraphs, check to see if you have supported your points adequately. Also check for paragraphs that present fragments of a full development, and so should be unified for logical flow.

Occasionally a one-sentence paragraph can be used for EMPHASIS, but not more than once in six pages. Occasionally a one-sentence paragraph also serves as a transition or an introduction, but again it should not occur too often.

For related writing problems, see SENTENCE LENGTH.

PARAGRAPHS

In legal writing, each paragraph should focus on only one point, and each should have a topic sentence that states that point, often at the beginning of the paragraph. In other disciplines, such as literary criticism, this more obvious form of logical ORGANIZATION is often disfavored, but obvious organization is rarely criticized in legal writing. Instead, your reader will be grateful to you for making it easy to see the point. For example, in the following paragraphs, the points are much clearer when two paragraphs are used, one for each point made, and when each point is stated in a topic sentence at the first of the paragraph.

To complain about the illegality of a search, the defendant must, as the State correctly asserts, have an expectation of privacy in the place searched. <u>United States v. Park</u>, 999 U.S. 314, 316 (1996); <u>United States v. Toyle</u>, 999 U.S. 115, 118 (1000). The State implies that solely because the defendant's office, desk, and files were within a public building, he knowingly exposed them to the public. This is incorrect. The uncontroverted testimony in this case established that defen-

dant did expect his office, desk, and files to be private because he exercised exclusive use and control over those areas and in things present in those areas. (R. 207–209).

This expectation of privacy must be justified under the law. In this case, the defendant was justified in expecting privacy in his private office. There was no free public access to these areas. The sole fact that a private office is located in a public building does not satisfy the "plain view" doctrine as restated in <u>United States v. Peabody</u>, 999 U.S. 22, 26 (1996). The trial court in this case thus found that defendant had rights guaranteed by the fourth amendment of the United States Constitution and by article I, section 2 of the Constitution of the State of Iowa, and that these rights were violated.

rather than

The trial court in this case found that defendant had rights guaranteed by the fourth amendment of the United States Constitution and by article I, section 2 of the Constitution of the State of Iowa, which were violated. To complain about the illegality of a search, the defendant must, as the State correctly asserts, have an expectation of privacy in the place searched. <u>United States v. Park</u>, 999 U.S. 314, 316 (1996); <u>United States v. Toyle</u>, 999 U.S. 115, 118 (1996). The State implies that because the defendant's office, desk, and files were within a public building, he knowingly exposed them to the public. This is simply not the fact in this case. The uncontroverted testimony indicates defendant did expect his office, desk, and files to be private and that he exercised exclusive use and control in these areas (R. 207–209). There was no free public access to these areas. The location of a private office in a public building does not satisfy the plain view doctrine as restated in <u>United States v. Peabody</u>, 999 U.S. 22, 26 (1996). Further, the defendant's expectation of privacy in his private office is justified under the law.

For related information, see ONE–SENTENCE PARAGRAPHS; TOPIC SENTENCES; PARAGRAPH LENGTH; OUTLINES; ORGANIZATION; TRANSITIONS; and ORGANIZATION, SMALL–SCALE.

PARALLEL CITATIONS

See CITATIONS, PARALLEL.

PARALLELISM

See PARALLEL STRUCTURE; LISTS, STRUCTURE OF; and EMPHASIS.

PARALLEL STRUCTURE

Parallel structure means using the same grammatical structure for things that are logically parallel. For example, parallel adjectives can describe parallel qualities.

Defendant was hostile, abusive, and violent.

Parallel prepositional phrases can describe parallel situations.

Plaintiff admits he was driving without his license, without his lights on, and with an open six-pack of beer in the front seat.

Parallel structure creates a grammatically transparent framework that allows substantive points to shine through in clear relation to each other. This structure is extremely useful in legal writing because it simplifies syntax and focuses on substance. Therefore, three common places to use parallel structure are in lists, in comparisons or contrasts of cases, and in persuasive writing to add emphasis.

1. Use parallel structure in lists.

The plaintiff parked his car, turned the wheels toward the curb, and set the handbrake.

This point was established in the testimony of the defendant, of the police officer investigating the accident, and of a passerby who observed the accident.

Parallel structure is also useful for emphasizing the logical parallels between the items in a list, such as in the following list of facts. See EMPHASIS.

The trial court found that Cox Realty displayed the Realax logo at its office, signs, and forms; that Cox's employees each wear a blue blazer with the Realax logo on it; and that Cox Realty benefits from nationwide advertising identifying Realax franchises as "local professionals."

2. Use parallel structure to compare or contrast cases. One place where parallel structure is particularly desirable is in the analogy of two similar cases, as shown by the following example taken from the middle of a paragraph.

In <u>Rickaby</u>, the court found that the plaintiff's reputation in the community was not impaired even though the employer disclosed his reasons for discharging the employee in a judicial proceeding. Similarly, in this case Elmore's reputation in the community has not been impaired merely because the employer disclosed her reasons for discharging Elmore in conferences with union officials.

As this example shows, using accurate TRANSITIONS, such as *similarly*, can also enhance the point of the parallel.

Parallel structure can also underscore a contrast. By making similarities obvious, parallel structure allows the differences to stand out.

> **In <u>Rickaby</u>, the court found that the plaintiff's reputation in the community was not impaired even though the employer disclosed his reasons for discharging the employee in a judicial proceeding. In contrast, Elmore's reputation was impaired, because his employer not only disclosed her reasons for discharging Elmore in conferences with union officials but also disclosed those reasons at an office party and in a reference letter written to Elmore's prospective employers.**

For more information on this technique, see COMPARISON.

3. Use parallel structure to add emphasis. In the following example, two points support the implied point that the defendant deserves no sympathy. The parallel structure of *failed to schedule, failed to have* and *failed to warn* thus reflects the logical parallels of the content and also allows the writer to use REPETITION to emphasize a point.

> **The defendant company failed to schedule routine maintenance for the press, failed to have a technician check the press when operators complained of its malfunction, and failed to warn the plaintiff about those malfunctions.**

For more information on this technique, see EMPHASIS.

PARAPHRASE

Paraphrasing means restating someone else's ideas in your own words. There is nothing illegitimate about paraphrasing as long as you give credit when you have used a specific source, such as on opinion or article, and as long as you avoid misstating the original point. Paraphrasing is more useful than quoting when the original language is hard to understand, is lengthy, or incorporates other information that could confuse your reader.

> **The court stated that it must intervene in this case to resolve the issue of mutuality despite the emotional pleas for freedom of contract.**

changed from the original

> **Despite the defendant's emotional plea regarding the centrality of upholding contracts to the free working of a democracy, we cannot ignore the plaintiff's complaint. In this case, the court must intervene; the issue of mutuality, not to mention that of duress, requires that the court examine both the contract's wording and the parol evidence surrounding the signing of that contract.**

Quote only when the exact language is needed, as when discussing the interpretation of a phrase in a statute, or when you could not say it better yourself, as with an apt and relevant phrase in an opinion.

In writing MEMOS or BRIEFS, it is permissible to quote a commonly used rule, without quotation marks, as long as you use a Pinpoint Cite.

> **Use of a criminal defendant's silence for impeachment purposes violates the defendant's due process rights. <u>Boyle v. Kentucky</u>, 999 U.S. 810, 817 (1996).**

For more information, see QUOTATIONS WHEN TO USE. For related information, see UNDERLINING, subsection 5 and PINPOINT CITES.

PARENTHESES

Use parentheses in legal writing only in the situations listed below. If the matter is important enough to be in the text, it should be stated outside the shadow of parentheses. Additionally, avoid overuse of parentheses because it can create the impression that the writer is disorganized. For related information, see PARENTHETICALS.

1. When to use parentheses.

(a) Use parentheses to enclose information useful to the reader if that information is not an integral part of the text itself. For example, use parentheses to refer to the transcript, such as *(Tr. 37)*, or an appendix, such as *(See Appendix A)*.

> **The defendant testified he had never seen the plaintiff (Tr. 349).**

or

> **The defendant testified that he had never seen the plaintiff (See Appendix A).**

(b) Use parentheses to introduce abbreviations. For example, if one of the parties in your brief is *Leitner Systems, Inc.*, and you want to use *LSI* in the text, write out the complete name the first time you use it and then put the abbreviation in parentheses afterwards.

> **Leitner Systems, Inc. (LSI).**

Do not state *hereinafter referred to as* before the abbreviation. See LEGALESE.

(c) Use parentheses in drafting contracts to enclose a numeral repeating a number spelled out.

> **For the sum of five hundred dollars ($500)** . . . .

(d) Use parentheses to enclose examples when the examples are necessary but do not require a separate definition. See UNOBTRUSIVE DEFINITIONS.

> **Crimes against persons (murder, rape, and the like) are usually considered more serious than crimes against property.**

2. How to punctuate within parentheses.

If they are written inside another sentence (*this is an example of a parenthetical sentence inside another sentence*), parenthetical sentences do not begin with capital letters or end with periods; but when other punctuation marks are appropriate, they are used (*do you understand this rule?*). If they are written outside other sentences, parenthetical sentences begin with capital letters and end with periods inside the parentheses.

> **Defendant's car was parked facing north. (R.P. 31.)**

or as a parenthetical within the sentence.

> **Defendant's car was parked facing north (R.P. 31).**

PARENTHETICALS

Parentheticals appear in specific places in legal writing to give the reader information about authority. Proper use of parentheticals saves time and text. While the Bluebook outlines all technical uses of parentheticals, the most helpful uses include the following.

1. Use parentheticals after basic citations to add information about the source.

> **Arnold v. Butters, 999 F. Supp. 111 (W.D. Wis. 1998) (holding that moral right is not cause of action for artist whose painting was separated into four pieces).**

For further reference, see Bluebook rule 1.5.

2. Use parentheticals after cases to indicate that the holding is not the single clear holding of a majority of the court, or to indicate the weight of authority.

> **State v. Blunt, 999 U.S. 99 (1999) (per curiam) (holding that an "indicia of reliability" is necessary for an informer's information to support a search warrant).**

For further reference, see Bluebook rule 10.6.

3. Use parentheticals in statute citations to convey the following information.

(a) Use them to show the code location of statutes cited to session laws or secondary sources.

> Popular Names Act of 1999, Pub. L. No. 102–113, 999 Stat. 111 (codified at 99 U.S.C. §§ 2222 to 2232 (1999)).

(b) Use them to give the unofficial section when an unofficial code is numbered differently from an official code and when the section does not yet appear in the official code.

> Mich. Comp. Laws § 999.09 (1990) (Mich. Stat. Ann. § 111.01 (Callaghan 1999)).

(c) Use them to identify useful dates, such as the effective date of a statute.

> Alaska Stat. § 99.09.090 (1999) (effective July 1, 1000).

(d) Use them to indicate the repeal, amendment, or prior history of a statute.

> 99 U.S.C. § 999(b) (1999) (repealed 2001).

(e) Use them to give any other relevant information about a statute.

> 99 U.S.C. § 999(b) (1999) (requiring IRS agents to give proper notice of auditing procedures to those being audited).

For further reference, see Bluebook rules 12.6 and 12.7.

PARTICIPLES

See VERBS, TENSES.

PARTS OF A SENTENCE

See SENTENCE, PARTS OF.

PARTS OF SPEECH

Parts of speech is the grammatical term used to summarize the eight categories into which all words are divided. These eight categories include NOUNS, PRONOUNS, ADJECTIVES, VERBS, ADVERBS, PREPOSITIONS, CONJUNCTIONS, and INTERJECTIONS.

PASSIVE VERBS

See PASSIVE VOICE and ACTIVE VOICE.

PASSIVE VOICE

In general, use ACTIVE VOICE rather than passive, both in OBJECTIVE WRITING and PERSUASIVE WRITING, because the active voice keeps the reader's eye moving forward and clarifies both the subject and the action. Active voice thus promotes CLARITY and PRECISION.

Passive voice, on the other hand, makes the reader's eye move backwards because the subject of the sentence receives the action, rather than causes the action. As a result, passive voice forces the reader to stop at the end of the sentence and think back through the sentence to sort out who did what.

The plaintiff was hit by the defendant. [passive voice]

but

The defendant hit the plaintiff. [active voice]

A decision was made by the court. [passive voice]

but

The court made a decision. [active voice]

or

The court decided. [active voice]

Passive verbs also sometimes leave the actor out of the picture.

The plaintiff was hit.

A decision was made.

This use of passive voice often creates ambiguity. For example, the following regulation would be inadequate if it did not specify who has the responsibility for the clean-up.

Any manufacturer who generates toxic waste must dispose of that waste by one of the following means.

rather than

Toxic waste must be disposed of by one of the following means.

Passive voice is useful, however, in four specific situations. In legal writing, use it consciously and for these reasons only; otherwise eliminate it.

1. Use passive voice to de-emphasize unfavorable facts or law. For example, the attorney for the defense might want to write the following.

The plaintiff was assaulted by the defendant.

The attorney for the prosecution, however, might write the following.

The defendant assaulted the plaintiff.

2. Use passive voice to hide the identity of the actor.

A decision was made to cut your salary.

Here passive voice avoids telling who made the decision.

3. Use passive voice when the subject is very long. In this situation, using passive voice creates a more readable sentence because the active voice would put the subject and verb so far apart that the sentence would be too hard to read.

> **This action is required by statutory law, by the common law principle of due care, and by a general sense of justice.**

rather than

> Statutory law, the common law principle of due care, and a general sense of justice require this action.

4. Finally, use passive voice when the subject is much less important than the object.

> **Freedom of speech cannot be encumbered by concerns of propriety.**

rather than

> Concerns of propriety cannot encumber freedom of speech.

For related information, see ACTIVE VOICE.

PAST PARTICIPLES

Past participles are the *-ed* form of regular verbs, such as *decided, moved, assaulted.* Irregular verbs form past participles differently, such as *held, gone,* and *been.* See VERBS, PARTICIPLES; VERBS, TENSES; and VERBS, IRREGULAR.

PAST PERFECT TENSE

See VERBS, TENSES.

PAST PROGRESSIVE TENSE

See VERBS, TENSES.

PAST TENSE

See VERBS, TENSES.

PEOPLE OR PERSONS?

Use *people* to refer a group of individuals collectively. Use *persons* when referring to a small and specific number.

> **All people of this country have constitutional rights.**

but

> **Defendant has assaulted nine persons in the last month.**

211

PER

Per means for each and is useful when talking about ratios.

The defendant company promised different rates of pay to different sales personnel, ranging from the $5 per call paid to secretaries who worked in the company headquarters, to $1 per call paid to employees who made the calls from their homes.

Per should not be used, however, in other contexts.

Regarding our previous request for payment, ...

rather than

As per our previous request, ...

PERCENT OR PER CENT?

Use percent, which is preferred by most authorities.

PERFECTIONISM

Perfectionism can be the enemy of creative thought. Relegate your perfectionism to REVISING, REWRITING, and POLISHING in the WRITING PROCESS. In PREWRITING, contain your perfectionist tendencies by balancing time constraints against scholarship and by concentrating on substantive ideas rather than the methodology of note taking, outlining, and other prewriting tasks.

When WRITING, do not allow your perfectionist editing voice to restrict your creative writing voice. Try not to perfect each sentence as you go, but rather try to write the entire paper without revising. This will allow your ideas to flow more smoothly as you focus on content, not form. Then go back to perfect your paper in the REWRITING, REVISING, and POLISHING stages. In those stages, let your perfectionism work within your time restraints.

For further help, see WHEN TO STOP. For a discussion of related problems, see PROCRASTINATION; WRITING BLOCKS; GETTING STARTED; and DEADLINES, MEETING THEM.

PERFECT TENSES

See VERBS, TENSES.

PERIOD OR QUESTION MARK?

See QUESTION MARKS.

PERIODS

Periods have three common uses in legal writing.

1.   Periods as ends to sentences.

If your sentences routinely run for more than four lines of text, use more periods.   See SENTENCE LENGTH and READABILITY.

2.   Periods with abbreviations.

When an abbreviation comes at the end of a sentence, use just one period.

The meeting is scheduled for 9:00 p.m.

3.   Periods in parentheticals.

If they are written inside another sentence (*this is an example of a parenthetical sentence inside another sentence*), parenthetical sentences do not begin with capital letters or end with periods; but when other punctuation marks are appropriate, they are used (*do you understand this rule?*).   If they are written outside other sentences, parenthetical sentences begin with capital letters and end with periods inside the parentheses.

Defendant's car was parked facing north.   (R.P. 31.)

or

Defendant's car was parked facing north (R.P. 31).

4.   Periods with quotation marks.

A period goes inside quotation marks, even if the period is not part of the quote.

The term on which we must focus is "intent."

This rule is the same for both double quotation marks ("—") and single ones ('—').   The rule is not meant to reflect logical concerns, but rather graphic ones.   It looks funny to see the period sitting out there alone.

One exception to this rule is LEGISLATION, where periods are treated like all other punctuation marks.

PERSON: FIRST, SECOND, OR THIRD?

First person is *I* or *we*, second person is *you*, and third person is *he, she, it,* or *they*.   Because person identifies the reader and writer, knowing the AUDIENCE determines which to use.   In any given piece of legal writing, choose one person and use it consistently throughout.

1.   Use first person singular, *I*, when giving a personal opinion.   Use first person plural, *we*, when including the reader in the scope of the discussion or when representing the collective opinion of several specific people, as in a letter that speaks for a law firm.

I suggest we try to settle this out of court.

We can argue that a five-month-old fetus is viable, but this issue will probably go to the Supreme Court.

Avoid the editorial or royal *we* because it can be ambiguous. Instead, use *I* or avoid referring to any persons.

I understand your dilemma.

rather than

We recognize your dilemma.

The second element of first degree murder is intent.

rather than

We must next consider the second element of first degree murder.

2. Use second person, *you*, to address the audience directly, when appropriate. For example, GENERAL OPINION LETTERS and other correspondence may include *you* because they require a more personal TONE.

You asked that I write to you about the legal consequences of your unfortunate accident.

Avoid using second person when addressing a court.

Granting this motion is appropriate for three reasons.

rather than

You ought to grant this motion for three reasons.

3. Use third person most often in legal writing, in BRIEFS, MEMOS, MOTIONS, and most formal documents. Identify parties in the third person, your clients as well as their opponents.

Defendant pled not guilty; he denies all charges.

The law favors the plaintiffs in this class action, so they will likely move for a summary judgment.

Respondent further contends that all the facts are not properly before the court.

PERSONAL REFERENCES

Personal references are appropriate in legal writing only if the reader and writer are familiar with each other. Avoid them otherwise; they impair both credibility and meaning.

Although Plaintiff argues that there is a dispute as to the material facts, the affidavits show otherwise.

or

The affidavits show there is no dispute as to the material facts.

rather than

> Attorney Cromwell on page sixteen of his brief argues incorrectly again that there is a dispute as to material facts.

For related information, see I, TONE, and TONE IN LETTERS.

PERSONS OR PEOPLE?

See PEOPLE OR PERSONS?

PERSUASIVE LETTERS

Persuading a legal reader to do or decide something in your favor is a bit like finding your way through a mine field; you are trying to reach a certain point without setting off any unfortunate reactions. For this reason, persuasive letters will not be as predictably structured as other GENERAL CORRESPONDENCE LETTERS. In all persuasive letters, however, you will need to make three decisions: (1) what arguments to use, (2) what organization to use for those arguments, and (3) what tone to take. The following guidelines should help you make these decisions.

1. Choosing arguments.

In general, choosing arguments for persuasive letters will take time and care because you must tailor your argument and tone to suit the individual circumstances. Choose not what persuades you, but what will persuade your reader. For example, if you are trying to persuade a party to settle out of court, do not use threats when you think the party would view those threats as a challenge and submission as a weakness. Instead, you might explain that an early settlement might bring better results for the client than a later, more costly, trial.

Similarly, if you think that the reader is someone motivated by certain values or goals, try to explain how the action you recommend is consistent with those values or goals. For example, you might argue that paying a bill is essentially the same as keeping a promise. Try to help the reader feel good, or at least not defeated, about taking the action you recommend.

2. Organizing.

The same organization used for other bad news letters will work here. See BAD NEWS, GIVING IT.

Start with a paragraph that sets the tone of the letter, such as the following kind tone.

> **Throughout the years, Everly Auto Parts has valued Morgan Auto as a customer. Because Everly hopes to maintain this solid working relationship, Bob Everly has asked me to**

> write to you concerning the rather large outstanding balance in your account.

Alternatively, you may choose a tough tone.

> **Despite receiving three statements from my client, Everly Auto Parts, your company has not yet paid the balance of $2,015 owed for parts purchased four months ago.**

Or you may choose something in between.

> **My client, Everly Auto Parts, has asked me to write to you concerning the outstanding balance on your company's account.**

Do not go on too long, however, because a lengthy introduction can make the writer look rather timid or can make the reader impatient.

At the end of the first paragraph or the beginning of the second, state your point. Write this sentence with care; it must be unambiguous and yet unoffensive if possible.

> **Everly will not be able to extend further credit to your company until this balance has been paid.**

Then launch into your reasons, which may go on for several paragraphs. Make one point at a time, rather than rambling back and forth between several points. See PARAGRAPHS.

> **Everly Auto Parts, as a general policy, limits credit to any company to .... Additionally, ...**

In the last paragraph close politely, or at least civilly.

> **Everly Auto Parts will appreciate your prompt payment of this outstanding balance and looks forward to your continued patronage.**

3. Establishing tone.

In general, use an unemotional, polite TONE. In most legal writing situations, the emotions you would arouse would work against you rather than for you. There are some exceptions to this, such as fund-raising letters to sympathetic constituents or letters advising clients to do what they want to do already. Even here, however, you will usually want to present yourself as a logical, reasonable person who, even when impassioned about a cause, is still capable of making a coherent, logical argument. For a discussion of related points, see TONE, EMPHASIS, PERSUASIVENESS, and COHERENCE.

PERSUASIVE WRITING

Writing persuasively is writing to create a desired outcome with a specific AUDIENCE. In legal writing, this may be persuading a trial court to rule positively on a motion, persuading an appellate court to remand a case, or persuading a fellow attorney that a settlement will be in the best interests of both your clients. Be clear on the PURPOSE of your persuasion, because that purpose will guide your choices throughout the WRITING PROCESS, from choosing CONTENT, strategy, and ORGANIZATION to REVISING for EMPHASIS. When PREWRITING persuasively, begin with the following two steps.

1. FOCUS on your AUDIENCE.

Choose the strategy and CONTENT that will persuade the individual readers you are addressing. When writing a brief, ask yourself what questions this court will ask and how the law supports resolving those questions in your client's favor. Do not assume that the exact arguments that prevailed at one level in the court system will prevail at the next level. Trial courts emphasize precedent, appellate courts emphasize legal errors, and courts that review constitutional issues may emphasize long-term effects, precedent, or public policy. So when deciding a criminal case, a trial court might be convinced by a careful comparison of your client's facts to the facts of previous cases; but an appellate court reviewing the same case might be convinced only by arguments that the trial court erred in its reasoning. For related information, see STANDARD OF REVIEW. For a more thorough discussion of persuasion in briefs, see Mary B. Ray & Barbara J. Cox, *Beyond the Basics: A Text for Advanced Legal Writers* (West 1991).

2. Structure your argument to convince your audience.

Choose the structure that is most logical and convincing to this audience. When ordering your issues, begin with the threshold issue if there is one; do not violate the reader's sense of logical progression. But if issues are independent, then begin with your most compelling argument for a strong first impression. If one of three arguments is weaker than the others, place it between the others, so that it is not emphasized by being in either the first or the final position.

When stating and presenting each issue, begin with an affirmative statement of your position.

> **The plaintiff provided adequate warning. Twice he tried to reach the defendant by telephone before leaving messages when no one answered.**

Avoid letting your opponent's arguments dictate your structure; use the structure that best suits your position.

Within PARAGRAPHS and PARAGRAPH BLOCKS, subordinate their arguments through careful use of SUBORDINATE CLAUSES, subheadings, or paragraphs placed in the middle of a larger paragraph block. Retain your focus on your client's position. Although you may need to refer to your opponent's position in the course of your argument, do not dwell on it.

217

> **The plaintiff gave adequate warning. She telephoned repeatedly, and left messages on the defendant's answering machine on two occasions.**

Beginning with a statement of the opposition's position would create a defensive tone and make your organization dependent on the other side's position.

> The defense argues that plaintiff gave no warning. This is not the case, however, because the plaintiff left messages on the defendant's answering machine on two occasions.

For related organizational strategies, see BAD NEWS, GIVING IT and BAD NEWS, SOFTENING IT.

REVISING persuasively entails the use of many specific techniques, none of which alone makes an obvious difference but all of which, when working in harmony, create a masterful piece of persuasion. Each of these techniques takes practice to master. Therefore, choose two or three from the following list and incorporate those into your writing habits. Then, as you master those, add new ones to your repertoire.

3. Use concrete words.

Concrete words create clearer images in the reader's mind than abstract ones, and those clearer images are more memorable. For example, *a 1965 black Stingray* is more memorable than *vehicle*. This tool is especially useful in drafting fact situations for BRIEFS, because you can use concrete words for facts that favor your client and abstract ones for facts that you want to de-emphasize. For example, if you are de-emphasizing the illness of a testator and the medications she was taking, you might write the following.

> **Because Julia Easley had a history of arthritic and cardiovascular diseases, she was taking a variety of medications.**

If, however, you were trying to emphasize the illness and the medications, you might write the following.

> **Julia Easley's health was poor. She suffered from excruciating tension headaches (R. 925), and during the past year she experienced increasing cardiovascular problems, cataracts, arteriosclerosis, and other problems (R. 928–53). She was also on a large and complex daily regimen of drugs (R. 454). Daily she took three kinds of barbituates: Tuinal (R. 1115–16), Fiornal (R. 1113), and Fiornal with Codeine (R. 1113–14). Additionally, she took greater-than-normal daily dosages of Triavil (R. 114–15), a specialized compound tranquilizer formulated and normally prescribed for mental depression (R. 1148–49).**

4. Choose the most appropriate term of address.

This choice is related to the choice of concrete or ABSTRACT NOUNS. In a brief, if you have a situation where your client is a sympathetic figure and the opposition is not, use names such as *Ms. Jones* or *Julia Easley*, for both parties. This will gently remind the reader of the real people involved here. If the facts are not sympathetic to your client and you are making an argument based more on the impersonal logic of the relevant law, then use generic terms, such as *Plaintiff* and *Defendant*. Use the same kind of term for both sides, however: using *Ms. Jones* for the defendant but then using *Plaintiff* would be too confusing and too obviously biased, even if it seemed appropriate.

5. Repeat key words.

If you want to emphasize a word, repeat it. This is most often useful in the argument section of a brief.

The defendant <u>abused</u> the privileges offered him; he <u>abused</u> the procedures designed to protect him.

When repeating a term, however, make sure that the idea represented by the term is indeed one you do want to emphasize. For example, repeating *clearly* will create a distraction, not effective EMPHASIS.

Also remember that the effect of a repeated word grows exponentially, rather than linearly. That is, if you use a word twice, it is given perhaps four times the emphasis, not just two. So do not overdo it. This is a place where reading it aloud may work a disservice; you may hear yourself repeating a theme like the master orator Martin Luther King did, but your reader, not hearing your impassioned pauses and intonations, may instead find it amusing. Let your eye and common sense guide you. See also REPETITION.

6. Repeat sentence or phrase structures.

This tool is particularly useful when analogyzing cases (see COMPARISON) but is also useful and subtly dramatic in CONCLUSIONS and sometimes in fact sections. Repetition of structure creates a sense of rhythm and anticipation. To some extent, it telegraphs to the reader what is coming, so that the reader gets a sense of completion when the expected information arrives.

At best, the City confused its argument by trying to do too much without a full explanation. At worst, the City contradicted itself by misapplying the law.

But this expectation can turn to boredom, so again avoid overdoing it.

7. Adjust sentence length.

SHORT SENTENCES are emphatic. Therefore use them for points you want to emphasize, but do not use them for unimportant points.

This tool is particularly useful in fact situations, where tools involving word choice are often limited.

> **Julia was uniformly described by all the witnesses who had personally known her as a strong-willed, positive, and independent woman. <u>The plaintiff himself called her "independent and abrupt."</u>**

It is also useful in arguments.

> **The major purpose of the trial court's established procedures is to give the litigants a fair opportunity to address their claims and have them resolved by a court of law. <u>The petitioners here had eight years of opportunity.</u> Therefore, their current procedural arguments . . . .**

Several short sentences in a row create a choppy, rather impatient or angry tone. Sometimes this can have a useful effect.

> **The major purpose of the trial court's established procedure is to give the litigants a fair opportunity to address their claims and have them resolved by a court of law. <u>That purpose was met here. The litigants had eight years of opportunity. In this context, their arguments on appeal are particularly specious.</u>**

Three sentences is about as far as you should push the series. Any more and the court might sense an intemperate tirade. After a series of short sentences, return to sentences of normal length and make a scrupulously objective statement of your reasoning.

8. Insert information into a sentence with care.

If you want to use a point to set the stage for a punch line, put that point in an introductory phrase at the beginning of a sentence.

> **<u>Despite the difficulty of this test</u>, the gravity of the situation required that it be done.**

If you want to de-emphasize a point, put it in an added phrase at the end of the sentence, like an afterthought.

> **The minority arrived at the same conclusion, <u>although for different reasons.</u>**

When you do this, make sure that the word at the end of the sentence is not one you want to de-emphasize. For examples and more details on this technique, see SENTENCE STRUCTURE, subsection 7.

9. Place key phrases at the beginning or end of a paragraph or a sentence.

In general, words at the beginning or end get more attention than those in the middle. In legal writing, things at the beginning have a slight edge because you are never sure the busy and often-interrupted legal reader will finish reading your document with care. While revising, scan your TOPIC SENTENCES to see if the first half-line of each paragraph includes the KEY TERMS of the paragraph. Avoid starting a paragraph with dates or case names unless you have a reason to emphasize that date or name.

> **Evidence of this concern showed up in the defendant's letter dated January 12, 1980, which stated** . . . .

rather than

> On January 12, 1980, the defendant wrote a letter that showed evidence of this concern when it stated . . . .

For related information, see POSITIONS OF EMPHASIS.

10. Use subtly emotional language, rather than overly emotional.

Emotional language should persuade, not lose, the reader. Therefore choose words precisely to fit the persuasive approach you are taking. Emotional words are not just positive or negative; instead, each word falls somewhere on a continuum between extremely positive and extremely negative. For example, one person who decided to maintain a position on an issue could be described as *ever-faithful*, *steadfast*, *unwavering*, *unchanging*, *stubborn*, or *pigheaded*. In legal writing, choose words that fall closer to the center of the continuum to color your meanings, but avoid the extremes. For example, if trying to show that someone was overmedicated and thus not capable of making a will, write the following.

> **Julia Easley was on a large and complex daily regimen of drugs, including** . . . .

rather than

> Julia Easley was drugged into oblivion daily.

Write the latter only if your facts establish that as her literal state.

Also avoid overly emotional language because it draws the reader's attention to the emotional level of the writing itself, rather than to the content of the persuasive argument. For example, many extremely emotional words, such as *blockhead* or *disaster*, can impair the writer's credibility in court, where another lawyer can point out the silliness of the overstatement.

Finally, avoid overly emotional language because it may be limited by the constraints of legal writing. For example, many words with emotional overtones, such as *derelict* or *nuisance*, are also TERMS OF ART that must be used with PRECISION, whether or not the emotional overtone is appropriate.

11. Play one persuasive technique against another.

As you are applying these tools, you may find some contradictions; applying one principle means you violate another. Practice playing these techniques against each other to get just the effect you want.

12. Avoid overdoing.

Any of these persuasive techniques can be overdone. If you tend to overdo, use Marilyn Monroe's technique to solve the problem. This may be apocryphal, but it has been said that Marilyn tended to overdo it on accessories when she dressed up. To compensate for this, she kept a full length mirror in her entry. Before she left the house, she would walk away from the mirror and then turn quickly to look at her image. She would then take off the first accessory that caught her eye. Similarly, as you read over your last draft of a persuasive piece, take out the most obvious persuasive tools you have used. After all, it worked for Marilyn. Few would have called her overdressed.

PHENOMENA OR PHENOMENONS?

Most dictionaries list either as the acceptable plural of *phenomenon*, but *phenomena* is preferred.

PHRASES

A phrase is a group of words working together, such as prepositional phrases, *in this case*; noun phrases, *the experienced supervising attorney*; and verb phrases, *had been reviewing*. In contrast, a clause is a phrase that includes both a subject and verb.

S   V

The supervising attorney had been reviewing the case.

For an explanation of the use of phrases, see SENTENCE, PARTS OF and SENTENCE STRUCTURE. For related information, see CLAUSES.

PIE CHARTS

See GRAPHICS, WHICH FORM TO USE, subsection 1.

PINPOINT CITES

Pinpoint cites are those cites that include the exact page on which the quote, proposition holding, or rule is found. Use pinpoint cites to show your reader the exact source of important points. Pinpoint cites are used more frequently than general cites because most cites refer to quotes, propositions, holdings or rules. When required to use parallel pinpoint cites, indicate a specific page for both the official reporter and the unofficial reporter or reporters.

In custody disputes, the appellate court will reverse the trial court only where there is an abuse of discretion. In re Marriage of Smith, 94 Wash. 2d 369, 371, 333 P.2d 43, 44 (1999).

> Where there are no exigent circumstances, police must obtain a search warrant before searching the premises. <u>Id.</u> at 486, 483 P.2d at 58.

For other examples of formats for pinpoint cites, see CITATIONS. For related information, see CITATIONS, PARALLEL.

PLAGIARISM

Plagiarism is copying someone else's ideas or words and claiming them as your own. In legal writing, this is as unacceptable as it is in any other kind of writing. But do not confuse plagiarism with paraphrasing; it is perfectly permissible to paraphrase someone else's words, that is, to put their ideas in your own words and then to acknowledge the source of that idea. Thus you may PARAPHRASE and then cite to the authority for any holding, proposition, rule, quotation, or point of law.

But do not use paragraphs and organization from a law review article in place of your own writing. You may quote passages from law review articles verbatim, but they must be marked as quotes and cited. For related information, see QUOTATIONS, HOW TO PUNCTUATE.

PLAIN ENGLISH

In legal writing, plain English is English that is simple, clear, and readable. Many states require plain English in any kind of consumer document. If the document is not drafted in plain English, the consumer has grounds to sue for malpractice against the drafter of the document. Check your jurisdiction for its specific laws on plain English, but in general free your writing of JARGON, LEGALESE, and any undefined terms that will send a reader scurrying to a dictionary. For ways to revise for plain English, see READABILITY, CLARITY, and SIMPLICITY. See also PLAIN MEANING and UNOBTRUSIVE DEFINITIONS.

PLAIN MEANING

Plain meaning is that method of construing statutes that interprets each term by its dictionary meaning. This is a very literal interpretation and is often the point of departure for interpretation of a statute. For example, when a court is interpreting a statute for the very first time and there is little or no legislative history, the court may resort to the dictionary meaning of each word in the statute in order to apply the statute to the facts before the court.

Therefore, as it relates to legal writing, plain meaning becomes important in drafting legislation. Be sure that each term you use in drafting the statute stands up under the dictionary's scrutiny. See LEGISLATION.

PLEADINGS

Legal pleadings serve varied purposes. For example, a complaint may start the litigation process, frame a dispute, encourage the opponent to negotiate, and stop the running of the relevant statute of limitations. An answer may help the parties see what facts are at issue and notify the plaintiff of the defendant's general strategy. A cross-complaint may introduce a new party to the action or put the original plaintiff on the defensive.

Whatever purpose your pleading serves, following these steps will help you produce an effective document.

When PREWRITING, do each of the following.

1. Record deadlines on your calendar and schedule enough time to consider thoroughly the substance and strategy of the case. For more on this, see TIME MANAGEMENT.

2. Clarify your goals and strategy early in the process, so you include all needed information in your pleading while omitting unnecessary details.

3. Research your facts and law thoroughly to avoid costly errors. Allocate enough time for this, because you need to think through the case to the appeal level before you draft the pleadings.

Be sure to consider the following questions at some time during your WRITING PROCESS, although it may be in PREWRITING, WRITING, or REWRITING.

4. Does the pleading include enough information to withstand adverse motions?

5. Does it include all information needed, so that no likely arguments are waived?

When REWRITING, ask the following questions.

6. Does the pleading make only one point per paragraph?

7. Is it organized inductively, so that paragraphs asserting the evidence to support an element precede the paragraph stating that the element has been established? For examples, see COMPLAINTS and ANSWERS.

When REVISING, consider the following questions.

8. Is each paragraph worded specifically enough to withstand adverse motions, yet generally enough to maintain some flexibility later in the legal process?

9. Are all dates, numbers, names, addresses, and other particulars accurate?

10. Are all assertions free of AMBIGUITY?

When POLISHING, do the following.

11. Check caption, signatures, and all other parts to make sure all court-required forms and conventions are followed.

12. Check spelling, punctuation, and other grammatical and mechanical concerns. For more detail on this, see POLISHING.

PLURALS OF NAMES

When making a name plural, add an *s*.

There are three Marys in the firm.

When the name ends in *s*, add *es*.

The Joneses are tenants in common.

Resist any urge to create any other variation by analogy from other common nouns.

The Zimmermans have both reviewed the will.

The Olympuses are joint tenants.

The Chanticleers all have equal shares in their company.

The wording of the will is ambiguous because the family includes two Jameses.

rather than

The Zimmermen have both reviewed the will.

The Olympi are joint tenants.

The Chanticleer all have equal shares in their company.

The wording of the will is ambiguous because the family includes two James's.

P.M.

It is written *p.m.* and is used only after a number, as in *7:15 p.m.* When it appears at the end of a sentence, only one period is used, as in the previous sentence.

POINT HEADINGS

Point headings, also known as argument headings, are conventions in argumentative writing designed both to tell the reader the legal point made in a section of the argument and to outline the reasons supporting that legal point. Point headings also appear in the tables of contents of APPELLATE BRIEFS. In any brief, the point headings, when read together, should give the reader an outline of the writer's argument.

1. Content and format for point headings.

Main point headings should correspond to the ISSUE STATE-MENTS. They provide the answer to the legal question asked in each issue, and so there should be a point heading for every issue. Use capital letters, single space, and use a Roman numeral. Include the legal point and the reason if there are no subheadings or multiple reasons; include only the legal point if subheadings will indicate the reasons.

> **I. THE TRIAL COURT ABUSED ITS DISCRETION WHEN IT AWARDED CUSTODY TO AN ALCOHOLIC MOTHER.**

or

> **I. THE TRIAL COURT ERRED IN DENYING PLAINTIFFS' JURY INSTRUCTION ON DEFECTIVE BRAKES BE-CAUSE SUBSTANTIAL EVIDENCE INTRODUCED AT TRIAL SUPPORTS THIS THEORY OF PLAINTIFFS' CASE.**

Include enough LEGALLY SIGNIFICANT FACTS to make your argument specific to this case, but avoid cluttering the point heading with so many facts that it becomes too long.

Subheadings are used to give more specific reasons for the main legal point. Usually a paragraph or two of summarizing text follows a main heading, and then the first subheading follows that text. In subheadings, you may indent and capitalize the first letter of each main word, as in a book title; add underlining or bold face if it is customary in your jurisdiction. Or you may use some other graphic device that distinguishes it from major headings, sub-subheadings, and the rest of the text.

> **A. The Trial Court Did Not Consider the Best Interests of the Children Because It Ignored Mrs. Davis' History of Alcohol Abuse.**

Sub-subheadings give particulars of the argument under the sub-heading, and appear most often in appellate briefs. Use sub-subheadings to highlight important points in your argument, but limit them to six at the most. Overusing them may make the brief look more like an outline than a cohesive argument.

Indent the sub-subheading and capitalize only the first word. Precede it with an arabic numeral.

> **1. Mrs. Davis has been arrested repeatedly for drunken driving.**

2. Techniques for writing point headings.

226

(a) Make one legal point in each heading.

(b) Use a strong, accurate connecting word, such as *because*. See TRANSITIONS.

(c) Include a summary of the reason for the main legal point.

> **I. THE TRIAL COURT ERRED IN DENYING PLAIN-TIFFS' JURY INSTRUCTION ON DEFECTIVE BRAKES BECAUSE SUBSTANTIAL EVIDENCE IN-TRODUCED AT TRIAL SUPPORTS THIS THEORY OF PLAINTIFFS' CASE.**

(d) Use PERSUASIVE WRITING, concentrating on strong SUB-JECT–VERB COMBINATIONS and eliminating unneeded MODI-FIERS.

(e) Make the point heading no longer than four single-spaced lines, if possible.

(f) Use PARALLEL STRUCTURE in all main headings and in all subheadings.

POINT OF VIEW, OBJECTIVE OR PERSUASIVE?

Point of view in legal writing travels along the spectrum from objective to persuasive. The writer's point of view tends toward the objective, or neutral, in MEMOS, OPINION LETTERS, CORRESPON-DENCE LETTERS that give information, and law review articles that synthesize or summarize information. Using a more objective point of view allows the writer to remain detached from the decision while informing the reader of the law and predicting any outcome or change in trends.

The point of view tends toward the persuasive in memoranda of points and authorities, PRETRIAL BRIEFS, TRIAL BRIEFS, APPEL-LATE BRIEFS, some law review articles, and some general correspon-dence letters. The purpose of using the persuasive point of view is to persuade the AUDIENCE to accept the writer's argument.

Do not mix the two points of view; remain consistent throughout any given piece of writing. For advice on ways to establish these points of view, see OBJECTIVE WRITING and PERSUASIVE WRITING. For related information, see MEMORANDUM OF POINTS AND AUTHOR-ITIES.

POLICY

Policy refers to matters outside the literal rules and procedures of the law. These matters may include factors such as social change, economic conditions, or unjust results from a literal interpretation of the law. For example, if a state introduced laws for uninsured motorists but in the process created a gap in protection against under-insured motorists, attorneys might argue that, as a policy matter, consumers should be protected from all improperly insured motorists and not just a subgroup.

Often *policy* questions arise in appellate arguments when one party desires the law be reinterpreted in response to changing social or economic values. For related information, see DISCUSSION SECTION, APPLICATION, and EQUITY.

POLISHING

Polishing, the last step in the WRITING PROCESS, includes checking for citation, grammatical, and typographical errors. Always polish your documents. The legal reader is concerned with detail, so failure to polish the presentation can undermine the legal writer's credibility and can erode the document's meaning.

To insure time for polishing, work backward from the deadline and give yourself a reasonable amount of time to polish smaller details. For example, for a brief, allow an hour; for a memo, thirty minutes; for a short letter, ten.

Develop your own system for polishing, but make sure each aspect gets enough time. You might try the following system.

1. Read from front to back once for each of the following.

(a) omission of any words, such as *not*;

(b) punctuation; and

(c) typographical errors.

2. Read from back to front just for correct citation form.

3. Reread just for spelling and errors a spell checker will not catch, such as incorrect or missing words. For related information, see MISSPELLINGS, HOW TO AVOID.

4. Reread for any problem peculiar to your own writing, such as dangling modifiers, overuse of *however*, or improper use of SEMICO-LONS.

5. Read with a ruler, read aloud, read in small out-of-order pieces, or find some other way to read carefully so you will concentrate on every word to ensure its correctness.

POSITIONS OF EMPHASIS

Positions of emphasis are locations in a written text that get more attention than the text in general. They include the beginnings and ends of sentences, paragraphs, sections, and entire works. Use these positions of emphasis to convey major legal points and arguments; all points that you want to emphasize should be at a position of emphasis, with less important or unfavorable information placed in between.

> **The best interests of children are of paramount concern to courts in custody disputes.**

rather than

> Most courts consider the best interests of children in custody disputes to be of paramount concern.

> **Although the trespassers caused much physical damage, their purpose was not to cause mental anguish.**

rather than

> The trespassers caused much physical damage but causing mental anguish was not their purpose.

POSSESSIVES

In the law, possessives become important to PRECISION, such as *daughter's half* or *daughters' half* of an estate, so make sure you follow these rules.

1. Add an apostrophe and an *s* to make a singular noun possessive.

   John's = belonging to John.

   plaintiff's = belonging to a plaintiff.

   statute's = belonging to a statute, as in *statute's language*.

2. Add only an *s* to singular pronouns to make them possessive.

   its = belonging to it. **It's** = it is. *Its'* is never correct.

   yours = belonging to you.

   hers — belonging to her.

3. Add only an apostrophe to singular or plural nouns ending in *s* already.

   Jones' = belonging to one Jones.

   Joneses' = belonging to all the Joneses.

   plaintiffs' = belonging to all the plaintiffs.

Some authorities allow adding an apostrophe and an *s* to plural nouns, such as *Jones's*. Whatever your choice, be consistent.

4. Add an apostrophe and an *s* to a plural noun that does not end in s.

   women's = belonging to women.

   For related information, see APOSTROPHES.

PRECISION

Precise writing says exactly what is meant, nothing more and nothing less. It thus focuses the reader on the writer's specific point.

In order to be precise, try to answer constantly the question, *What does this mean?*

The following revision techniques can help you increase precision. For the closely related problems caused by inaccurate word choice, see ACCURACY.

1. Make sure the subject-verb combination in your Question Presented or issue says precisely what you mean, including the legal question and the LEGALLY SIGNIFICANT FACTS.

> **Under Missouri tort law, <u>did a five-year-old intend</u> to assault an elderly woman when he pulled a chair out from under her as she was sitting down?**

rather than

> Under Missouri tort law, <u>did assault occur</u> when a five-year-old pulled a chair out from under an elderly woman as she was sitting down?

Did intend refers to the specific legal question being asked, and *five-year-old* refers to the specific facts of this case.

> **The issue appellant raises on this appeal is whether <u>the trial court erred in applying the statute</u> when it summarized its findings <u>in only one sentence</u>.**

Trial court erred in applying the statute refers to the error raised on appeal, and the statement *in only one sentence* refers to the legally significant facts of this case. For more help, see QUESTION PRESENTED, SUBJECT–VERB COMBINATIONS, and ISSUE STATEMENTS.

2. In MEMOS, make sure the Brief Answer indeed gives an answer to the Question Presented and explains that answer by giving reasons specific to this case.

> **No; the five-year-old did not intend to assault the elderly woman because a five-year-old is not capable of forming intent.**

or

> **Yes; the trial court erred because the statute requires the trial court to make specific findings of fact on each subpart of the statute.**

For more information, see BRIEF ANSWERS.

3. In argumentative writing, make sure the POINT HEADINGS use appropriate TERMS OF ART and are free of vague or overly general words.

> **THE TRIAL COURT ABUSED ITS DISCRETION IN FAIL-ING TO SUPPRESS THE EVIDENCE BECAUSE THE GUN**

WAS PRODUCED AS THE RESULT OF AN ILLEGAL SEARCH OF MS. OLSEN'S APARTMENT.

rather than

THE TRIAL COURT ERRED BECAUSE THE SEARCH WAS IM-PROPER.

4. Make sure the STATEMENT OF FACTS or STATEMENT OF THE CASE contains all of those facts used in the analysis. Other than these legally significant facts, make sure that the statement contains only those other facts essential to establish context, such as BACKGROUND FACTS and EMOTIONALLY SIGNIFICANT FACTS.

5. Use PINPOINT CITES for any rule, holding, proposition, quotation, or specific reference.

> **An implied duty exists not to make changes in the work that would render the work a false attribution. Williams v. ABC, 938 F.2d 14, 16 (2d Cir. 1996).**

6. Make exact any references to the record, to dates, to numbers, and to authority.

> **Plaintiff signed the contract on June 22, 1993. (CP 36.)**

7. In general, use concrete and specific words rather than abstract or general ones.

> **The defendant said that he had a gun as he grabbed Ms. Delaney's arm and poked her in the back.**

rather than

The defendant said he was armed as he accosted the victim.

Use the latter version only if you mean to obscure the facts. For related information, see EMPHASIS and PERSUASIVE WRITING, subsection 2.

PREDICATE

See SENTENCE, PARTS OF.

PREFIXES, WHEN TO HYPHENATE

See HYPHENS.

PREPOSITIONAL PHRASES

A prepositional phrase is a group of words that work together to show the relationship of a noun or pronoun to the rest of the sentence. This noun or pronoun is called the object of the preposition. A preposition, which is always the first word in a prepositional phrase, shows how the rest of that phrase is logically related to the sentence.

PREPOSITIONAL PHRASES

Examples of prepositions are *of, to, on, off, between, through, in, at, without, over,* and *under.* The following examples of prepositional phrases illustrate the variety of information they can convey.

> **He built the house <u>with his own hands</u>.**

> **All nonresidents living <u>in Illinois for more than three months of a calendar year</u> must complete the following section.**

> **The contract will have been signed <u>by that date</u>.**

> **The settlement seems reasonable <u>in light of the facts</u>.**

For more information, see PREPOSITIONS.

PREPOSITIONS

Prepositions go before NOUNS, PRONOUNS, or phrases working as nouns (that is the *pre-*), and show the relationship of that noun, pronoun, or phrase to the rest of the sentence (that is the *-position*). Prepositional phrases thus begin with a preposition and end with a noun or pronoun; the noun or pronoun at the end of the phrase is called the object of the preposition.

> **in the car, beyond the cost, of this litigation, without his testimony**

Prepositional phrases are useful and necessary, but watch for three problems when using them.

1. Avoid using many in a row. Prepositional phrases have a rhythm something like that of a slow waltz, and many of them in a row can waltz your reader right off to sleep.

> **The department is required to submit a written explanation if income deviates substantially from predicted income in 1984.**

rather than

> The department is required to submit a written explanation in the case of deviations of substantial size from the predictions of income for the calendar year of 1984.

2. Avoid using a prepositional phrase when a shorter grammatical phrase could do as well.

> **If the hearing is delayed,** ....

rather than

> In the event of the occurrence of a delay of the hearing, ...

See CONCISENESS, NOMINALIZATIONS, and PREPOSITIONAL PHRASES.

3. Use the objective case (such as *me, us, him, her,* or *them*) of a pronoun that is the object of a preposition.

This written contract between you and me should help us avoid any confusion in the future.

rather than

This written contract between you and I should help us avoid any confusion in the future.

PRESENT PARTICIPLES

See VERBS, TENSES.

PRESENT PERFECT TENSE

See VERBS, TENSES.

PRESENT PROGRESSIVE TENSE

See VERBS, TENSES.

PRESENT TENSE

See VERBS, TENSES.

PRETRIAL BRIEFS

A pretrial brief is any brief written in support of or opposition to a pretrial motion. A pretrial brief uses PERSUASIVE WRITING to inform the reader of the law and to persuade the reader to accept the client's position, and it is usually filed with the Notice of Motion and Motion or shortly thereafter. For related information, see MEMORANDUM OF POINTS AND AUTHORITIES, NOTICE OF MOTION, and MOTIONS.

Check your jurisdiction for the particular FORMAT requirements. See BRIEFS for a sample format.

PREVIOUS TO

Usually you can substitute *before* for greater READABILITY and CONCISENESS.

PREWRITING

Prewriting includes all work done before writing the first substantial draft of any paper. Clear thought and focused effort at this stage will save hours of time in the later stages of the WRITING PROCESS: WRITING, REWRITING, REVISING, and POLISHING. In a research project, prewriting includes the first five steps of the RESEARCH

STRATEGY, taking NOTES on the research found, in some cases PROCRASTINATION, thinking, and outlining or some other means of ORGANIZATION. See OUTLINES or ORGANIZATION FOR THOSE WHO CAN'T OUTLINE.

Organization is the key to successful prewriting. As soon as possible, categorize the sections and subsections of your problem so that the work can be done in compartments. For example, if you are writing a three-issue appellate brief, you might organize your prewriting by those three issues and work on only one issue at a time.

Some writers prefer to begin the writing process by writing a very rough preliminary draft as soon as possible, rather than beginning with other prewriting activities. If you are one of these writers, you may apply the techniques below after your preliminary draft.

If you are comfortable with prewriting activities, be careful not to stay in this stage so long that writing, rewriting, and revising are shortchanged. The following techniques can help make your prewriting stage successful.

1. Think before you go to the library. In particular, do some version of the first five steps of the RESEARCH STRATEGY CHART first.

2. Make the library work to your advantage by planning your research the way you might plan a trip to the grocery store: before you go, list the books you want to use and order the list.

3. Have your system of note-taking ready to go before you go to the library. See NOTES.

4. Allow yourself to think about the problem even when you are not writing notes; if a good idea comes to your head, jot it down so you can easily file it with its issue.

5. Try to list or outline the important points that you want to make under each issue. Even though this list may be flawed, it will help you focus your research. See OUTLINES.

6. Allow yourself always to make your own comments and commentary as you take notes, to help you pull the pieces together in your own mind.

7. Pull all the pieces together by letting the law itself dictate the organization; resist using a pre-programmed organizational scheme, but instead respond to the organization of the law. For example, you might discover several elements to a rule and use them as subdivisions. Or you might have only one test to be applied to the facts in one unit.

PRINCIPLES OF GOOD LEGAL WRITING

The following checklist is designed to provide a brief overview and reminder of the principles of good writing. For specific detail on how to incorporate each of these principles in your writing, see the cross-referenced entries.

1. Principles regarding the WRITING PROCESS.

   (a) PREWRITING.

   Good writing is good thinking. Make sure you have done enough of the second before you start the first. See also OUT-LINES and ORGANIZATION FOR THOSE WHO CAN'T OUT-LINE.

   (b) WRITING.

   At this stage, focus on getting it written, not getting it right. Let your thinking flow onto the page in the first draft, without stopping to edit.

   (c) REWRITING.

   Rework main ideas and large-scale organization. Add content if necessary. See ORGANIZATION, LARGE–SCALE and ORGA-NIZATION, SMALL–SCALE.

   (d) REVISING.

   Reconcile yourself to the fact that it will take several passes over the text to get it right. Revise for ACCURACY, CONCISE-NESS, READABILITY, TONE, and EMPHASIS. In particular, revise POINT HEADINGS, ISSUE STATEMENTS, TOPIC SEN-TENCES, and CONCLUSIONS, because your reader will pay special attention to these parts of any legal document.

   (e) POLISHING.

   Use whatever technique works for you: moving back to front, reading through separately for each kind of revision needed, reading aloud, or working section by section. Check such things as COMMAS, spelling, and FORMAT.

2. Principles regarding the quality of the final product.

   (a) Content.

   (i) Select and carefully present all issues relevant to the scope of the paper, with the subjects and verbs presenting the legal question. See ISSUE STATEMENTS.

   (ii) In MEMOS, make sure the BRIEF ANSWERS each contain the answer and the reasons for it; in BRIEFS, make sure the POINT HEADINGS contain the legal points and major reasons.

   (iii) Include all relevant constitutional provisions, statutes, regulations, and cases.

(iv) Synthesize general RULES from the statute and the cases interpreting it, or the common law rule from the cases. Describe the law completely but concisely.

(v) Apply the law carefully to facts of this case; balance strengths against weaknesses. See APPLICATION.

(vi) Make sure you have adequately examined POLICY and EQUITY.

(vii) Make sure the Conclusion makes a strong prediction based on the information in the DISCUSSION SECTION of a memo, or specific prayer for relief based on the ARGUMENT SECTION of a brief.

(b) Purpose.

(i) Consider the AUDIENCE and tailor the paper to the audience's request.

(ii) Keep TONE and POINT OF VIEW consistently objective in a memo, consistently persuasive in a brief. Avoid editorializing or becoming overly dramatic.

(iii) Make sure the writing is easy for the reader to follow, with clear TRANSITIONS and strong, LOGICAL LINKS. See READABILITY.

(iv) Avoid losing the reader by either skipping steps in reasoning or by overexplaining. Also make sure WORD CHOICE is consistent and accurate. See ACCURACY.

(c) ORGANIZATION and STYLE.

(i) Check organization on all levels: overall, within a section, within a paragraph, and within a sentence. Make sure each subpart is carefully planned and connected to its neighbors. See ORGANIZATION, LARGE–SCALE; ORGANIZATION, SMALL–SCALE; ORGANIZATION; and CONNECTIONS, MAKING THEM.

(ii) Make every word count. See CONCISENESS. Also use ACTIVE VOICE whenever possible.

(iii) Give every paragraph a purpose and say it in the topic sentence. See PARAGRAPHS and TOPIC SENTENCES.

(iv) Use techniques of EMPHASIS, SENTENCE STRUCTURE, and WORD CHOICE to refine your STYLE.

(d) POLISHING.

(i) Do a final check for details; try reading backwards if it helps. Check GRAMMAR, PUNCTUATION, SPELLING, WORD USAGE, and CITATIONS.

(ii) Check to see that all cites conform to the Bluebook or your jurisdiction's citation form.

PRIOR TO

Prior to sounds a bit stuffy and can be ungrammatical. To avoid *prior to*, use *before*.

Before the accident, he ran three miles each morning.

rather than

Prior to the accident, he ran three miles each morning

Or use *to*.

To receive this summary of past complaints, the consumer must file . . . .

rather than

Prior to receiving this summary of past complaints, the consumer must file . . . .

PROCEDURAL OR SUBSTANTIVE?

Use these terms precisely, because the distinction between them is critical in legal writing. *Procedural* refers to legal method, or the legal machinery for carrying on a suit. This machinery includes pleading, evidence, process, and similar practical matters. For example, the question of whether a court has jurisdiction over a particular suit is a procedural question; the question of whether post-verdict motions were filed on time is also procedural.

Substantive refers to the law itself, which regulates and defines the rights and duties of parties to the suit. For example, a defendant's right to be represented by counsel is a substantive right; a party's right to bring an action for wrongful death is also a substantive right.

Often substantive rights are referred to as the merits of a case. For example, to say *The judge is ready to make a decision on the merits*, is to say that all the procedural matters have been settled so that the court may judge the remaining issues on the basis of the parties' duties and rights.

PROCESS AND PRODUCT COMPARED

The writing product is the document itself, which is subject to scrutiny and evaluation by your AUDIENCE and those who evaluate your performance, whether supervisors, clients, judges, or professors. To assist and even impress them, your product must exhibit ACCURACY, PRECISION, and CLARITY, regardless of the constraints imposed on you by less-than-ideal conditions.

In contrast, your writing process is your personal way of getting the job done. It includes every aspect of your work, such as your time allocations for different tasks, your order for doing these tasks, and your style of interacting with others involved in the project. It is affected by your habitual ways of completing all the tasks involved in your WRITING PROCESS, such as ordering your RESEARCH STRATEGY, WRITING with dictaphone or computer, and proofreading. It is also affected by external factors that vary with the situation, such as your client's demands, your supervisor's agenda, and your energy level on the day you write.

Although your process is not generally scrutinized by others, it deserves your personal scrutiny because it can dramatically affect the product. Refining your legal writing process, particularly noting how it may differ from nonlegal writing processes, also has personal benefits; it can make you more effective, efficient, and confident. For ways to make this evaluation, see WRITING PROCESS.

PROCRASTINATION

Procrastination works if it is incubation, fails if it is empty postponement. To make procrastination work for you, do the following.

1. Do short PREWRITING tasks early and then think. For example, write the Questions Presented as soon as you begin working on a memo and then think about them. Alternatively, gather the research, read it, and then think about it.

2. A little later, brief the cases or take whatever notes work for you. Let the problem sit a while to let it breathe, turn over, move about in your mind. Then jot down ideas as they come to you and put them in your files. See BRIEFING CASES and NOTES.

3. Set a time for completing the research and writing an outline. However cursory this outline may be, this step will usually force the procrastinating to end and the organizing to begin. This is the hardest step to take, but you must take it; skipping it can ruin worthwhile incubating. See OUTLINES and ORGANIZATION FOR THOSE WHO CAN'T OUTLINE.

4. Similarly, set a time to have the draft to a typist, even if you are the typist. By putting interim deadlines on your calendar and tying them to another person or task, you force yourself to avoid further procrastination by sheer embarrassment. If you do your own typing, try to find someone who will be a listener or a reader for your paper at a specific time, again so you have a deadline tied to another person.

5. Finally, schedule many small interim deadlines instead of just the final one and stick to your schedule. This will break down your temptation to postpone.

For related information, see WRITING PROCESS, TIME MAN-AGEMENT, WRITING BLOCKS, SAYING *NO*, GETTING STARTED, and WHEN TO STOP.

PROFESSIONAL POSTURE

To write effectively, you must keep focused on your document's PURPOSE, AUDIENCE, and SCOPE. But realistically, you will also be affected by another goal, which is leaving the reader with a good impression of you as a writer, a lawyer, and a person. Rather than denying that goal or letting it overshadow your other goals, include it within your FOCUS.

You can create a good impression by communicating an appropriate professional posture in the document. That posture includes your professional responsibility and your personal style.

Your professional responsibility varies as the particular situation and legal document vary, so take time to ascertain your responsibilities in each situation; then make sure you meet them. For example, in an OPINION LETTER, you have a duty to remind the client that the choice is finally up to him or her, even though you recommend one particular course of action. Therefore, take care to explain with equal clarity both the reasoning behind your advice and the limits of your role as advisor. Explain so clearly and completely that your reader could make an informed decision either way. In a BRIEF, you have a duty in most jurisdictions to acknowledge a precedent that seems unfavorable to your case. To meet that duty, cite the case but also argue that it is distinguishable based on different facts or reasoning.

Besides meeting your professional responsibility, you may want to communicate a personal style. For example, compared to other attorneys, you may be more formal or informal, personal or impersonal, impassioned or unemotional.

You will probably adjust this style somewhat in each document you write, just as you adjust your manner of speaking when talking to different people. For more on this, see AUDIENCE. For ways to communicate your personal style, see TONE.

PROGRESSIVE TENSES

See VERBS, TENSES.

PRONOUN REFERENCE

See AMBIGUITY, Subsection 2.

PRONOUNS

Pronouns take the place of nouns, and they have many uses.

He is the officer who gave me a ticket.

Without it, they have no case.

The plaintiff must take the responsibility upon himself.

Each of you should write to your senator.

For answers to common problems with pronouns, see the following subsections.

1. When to use commas with relative pronouns.

Relative pronouns, one subcategory of pronouns, deserve special attention because they are used frequently in legal writing and their proper use is often crucial to ACCURACY. Relative pronouns include *who, whose, that, which, whoever, whichever,* and *whatever*. These relative pronouns introduce subordinate clauses, or groups of words that include a subject and verb but cannot stand by themselves as sentences.

Your car, which was still in the lot at midnight, was towed.

This issue was resolved by the court in Barker v. Holmes, which stated ....

Any nonresident who has lived in the state for more than three months must fill out this portion of the form.

All cars that remain in the lot after 10:00 p.m. will be towed.

All operators whose licenses expire this month must show the supervisor their renewed license.

Sometimes a subordinate clause adds extra information to the sentence but is not essential to the accuracy of the sentence. To punctuate this clause correctly, place commas before and after the subordinate clause.

Your car, which was still in the lot at midnight, was towed.

Sometimes, however, a subordinating clause is essential to the meaning of the sentence because the clause narrows the subject, or restricts the meaning of the subject. In this situation, removing the subordinate clause would make the sentence inaccurate. To punctuate this kind of subordinate clause correctly, do not put commas before or after the clause.

All cars [ ] that remain in the lot after 10:00 p.m. [ ] will be towed.

Any nonresident [ ] who has lived in the state for more than three months [ ] must fill out this portion of the form.

240

All operators [ ] whose licenses expire this month [ ] must show the supervisor their renewed license.

2. When to use *who* or *whom*.

Use *who* as a subject, *whom* as an object. First, use *whom* as the object of a PREPOSITION.

To whom did you present the question about the gun?

Second, use *whom* as the object of a verb.

Whom did you see on the night of the incident?

Finally, use *whom* as the subject of a complementary infinitive.

Defendant is the person whom the plaintiff saw on the night of the crime.

Use *who* as a subject of a sentence or of a clause.

Who took my shoes?

You are the person who called me yesterday.

3. When to use *he*, *she*, or *they*.

Use *they* only when referring to a plural noun. Use *he or she* when you are referring to one person but do not know the sex of the person. For more on this question, see SEXIST LANGUAGE, WAYS TO AVOID.

PROPER NOUNS

Proper nouns are names of specific persons, organizations, publications, and so forth. *Helen Harris, American Bar Association, Texas Law Review.* Capitalize them.

PROVIDED THAT

Replace this phrase with *if* for greater CONCISENESS and CLARITY.

Our client has the contractual right to reject any shipment if she notifies Norcross of her decision within forty-eight hours of receiving that shipment.

rather than

Our client has the contractual right to reject any shipment provided that she notifies Norcross of her decision within forty-eight hours of receiving that shipment.

Sometimes *provided that* may have been used to introduce something that will most likely happen; then you may replace it with *when*.

The transfer of ownership will occur at closing, when the seller provides the title and the buyer pays the full purchase price.

241

rather than

> The transfer of ownership will occur at closing, provided that the seller provides the title and the buyer pays the full purchase price.

PUNCTUATING LISTS

See LISTS, STRUCTURE OF.

PUNCTUATION

Punctuation rules are extensive and particular but critical to ACCURACY. For ways to punctuate sentences, see PERIODS, SEMICOLONS, COLONS, EXCLAMATION POINTS, and QUESTION MARKS. For ways to punctuate phrases within a sentence, see COMMAS, DASHES, SEMICOLONS, and COLONS. For ways to punctuate lists, see LISTS, STRUCTURE OF. For ways to punctuate quotes, see QUOTATIONS, HOW TO PUNCTUATE. See also HYPHENS and APOSTROPHES.

PURPOSE

Have one in mind before you get too far along in the WRITING PROCESS. Although you may brainstorm a first draft or some notes, take time to think about why you are writing as well as what you want to say and to whom you will say it. Take time to be honest with yourself about your purposes: there may be many. For example, you may be writing to impress a new boss as well as to advise on a decision. This honesty often does not mean you state these purposes explicitly in the document, but it will nevertheless make your writing more effective and more efficient. You may want to write your primary and secondary purposes, and refer to them throughout WRITING, REWRITING, and REVISING. The following list may help you more clearly define your purposes.

- inform the client
- persuade a judge
- advise on a decision
- suggest a change in the law
- advance a new theory
- settle a dispute
- impress your boss
- get a promotion
- complete a transaction
- assist the decisionmaker
- collect a bill
- keep a record
- suggest a solution
- set a meeting
- codify case law
- preserve a document against litigation
- get action from the reader, client, or opposing counsel
- pressure someone into action

For more information on how to develop your purpose, see GETTING STARTED, OUTLINES, ORGANIZATION FOR THOSE WHO CAN'T OUTLINE, and AUDIENCE.

QUESTION MARK OR PERIOD?

See QUESTION MARKS.

QUESTION MARKS

You know to use question marks with questions. The problems occur with sentences like the ones that follow.

The question is whether this term applies to the facts of this case.

A period, not a question mark is used.

The boy, when confronted by the clerk, said only, "Who, me?"

No period is used after the question mark.

Can the issue be raised? is the question.

A question mark is used mid-sentence, after the question, but a period is used at the end of the sentence. This structure is rare and thus looks odd to most readers; try rewording the sentence whenever you can to avoid putting a question mark in the middle, even if it is grammatically correct to do so.

The question is, "Does this term apply to the facts of this case?"

A question mark, not a period, is used.

May we hear from you within one week.

Here the choice between a period and a question mark is a tactical one. When you are asking a question but implying a demand, you may use a period.

See also QUOTATIONS, HOW TO PUNCTUATE for handling question marks and quotation marks together.

QUESTION PRESENTED

The lens of the legal analyst's camera, the Question Presented focuses on the specific question to be answered in a legal memo. The issue statement in a persuasive piece of writing is also sometimes called a Question Presented. In its objective form, the ideal Question Presented outline the memo because it has three parts: (1) the general rule of law governing the question, (2) the legal question to be answered in this situation, and (3) the LEGALLY SIGNIFICANT FACTS necessary for the analysis.

Under Fed. R. Clv. P. 4(d)(1), Summons: Personal Service, was a notice effective when it was delivered to defendant's wife and when defendant did not reside at his wife's address, but moved back in with her one week later?

These three parts are combined and written in either question form or *whether* form. The *whether* form enjoys common use among established lawyers, but it is grammatically incorrect because it is an incomplete sentence. The *whether* form also implies a statement rather than a question and can add extra words. In either form, keep subject and verb close together to increase READABILITY.

> **Whether notice was effective under Fed. R. Civ. P. 4(d)(1), <u>Summons: Personal Service</u>, when it was delivered to defendant's wife and when defendant did not reside at his wife's address but moved back in with her one week later.**

Put the legally significant facts at the end of the Question Presented so that the reader is focused by moving from general to specific. Placing the legally significant facts at the end also helps keep the question readable because it places the list at the end of the sentence. See LISTS, STRUCTURE OF.

Check with your reader to see if the particular facts of your case should be included in the Questions Presented, which will focus the questions on the client's situation. Your reader may prefer that the facts be stated in general terms so the memo is easier to use as a reference in future cases. For related information, see ISSUE STATEMENTS.

QUOTATION MARKS

Use quotation marks for quotes of forty-nine words or less. Also use quotation marks to indicate that you are referring to a word itself, rather than the thing the words stand for, as in the following example.

> **"Hearsay" refers to a statement, other than one made by the declarant while testifying at the trial or hearing, offered in evidence to prove the truth of the matter asserted.**

For related information, see QUOTATION MARKS OR INDENTED QUOTES? and QUOTATIONS, HOW TO PUNCTUATE.

QUOTATION MARKS IN LEGISLATION

See LEGISLATION.

QUOTATION MARKS OR INDENTED QUOTES?

Use quotation marks around direct quotes of forty-nine words or less and around titles of articles. When a direct quote is longer than forty-nine words, indent it, single-space it, and omit quotation marks. The only time you will use quotation marks in an indented, single-spaced quote is when there is a quote within the indented quote. See also QUOTATIONS, HOW TO PUNCTUATE.

QUOTATIONS, HOW TO PUNCTUATE

These rules are picky and extensive but worth observing. It is important to be accurate in legal writing, and particularly important to be accurate when quoting. These rules include (1) when to use quotation marks, (2) when to indent, (3) when to use a comma before a quote, (4) how to use other punctuation marks with quotation marks, (5) when to use single quotation marks, (6) when and how to underline parts of a quote, (7) how to mark changes in a quote, (8) how to mark omissions from a quote, and (9) how to maintain credibility when editing a quote.

1. When to use quotation marks.

Use quotation marks to mark any direct quote. When the quote is forty-nine words or less, put it in quotation marks.

The court reasoned that "any error must in this situation be material."

Also use quotation marks to indicate that a word is being used to refer to the word itself, rather than to the meaning of the word. Thus, put quotation marks around a word when you could insert *the term* or *the word* before that word.

The court focused on "reasonable" when interpreting the meaning of this clause in the contract.

Avoid using quotation marks to indicate slang, sarcasm, irony, or anything other than direct quotes or words used as words. The precision of legal writing requires the precise use of punctuation, including quotation marks. If you feel uncomfortable using a word because it is informal or ambiguous, change the word rather than putting it in quotation marks.

The attorney's complaint about the secretary's typographical errors cannot be considered slander.

rather than

The attorney's complaint about the secretary's "typos" cannot be considered slander.

2. When to indent.

When the quote is longer than forty-nine words, indent it and type it single-spaced. Put the citation on the first line of text following the quote, rather than within the indented quote itself.

The court in this case addressed the issue of mutuality.

> **Despite the defendant's emotional plea regarding the centrality of upholding contracts to the free working of a democracy, we cannot ignore the plaintiff's complaint. In this case, the court must intervene because the issue of mutuality, not to mention that of duress, requires that the court examine both the con-**

tract's wording and the parol evidence surrounding the signing of that contract.

Hartman v. Legler, 986 F. Supp. 192 (S.D. Ind. 1999).

3. When to use a comma before a quote.

Use a comma if the phrase before the quote introduces it.

She said, "I killed him."

If the quote is an integral part of the larger sentence, do not use a comma.

He said "killed," not "stabbed."

4. How to use other punctuation marks with quotation marks.

Quotation marks go outside commas and periods, even if the comma or period is not part of the quote.

The term on which we must focus is "intent."

This rule is the same for both double quotation marks ("—") and single ones ('—'). The rule is not meant to reflect logical concerns, but rather graphic ones. It looks funny to see the period or comma sitting out there alone.

One exception to this rule is LEGISLATION, where periods and commas are generally treated like all other punctuation marks. As always, check and follow your jurisdiction's rules. Another exception is British English, which also puts commas and periods outside the quotation marks when they are not part of the quote.

All other punctuation marks go inside the quotation marks if they are part of the quote, outside if they are not.

Common law recognized a defense to a privacy action where "the incident was a public concern and record"; however, the statutory policy had in effect eliminated this defense.

The semicolon is not part of the quote, so it goes outside the marks.

Smith reports "a majority of the jurors thought 'infer' meant 'assume'!"

The exclamation point is part of the quote, so it goes inside the quotation marks. *Infer* and *assume* refer to the words as words, rather than the concepts the words describe, and so are put in quotation marks. Single marks are used because the words are within another quote. For related information, see EXCLAMATION POINTS.

5. When to use single quotation marks.

In the United States use single quotation marks only for quotes within other quotes.

The defendant said, "He told me to 'get lost.' "

6. When and how to underline parts of a quote.

Underline to add emphasis to the key phrase in QUOTATIONS long enough to be indented and single-spaced in the text. Underlining may encourage the legal reader to read the long quote by making it more visually pleasing. When you underline, add *(emphasis added)* after the citation.

> **As this court itself has stated, "[T]he court must intervene because the issue of mutuality, not to mention that of duress, requires that the court examine <u>the parol evidence surrounding the signing</u> of the contract." <u>Durant v. Colt</u>, 945 F. Supp. 041 (D.D.C. 1004) (emphasis added).**

When the quote is indented, put the cite and *(emphasis added)* on the first line of text following the indented quote, not within the indented quote itself.

7. How to mark changes in a quote.

In general, use BRACKETS to mark any changes you make in the wording of a quote.

(a) If you are changing or adding a word to a quote to make it fit grammatically into your sentence, put brackets ([ ]) around that word.

> **As the court explained, "Despite the defendant's emotional plea regarding the centrality of upholding contracts to the free working of a democracy, [the court] cannot ignore the plaintiff's complaint."**

changed from the original

> **Despite the defendant's emotional plea regarding the centrality of upholding contracts to the free working of a democracy, we cannot ignore the plaintiff's complaint.**

(b) If you are adding or changing a letter within a word, put brackets around the part of the word changed. Even if all you do is change a letter from lower case (a) to upper case (A), you must put brackets around the change.

> **The court made this explicit when it said, "[W]e cannot ignore the plaintiff's complaint."**

changed from the original

> **Despite the defendant's emotional plea regarding the centrality of upholding contracts to the free working of a democracy, we cannot ignore the plaintiff's complaint.**

(c) If you are adding SIC, put it in brackets. Add *sic* when you want to inform the reader that the error in the text was in the original, rather than being an error you made when copying the quote.

"In this cause [sic], Ms. Hofner did not realize she was waiving this right."

8. How to mark omissions from a quote.

In general, use ELLIPSES to mark any omissions you make in a quote. An ellipsis is a series of three periods with spaces between them (. . .). To be accurate, you must not only use ellipses to mark any omissions; you must also use accurate spacing and punctuation before and after the ellipses, as the following rules explain. These rules are intricate, but important and useful to the careful reader. If ellipses are used accurately, the reader can tell exactly what changes you made in the original without having to look up the original.

(a) If you are omitting a word or words within one sentence, put a space before and after the ellipsis.

"The issue of mutuality . . . requires that the court examine both the contract's wording and the parol evidence surrounding the signing of the contract."

changed from the original

The issue of mutuality, not to mention that of duress, requires that the court examine both the contract's wording and the parol evidence surrounding the signing of the contract.

(b) If you are omitting the rest of an entire sentence, put a space before the ellipsis and a space and period after the ellipsis. This fourth period represents the period at the end of the original sentence.

"There can be no negligence without duty . . . ."

changed from the original

There can be no negligence without duty, and in this case there is no duty.

(c) If the sentence quoted ended with a question mark or exclamation mark, use that mark rather than a period after the ellipsis.

"The jury thought 'imply' meant 'assume' . . . !"

changed from the original

The jury thought "imply" meant "assume" in this situation!

"Did the defendant take all reasonable precautions . . . ?"

changed from the original

Did the defendant take all reasonable precautions before starting up the mower?

(d) Similarly, if you are omitting the rest of one sentence and then continuing the quote at the first of the next sentence, put a space before the ellipsis, and a space and period after the ellipsis. After the fourth period, add two spaces and then begin the next sentence, just as you would after the period at the end of any other sentence.

> **"The court cannot base its decision on sympathy** .... **There can be no negligence without duty** ...."

changed from the original

> **The court cannot base its decision on sympathy, no matter how great that sympathy may be. There can be no negligence without duty, and in this case there is no duty.**

Again, if the sentence you are editing ended with a question mark or exclamation point, repeat that mark instead of the fourth period.

(e) If you are quoting the end of a sentence, omitting one or more sentences, and then continuing the quote with a later sentence, do the following. First, put a period, question mark, or exclamation point immediately after the last word of the quoted sentence right before the ellipsis, just as you would have done if you were not omitting sentences. Second, put in one space and then the ellipsis. Third, space once and then begin the next quoted sentence.

> **In this case, the court must intervene.... The issue of mutuality, not to mention that of duress, requires that the court examine both the contract's wording and the parol evidence surrounding the signing of that contract.**

changed from the original

> **In this case, the court must intervene. Despite the defendant's emotional plea regarding the centrality of upholding contracts to the free working of a democracy, it cannot ignore the plaintiff's complaint. The issue of mutuality, not to mention that of duress, requires that the court examine both the contract's wording and the parol evidence surrounding the signing of that contract.**

(f) If you are quoting the end of a sentence, omitting one or more sentences, and then continuing the quote mid-sentence, follow the same procedure explained in subsection (d), but also put brackets around the first word after the ellipsis if you are changing that letter from lower case to upper case.

> **In this case, the court must intervene.... [M]utuality requires that the court examine both the contract's wording and the parol evidence surrounding the signing of that contract.**

changed from the original

> **In this case, the court must intervene. Despite the defendant's emotional plea regarding the centrality of**

249

upholding contracts to the free working of a democracy, it cannot ignore the plaintiff's complaint. The issue of mutuality requires that the court examine both the contract's wording and the parol evidence surrounding the signing of that contract.

(g) Never use an ellipsis at the beginning of a quote, even if you have omitted the first word or words of the quoted passage. The ellipsis is unneeded because the fact that the first word of the quote was not originally capitalized is sufficient to indicate that words have been omitted.

[T]here can be no negligence without duty.

rather than

. . . there can be no negligence without duty.

changed from the original

As the defense so aptly argued, there can be no negligence without duty.

9. How to maintain credibility when editing a quote.

Avoid extensive editing of quotes, even though you now know how to do it accurately. If you use ellipses and brackets extensively, the reader will find the quote awkward to read and will probably suspect that you are misrepresenting the original idea. The solution in this situation is not to omit ellipses and thus sacrifice ACCURACY; it is to PARAPHRASE or to find another quote that fits the situation without needing such extensive surgery.

The court stated that it must intervene in this case to resolve the issue of mutuality despite the emotional pleas for freedom of contract.

rather than the edited version

Despite the . . . emotional plea regarding . . . upholding contracts to the free working of a democracy, [the court] cannot ignore the plaintiff's complaint. . . . [T]he court must intervene; the issue of mutuality . . . requires that the court examine both the contract's wording and the parol evidence . . . .

changed from the original

Despite the defendant's emotional plea regarding the centrality of upholding contracts to the free working of a democracy, we cannot ignore the plaintiff's complaint. In this case, the court must intervene; the issue of mutuality, not to mention that of duress, requires that the court examine both the contract's wording and the parol evidence surrounding the signing of that contract.

QUOTATIONS, LONG

See EXTENDED QUOTES.

QUOTATIONS, WHEN TO USE

Use quotations if the particular phrasing is central to your issue, such as phrases including TERMS OF ART or key passages from the applicable statute. Otherwise use quotes only if the answer to each of the following questions is *yes*.

1   Does the quotation contain information directly pertinent to the point?

2.   Is the quotation no longer than one long **paragraph**, unless content requires all of it?

3.   Does the quotation communicate the information more clearly than you could, even in an accurate PARAPHRASE?   Alternatively, does this quotation communicate the information more eloquently than you could in a paraphrase?

See also QUOTATIONS, HOW TO PUNCTUATE and EXTENDED QUOTES.

QUOTE WITHIN A QUOTE

See QUOTATIONS, HOW TO PUNCTUATE, subsection 5.

RAMBLING

To avoid this problem, see ORGANIZATION, PARAGRAPHS, OUTLINES, and ORGANIZATION FOR THOSE WHO CAN'T OUT-LINE.

RE

You may use *re* in subject lines for letters or memos, but do not use it in the text of the letter or memo. Instead use *regarding*.

READABILITY

Many factors work together to enhance the readability of a document. Here is a checklist of some of the most useful ones.

1.   Use shorter sentences.

Check to make sure that your sentences do not habitually run more than three-and-one-half lines. One easy way to do this is to put a slash after each period in the draft. You can do this without actually reading the text; just skim for the periods. Then, looking at where the slashes fall, check for places where there are several long sentences in a row. Divide at least some of these into shorter sentences.

> **You may decide that the testimony of one witness is entitled to greater weight than that of another witness, or even of several witnesses. In weighing the evidence, you may consider your own knowledge, observations, and life experiences.**

rather than

> In weighing the evidence, you may consider the testimony of one witness as entitled to greater weight than that of another witness or several others, your own knowledge, what you have observed, and the experiences you have had in life.

If a sentence contains a list at the end, it may not need to be divided. For ways to handle the list, see the next subsection.

2. Use clear and logical lists.

Careful structuring of lists greatly increases readability. First, always make sure that the elements of your list are both logically and grammatically parallel.

> **The defendant moved his car into the left lane to pass, lost control on the snow-packed pavement, slid back into the right lane, and collided with the plaintiff's truck.**

rather than

> The defendant moved his car into the left lane to pass, was losing control, slid back into the right lane, and caused injury to the plaintiff when he hit her truck.

Then structure your sentence so that the list comes at the end. Additionally, when the list is long or complex, use signals, such as parenthetical numbers or tabulation, to help the reader see immediately the structure of the list.

> **In justifying the exclusion of expert psychiatric evidence, the court discussed (1) maintaining the integrity of the bifurcated trial procedure, (2) avoiding allowing the guilty to go free, and (3) preserving the defendant's right against self-incrimination.**

rather than

> The court discussed maintaining the integrity of the bifurcated trial procedure, avoiding allowing the guilty to go free, and preserving the defendant's right against self-incrimination in justifying the exclusion of expert psychiatric evidence.

For more detail about ways to do this, see LISTS, STRUCTURE OF.

3. Use familiar words.

Use words that your reader will understand without having to resort to a dictionary.

> **Counsel, by using apt wording and artful presentation, minimized this weak point in her argument.**

rather than

> Counsel, by applying her verbal acumen and felicitous propensity for oratory, accomplished a feat of legerdemain regarding this conceptual proposition.

Unusual words, even if the reader does know what they mean, force the reader to stop and think. Busy legal readers usually will not stop mid thought to ponder the nuances of an individual word, and so your meaning may be lost. For more information, see FLOWERY LANGUAGE.

4. Use consistent wording.

Use the same term for the same concept throughout the document; do not change it just for VARIETY.

> **The defendant proposes that his repair of the water heater was adequate. This proposal, however, ...**

rather than

> The defendant proposes that his repair of the water heater was adequate. This suggestion, however, ...

Using consistent terms aids readability by helping the reader know immediately that you mean the same thing. For more on this point, see REPETITION.

5. Keep the subject and verb undivided and focused on your point.

Keep the subject within seven words of the verb and make sure the subject and verb state the main point of the sentence.

> **If this case were retried, the result would be different because of the combination of the numerous defects in the proceedings below and the newly discovered evidence.**

rather than

> The total effect of the numerous defects in the proceedings below, which in combination with the newly discovered evidence referred to above creates a miscarriage of justice, would if this case were to be retried under optimum circumstances produce a different result.

In the second example, the subject (*effect*) is divided from the verb (*would produce*) by twenty-four words, and the two words of the verb (*would* and *produce*) are divided by ten words. By the time the reader finally finds the verb, the subject will be forgotten and the reader will have to re-read the sentence several times to find it. For more ways to restructure sentences, see SENTENCE STRUCTURE.

Additionally, PRECISION is lost when the subject and verb do not clearly state the writer's point. In the previous example, *effect would produce* does not state the reader's main point. Moving the subject and verb together would have exposed this problem to the writer, who could then revise it to *the result would be different*. For more on this see SUBJECT–VERB COMBINATIONS. For related problems, see AGREEMENT, SUBJECTS AND VERBS.

6. Use precise transitions.

Use transitions that convey exact connections. For example, use *nevertheless* only when *nevertheless* is the logical connection between the two thoughts.

> **The litigation may cost more than the amount our client could recover if she wins the suit. Nevertheless, she has chosen to pursue her claim.**

rather than

> The litigation may cost more than the amount our client could recover if she wins the suit, although she has chosen to pursue her claim.

In the second example, using the wrong transition confuses the reader. For more on this and for a list of transitions, see TRANSITIONS.

7. Use consistent word signals.

If you use *second*, make sure that you used *first* earlier. Similarly, if you used *not only*, use *but also* later. Without these parallel signals, the skilled reader is left frustrated, like the waiting listener who hears one shoe drop but never hears the second. For related information, see CONJUNCTIONS and CONNECTIONS, MAKING THEM.

8. Accurate and adequate punctuation.

PUNCTUATION marks are the road signs of legal writing, and inaccurate punctuation can lead to wrong turns. Revise once just for accurate punctuation. For more information on punctuation needed but often omitted, see COMMAS and SEMICOLONS. For ways to spot these problems, see REVISING.

READER

See AUDIENCE.

READING OPINIONS

See OPINIONS.

REALLY

Really means *in reality* or *indeed*. It is overused, so avoid it unless it accurately conveys your meaning. Because *really* is used frequently and loosely in informal speech, it is probably best to replace the word with *in reality* in formal legal writing.

REASONING

Reasoning refers to the process by which a court or lawyer analyzing the law moves from a general proposition of law to a specific conclusion. This process is called deductive reasoning and is usually based on a syllogism. The legal reader is particularly interested in each step of the reasoning process, so consider the following when presenting your reasoning

1. Make the presentation of the general RULES thorough and precise. For example, if the entire statute is necessary for analysis, include the entire statute at the beginning of the reasoning process; if several cases must be synthesized to pull together one rule, synthesize them at the beginning of the analysis.

2. Explain any relevant exceptions to the rule.

3. Provide examples of previous applications of the rule.

4. Explain the LEGALLY SIGNIFICANT FACTS in the case being analyzed and show how those facts fit under the rules and the exceptions. Explain how this case compares to the examples.

5. Explain how this application results in the conclusion.

Remember to consider this list but not to follow it mechanically, because legal reasoning is a complex process, unique to each problem. For related information, see SYLLOGISMS, DISCUSSION SECTION; and ARGUMENT SECTION. For more suggestions on how to build reasoning, see Pierre Schlag and David Skover, *Tactics of Legal Reasoning* (Carolina Academic Press 1986).

RECOMMENDATIONS

Recommendations are appropriate in the Conclusion of a memo when the memo's purpose is to analyze the law and to predict the outcome in the context of pretrial discovery. Often the reader, another person in the same office, has assigned the writer the job of analyzing the law so that the reader can make a decision about a particular pretrial activity. For example, a partner might assign an associate to write a memo on whether or not the partner should move for summary judgment in a case. The associate should make the recommendation as specific as possible, after explaining the reasons in the DISCUSSION SECTION.

Similarly, an attorney might recommend certain action in an opinion letter. This recommendation should be within the realm of professional, not personal, advice. See MEMOS, OPINION LETTERS, and OPINION OR ADVICE?

RECORD, CITING TO IT

Cite to the record in the STATEMENT OF THE CASE in pretrial, trial, or appellate BRIEFS. Be scrupulous about using PINPOINT CITES in the references so the reader can quickly locate exact passages. For the reader's convenience, also refer to the record in the ARGU-MENT SECTION if the reader might need to check sources.

Check your jurisdiction for the appropriate format for these citations to the record. Some prefer parentheses, *(Tr 38)*, some use none, *CP 19*, and others use periods, *R. 76*. For related information, see Bluebook rule P.7, CITATIONS, and CITATIONS, PARALLEL.

RECUR OR REOCCUR?

The difference in meaning between these two words is slight, but in some contexts it is important. *Recur* implies that the event happens repeatedly; *reoccur* implies that the event is repeated only once.

REDUNDANCY

See CONCISENESS. For related information, see REPETITION.

REFERENCES

See CITATIONS; FOOTNOTES; and RECORD, CITING TO IT.

REFERENTS

See ANTECEDENTS.

REGARDLESS OR IRREGARDLESS?

Regardless, always.

REJECTION LETTERS

See BAD NEWS, SOFTENING IT and BAD NEWS, GIVING IT, subsection 1.

REOCCUR OR RECUR?

See RECUR OR REOCCUR?

REPETITION

Repetition by careful design works in legal writing. Rather than avoiding repetition absolutely, avoid it only when it does not have one of the following uses.

1. Use repetition when it is needed for ACCURACY.

If you mean *contract*, do not shift to *document* or *agreement*. Changing terms confuses legal readers, who will think that you must mean something else if you changed terms.

2. Use repetition when it is needed for READABILITY.

For example, repeating the same first word at the beginning of each item in a list can be very helpful to the reader when each item in the list is long. See LISTS, STRUCTURE OF.

> **Any proposed method for reducing marital status discrimination <u>must</u> reflect the statutory complexity creating discrimination, <u>must</u> avoid reproducing the undesirable effects of the current taxation structure, and <u>must</u> show awareness that compromising one or more important policy goals is necessary in any tax scenario.**

3. Use repetition as a transition to logically dovetail two sentences or paragraphs.

Repeating a key word from a previous sentence or paragraph shows how the idea that word represents fits in with the idea of the new sentence of paragraph.

> **Environmental Impact Studies could be handled similarly without <u>delaying</u> the hearing.**
>
> **Even if there were some <u>delay</u>, ...**

4. Use repetition when it is needed for EMPHASIS.

Sometimes the very fact that a repeated word gains attention can be an advantage. For example, you may repeat a word or structure that states a dramatic or important point.

> **The defendant stated this intention to his girlfriend. He stated it to his coworkers. He stated it to the cabdriver who took him to the airport.**

For related techniques, see ALLITERATION.

5. Use repetition when it is required by format or convention.

It is appropriate to repeat content from the main text in some circumstances. For example, conclusions and introductions, which summarize the body of a text, must by definition repeat content and KEY TERMS, if not whole sentences. Similarly, you will necessarily need to repeat some information when you write captions for APPENDICES, GRAPHS, or TABLES.

REPETITION OF SOUNDS

See ALLITERATION and ASSONANCE.

REQUESTS FOR PAYMENT

There are four do's here. First, do consciously decide what you want. If you want money, focus on that and set aside your moral outrage at the way you have been treated. In contrast, if you really want to express your moral outrage, do so in temperate language. Realize, however, that this expression may not do much to help you get your money.

Second, do consider the possible motivations your reader may have and try to employ those motivations to get what you want. Choose not what persuades you, but what will persuade your reader. For example, if you are trying to persuade a party to settle out of court, do not use threats when you think the party would view that threat as a challenge and submission as a weakness. In that situation, you might instead explain that the cost of litigation would exceed the cost of settlement. Similarly, if you think that the reader is someone motivated by certain values, try to explain how the action you recommend is consistent with those values. For example, you might argue that paying a bill is essentially the same as keeping a promise. In short, try to explain how the action you recommend is consistent with some goal the reader has. Try to help the reader feel good, or at least not defeated, about taking the action you recommend.

Third, do consciously decide what TONE you want to create. For example, do you want to be nice, giving the reader the benefit of the doubt, or do you want to be tough? If you want to be nice, you may use kind opening and closing paragraphs. For more on this, see BAD NEWS, SOFTENING IT. If you want to be tough, you may use shorter sentences and impersonal language. For more on this, see TOUGH, SOUNDING THAT WAY. For related information, see TONE IN LETTERS.

Finally, do make sure what you say is literally correct. Satiric comments or broad hints can be misread easily and can lead to further delays in getting the results you want. Do not resort to diatribe, even if your anger is completely justifiable. Lay out in objective language the facts, the options, and the results. Similarly, do not make empty threats; if your reader knows or finds out that one threat is empty, he or she may assume that later ones are empty too. See EMOTIONAL LANGUAGE.

RESEARCH STRATEGY CHART

The following ten-step Research Strategy Chart is designed to maximize your efficiency in the process of finding all the sources necessary to complete your research task. The first five steps take place before you leave your desk. Fight the temptation to run to the library without having completed this portion of the strategy. The preliminary issue statement is particularly important because it helps you focus your research from the very beginning. It is essential to do this before you leave for the library, so you can decide what books you should go to first, second, third, and so on. This saves the time spent wandering from one book to another.

For further elaboration on each step, see the specific pages cited to in Christopher Wren & Jill R. Wren, *The Legal Research Manual: A Game Plan for Legal Research and Analysis* (A. R Editions 2d ed. 1986). These cites are noted by *LRM*, followed by the specific page number.

RESEARCH STRATEGY CHART

At your desk

Step 1. Collect the facts.

Just as a journalist does, make sure you know the who, what, when, where, why and how of the facts. You can collect the facts by reading the complete file or transcript, taking notes during a client interview, doing your own discovery, and talking directly to the client. *LRM* 30.

Step 2. Analyze the facts.

Using whatever system you prefer or have, such as *West's* or *Lawyers' Co-op*, group the facts into their general categories. For West, use *Parties, Objects, Basis, Defense,* and *Remedy*. For Lawyers' Co-op, use *Things, Acts, Persons,* and *Places*. Give each category a page or column. Transfer your facts from Step 1 to these columns. Then brainstorm synonyms and antonyms for the facts in each column. These terms become your search words.

Step 3. Formulate a preliminary issue statement.

A. This can be done before you know the law by following a format that goes from general to specific, using the key words *under, did,* and *when,* as follows:

Under Missouri assault law, [general law—indicate as specific a category as you can without doing any research]

did Fred assault Harvey [legal question]

when he waved an unloaded gun in Harvey's face

[legally significant facts]?

The first part of the question tells you what books to look under, such as the Missouri Statutes Annotated index. The second part tells you what topic to look under in the book, such as *assault*. The third part tells you how to filter through the summaries of the cases found in the annotated statutes. For example, you would look for *cases involving a loaded gun or an unloaded gun waved in the vicinity of someone or in someone's face.* You can eliminate those cases whose summaries do not indicate a similarity to these legally significant facts.

B. Organize the issues logically. For example, put threshold issues such as *standing* first. *LRM* 37.

Step 4. Verify jurisdiction.

Make sure you know whose law applies. You can look at court papers in a case to make sure you know what court or even what judge is hearing the case. If there is a potential conflict of laws question or a question about whether federal or state law applies, make resolving the jurisdiction question the first issue when you begin your research.

Step 5. Make a research plan.

Map out where you will go first, second, and so on. It is crucial to think this through before you start researching to avoid wasting time wandering from shelf to shelf or from database to database at the computer. For example, after you look through the annotated statutes, you might plan to go to the Missouri Digest, then to the Missouri Patterned Jury Instructions, and then to SHEPARD'S.

At the library

Step 6. Find the law.

The purpose of this step is to make sure you find all relevant primary sources, provisions, statutes, regulations, and cases. If you were given a statute or case name, for example, you might start with A. If you were not given a known authority, you might start with B. And if you are completely unfamiliar with the area of law, you might start with C.

A. Known authority.
   (1) Statute or regulation. *LRM* 51.
      (a) Go to the statutes or regulations annotated for that jurisdiction.
      (b) Shepardize in the appropriate volume.
      (c) Check looseleafs if researching administrative regulations.
      (d) Do a computer search if available.
      (e) Check pocket parts and supplements.
   (2) Case. *LRM* 53.
      (a) Find the volume containing the case and review the headnotes.
      (b) Choose the headnotes that are pertinent and note the topic title and key or section number.
      (c) Retrieve the digest volume containing that topic and turn to the topic and section number; you now have all the published cases about that topic.

(d) Check the pocket parts.

B. Descriptive word or fact word.
   (1) Statute or regulation. *LRM* 46.
      (a) Take the list developed in Step 2 and look up those words in the index to statutes or regulations to see if there is a statute or regulation on that subject.
      (b) If so, follow steps listed in A(1) above.
   (2) Case. *LRM* 49.
      (a) Find the appropriate digest for that jurisdiction.
      (b) Take the list developed in Step 2 and look up those words in the index to the digest.
      (c) Move from the index to those topics in the digest.
      (d) Check pocket parts.
      (e) Use the words from your list to write a query and search the computer database.

C. Encyclopedias, treatises, and other sources useful for your own background. *LRM* 65.
   (1) Check the *A.L.R.* Quick Index. Use descriptive words; you may find a gold mine here if there is an annotation on your topic.
   (2) Check the *Index to Legal Periodicals* and the *Current Resources Index* for law review articles. Also check *C.J.S., Am.Jur.,* and the *Restatements*.
   (3) Check your library book catalogue for treatises on relevant topics.

Step 7. Read the law (before you copy it).
A. Evaluate internally. *LRM* 79.
   (1) Statute.
      (a) Evaluate the language of the statute itself.
      (b) Is there a general factual similarity to this case?
      (c) Is there ambiguity in the legislative intent that favors this case?
      (d) Does the statute's context give it a focus applicable to this case?
      (e) Does the statute's legislative history illuminate its meaning?
      (f) How do the canons of construction augment the statute's meaning? *LRM* 87–88.
   (2) Case.
      (a) Is there a factual similarity to this case?
      (b) Is the RULE pertinent and useful?
      (c) Is there a general similarity that is useful if the facts are recharacterized?
      (d) Does the POLICY provide a useful basis for argument?

B. Evaluate externally. (See Step 8 below.) *LRM* 89.
   (1) Current status.
      (a) Has the statute been invalidated, repealed, or amended?

        (b) Are these subsequent interpretations of cases useful to this case?

    (2) Extend the law.

        (a) Can a new rule or innovative twist be formulated?

        (b) Is the statute a codification or a departure from previous rules?

        (c) Has a novel policy or doctrine emerged?

Step 8. Update the law.

    A. Shepardize. *LRM* 95.

        (1) Find the right set of Shepard's.

        (2) Collect all the necessary volumes (see box in front cover of each volume).

        (3) Find the correct tables for your statute or case.

        (4) Find the volume and page number, or statute number.

        (5) Examine entry. For more detailed assistance, see SHEPARD'S.

    B. Check the pocket parts and supplements.

    C. Check the looseleaf reporter services.

    D. Do a computer search. *LRM* 133. See COMPUTERS FOR RESEARCH.

    E. Check other possible sources, such as newspapers, for recent opinions or references to the source.

Step 9. Take effective notes.

    A. Have a system and write out the plan. See NOTES. *LRM* 123.

    B. Reread your preliminary issues periodically to maintain your focus.

    C. Record full CITATIONS in proper form.

Step 10. Ask or call.

    Sometimes information is not easily available in print or your library does not have it. You may then find it more useful and efficient to ask esoteric questions of your librarian, the supervising attorney, another associate who has worked on similar cases, or an expert in the field. You may also find it more efficient to call sources, such as agencies that have set up a number for asking questions.

RESPONDENT

Respondent can be used as either a PROPER NOUN or a generic description, like *Appellant, Defendant,* and *Plaintiff.* When used as a proper noun, it should be capitalized and used without an article.

Respondent objects to Appellant's characterizing the case as a simple one.

When used generically, it should not be capitalized, and the article should be used.

The respondent filed the brief well within the time limits.

Lawyers use *respondent* both ways, so check the conventions of your office or particularly of your AUDIENCE. If your readers have no preference, choose whatever you prefer, but be consistent throughout the document. Avoid choosing the proper noun solely for CONCISENESS; omitting *the* will shorten your document but may create a telegraphic or harsh TONE.

RESTRICTIVE PHRASES

See THAT OR WHICH?

REVISING

Revising occurs after REWRITING in the WRITING PROCESS. During rewriting, you settled the document's content and organization; now you are free to concentrate on the expression of that content. Revising your expression includes refining small-scale organization, SENTENCE STRUCTURE, TRANSITIONS, PARAGRAPHING, GRAMMAR, and PUNCTUATION. For related information, see ORGANIZATION, SMALL–SCALE.

There are two things to remember about revising. First, do not revise while you write; this slows down both the writing and the revising processes. When you are writing, concentrate solely on your ideas, no matter how unpolished your writing may seem. Revise later. Second, when you revise, do it in stages. It is exhausting and inefficient to try to revise on every level at once. You can subdivide the time available for revising into categories that move from general writing problems to more specific ones. For ideas on what categories to use when, see WRITING PROCESS CHECKLIST, subsection 4.

REVISING THE WRITING OF OTHERS

See EDITING.

REWRITING

Rewriting follows the WRITING stage in the WRITING PROCESS, and it addresses content, large-scale organization, logic, and coherence. This is the stage where criticism takes over from creativity and the text starts moving from a writer-oriented first draft toward a reader-oriented final draft. But unlike REVISING, at this stage the writer is still concerned primarily with the document's legal aspects and its ideas rather than their final expression.

Rewriting should be done separately from the other stages in the writing process because the tasks it involves deserve specific attention.

263

It should also be done separately so that the writer concentrates on criticizing the content, not its expression. The most common mistake many writers make, one that costs them hours and hours, is to write, rewrite, and revise simultaneously. Some writers even try to polish. This approach forces the id of creative thought to clash with the super-ego of correction, an impossible and insufferable pairing. The result is often WRITER'S BLOCK. No wonder.

To focus instead on first things first, set aside a substantial amount of time to make sure that all possible ideas appear in the draft and that the content is accurate and thorough. This is when you check the document to make sure it fulfills its PURPOSE, answers the AUDI-ENCE's questions, includes all relevant law and facts, contains all points necessary in the LEGAL ANALYSIS, encompasses the appropriate SCOPE, and uses logical ORGANIZATION. For specific questions to ask during rewriting, see WRITING PROCESS CHECKLIST, subsection 3. The following list offers techniques to use as you ask those questions.

1. Decide on a central theme or message. Your thinking may have evolved as you drafted. Make your final decisions in this stage.

2. Check scope by filling in holes. Add any information or steps in the reasoning that are missing. But also fight the temptation to include information just because you have researched it or like it; if the reader does not need it, omit it. In general, delete repetition of content that is not needed for TRANSITION, EMPHASIS, or FORMAT.

3. Compare your original organization from prewriting to the result you read now. Make sure organization matches the theme. Also make sure that the subparts explain that theme and convey your message.

4. When you are sure that the paper is complete and unrepetitive, rearrange the parts in the order best suited to your audience and purpose. If necessary, abandon an organizational scheme that is not working. You may want to revisit the alternative versions you created during prewriting to make sure you have chosen the best one.

Once you have settled on an overall plan, use the following techniques to align and unify the document.

5. Check the HEADINGS, subheadings, and POSITIONS OF EMPHA-SIS to make sure that each indicates what part of the whole is about to follow and how it connects to the previous section or the overall message. Move paragraphs as needed until the order is correct and the headings reflect that order.

6. Check first sentences to make sure they contain concrete information that introduces each paragraph's ideas, connect to the previous paragraph, or clearly indicate any departure from a previous topic. Also make sure they echo TERMS OF ART where appropriate to carry

your message throughout the document. If someone speed-reads your document, they will look at first sentences.

7. Read aloud any sections that are not working if you have looked at the document too many times. Listen for ideas, connections, or omissions that would be jarring to a listener or reader. You may hear problems that you cannot see.

In summary, concentrate instead on the overall picture and on concise content. Avoid revising at this stage. You may be able to fix a term or a typographical mistake here and there, but be careful not to be drawn away from the legal and logical tasks of this stage. Do not waste time fixing a sentence you may later delete. It will waste time and later leave you tempted to keep the sentence even when it should be omitted. Instead, when you are satisfied that everything needed is present and in an overall logical order, then move to revising.

RHETORICAL QUESTIONS

Rhetorical questions, which have either an obvious answer or no answer, usually irritate legal readers and invite them to question your point. Therefore, avoid them. Ask questions only in your ISSUE STATEMENTS or QUESTION PRESENTED; give the answers to those questions in your ARGUMENT SECTION or DISCUSSION SECTION. To make a rhetorical point, state it in declarative sentence form.

RHYMES

Avoid them in legal writing unless you intend to be humorous and the humor is appropriate to the content and AUDIENCE. You may, however, use ALLITERATION if you use it with discretion.

ROUGH DRAFTS

See WRITING and WRITING PROCESS.

RULES

Legal rules are statements of law that provide the basis and structure for legal analysis. They are often general principles that can be applied to several situations, such as constitutional provisions or statutes. Sometimes they are derived from cases, where a judge has used a common law principle as the basis for the analysis. When a rule derives from cases, the writer must determine what rule previous courts used by looking at the court's foundation for its reasoning. When a rule is not explicitly stated, the writer must synthesize previous holdings to establish the general rule to be applied in this case. See SYLLOGISM, SYNTHESIS, and HOLDINGS.

Rules fall into a hierarchy of authority. Thus, if a constitutional provision is involved in your issues, it should be discussed first. If a statute is involved, it should come next, or first if no constitutional provision is involved. Case law comes last. If there is no constitutional provision or statute, then case law provides the rules. Consider the following in presenting the rules.

1. Place rules at the beginning of your DISCUSSION SECTION, ARGUMENT SECTION, or explanation in OPINION LETTERS.

Because legal rules provide the structure for your analysis or argument, the legal reader needs to know those rules right away. Similarly, the reader needs to know the rule's source, so cite accurately and thoroughly.

> **All citizens are protected from unreasonable searches not only in their homes, but wherever they have a right to be. Wash. Const. art. I, § 7.**

> **The Plaintiff's recovery is barred when the plaintiff's negligence exceeds the defendant's negligence. Or. Rev. Stat. § 18.470 (1999).**

> **Jury misconduct occurs when a juror supplies information to other jurors that is outside the recorded evidence of the trial and not subject to the protections and limitations of court proceedings. Salverson v. Anderson, 99 Wash. 2d 746, 752, 913 P.2d 827, 830 (1999).**

2. Decide how case law presents a rule.

For example, a case may explicitly state the definitive rule; if so, you may cite the case singly as the source of that rule. Or several cases may be synthesized to form the rule; if so, you must cite those cases separately, each standing for a proposition that contributes to the rule. Finally, several cases may provide a rule plus exceptions; if so, you should cite the case giving the rule first, with the cases giving exceptions after.

3. In constructing your rule from cases, synthesize when needed.

Synthesizing a rule means pulling pieces from several cases together. Courts do not always state these rules because they rule on specific factual situations and thus do not need to pull the larger rule together. As a result, you must try to do the synthesizing yourself when the courts have not done it. To do this, step back from the pieces and try to see the larger picture. Then characterize that picture in your own words as a topic sentence. (See TOPIC SENTENCES.) Follow this sentence with the sections of the cases that create this picture, and give appropriate citations.

4. When constructing a rule from cases, include exceptions.

Remember that any rule may have exceptions so, after making sure that the rule and its source are clear to the reader, follow with the exceptions.

5. Check for ACCURACY and LOGICAL LINKS.

Your presentation of the law outlines the structure of your entire analysis, argument, or explanation, so make sure the rules are accurately presented. Check for logical links between subparts, so that the reader knows exactly how the rule works when applied. Then you are ready to follow this logic in applying the rules to the facts of your analysis.

SAID

Substitute *this, that,* or a more detailed description.

This document was signed by the plaintiff.

rather than

Said document was signed by the plaintiff.

Arcane legal language includes *said* as an adjective; do not use it that way. Similarly, *said* was once used in legal documents to say, *I mean the one mentioned above, in contrast to any mentioned below or elsewhere.* But often no other one was mentioned, so *said* was nonsensical. When you need to distinguish one item from another, simply repeat the designation used earlier.

the 1985 contract

rather than

the said contract

For related information, see SUCH.

SALUTATIONS

The salutation is the line beginning with *Dear* that traditionally introduces the text of a letter. There are three common questions about salutations: (1) whether to include them, (2) how to write them when you do not know the sex of the reader, and (3) whether to punctuate them with commas or semicolons.

1. Including or omitting the salutation.

In general, include the salutation. Some writers omit the salutation in business letters, substituting instead a subject line, and this is not technically wrong. Omitting the salutation, however, makes the letter seem rather abrupt and impersonal, which is not the tone you usually want in a letter. For more on this generally, see TONE IN LETTERS.

2. Writing non-sexist openings.

If you do not know the sex of the person to whom you are writing, substitute the name without a title of *Mr.* or *Ms.*

Dear D. A. Young:

Dear Terry Holmes:

If you do not know the name, use the person's title or some appropriate generic term.

Dear Administrator:

Dear Client:

If you cannot come up with a generic term, you may use the following.

Dear Sir or Madam:

Use *Dear Sir* only when you are sure the reader is male.

3. Choosing commas or colons.

Use colons in business writing. If you are writing something that is a social courtesy, such as a thank you note or an expression of congratulations, you may use a comma. A colon would also be appropriate, except in a note that is much more personal than businesslike in tone.

SARCASM

Do not use sarcasm in legal writing; it is too easy for the reader to take it literally. Even if the reader catches your sarcastic TONE, that tone is usually inappropriate in legal writing. In general, sarcasm is only effective when writing to readers who already whole-heartedly agree with your position.

SAYING *NO*

Saying *no* to requests to do additional work may be hard for you, as it is for many lawyers. But maintaining a good quality to your writing will require you to learn how to do it. Taking on all requests eventually forces you to do mediocre work, which will damage your CREDIBILITY and reputation. In contrast, saying *no* when appropriate keeps the quality of your work high and may win you respect. To help you know when you cannot take on more tasks, stay aware of your deadlines and workload.

Depending on the PROFESSIONAL POSTURE you choose to project, you can refuse gently (*I would love to, but I don't think I can do a good job...*), firmly (*I cannot do that for you. I'm sorry.*), with limits (*Yes, I can do that for you but not until six weeks from now.*), or you can flatter (*Of all the people I enjoy working with, you are the one I enjoy most. But I cannot do it for you this time. Please ask again.*).

If you know that your refusal will cause you problems or create tension, try asking to be used as a back-up (*This is very inconvenient for me right now. Can you find someone else? If not, then get back to me.*) or give a long-term *no* (*I will do this last project for you, but I cannot be called upon with such short notice in the future.*) Find ways that work best with your personality and that of your associates. For related information, see MANAGING OTHER WRITERS, PERFECTIONISM, PROCRASTINATION, TIME MANAGEMENT, and WRITING PROCESS.

SCARCELY

Scarcely is an adverb that means *barely* or *assuredly not*. As such it has a negative meaning and should not follow another negative.

The defendant could scarcely deny the charges.

rather than

The defendant couldn't scarcely deny the charges.

Place *scarcely* just before the word or group of words that it modifies.

The defendant heard the pronouncement of sentence with scarcely a change in demeanor.

rather than

The defendant heard the pronouncement of sentence scarcely with a change in demeanor.

SCHOLARLY WRITING

Scholarly papers differ from other kinds of legal writing in AUDIENCE, PURPOSE, scope, technical details, and FOOTNOTES, all of which in turn affect your WRITING PROCESS. The following subsections help you identify these differences and how they affect the product. For specific ways to check the product, see SCHOLARLY WRITING CHECKLIST; for ways to adapt your process, see SCHOLARLY WRITING PROCESS. For related information, see PROCESS AND PRODUCT COMPARED.

1. Audience

As a scholar, you write for several types of readers. At the least, these readers expect creativity and demand careful and thorough treatment of the topic. Beyond that, some readers are other scholars, who are interested in the careful treatment of a narrow topic with exhaustive research contained in the footnotes. Others are practitioners, who often want practical answers to specific questions within one jurisdiction. Your readers may include any of the following:

(a) scholars and experts who know this topic very well,

(b) practitioners who are looking for innovative arguments,

(c) judges who want to be brought up to date on this topic,

(d) nonlawyers who want to understand this topic,

(e) editors who want excellence in their publication,

(f) future scholars looking for examples of creative analysis and thorough research,

(g) prospective future employers looking for original analysis and good writing, and

(h) faculty committees evaluating for tenure.

You need to keep these diverse readers in mind as you create the purpose and synthesize the substance of the paper. To do this, you might try to imagine all your potential readers gathered in one room; then create the TONE, ORGANIZATION, STYLE, and thesis that will satisfy both the most confused and critical readers' needs. See AUDIENCE.

Alternatively, you may choose one primary audience and write for that audience through the first draft and first stages of REWRITING. Then, in later stages of rewriting, adjust your ORGANIZATION to accommodate your other, secondary AUDIENCES. Thus you might (1) insert paragraphs that answer questions these readers may raise, (2) replace technical terms or add definitions of some TERMS OF ART, or (3) move some extensive technical details to TABLES, FOOTNOTES, or subsections so the readers who want to may easily skip over this detail and still follow your article.

2. Purpose

A scholarly paper may serve several purposes. For clearer focus, decide which purpose is uppermost. Write it down, then use that statement to maintain your FOCUS as you research, write, revise, and work through footnotes. While the following list is not exhaustive, use it to help identify specifically the purposes of your paper.

(a) to synthesize a body of law not yet drawn together,

(b) to criticize or support a recent opinion,

(c) to provide a reference on this area of the law,

(d) to expand a field of knowledge by offering a new direction,

(e) to criticize a theory or argument made by another scholar,

(f) to predict developments in the law,

(g) to suggest changes in the status of the law,

(h) to organize and clarify a confusing array of issues,

(i) to propose or advocate a plan of action on a legal issue,

(j) to secure tenure, or

(k) to secure clients.

No matter what the purpose, your thinking should be original, creative, innovative, and useful. You might keep in mind the question, "SO WHAT?" as you develop the paper's purpose, so you can relate each point to the overall purpose.

3. Scope

When you have determined the purposes, consider the scope that your purposes dictate. Write down a target page length; that number may help to keep your message manageable. Then ask yourself whether or not you can achieve your stated purposes in this amount of space. Narrow or broaden your topic accordingly so your audience will easily comprehend your message, the relevance of your research, and the originality of your commentary.

4. Technical Details

Before you begin researching, become familiar with your citation guide's current edition. This will enable you to record the full citations correctly as you find them. Having to return to the sources solely for citation information is time-consuming and irritating.

5. Footnotes

If you are doing traditional scholarly writing, use footnotes for any of the following three purposes: to give authority for all unoriginal propositions, to expand on authority by offering several other sources, or to add necessary details. For a more complete list of how to use footnotes, see SCHOLARLY WRITING CHECKLIST.

Avoid using footnotes to write another paper within this text, to argue with yourself, to record irrelevant sources, or to substitute for deciding where to put some information or analytical point. Footnotes should enhance the paper, not salve the writer's frustration at researching an unused source. Above all, do not diminish the impact of your analysis by making footnotes longer than the text.

SCHOLARLY WRITING CHECKLIST

As you refine your scholarly paper during REWRITING and REVISING, create your own checklist for the document, perhaps with the help of your editors or some of your readers. Use the following questions to get yourself started.

1. AUDIENCE

Does the paper take into account all intended audiences? For information on various readers, see AUDIENCE, CONTEXT–INDEPENDENT WRITING, REWRITING, and SCHOLARLY WRITING, subsection 1.

(a) Does the paper take into account your readers' backgrounds and how much information or expertise they already have?

(b) Is the paper layered where appropriate, so that readers can use the general or specific sections that are most useful to them? Does it use HEADINGS, FOOTNOTES, or PARAGRAPH BLOCKS so that the reader can easily identify each part's role in the whole? See also UNOBTRUSIVE DEFINITIONS; ORGANIZATION, LARGE–SCALE.

(c) Will any reader, at any point, not misunderstand the writer? For ways to keep the paper unambiguous, see ACCURACY, AMBIGUITY, TOPIC SENTENCES, and CONNECTIONS, MAKING THEM.

2. PURPOSE

(a) Is the purpose clear? For example, does the paper synthesize, summarize, clarify, or criticize? See SCHOLARLY WRITING, subsection 2.

(b) Is your purpose explicit or implicit in your message? Is the message captured in a precise and explicit thesis statement?

(c) Is the purpose explained early enough to satisfy the reader?

(d) Is the document's POINT OF VIEW clear at the outset? Is it consistent and unified throughout the document? Is it primarily persuasive or informative?

3. CONTENT

(a) Is the paper original, analytical, and creative, and not just descriptive?

(b) Is the research thorough enough to support the thesis statement and to be useful to the reader?

(c) Have all legal materials been accurately synthesized to support the thesis? Do all parts of the paper support the thesis?

(d) Are all relevant views on the topic presented accurately?

(e) Is extraneous or unhelpful material omitted?

(f) Do footnotes function properly, such as in the following ways:

(1) give authority for all unoriginal propositions;

(2) expand on one authority by offering other, related sources where appropriate;

(3) add detail, explanation, or definitions needed by the uninitiated reader;

(4) add detail for the reader using the paper as a scholarly tool;

(5) give the text of a statute, regulation, quote, or specific source being discussed?

4. ORGANIZATION

(a) Does the structure flow from substance?

(1) Are the parts of the whole congruent with some logical rationale? For example, some rationales used include parts used in previous cases, parts used in a statute, parts used in other legal documents, parts of an overall process, or different causes of one effect.

(2) Does the paper keep to that organization throughout, rather than shifting midstream?

(3) Is each section internally logical?

- Do paragraphs within each section connect to each other?

- Is each paragraph logically structured? Deductively? Inductively? Other?

- Are sentences organized logically, e.g., subordinate ideas are subordinated, main ideas appear in main clauses, and PARALLEL STRUCTURE is used to present like ideas?

(b) Is the structure obvious to any reader?

(1) Does the Introduction present a blueprint for the paper?

(2) Is each section's relationship to the thesis statement clearly reflected by its order in the organization?

(3) Is each section connected accurately and clearly both to the thesis and to previous and subsequent points?

5. PHRASING or STYLE.

(a) Are TERMS OF ART presented in the thesis statement and echoed throughout the document?

(b) Is phrasing clear?

(1) Is WORD CHOICE precise?

(2) Is PLAIN ENGLISH used, JARGON and LEGALESE omitted?

(3) Are subjects and verbs generally concrete?

(4) Do SUBJECT–VERB COMBINATIONS carry your message, remind the reader of the thesis?

(c) Is text readable?

(1) Is there no more than one main point per sentence?

(2) Are TOPIC SENTENCES generally the first sentences of paragraphs?

(3) Is PASSIVE VOICE avoided unless needed?

(4) Are NOMINALIZATIONS minimized or avoided?

(5) Are subjects and verbs close together?

(d) Does phrasing emphasize key points?

(1) Are key points made in POSITIONS OF EMPHASIS?

(2) Is REPETITION used effectively where appropriate?

(3) Does PARALLEL STRUCTURE reveal parallel ideas?

(4) Do SHORT SENTENCES make emphatic points or catch reader's attention? See SENTENCE LENGTH and SENTENCE STRUCTURE.

(e) Do all wording changes flow together to create an eloquent whole?

(1) Are all emphatic techniques reinforcing the content, rather than distracting from it?

(2) Are no phrases or techniques overused, so that they draw the writer's attention to the phrase itself?

(3) Is emphasis focused on key points, rather than invoked too much or indiscriminately?

6. MECHANICS

(a) Is GRAMMAR correct?

(b) Is PUNCTUATION correct?

(c) Are CITATIONS correct?

(d) Are all typographical errors corrected?

SCHOLARLY WRITING PROCESS

When working on a scholarly paper, your writing process will likely change because the PURPOSE, SCOPE, AUDIENCE, and DEADLINES for a scholarly paper differ from those used in practice. You will often have much longer to write a scholarly work than to write practical documents. You may not be given a topic, so you will need to add a step in the process for preliminary research to identify your topic. Thus your research will be more comprehensive, your writing will include more detail, and your rewriting may require more reorganization because of the paper's broader SCOPE.

Further, you will need more time to make sure that a scholarly paper is original, creative, interesting, thorough, and useful. Your scope may be broader or deeper, your CREDIBILITY more at stake, and your audience more diverse in experience and background. To adapt comfortably to these differences, you might want to include the following steps in your process.

1. Set your deadlines.

Set both your final and interim deadlines, and write them on your calendar. Take time to consider how this project will blend with your other work; keep balance in your schedule. When setting interim deadlines, you might include the following steps:

- Topic Selected
- Preemption Check Completed
- Research Completed
- Notes Completed
- Outline Drafted
- First Draft Completed, with Footnotes
- Further Research Completed
- Draft Rewritten for Organization, Content; Matched to Topic, Purpose, Audience, Scope
- Draft to Editor, or other reader
- Draft Revised
- Second to the Last Draft Completed
- Footnotes Checked for Accuracy and Citation Form
- Final Draft Completed

2. Select a topic.

Check the subject index in a secondary finding source such as the Index to Legal Periodicals, the Current Resources Index, Infotrac, Dialog, or Nexis. Read for a general understanding of topic that interests you, and take notes on specific ideas that catch your interest. Narrow your topic until it fulfills a scholarly purpose and is timely, useful, and interesting. See SCHOLARLY WRITING, subsections 1–3, and SCHOLARLY WRITING CHECKLIST, subsections 1 and 2.

If you have not done so already, state the topic in a thesis sentence, even if you do not use this exact statement in the paper. This one statement will help you retain your FOCUS throughout the process and should prevent you from going too far afield in your research.

3. Do a preemption check.

If you wish to publish the paper or if your reader expects originality, check to make sure your topic has not been preempted by another writer. You must do an exhaustive search of scholarly materials. Plan for a sufficient amount of time to do this, knowing it will be well-invested. The search will complete the research you started in your topic search and begin the research you will use in your paper.

If someone has come close to your topic, modify it so it adds something new. For example, you may have to create a theory, propose a statute, or offer a new synthesis. If you cannot add anything new, abandon the topic and try another.

4. Reconsider PURPOSE and SCOPE.

When you have secured and sufficiently modified your topic, identify more specifically your purpose and scope. See SCHOLARLY WRITING, subsections 2 and 3. List several possible purposes and decide which is uppermost; relate your ideas to your list throughout the process. Then identify the scope you expect to cover on your topic, and the page length. Similarly remind yourself of scope as you develop the project so you can adjust the topic if it becomes too narrow or broad.

5. Take accurate notes.

In particular, note TERMS OF ART, phrases that contribute to the development of your proof or criticism, and arguments that need refutation. Use the terms you capture in your notes to develop and refine the language of your thesis sentence.

If you are comfortable doing so, sketch an outline as you take notes. The outline should combine an accurate picture of your topic with your original idea about it. As you sketch, build logical connections between the research and your message, keeping the purpose and scope in mind. See ORGANIZATION. This is a good time in your process to get feedback, so you might want to go over the outline with your editor or professor.

6. Make a drafting plan.

You may want to draft in pieces, concentrating fully on each piece, or draft in one sitting. For example, if you have a historical background section, you might want to draft that in one sitting. Or if you are developing your argument, you might want to draft that without stopping. You may even want to draft the whole article all at once so you are forced to synthesize the document fully. Your topic can change so much that it loses its force and integrity, so be flexible enough to change your plan to suit the paper, but realistic enough to meet your deadline.

7. Begin drafting well ahead of a first draft deadline.

Because of its detail and length, scholarly writing requires more time. For example, you will need more time deciding what to include because you will have so many sources. Beware of procrastination at this point. If you are having trouble writing, see WRITING BLOCK, WRITING, PERFECTIONISM and PROCRASTINATION.

8. Decide how to use your footnotes.

Some writers are comfortable including the full citation and writing the whole footnote as they draft, which a strong OUTLINE will permit. Others add footnotes when REWRITING or in the early stages of REVISING. Avoid the other extreme of writing all footnotes after you have completed the draft; they will take too long to write and may be analytically divorced from the main text. See SCHOLARLY WRITING, subsection 5.

9. Plan for multiple redrafts.

Keep aware of the final deadline and pace yourself so you can redraft as much as necessary to explore the topic comfortably. You may need several drafts during REWRITING, for example, to get the content and logic to fit your purpose and message. You may need as many drafts for REVISING to capture TONE and VOICE.

10. Ask for comments and criticisms on the paper.

To gain specific advice, you might want to send a cover memo with the paper asking questions about the draft and how to handle particularly troublesome places. The reader, by responding to your specific questions and adding other comments, will offer valuable evidence of audience reaction. Then you can adjust the draft to make it clearer. If you have more than one reader, compare suggestions and pay special attention to the common points. Attend to the problem the readers see; if you disagree with their solutions, fashion one that is better. Criticism from many readers should strengthen your paper, make it more accessible to a variety of readers, and offer you more writing techniques. For ideas on how readers may react, see EDITING.

11. Read the paper once just for technical details.

Refresh yourself on accurate Bluebook usage and make sure that every citation is accurate and correct. You might want to work backward or on the second half of the paper first, where there are usually more mistakes. For more techniques, see POLISHING.

SECTION

Section should always be spelled out when it begins a sentence. In text, also spell out *section* except when referring to a U.S. Code provision or a federal regulation. For further reference, see Bluebook rules 6.2(b) and 12.9. If you have the symbol *§* on your typewriter or word processor, use that symbol in footnotes and cites. Use *s.* or *sec.* only if your jurisdiction permits.

SELF– OR SELF?

Use *self-* when adding it as a prefix to another noun: *self-interest*, *self-serving*, and *self-sufficient* Use *self* as the first syllable in words such as *selflessness*, *selfish*, and *selfsame*. For related information, see HYPHENS.

SEMICOLONS

Semicolons have two uses.

1. You may use a semicolon instead of a period between two sentences if those sentences are closely related logically but could each stand as complete sentences.

The Plaintiff did not intend to destroy another's property; he broke the window only because he saw flames inside the house.

Avoid, however, allowing yourself to use semicolons without clarifying the logical relationship of your points.

This action violated Tremont's rights to both freedom of speech and due process.

rather than

This case involves not only freedom of speech, but also due process; each of these issues indicates that Tremont's rights were violated.

Do not use a comma between two independent clauses unless a conjunction such as *and* follows the comma. This error occurs frequently when *however* connects the clauses.

Cutts denied being at the scene of the crime; however, he admitted having been there two hours earlier.

rather than

Cutts denied being at the scene of the crime, however, he admitted having been there two hours earlier.

2. You must use a semicolon, instead of a comma, at the end of each element in a list if a comma occurs within any one element in the list.

The Company warrants for one year that its compressors (1) are free from defects in material and workmanship; (2) have the capacities and rating set forth in the Company's catalogs, provided that no warranty is made against corrosion, erosion, or deterioration; and (3) meet all relevant federal safety standards.

The Company is not liable for any delay in performance due to any of the following:

(1) any act of God, including but not limited to floods, epidemics, fires, storms, or earthquakes;

(2) any acts of others beyond the reasonable control of the Company, including but not limited to strikes or other labor disturbances, riots, wars, acts of civil or military authority, or acts of the Customer; and

(3) any cause beyond its reasonable control, including but not limited to delays in transportation, inability to obtain necessary materials or components, or labor shortages.

The semicolon helps the reader see where each item on the list begins and ends.

Do not use a semicolon at the end of each element in a list solely because the list is tabulated rather than run in text. Commas are still sufficient if there are no commas within any of the items listed.

"Remanufacturing equipment" included the following processes:

(1) disassembly to a predetermined standard established by the Manufacturer for each model,

(2) cleaning,

(3) refinishing,

(4) inspecting and testing to new machine test standards,

(5) installation of all retrofits, and

(6) operational testing.

For related information, see CLARITY; TRANSITIONS; HOWEVER; and LISTS, STRUCTURE OF.

SENTENCE LENGTH

In general, avoid making sentences longer than three lines of text. The one exception to this is sentences containing lists, which are easier to read because of their more obvious structure.

A doctor may forego disclosure to his patient if any of the following situations occur: (1) if the patient is unconscious, incompetent, or otherwise incapable of understanding the information; (2) if the patient is a minor; (3) if in the doctor's opinion the information would have a disproportionately adverse reaction on the patient's ability to make a rational decision; or (4) if an emergency exists which allows no time to safely consult with the patient.

One handy way to check sentence length is to scan several pages of your text and mark slashes after each period, which you can do without actually reading the text. Then look at the slashes. If you see several sentences in a row that run more than four lines, try to shorten at least one.

Similarly, if you see several sentences in a row that are one line long, try to combine two of them or make some other changes. This will help avoid a choppy tone. Occasionally, however, you may want this choppy effect.

The major purpose of the trial court's established procedure is to give the litigants a fair opportunity to address their claims and have them resolved by a court of law. <u>That purpose was met here. The litigants had eight years of opportunity. In this context, their arguments on appeal are particularly specious.</u> ...

For related information, see SENTENCE STRUCTURE; SHORT SENTENCES; and TOUGH, SOUNDING THAT WAY.

SENTENCE, PARTS OF

Knowing the parts of a sentence can help you understand SENTENCE STRUCTURE, which in turn can help you write sentences that convey your meaning clearly and emphasize your points effectively. If you have trouble identifying such things as verbs or indirect objects, this quick overview may help.

1. Verb.

Each sentence has at least one verb. The verb expresses either an action, such as *hit* or *received*, or a state of being, such as *is* or *seemed*. The verb may be one word, such as *signed* or *appeared*, or more than one word, such as *must complete* or *will have been signed*. When the verb contains more than one word, it is called a *verb phrase*.

The following verbs express an action.

Faulkner <u>signed</u> a waiver of rights form.

All nonresidents living in Illinois for more than three months of a calendar year <u>must complete</u> the following section.

The defendant <u>agreed</u>.

The contract <u>will have been signed</u> by that date.

The trial court <u>determined</u> that the defendant's statements were voluntary and <u>admitted</u> them at trial.

The following verbs express a state of being.

The settlement <u>seems</u> reasonable in light of the facts.

The plaintiff <u>is</u> a former employee of Stills, International.

In this case, nevertheless, the problem <u>exists</u>.

For more information see VERBS, TENSES; VERBS, AUXILIARY; VERBS, IRREGULAR; VERBS, LINKING; VERBS, MOODS; or VERBS, PARTICIPLES.

2. Subject.

Each sentence has at least one subject. The complete subject is the person, thing, or idea about which the verb speaks, and may be one word or many.

<u>Faulkner</u> signed a waiver of rights form.

<u>All nonresidents living in Illinois for more than three months of a calendar year</u> must complete the following section.

<u>The defendant</u> agreed.

<u>The contract</u> will have been signed by that date.

<u>The trial court</u> determined that the defendant's statements were voluntary and admitted them at trial.

<u>The settlement</u> seems reasonable in light of the facts.

<u>The plaintiff</u> is a former employee of Stills, International.

<u>The defendant's statements</u> were voluntary.

The simple subject is the main word in the complete subject.

All <u>nonresidents</u> living in Illinois for more than three months of a calendar year must complete the following section.

280

3. Predicate.

Each sentence has a predicate. The predicate is the part of the sentence that says something about the subject.

All nonresidents living in Illinois for more than three months of a calendar year must complete the following section.

The defendant agreed.

The trial court determined that the defendant's statements were voluntary and admitted them at trial.

The contract will have been signed by that date.

The settlement seems reasonable in light of the facts.

The plaintiff is a former employee of Stills, International.

The defendant's statements were voluntary.

Every predicate includes at least one verb, and it may include any or all of the following: direct objects, indirect objects, prepositional phrases, and participial phrases.

4. Direct Object.

A direct object is the person, object, or idea receiving the action of the verb.

The plaintiff built the house with his own hands.

Faulkner signed a waiver of rights form.

The defendant's action destroyed that right.

All sentences have a subject and predicate, but not all have a direct object.

5. Indirect Object.

An indirect object receives the direct object, rather than the action of the verb.

The plaintiff gave the defendant the house when she agreed to cohabit.

Here, *the defendant* received the house, and thus is the indirect object. *The house* is the direct object, because it was the object of the verb, *gave*. Not all sentences have an indirect object.

6. Prepositional Phrase.

A prepositional phrase is a group of words that work together to show the relationship of a noun or pronoun to the rest of the sentence. This noun or pronoun is called the object of the preposition. A preposition, which is always the first word in a prepositional phrase, shows how the rest of that phrase is logically related to the sentence. Examples of prepositions are *of, to, on, off, between, through, in, at, without, over,* and *under.* The following examples of prepositional phrases illustrate the variety of information they can convey.

He built the house with his own hands.

All nonresidents living <u>in Illinois for more than three months of a calendar year</u> must complete the following section.

The contract will have been signed <u>by that date</u>.

The settlement seems reasonable <u>in light of the facts</u>.

7. Participial Phrase.

A participial phrase is a group of words that work together to show the relationship of some action to the rest of the sentence. A participle, which is always the first word in a participial phrase, is either the *-ed* or *-ing* form of a regular verb, *(followed, following, covered, covering)* or the past tense or *-ing* form of an irregular verb *(held, holding)*. The following examples illustrate how participial phrases can be used in a sentence.

The boat, <u>built by Mr. Tremat</u>, should not be considered community property.

The attorney focused her argument on this issue, <u>building carefully on these facts</u>.

<u>Covered by snow</u>, the edge of the ditch was not visible.

The statute <u>covering this issue</u> is unambiguous.

This right, <u>held inviolate since the founding of our country</u>, must not now be extinguished.

Any court <u>holding on this issue</u> must address the elements of the statute.

8. Clause.

A clause is a group of words that includes both a subject and a predicate.

  subject   predicate
<u>The trial court</u> <u>determined this issue</u>.

In contrast, a phrase does not include both a subject and a predicate.

a case of first impression

determining this issue

There are two kinds of clauses: independent (or main) and dependent. An independent clause can be set off as a sentence by itself.

The defendant knew or should have known this.

The company gave a free water heater to residential customers.

Every sentence must include at least one independent clause.

A dependent clause cannot by itself form a sentence because it is logically dependent on an independent clause.

> that the plaintiff would not be aware of the stock market usage of the phrase "passed its dividends"

> who installed electric space heating

This logical dependence is signalled by the CONJUNCTION that introduces the dependent clause, which is called a subordinating conjunction. For related information, see SUBORDINATION.

Make sure all dependent clauses are part of a larger sentence including an independent clause.

> **The defendant knew or should have known that the plaintiff would not be aware of the stock market usage of the phrase "passed its dividends."**

rather than

> The defendant knew or should have known. That the plaintiff would not be aware of the stock market usage of the phrase "passed its dividends."

> **The company gave a free water heater to residential customers who installed electric space heating.**

rather than

> The company gave a free water heater to residential customers. Who installed electric space heating.

For related information, see SENTENCE STRUCTURE.

SENTENCES, MAIN

See TOPIC SENTENCES.

SENTENCE STRUCTURE

Mastering the basics of sentence structure provides a valuable tool for effective writing. After you learn how to change the structure of a sentence, you can use that skill to emphasize or de-emphasize points, to increase READABILITY, to change the TONE of your text, and to clarify TRANSITIONS between paragraphs and sentences. For help identifying the grammatical parts of a sentence, see SENTENCE, PARTS OF.

What follows are explanations of four basic sentence structures (subsections 1–4) and examples and explanations of ways you can exploit those basics to create sentences that are both readable and effective (subsections 5–7).

1. Simple Sentence.

Grammatically, this sentence includes only one set of SUBJECTS and VERBS, although it may have many modifying phrases.

```
        S       V
This case involves three issues.
```

```
        S              S        V
Mr. Smith and his attorney will confer on the matter tomor-
row.
```

```
          S              S     V                    V
The defendant and his wife ransacked the house and took
items worth $3,000.
```

Strategically, use a simple sentence that has only a few words, usually fewer than ten, if you want the dramatic impact that a simple sentence can have.

> **The Court of Appeals refused to consider this argument because it "was not properly ... presented to the trial court." The court did not elaborate.**

2. Compound Sentence.

This structure includes two or more independent clauses joined by a conjunction, semicolon, or colon. An independent clause could be set off as a sentence by itself.

```
   S     V                          conjunction
There can be no negligence without duty, and in this case
  S   V
there is no duty.
```

```
   S     V                          semicolon
There can be no negligence without duty; in this case, no
  S   V
duty exists.
```

```
               S                  V    colon  S  V
In this case, one element of negligence is missing: there is no
duty.
```

This structure can create a one-two punch. This effect will be stronger if the second of the joined sentences is short. For related information, see CONJUNCTIONS, SEMICOLONS, and COLONS.

3. Complex Sentence.

In a complex sentence, one or more DEPENDENT CLAUSES are inserted into another sentence, which is the independent clause.

dependent clause

> **Because more married women entered the labor market as second earners,**

independent clause

more married couples were subject to the tax penalty.

The independent clause includes the main subject, verb, and object of the sentence. Because this is the structural heart of the sentence, you want to put your main information here.

More married couples were subject to the tax penalty.

Often you will want to use dependent clauses to add some background information, elaboration, or other less important points to the sentence. A dependent clause cannot by itself form a sentence because it begins with a subordinating word and thus is logically dependent on an independent clause.

because more married women entered the labor market as second earners

The complex sentence is useful because it allows the writer to show the logical interrelationship of two or more points while giving more emphasis to one point. As a result, the complex sentence is common in legal writing. To use it effectively, however, you must keep the complex sentence readable and logically structured.

This court interpreted this statute broadly in previous cases, when it applied the statute to parents of minor children, trustees of the estates of handicapped adults, and foster parents.

rather than

This court, when it in previous cases applied the statute to parents of minor children, trustees of the estates of handicapped adults, and foster parents, interpreted this statute broadly.

Avoid using complex sentences exclusively; also exploit the strengths of simple and compound sentences. Too many complex sentences make the text less interesting, because VARIETY is lacking. If all your sentences are complex, try restructuring some important points into simple sentences.

Also avoid overdoing the complexity of the sentence. In general, do not insert more than two dependent clauses in one sentence; doing so gives the reader a bite too big to chew. If you decide you must show the logical interrelationship of more actions, try putting those actions in separate sentences and using a connecting word or phrase that explains that logical interrelationship.

Waivers of constitutional rights not only must be voluntary; they must also be knowing, intelligent acts done with sufficient awareness of the relevant circumstances and likely consequences. Breckenridge v. United States, 900 U.S. 321, 323 (1999). Furthermore, waiver of the right to counsel cannot be presumed from a silent record. Kelstad v. Karney, 969 U.S. 506, 516 (1999).

For more on the use of the complex sentence, see subsection 7. For help connecting two sentences, see TRANSITIONS and CONNECTIONS, MAKING THEM.

4. Inverted sentence.

One final structure you can use occasionally is the inverted sentence. In this structure, some part of the predicate, such as the object of the verb, comes before the subject.

Imprudent it was, but not illegal.

rather than

It was imprudent, but not illegal.

In the inverted version of this sentence, the predicate adjective, *imprudent* is placed before the subject, *it*, rather than after the linking verb *was*. The inverted sentence is dramatic precisely because the parts of the sentence are out of their usual order. It is so dramatic, however, that it is hard to find an occasion to use it in legal writing without sounding self-conscious, as would be the case if someone said, *While coming to work today, an old friend I saw.*

5. Using subjects and verbs effectively.

Put your main point in the main subject and verb in your sentence. Conversely, de-emphasize points by putting them in DEPENDENT CLAUSES. For example, the following sentence emphasizes *he had slowed and was not accelerating* by making that the main subject and verb.

Although the defendant had not come to a full stop at the official stop sign, he had slowed to less than five miles per hour and was not accelerating at the time of the accident.

6. Choosing the best sentence structure.

In general, vary your sentence structure. This VARIETY should come naturally, however, out of the logical structures needed by your content. Never use a sentence structure that goes against the logical structure of your content. To do so is tantamount to signalling that you plan to move to the right lane on a freeway and then moving to the left lane instead. Even if the reader manages to keep up with you, that reader will be distrustful and unhappy. For more help in determining what structure fits your content, see subsection 7.

7. Inserting information in a sentence.

Although the unmodified, simple sentence is strong and effective, you will usually need to add more to the sentence because you need to add more information. There are three places where these extra phrases can be inserted.

(a) Insert extra phrases after the independent clause.

> This inflationary effect was especially marked for two-earner married couples, <u>whose income is aggregated for tax purposes</u>.

> Triavil offered no treatment or cure for tension headaches, <u>as testified by Dr. Paul Wyles</u> (R. 1159).

> The minority arrived at the same conclusion, <u>although for different reasons</u>.

This structure is the mainstay of communication because it is the easiest for the reader to follow. For example, in the following sentence you understand **the point immediately** because you got the independent clause right away, before getting the elaboration.

> **I saw an old friend while coming to work today.**

As such, this structure is useful for presenting routine information that needs no special emphasis.

> **This inequity affected more people in the early 80's when more married women entered the labor market.**

It is also useful for presenting information that is complex and thus must be presented in a simple form.

> **Unmarried individuals paid substantially greater taxes than married individuals between 1948 and 1969, in some cases more than 40% in excess of a married individual's tax on an identical income.**

(b) Insert extra phrases before the independent clause.

> <u>Until recently</u>, others have supported inserting legislative veto provisions in statutes covering most agency rulemaking.

> <u>Despite the difficulty of this test</u>, the gravity of the situation required that it be done.

This structure, a mainstay of storytellers, is useful when you want to create a touch of suspense. For example, after reading the following sentence, you expect more after hearing the introductory phrase.

> **While coming to work today, I saw an old friend.**

The change in structure alone tells the reader that this is the beginning of a story. You might use this touch of suspense to present either facts or an argument.

> **Pointing the gun at the teller, the defendant ordered her to fill the bag with cash.**

> **Because there was no timely notice, this opportunity for hearing provided no opportunity at all.**

Additionally, placing information before the independent clause is a useful way to provide a transition at the beginning of a paragraph. In the following example, the information placed at the beginning of the paragraph both reminds the reader of the topic of the previous paragraph and shows the reader how that topic relates to this paragraph.

> **Environmental Impact Studies could be handled similarly, without delaying the hearing.**

> **Even if there were some delay, that delay would present no procedural difficulties.**

Finally, placing information in a dependent clause before the independent clause can signal to the reader that the added information is less important than the independent clause.

> **Although there are three kinds of marital status discrimination, this comment focuses only on the marriage penalty.**

This structure can be useful when you need to include an unfavorable fact and you want to make that fact seem as unimportant as possible.

> **Although Mr. Allerton was in the room during the signing of the will, he was there only because it was his habit to sit in the living room while reading the evening paper.**

(c) Insert extra information in the middle of the independent clause.

> **Anorexics, <u>by failing to eat</u>, passively expose themselves to harm.**

This structure, a tool of orators, creates a very formal tone. For example, the following sentence sounds rather stuffy.

> **I, while coming to work today, saw an old friend.**

This structure is harder to read because to understand the main point the reader must remember the first part of the sentence, read the interrupting clause, and then reunite the last part of the sentence with the first in his or her memory. Therefore, avoid using the structure in sentence after sentence; give the reader breathing space between these difficult sentences. Also, avoid allowing the interruption to exceed seven or eight words. After that long an interruption, the reader would have to reread the sentence to get the point.

> **The burden is on the defendant to show, not just that the tax is excessive, but also that the defendant was taxed for more than its fair share.**

288

> These issues, controversial but crucial, must be resolved by this court.
>
> Dr. Barnard, who attended the plaintiff immediately after the accident, has testified that her internal injuries were caused by the faulty seatbelts.

For information in problems associated with long interruptions, see AGREEMENT, SUBJECTS AND VERBS.

SENTENCES WITH *AND*

See SENTENCE STRUCTURE, subsection 2 on compound sentences; LISTS, STRUCTURE OF; and COMMAS.

SETTLEMENT LETTERS

A settlement letter is a letter written to encourage a party to settle a case. It is usually written by one client's attorney and directed to the other client's attorney. A settlement letter is designed to inform the reader of the writer's argument and to persuade the reader to accept that argument. Consider the following in writing a settlement letter.

1. Choose the approach you think is most likely to influence the other attorney. For example, if you think the attorney can be persuaded gently, you might want to begin with a friendly opening, show you have considered the other side, and then build your argument, leading to the settlement offer. If you think this attorney would be more convinced by a stronger opening, start with the offer of settlement. For related information, see PERSUASIVE WRITING and AUDIENCE.

2. Make sure the attorney knows that you understand the other client's position. For example, if the client and attorney have already offered a settlement, remind them that you are aware of that offer, of how much it was, and that you are grateful for the offer.

3. Choose a TONE appropriate to the method of persuasion, such as tough if you expect unreasonable opposition, or friendly if you want them to be convinced that your offer is fair. For more information, see TONE IN LETTERS.

4. Follow a format that includes the following, adjusting the order and content to suit your purpose, tone, and audience:

(a) a heading,

(b) a salutation,

(c) an introduction that identifies the settlement purpose of the letter,

(d) your terms for settlement and the reasoning behind them,

(e) a course of action on the settlement matter,

289

(f) a specific directive to the attorney to call you or answer your offer of settlement,

(g) a closing. For help here, see CLOSINGS FOR LETTERS.

See also GENERAL CORRESPONDENCE LETTERS, PERSUASIVE WRITING, OPINION LETTERS, and TONE IN LETTERS.

SEXIST LANGUAGE, WAYS TO AVOID

The first thing to remember when avoiding sexist language is that it is legitimate and even desirable to use *he* or *she* when you are talking about a specific person, as you usually are in BRIEFS or MEMOS. Sexist language here would be to use *he* when referring to a woman or *she* when referring to a man.

Sometimes, however, you will be discussing general principles that apply to all persons. When a singular pronoun is needed in that situation, use *he or she*, or *she or he* if you prefer. If you find yourself awash in *he or she's*, you can use any of three techniques to avoid the pronoun problem.

1. Reword the phrase to omit the pronoun.

Anyone desiring a position with this firm should submit a resumé at the interview.

rather than

Anyone desiring a position with this firm should submit his or her resumé at the time of his or her interview.

2. Substitute *one* throughout the text.

One cannot apply for a loan if one does not have collateral.

rather than

A person cannot apply for a loan if he or she does not have collateral.

This technique, however, is hard to use gracefully. It often creates phrasing as awkward as the original *he or she*.

3. In general discussions, such as in law review articles, refer to people in the plural so that you can substitute *they* for *he or she*.

All attorneys must adjust their trial strategies in response to this ruling.

rather than

Each attorney must adjust his or her trial strategies in response to this ruling.

Do not, however, resort to using a plural pronoun to refer to a singular noun.

Anyone desiring a position should submit a resumé.

rather than

Anyone desiring a position should submit their resumé.

This use of the plural pronoun is not only grammatically incorrect, but also dangerously ambiguous. For example, *each child shall inherit an equal share of the land as long as they live* could result in confusion about what happens if one of the children dies.

Do not resort to using S/HE. It is convenient for the writer but not for the reader, who will stumble slightly over the term, substituting *he or she* to read the sentence. Always write with the reader's convenience in mind, rather than your own.

If you find that nothing you try sounds graceful, choose the accurate *he or she* rather than the inaccurate *he*. In legal writing, a conflict between accuracy and elegance should always be resolved in favor of accuracy. For avoiding sexist language when beginning a business letter, see SALUTATIONS. For related information, see AC-CURACY.

SHALL

In all legal writing except LEGISLATION, use *must* instead of *shall* to state that something must be done; use *may* when stating something that may be done. Legislation traditionally treats *shall* as establishing a requirement, and therefore *shall* is not ambiguous in that context. The general public, however, does not necessarily give *shall* this more specific reason. To them, *shall* is often an archaic or fancy version of *will*. They also may read *shall* as meaning either *must* or *may*, and thus it can be ambiguous.

I shall attempt to go over Niagara Falls in a barrel.

For this reason, *must* is usually the more precise choice.

S/HE

Resist the temptation. Use *he or she*, or *she or he* if you prefer. *S/he*, besides looking funny, is hard to read aloud, and anything that is hard to read aloud is hard to read silently. Write for the reader's convenience; the reader will be grateful. If *he or she* seems cumbersome to you, see SEXIST LANGUAGE, WAYS TO AVOID for other tactics.

SHEPARD'S

Shepard's Citations is indispensible for updating the law. It is also an excellent source for finding other cases relevant to your topic. *Shepard's* is the main resource book you can use to determine whether the source you are using has been overturned, distinguished, endorsed, or modified in any way. In other words, this lets you know if your source is still usable law. When using *Shepard's*, follow these steps.

1. Find the proper set of *Shepard's* in the library. For example, if you are updating a Third Circuit Decision, you should have *Shepard's Federal Citations.*

2. Make sure you have all the volumes; check the box in the lower right hand corner of the most recent volumes, which will tell you what volumes you need.

3. Find the correct tables, including the table for the parallel citation. For example, if you are using the *Minnesota Reporter* and Shepardizing a Minnesota case, make sure you also Shepardize its parallel citation in the *Northwest Reporter*; the tables are not identical.

4. Find the volume number of the statute, case, or law review article that you are using.

5. Find the beginning page or section number of that text.

6. Review the signals and the raised numbers. The signals, which are described in the beginning of each *Shepard's* volume, let you know if the case was subsequently overturned, if it has been distinguished from other cases, if there is a dissenting opinion, and so forth. The raised numbers refer to the specific HEADNOTES in the published case.

7. Note that there are differences in *Shepard's* for the type of law you might be Shepardizing. For example, cases, statutes, regulations, law review articles, ordinances, court rules, city charters, and constitutions are all Shepardized differently. Inspect the set you are using for specific guidelines.

See also RESEARCH STRATEGY, step 8; and UPDATING THE LAW. For more extensive detail in Shepardizing, see Christopher Wren & Jill R. Wren, *The Legal Research Manual: A Game Plan for Legal Research and Analysis* (A–R Editions 2d ed. 1986).

SHORT SENTENCES

Short sentences provide one of the most effective ways to emphasize a point.

This was an error.

He failed to do so.

The Court of Appeals refused to consider this argument because it "was not properly ... presented to the trial court." The Court did not elaborate.

Several short sentences in a row also create a clipped, no-nonsense tone.

My client, Ms. Ambrose, does not intend to pay this bill. She has no reason to pay this bill. She did not receive any

software from your company. She did not order any software from your company. Until receiving your bill, she did not know your company existed.

Avoid using short sentences for unimportant points or using several short sentences in a row when you do not want a clipped or exasperated tone. This will help you avoid creating any unintended EMPHASIS.

For related information, see SENTENCE STRUCTURE and TOUGH, SOUNDING THAT WAY.

SHOULD

Should has several meanings, and thus can create some AMBIGUITY. In the following sentence, for example, it could mean *ought, must,* or *may.*

The affidavit should be in our office at least five days before the scheduled hearing.

In general, legal writing needs the meaning of *must;* use *must* whenever that is your meaning.

The affidavit must be in our office at least five days before the scheduled hearing to insure the proceeding going forward.

Should can be useful when you want to imply that something was not done that should have been.

The police should have read him his <u>Miranda</u> rights before searching his car.

Should is sometimes used to imply doubt that something will happen in the future. But avoid this use, because this implication is ambiguous and thus may not be inferred by the reader.

The contract should arrive in our office by next Thursday.

You may consider using *should* for tact when the statement is an indirect request, although *ought* may actually be the precise choice.

To insure the proceeding going forward, the affidavit ought to be in our office at least five days before the scheduled hearing.

The safer route may be to make a direct request.

Please send the affidavit to our office at least five days before the scheduled hearing to insure the proceeding going forward.

When the statement is a comment on what may happen, use *may* rather than *should.*

The affidavit may arrive in our office several days before the actual hearing.

To increase readability, avoid using *should* at the first of a sentence when you really mean *if.* While *if* is precise because it can only mean that what follows is an *if . . . then* situation, *should* is less precise because it can introduce either a question or an *if . . . then* situation.

For related information, see VERBS, TENSES.

SIC

This is a Latin word that means *thus* or *so.* Use it within quotations to inform the reader that the error in the text was in the original, rather than an error you made when copying the quote. *Sic* is surrounded by brackets.

The police read defendant his <u>Mirenda</u> [sic] rights.

For related information, see QUOTATIONS, HOW TO PUNCTUATE.

SIGNALS

Signals are used before CITATIONS as shorthand to indicate their exact use. As such, signals replace unnecessary text, such as *the court held that* or *another court also agreed that.*

The Bluebook separates signals into four categories:

(1) signals that indicate support,

(2) signals that suggest a profitable comparison,

(3) signals that indicate contradiction, and

(4) signals that indicate background material.

Keep these four categories in mind and use the signals accordingly. For further reference, see Bluebook rule 1.2.

1. Signals that show supporting authority.

    (a) Citing without using any signal indicates that a cited authority clearly states the proposition, is the source of a quotation, or is the authority referred to in text. This is the cite used most often to indicate the direct support for the authority used in legal analysis.

    (b) *See* indicates that the cited authority clearly supports the proposition but does not say it explicitly. Use *see* when the proposition in the text is not directly stated by the cited authority but obviously follows from it.

    (c) *E.g.,* indicates that the cited authority is an example of another case that states the proposition; this signal also indicates that the cited authority is among several other authorities that also state the proposition, but that citing all of them would not be helpful or necessary. This signal can also be combined with other signals, such as *See, e.g.,* or *But see, e.g.*

(d) *See also* indicates that the cited authority adds source material that supports the proposition. Use this signal when you have already cited an authority that supports your proposition and you want to add other cites. It is often good to use PARENTHETI-CALS after these additional cites.

(e) *Cf.* means that the authority supports a proposition different from the main proposition you have stated, but sufficiently like that authority to lend support. Because this comparison needs explanation, use a parenthetical here as well.

(f) *Accord* indicates that the cited authority states or clearly supports the proposition, even when it has not been directly quoted. It is in accord with the text that has been quoted or referenced. For related information, see CITATIONS, STRING.

(g) *See generally* is used to refer to several sources that address the proposition or topic. Be careful not to overdo lists of authority. See CITATIONS, STRING.

2. Signals that show a comparison favorable to your point.

Compare ... [and] ... *with* ... [and] ... indicates a comparison that will support or illustrate the proposition stated in text. Again, this needs explanation, so use parentheticals.

3. Signals that show contradicting authority.

(a) *Contra* indicates that the cited authority directly states the opposite of the proposition. Use this where you would have used [no signal] for support, that is, if this authority is exactly opposite to the proposition.

(b) *But see* indicates that this authority clearly supports a proposition contrary to the main proposition. This would be used where *See* would have been used for support.

For related information, see CITATIONS; CITATIONS, PARALLEL; and CITATIONS, STRING.

SIMPLE SENTENCE

A simple sentence includes only one set of SUBJECTS and VERBS, although it may have many modifying phrases.

      S   V
This <u>case</u> <u>involves</u> three issues.

      S   S   V
<u>Mr. Smith</u> and his <u>attorney</u> <u>will confer</u> on the matter tomorrow.

295

S   S   V   V

The <u>defendant</u> and his <u>wife</u> <u>ransacked</u> the house and <u>took</u> items worth $3,000.

Strategically, however, use a simple sentence that has only a few words, usually fewer than ten, if you want the dramatic impact that a simple sentence can have.

The Court of Appeals refused to consider this argument because it "was not properly ... presented to the trial court." The court did not elaborate.

For related information, see SENTENCE STRUCTURE and SHORT SENTENCES.

SIMPLICITY

Simplicity has gained status in legal writing over the years, mostly because of the universal overload under which lawyers and judges operate; most legal readers want to finish the job and go home. Confine your presentation to the information essential to your case, nothing more and nothing less. Achieving the delicate balance between thoroughness and simplicity in your writing will win you respect and credibility.

To achieve simplicity, concentrate on (1) using TERMS OF ART and other KEY TERMS in subjects and verbs, (2) focusing issues specifically, (3) using clear and logical organization, (4) REVISING for CONCISENESS, and (5) using PLAIN ENGLISH, rather than LEGALESE or FLOWERY LANGUAGE. For specific suggestions, see REPETITION; PARAGRAPHS; WORD CHOICE; ORGANIZATION, SMALL–SCALE; ISSUE STATEMENTS; and SENTENCE STRUCTURE.

SINCE OR BECAUSE?

See BECAUSE OR SINCE?

SINGLE QUOTATION MARKS

Although writers in some other countries conventionally use single quotes ('___') instead of double quotes ("___"), the United States currently uses double quotes. Single quotes are used only for A QUOTE WITHIN A QUOTE.

For related information, see QUOTATIONS, HOW TO PUNCTUATE.

SINGULAR OR PLURAL?

When deciding whether to use the singular or plural form, always use the one that is grammatically accurate, even if it seems wordier or less smooth.

Each petitioner must sign his or her full legal name.

rather than the slightly less precise

All of the petitioners must sign their full legal names.

Use consistent numbers throughout.

Each petitioner must sign his or her full legal name.

rather than

Each petitioner must sign their full legal names.

When you may accurately use either singular or plural,

consider the following guidelines.

Use the plural *they* for any one of these reasons.

1. You want to distance the reader from the idea or persons the term represents.

Injured plaintiffs must file their claims before the statute of limitations runs.

2. You need to avoid using *he or she* too much.

Attorneys must file their complaints by the fourth day of the month in which they are requesting a hearing.

3. The point you are making applies logically to a class of people or a concept, rather than an individual.

The asbestos victims in this class action request monetary damages for several reasons.

Use the singular *he or she* for any of these reasons, when doing so does not cause distracting repetition.

1. You want to pull the reader closer to the idea or persons the term represents.

Each defendant must be held accountable for his or her part in this tragedy.

2. The point you are making applies logically to a concern for an individual rather than a class of people or a concept.

Unlike an older child, a toddler cannot describe a parent's abusive actions. But he or she can feel the results of the abuse, and may be permanently harmed.

SLANG

Avoid using slang in legal writing because it is too informal and often too imprecise.

SLANTED LANGUAGE

See EMOTIONAL LANGUAGE.

SLASH

The only time you should use a slash (/) in legal writing is when you are writing a form in which the person signing is to mark out the inappropriate word, as in *Mr./Ms./Mrs./Miss*. For related information, see AND/OR and SEXIST LANGUAGE, WAYS TO AVOID.

SMOOTHNESS

See COHERENCE, EMPHASIS, and CLARITY.

SO

So has several different meanings and thus must be used carefully to avoid potential ambiguity. For example, when used as a conjunction, *so* can introduce a clause stating a consequence of the point stated before *so*.

The defendant was in the hospital at the time, so he could not have been at the meeting.

When *so* introduces a clause stating a consequence, substitute *and as a result* if *so* could be ambiguous.

The defendant was in the hospital at the time, and as a result he could not have been at the meeting.

So can also introduce a clause stating the purpose of the point stated before *so*.

Mrs. Williamson asked for the check to be mailed to her mother's home so her husband could not intercept it.

To avoid ambiguity, substitute *so that* when you are introducing a clause stating a purpose.

Mrs. Williamson asked for the check to be mailed to her mother's home so that her husband could not intercept it.

So may also intensify an adjective or adverb.

So serious was the oversight that, had it not been caught by Ms. Abrahams, it would have cost the company millions of dollars.

The car moved so slowly that it created a traffic hazard.

SOMEBODY

Use *someone* instead in formal legal writing because *somebody* sounds informal. Like *someone*, *somebody* is singular and takes a singular verb.

Somebody claims to have seen defendant elsewhere that night.

SOMEDAY OR SOME DAY?

Someday means *at some future time*; *some day* means *a day in the past or the future*.

SOMEONE

Someone is singular and uses a singular verb and a singular pronoun.

If someone needs to contact me, he or she should call this number.

SOMETIME OR SOME TIME?

Use *sometime* to refer to an indefinite point in time.

This question will reoccur sometime in the future.

Use *some time* to refer to an indefinite quantity of time.

We need to spend some time identifying all the options we have when the question does arise.

SO WHAT?

You may have encountered this comment on your paper, or you may be feeling it about a point you are trying to make. Most legal readers ask, *So what?* whenever they read legal documents. Those readers have been taught to question each authority, each premise, each idea. They expect explanations, yet they also expect no extraneous information.

So what? usually indicates that the opposite has occurred: the reader has encountered an idea that is not fully developed or is extraneous. Or it may only seem so because it is inadequately connected to the overall message, to the previous point, or to the next point.

Make *So what?* work for you. Ask yourself that question during PREWRITING, as you decide what to include; during REWRITING, as you decide what is and is not essential to the analysis; and during REVISING, as you check your expression for accuracy. Answering the question throughout the document will ensure that no one in your AUDIENCE will have to ask it.

SPECIFICITY

See PRECISION.

SPELLING PROBLEMS

See MISSPELLINGS, HOW TO AVOID.

SPLIT INFINITIVES

An infinitive consists of *to* plus the verb. Some readers believe split infinitives are grammatically incorrect, so avoid splitting them when possible.

to move afterwards

rather than

to afterwards move

On rare occasions, however, a split infinitive will avoid ambiguities.

The mayor agreed to only suggest the alternative if the matter came up in committee meeting.

In this case, putting *only* before *to* would communicate that this was the only thing to which the mayor agreed.

The mayor agreed only ....

Putting *only* after *suggest* would communicate that this is the only alternative the mayor would suggest.

suggest only this alternative ....

When forced to make a choice like this, choose the clarity of the split infinitive over the elegance of the ambiguous unsplit version.

You may often find, however, that you can avoid the problem by restructuring the sentence altogether.

The mayor agreed that she would only suggest the alternative if the matter came up in the committee meeting. She would refrain from requesting it.

This is the safest route; your revised version will offend no one and still avoid ambiguity. If you choose to boldly split with this tradition, consider whether this minor rebellion will cost you CREDIBILITY with your reader, and then decide. For related information, see PRECISION; ACCURACY; and AMBIGUITY, WAYS TO AVOID.

SQUINTING MODIFIERS

A squinting modifier could be called shifty-eyed, because its gaze shifts indecisively between two different terms. Because it could be modifying either term, it creates AMBIGUITY.

The point the appellant is making logically applies to the Fourth Amendment claim.

Logically, as it is currently placed, could modify either *making* or *applies.* Often the phrase's position creates the ambiguity, and reordering solves the problem.

The point the appellant is making applies logically to the Fourth Amendment claim.

At other times clearer verbal signals may be needed.

The point, which the appellant has logically presented, applies to the Fourth Amendment claim.

STANDARD OF REVIEW

The standard of review is the standard by which appellate courts measure errors made by trial courts on specific legal issues. The standard of review differs with each legal issue and must therefore be discovered by researching that specific subject matter.

For example, an appellate court in one state might reverse a trial court in child custody matters if the trial court *abuses its discretion* by failing to make specific findings of fact under that state's statute. Derive the specific definition of the standard of review for your issues by examining the facts of each case in that subject area and determining the exact circumstances under which the court was willing to reverse the trial court. Those circumstances define what constitutes *abuse of discretion.*

In a similar case in another state, however, the appellate court might reverse the trial court only if the trial court has *manifestly abused* its discretion. Worse, your state may have two standards. This is because the term *standard of review* is relatively new and has only recently been singled out as a specific entity of analysis. If you find contradictory standards, inform the reader of the contradiction or choose that standard most recently used by the highest court in your state.

In writing an APPELLATE BRIEF, make sure you state for the court the standard of review for the issue you are appealing. Place the discussion of the standard of review at the beginning of each main section right after the point heading.

301

STATEMENT OF FACTS

This is one section in an objective memo. It may be placed either after the caption or after the QUESTION PRESENTED and Brief Answer. It contains both LEGALLY SIGNIFICANT FACTS and any BACKGROUND FACTS or EMOTIONAL FACTS needed to orient the reader to the information being analyzed in the memo. The writer may choose a chronological or topical organization, depending on the amount and kind of information to be presented. This section should be concise, giving only necessary information. For ways to do this, see CONCISENESS. For related information, see MEMOS, CAPTIONS, BRIEF ANSWERS, CHRONOLOGICAL ORGANIZATION, and TOPICAL ORGANIZATION.

STATEMENT OF THE CASE

The Statement of the Case section is used in persuasive legal writing, such as Memoranda of Points and Authorities, PRETRIAL BRIEFS, TRIAL BRIEFS, APPELLATE BRIEFS, or SETTLEMENT LETTERS. It is written in persuasive style and contains LEGALLY SIGNIFICANT FACTS, BACKGROUND FACTS, and EMOTIONAL FACTS. Often this section is divided into *Procedural History*, which outlines the procedural details of the case, and *Statement of Facts*, which gives the chronological or topical organization of the events leading to the motion, trial, settlement, or appeal. For related information, see PERSUASIVE WRITING, CHRONOLOGICAL ORGANIZATION, and TOPICAL ORGANIZATION.

STATISTICS

Whenever you use statistics, be sure they are logically connected to your legal reasoning, are well-documented, and advance the point you are making. Do not allow them to distract from your main PURPOSE.

Statistics are most often useful as support for an explicit contention. For example, you could support an assertion that a faulty taillight rarely causes injury with statistics on the number of accidents in which a faulty taillight was cited as a cause. To make its significance clear, you would then explain the significance of the statistic to your case. Thus statistics are usually best placed in the middle of a PARAGRAPH or PARAGRAPH BLOCK. Unless their significance is striking and intuitively clear, statistics are not as effective as opening or summary sentences.

Also consider your AUDIENCE and its particular reaction to statistics, if you can predict it. Statistics stir varied responses in readers. Although some readers revere statistics, others have a reaction similar to that credited to Disraeli: "There are three kinds of lies—lies, damned lies, and statistics." Thus their persuasive power is uncertain. For related information, see GRAPHICS, WHEN TO USE and GRAPHICS, HOW TO USE.

STATUTE DRAFTING

See LEGISLATION.

STRING CITES

See CITATIONS, STRING.

STRUCTURE

See SENTENCE STRUCTURE or ORGANIZATION, LARGE-SCALE.

STUFFY LANGUAGE

See PLAIN ENGLISH, FLOWERY LANGUAGE, and TONE.

STYLE

In legal writing, style refers primarily to objective or persuasive style. The first appears in MEMOS and OPINION LETTERS, the second in BRIEFS and SETTLEMENT LETTERS.

Style is also used to refer to grammar rules, which have to be followed, such as rules regarding usage, PUNCTUATION, verb tenses, and SUBJECT–VERB AGREEMENT. See BENDING THE RULES.

Finally, style may refer to a writer's personal method of presentation, which has developed throughout his or her writing experience. As clothes reflect your personal tastes, so your written product reflects your personal level of formality, your choice of TONE, and your patterns of ORGANIZATION. For a discussion of aspects of writing that influence your style, see OBJECTIVE WRITING, PERSUASIVE WRITING, WORD CHOICE, POSITIONS OF EMPHASIS, SENTENCE STRUCTURE, TONE, and TONE IN LETTERS.

Focus on these aspects one at a time to become comfortable and versatile with each. Begin with the basics: sentence structure and word choice. As versatility develops with these basics, keep adding other skills to develop your objective, persuasive, and scholarly styles. Gradually, these skills will merge into a pattern that is your own style.

Do not, however, become preoccupied with the problem of developing or losing your personal style. Instead, focus on mastering the

S

various aspects of good writing. From this seed of individual mastery, your personal style will blossom naturally and inevitably.

SUBHEADINGS

See POINT HEADINGS and HEADINGS.

SUBJECT

See SENTENCE, PARTS OF, subsection 2.

SUBJECT–VERB AGREEMENT

Sometimes, when the subject and verb are far apart in a sentence, the writer accidentally uses a plural verb with a singular subject, or a singular verb with a plural subject.

In the interviews, <u>each</u> of the many therapists currently finding their practice restricted by these recent holdings <u>is</u> [not <u>are</u>] less likely to be willing to treat these patients.

One good way to avoid having this happen is to avoid putting more than seven words between your subject and verb. This will not only help you avoid agreement problems, but will make your writing more readable. See READABILITY.

SUBJECT–VERB COMBINATIONS

Subject-verb combinations help move the legal reader along when they are specific and concrete; they halt and reverse the reader when they are vague and abstract. Because the subject and verb are the main part of the sentence, try to place important information in your subjects and verbs; concentrate especially on using TERMS OF ART and KEY TERMS. Do not waste subjects and verbs on information that is unimportant to the reader.

The <u>show-up I.D. negated</u> the effect of capturing the defendant one block from the crime.

rather than

The <u>court stated</u> that the show-up I.D. negated the effect of capturing the defendant one block from the crime.

In this example, the legal point is more important than the narration that the court stated it. Use a citation to give that information.

Also avoid abstract combinations like *it is*, *there is*, *there were*. Use nouns instead of those pronouns, specific verbs instead of those verbs of being.

> **False imprisonment occurs** when a person is restrained without his or her consent.

rather than

> **There is false imprisonment when a person is restrained without his or her consent.**

For related information, see CONCRETE NOUN, TERMS OF ART, and CONCISENESS.

SUBJUNCTIVE TENSES

See MOODS.

SUBORDINATING CONJUNCTIONS

See CONJUNCTIONS; EMPHASIS; SUBORDINATION; and BAD NEWS, SOFTENING IT.

SUBORDINATION

You are subordinating when you make one point in a sentence depend structurally on another point.

> **Although our client did not look both ways immediately before stepping into the street, this fact alone is not enough to constitute contributory negligence.**

The writer here subordinates a fact that works against his case by placing it in a dependent clause beginning with *although*. Similarly, the following sentence downplays an unfavorable fact by putting it in a dependent clause beginning with *even though*.

> **Even though he had not come to a full stop at the stop sign, the defendant had slowed to less than five miles per hour and was not accelerating at the time of the accident.**

See also SENTENCE, PARTS OF; BAD NEWS, SOFTENING IT; and EMPHASIS.

SUBSTANTIVE OR PROCEDURAL?

See PROCEDURAL OR SUBSTANTIVE?

SUCH

Avoid using *such* as an unnecessary adjective, which is sometimes used in arcane legal writing. Substitute *this, that,* or a more detailed description.

> **This document was signed by three witnesses.**

rather than

Such document was signed by three witnesses.

SUMMARY OF THE ARGUMENT

The Summary of the Argument is a separate section used in long briefs to state the gist of the writer's arguments without referring to authority. The section appears just before the Argument. The purpose of this section is to pull together the writer's arguments without stopping the flow with references to details of authority. Thus at one glance the reader can understand the writer's argument.

A general rule for writing summaries is to use one paragraph per issue. Make sure you state the Summary of the Argument in your own words, as if you were making an oral presentation, rather than solely quoting cases.

Writing a Summary of the Argument can be a good way of GETTING STARTED. Even if this summary is not included in the final product, it can help you focus issues, answers, and explanations. For related information, see ISSUE STATEMENTS, BRIEFS, and APPELLATE BRIEFS.

SUPPORT

The legal reader generally does not believe any assertion that is not backed by authority such as case law, statutes, or regulations. Therefore, support your assertions wherever possible. In a BRIEF, for example, if you are illustrating why your client should have been able to breach a restrictive covenant, give examples of cases where others have breached a restrictive covenant and show the legal, factual, economic, or policy similarities to support your position. When REWRITING, read your document to make sure you have not made assertions that are not connected to authority. See ANALYSIS, APPLICATION, SYLLOGISM, SYNTHESIS, and STARE DECISIS.

SYLLOGISMS

A syllogism is a form of deductive reasoning that consists of a major premise, a minor premise, and a conclusion. It moves from general to specific.

Major premise: All dogs have four legs.

Minor premise: Spot is a dog.

Conclusion: Therefore Spot has four legs.

Syllogisms are similar to the logical structure used most often in legal writing. The major premise is created by the law itself, which is the rule or rules governing the specific situation. The minor premise is created by the application of RULES to the specific facts of the case being analyzed. The conclusion is the result, whether it be a prediction, as in a memo; a holding, as in opinion; or a request for relief, as in the ARGUMENT SECTION of a brief.

Major Premise: False imprisonment occurs when there are words or acts intended to confine, there is actual confinement, and there is awareness by the plaintiff that he or she is confined.

Minor Premise: Martin told Knight he intended to keep him in the car, he did keep Knight in the car for seven hours, and Knight knew he could not get out of the car.

Conclusion: Martin falsely imprisoned Knight.

When reading cases, make sure that you yourself understand the connection among all three parts of the syllogism. If the connections are faulty, these holes in the reasoning may allow you to distinguish the case from the case that you are advocating; you can then fill the holes according to your own reasoning and perhaps reach a different result.

When writing, make sure your reader understands the connections among these three parts. For more suggestions on how to build reasoning, see Pierre Schlag & David Skover, *Tactics of Legal Reasoning* (Carolina Academic Press 1986). For writing techniques that help show the connections, see CONNECTIONS, MAKING THEM.

TABLES

See GRAPHICS, WHICH FORM TO USE, subsection 5.

TACT

See BAD NEWS, GIVING IT; BAD NEWS, SOFTENING IT; TONE; and TONE IN LETTERS.

TAKING NOTES

See NOTES.

TENSES

See VERBS, TENSES.

TERMS OF ADDRESS FOR COURTS

See JUDGES, HOW TO ADDRESS.

T

TERMS OF ART

Terms of art are those terms used specifically in the law to describe legal theories, RULES, or doctrines. They are the words that carry the most weight in legal writing and the words on which the legal reader focuses. Because of their importance to the legal reader, terms of art should be used as subjects and verbs.

The Parol Evidence Rule prevents admission of this evidence.

Terms of art should also be used at POSITIONS OF EMPHASIS, such as the beginnings or ends of sentences.

Plaintiff brought an action under the theory of res ipsa loquitur.

The police escaped the strict requirements of the search and seizure rule by claiming that they were operating under exigent circumstances.

Washington is one of a minority of states to use the Family Car Doctrine.

Terms of art should always be used in the legal questions of QUESTIONS PRESENTED or ISSUE STATEMENTS. Make sure they are used precisely as intended under the authority specific to them.

Under the exigent circumstances exception to the Fourth Amendment, were police in "hot pursuit" when defendant had sold drugs to an undercover officer four hours before the search and had not left the premises?

Under Washington tort law, can a five-year-old commit an intentional tort when he pulls a chair away from an elderly lady who is in the process of sitting down?

Use Latin terms when they are terms of art, such as *res ipsa loquitur*. Do not, however, use them when they can be replaced by plain English. For example, use *before* rather than *a priori*. Similarly, terms such as *hereinafter* or *aforesaid*, are LEGALESE, not terms of art.

THAT NEEDED?

Omit *that* only if doing so will not confuse the reader.

Mr. Salovar agreed he would pay the overtime costs.

or

Mr. Salovar agreed that he would pay the overtime costs.

but

The court decided that the ruling was an abuse of discretion.

rather than

The court decided the ruling was an abuse of discretion.

If you have difficulty determining when the omission of *that* would confuse the reader, try the following test. First write the sentence without *that*.

The prosecution found the key here was the defendant's own admission.

Then put your finger over everything that comes after the first noun or pronoun following the verb. If the uncovered portion would not make sense by itself, you may omit *that*, as in the following example.

The defendant believed his safety procedures were adequate.

Here, *the defendant believed his safety procedures* would not make sense by itself, so *that* is not required.

If, however, the uncovered portion could make sense by itself to the reader but is incorrect, as in this example, you need to add *that* to avoid confusion.

The prosecution found that the key here was the defendant's own admission.

For related concerns, see THAT OR WHICH?

THAT OR WHICH?

In legal writing, especially legal drafting, maintaining a distinct meaning for *that* and *which* is useful. This remains true even though many writers in other fields do not bother to use these terms so carefully.

1. Use *that* when you are adding a phrase to narrow the range of items covered by a word.

All cars that remain in the lot after 10 p.m. will be towed.

[R]emain in the lot after 10 p.m. narrows the range of *cars* under discussion, so *that* should introduce the phrase. Do not put commas before or after this narrowing phrase. This punctuation rule is important, because even more general writing still observes this distinction.

2. Use *which* when you are adding a phrase that does not limit the range of items covered by the word it modifies.

Your car, which was still in the lot at midnight, was towed.

The range included in *your car* is not limited by the following phrase, so *which* is the correct word to begin the phrase. Do put commas both before and after a *which* phrase. The commas work like parentheses, showing that the phrase could be lifted from the sentence without changing the essential meaning. In summary, if a comma, *which*; if not a comma, *that*.

3. For ACCURACY, use both commas and *which* to distinguish non-limiting phrases from limiting ones. If you do not, your sentences may suffer from AMBIGUITY.

The taxes, which have been paid, should not appear on this statement.

or

The taxes that have been paid should not appear on this statement.

rather than

The taxes which have been paid should not appear on this statement.

In the first version, all the taxes have been paid. In the second, some of the taxes have been paid. In the last version, however, you are not sure if all or part of the taxes have been paid.

4. *Which* can be substituted for *that* when two *that's* appear in a row.

That which is good is not always pleasant; that which is pleasant is not always good.

rather than

That that is good is not always pleasant; that that is pleasant is not always good.

When possible, however, revise to avoid *that which*, which is rather awkward to read.

THE

Do not omit *the*, *a*, or *an* solely to gain conciseness.

The owner of the car gave the keys to Hendricks, who was supposed to move the car to a legal parking spot.

rather than

Owner of car gave keys to Hendricks, who was supposed to move car to legal parking spot.

Omitting these articles will give the text an abrupt tone, like a telegram, and will decrease the text's READABILITY.

THEIRS OR THEIR'S?

Theirs, always.

THERE IS OR THERE ARE?

The answer to this question depends on the word that follows the verb, the PREDICATE adjective. If it is plural, use *are*.

There are twelve members on each jury in this state.

If it is singular, use *is*.

There is one alternative we have not yet discussed.

Sometimes the choice is not so obvious with more abstract nouns. For example, either of the following sentences is correct.

There are precedents for this line of reasoning, although they address different factual situations.

or

There is precedent for this line of reasoning, although the cases establishing this precedent address different factual situations.

For related information, see SINGULAR OR PLURAL? or NONE, SINGULAR OR PLURAL?

THERE IS ... THAT

Omitting this phrase when you can do so creates a more concise sentence.

No cases address this issue directly.

rather than

There are no cases that address this issue directly.

Similarly, revise to omit *it is ... that* and *there are ... that*. For related information, see CONCISENESS.

THEY OR *HE OR SHE?*

When choosing between the plural or singular form, first determine whether one of the two forms is required for ACCURACY.

If a member chooses to go forward with a grievance, he or she must explain that grievance in writing.

rather than

If members choose to go forward with a grievance, they must explain that grievance in writing.

The second version could be read to exclude an individual from bringing a grievance, and so would be unclear.

If accuracy does not limit you, you may use the plural form to avoid using *he* or *she* too much.

The members had the opportunity to air their concerns at the November meeting.

Use the plural number throughout the text as needed for consistency. For related information, see SINGULAR OR PLURAL?

311

THIS

This frequently creates ambiguity because it can refer to any idea or object and because it often starts a sentence.

You must ultimately make a judgment about the weight of the evidence. This judgment will help you decide what the verdict should be.

rather than

You must ultimately make a judgment about the weight of the evidence. This will help you decide what the verdict should be.

In the second version, it is not clear whether *this* refers to *judgment* or *evidence*. To avoid the problem, add the appropriate noun after *this*. For related information, see AMBIGUITY, WAYS TO AVOID, subsection 2.

THOUGH OR ALTHOUGH?

See ALTHOUGH OR THOUGH?

TIME MANAGEMENT

Writing well often involves managing your time, particularly when you have several projects to finish. Creating your own approach to time management will enhance your ability to accommodate your personal life while meeting your professional demands. To increase your writing efficiency and effectiveness, first follow three important rules: compartmentalize, concentrate, and condense.

1. Compartmentalize.

Pull together similar tasks, such as researching several short projects, dictating letters, or polishing outgoing documents. As much as you can, do similar tasks in one block of time. This approach eliminates unnecessary changeover time, and your mind can remain focused on each type of task.

2. Concentrate.

Having compartmentalized tasks, devote all of your attention to the compartment in front of you. You should find that your mind works more easily and quickly when you give it only one type of task at a time.

3. Condense.

After you have created compartments and increased your concentration, try to decrease the quantity of time you spend without jeopardizing the quality of the product. Unmonitored writing will expand to fill any amount of time available. Sometimes changing the medium will help; you might dictate letters rather than write them by hand, or revise on the word processor rather than literally cutting and pasting. Become more alert to ways that increase speed without causing unnecessary stress.

When you have taken command of these three tasks, you can then move on to improve your overall approach to managing your time. For example, you may want to add some of the following goals to your list.

4. Write down directions.

If you have had trouble understanding what is wanted of you, try writing directions down when you receive them. Then, if there is a question, you can refer to your notes rather than contacting your supervisor or retracing your steps. Similarly, if you give directions, write them down. Then, when you are busy, the person to whom the task has been delegated can continue to work without having to interrupt you. Writing precise directions can save hours of volleying between attorneys. It also saves start-up time reminding yourself where you should be going on the project.

5. Touch each piece of paper only once.

Try to avoid shuffling paper too much. When dealing with the miscellaneous papers that cross your desk, decide what to do with each piece of paper and avoid letting it pile up. That way, you will not feel overwhelmed by the sight of more paper adding to the papers you are producing. For example, as you read each day's mail, try to discard what you can, dictate or write needed responses, and take action or give directions for the action to others. Try to give each paper a home by filing it immediately, marking a deadline on it, or forwarding it to the person who should take action. You can also use computers to store documents, which may make finding them faster and easier.

6. Say *no*.

Know your own capacity as a writer, and try to decline projects that will overwhelm you or interfere with the quality of other projects. If you are under particular pressure from a supervisor, choose a gentle way to say *no* or set aside time to meet with that person in the future to discuss reasonable workload. See SAYING *NO* for specific suggestions.

7. Percolate, don't procrastinate.

Rather than putting a project aside when you receive it, try to begin immediately, even if you are only collecting the ingredients and turning on some energy. Take a few minutes to gather facts, hypothesize some issues, and note a possible research strategy. Then stop; leave those ideas while you work on another compartment. Percolating usually allows your mind to create better ideas than doing the project all at once does. In fact, it is often necessary to good legal analysis because it allows time for your ideas to steep. See PROCRAS-TINATION, PERFECTIONISM, and WRITING PROCESS.

8.   Use the calendar and the clock.

Know your major deadlines and pace yourself accordingly. Use the clock as a helpful friend who reminds you when the mind is wandering unnecessarily, when the meeting you are conducting is going too long, or when you are tempted to research longer than you should. Writing tasks often take longer than you anticipate, so set a realistic ending time before you begin.

9.   Delegate whenever you can.

Ask others to do tasks that they can, and save your time for matters only you can do. This can be a hard adjustment to make, especially if you are used to doing everything for yourself. For ways to do this, see EDITING and MANAGING WRITERS.

10.   Choreograph your day.

Use your high energy times for the most critical tasks or those you like least; use your low energy times for the least critical or those you like most. When your energy wanes, answer calls, hold meetings, or do other activities that will keep you awake. Then your day will become more even, rather than clustered around least favorite and most favorite moments.

Although you may see many changes you want to make in managing your writing time, implement changes gradually. This minimizes upset to either your own balance or that of your associates. You might start by changing your approach to one major writing project or by trying one new technique for a period. At the end of that project or period, assess the success of the change and revise your writing process as needed. If the change worked, try it next on two projects at once. Gradually, you can fold your new techniques into your schedule, and give yourself a year or more to transform yourself into an efficient and effective writer.

TITLES OF JUDGES

See JUDGES, HOW TO ADDRESS.

TO ALL INTENTS AND PURPOSES

Find a shorter way to say this idea or omit the phrase. If the sentence needs something more, try to find one word that makes your point.

Therefore my client is innocent.

rather than

To all intents and purposes, my client is innocent.

TO BE

To be, in its various forms, communicates a continuing state of being. When used appropriately, this verb does not add unnecessary words to the language. Therefore do not try to avoid using *was, were, are,* or *is;* instead avoid their overuse. *To be* has three main uses: (1) as a linking verb, (2) as a helping verb, and (3) as a statement of existence.

1. As a linking verb.

This is its most recognized use, where it often is the only verb in the sentence.

> **Strict interpretation of this statute <u>is</u> essential to the preservation of this doctrine.**

The problem with using this and other linking verbs is that they create a sentence without action. When used frequently, the writing itself stagnates and becomes uninteresting to read. To avoid this, use action verbs whenever it is logical to do so.

> **The motor stalled immediately after the plaintiff engaged the gear.**

rather than

> The motor was immediately inoperable after the driver engaged the gear.

2. As a helping verb.

Used as a helping verb with the *ing* form of another verb, a form of *to be* shows that an action occurred over a period of time.

> **The witness <u>was</u> operating a lawn mower at the time he reported hearing the scream.**

Often this communication of relative time is legally significant. This use of *to be* is needed, not wordy; it is also past progressive tense, not passive voice, so you need not avoid it for that reason.

To be does create the passive voice, however, when used as a helping verb with the *ed* past participle form of the main verb.

> **The lawn mower <u>was</u> operated by the witness.**

Passive voice is harder to understand and requires more words, so use it only when it is needed. For more on this, see PASSIVE VOICE.

3. As a statement of being.

This is the use seen least in legal writing.

> **She <u>is</u>.**

It may occasionally be useful, however, for EMPHASIS in PERSUA-
SIVE WRITING.

> **The witness has repeatedly testified that, since the attack, she
> is terrified by sudden noises. She is.**

For related information, see VERBS, TENSES.

TONE

Tone communicates the writer's point of view, or attitude toward
the reader and the subject matter. Choose a tone appropriate for the
medium, such as objective for office memos, persuasive for briefs,
friendly for informative client letters, or stern for tough settlement
letters. Then choose words and sentence structures to convey that
tone. For more specific information, see also TONE IN LETTERS.

Tone is established and conveyed through attention to many details. As the following subsections explain, you can convey tone
through (1) WORD CHOICE by choosing the appropriate subjects, verbs,
and MODIFIERS; by choosing appropriate TERMS OF ADDRESS; and
by choosing words that have the appropriate emotional overtone and
level of formality. You can also convey tone through (2) SENTENCE
STRUCTURE by making effective use of active and PASSIVE VOICE
and POSITIONS OF EMPHASIS, and by choosing appropriate SEN-
TENCE LENGTH, SUBJECT–VERB COMBINATIONS, and various
kinds of SENTENCE STRUCTURE.

1. Conveying tone through word choice.

(a) Choose appropriate subjects, verbs, and MODIFIERS. For example, in MEMOS, when you want to convey an objective and
businesslike tone, use TERMS OF ART as subjects and verbs to
keep the text focused on the issue being analyzed.

> **The <u>Family Car Doctrine holds</u> parents liable for their
> child's negligence.**

Keep modifiers to a minimum, and then use only factual, specific
information.

> **Jamison grasped Hendricks by the arm and led him to the
> door.**

rather than

> Jamison rudely grasped the unfortunate Hendricks by the left
> arm and inexorably led him slowly to the battered wooden
> door.

In BRIEFS, when you want to convey a persuasive and more
assertive tone, retain terms of art as subjects and verbs to help the
reader focus on your point. But also use stronger subjects and

verbs when stating favorable facts, that is, subjects and verbs that give the reader a vivid picture of those facts.

Jamison grasped Hendricks left arm and pulled him slowly toward the door.

When stating unfavorable facts, use weaker, more abstract subjects and verbs.

The defendant then took Hendricks by the arm and moved to the door.

Also use modifiers with subtle emotional connotations that favor your position.

Muttering threats, Jamison grasped Hendrick's bruised left arm and pulled him slowly toward the door.

But do not overdo, or you may hamper your credibility.

(b) Choose the appropriate terms of address.

In a memo or brief, you want to avoid terms of address that refer to yourself or the reader because the focus should be on the legal issues and the parties rather than on the attorneys or judges.

Granting a summary judgment is not justifiable in this case.

rather than

You must not grant a summary judgment because these facts preclude it.

In a letter to a client, however, you will often want to refer to yourself and the reader because you are indeed speaking as one person to another.

At our meeting on Tuesday, April 11, you asked me to give you a legal opinion on whether ....

rather than

In response to the request made on Tuesday, April 11, for an opinion on whether ....

If you avoid all personal references in letters, you create a distant, cold tone. You may want to use this cold tone occasionally, as in a tough SETTLEMENT LETTER, but it is not wise to use it with your current clients. For related information, see TOUGH, SOUNDING THAT WAY.

(c) Choose the appropriate level of formality.

In general, use more formal language in official documents, such as BRIEFS or OPINION LETTERS, because you want to sound respectful and serious. Use less formal language in other writing, such as MEMOS or GENERAL CORRESPONDENCE LETTERS, where you want to be readable and avoid being stuffy. For example, you might say the following in a conference with another attorney.

Helen Thomas bought her computer at the local Apex store.

But you might write it this way in a brief.

Ms. Thomas purchased her computer at Apex Computers, located at 417 Cherry Street.

Avoid creating a stuffy tone by using overly formal language, especially when describing everyday concepts.

the trash truck

rather than

the refuse management vehicle

2. Conveying tone through SENTENCE LENGTH and structure.

(a) For a clipped, no-nonsense tone, use shorter sentences.

My client, Ms. Ambrose, does not intend to pay this bill. She has no reason to pay this bill. She did not receive any software from your company. She did not order any software from your company. Until receiving your bill, she did not know your company existed.

(b) For a more conversational tone, use longer sentences with the subject and verb near the beginning of the sentence.

You asked me to research the possibility of recovering part or all of your down payment on a stereo you later decided not to purchase.

rather than

In our phone conversation, you stated that, after some consideration, you wanted to recover . . . .

or

You asked me to research a question for you. Specifically, you want to know if you can recover part or all of a down payment. The down payment was made for . . . .

(c) For a more formal tone, use some interrupting phrases in your sentence structure.

Anorexics, <u>by failing to eat</u>, passively expose themselves to harm.

This sentence structure is harder to read because to understand the main point the reader must remember the first part of the sentence, read the interrupting clause, and then reunite the last part of the sentence with the first in his or her memory. Therefore avoid using it in sentence after sentence; give the reader breathing space between these difficult sentences. Finally, never allow the interruption to exceed seven words. After that long an interruption, the reader would have to reread the sentence to understand the point.

For information on problems associated with long interruptions, see AGREEMENT, SUBJECTS AND VERBS. For related general information, see SENTENCE STRUCTURE. For related information, see TONE IN LETTERS; TOUGH, SOUNDING THAT WAY; BAD NEWS, SOFTENING IT; OBJECTIVE WRITING; PERSUASIVE WRITING; ARGUMENTATIVE WRITING; EMOTIONAL LANGUAGE; and STYLE.

TONE IN LETTERS

Tone is especially important in letters. As the tone of your voice creates an impression in the mind of the listener, so the tone of your letter creates an impression in the mind of the reader. Thus, although your tone in various letters may range from friendly to tough, it should always be within the limits of temperate, businesslike communication. A chatty tone will seem slightly unprofessional in all but purely personal letters. A tirade will also seem unprofessional, even in the toughest collection letter.

Within these limits, however, you must make your own choices, based on what is appropriate to the situation and what suits your personal communicating style.

Using tone effectively in letters involves three tasks: (1) choosing the appropriate tone, (2) creating that tone through word choice and sentence structure, and (3) keeping the tone consistent.

1. Choosing the appropriate tone.

Before you begin writing the letter, consider first what your relationship is to the reader. For example, if your reader is a judge or your supervisor at work, you will probably want to use a tone that is both businesslike and respectful. This means that you will state your points as concisely as possible but will not omit appropriate opening and closing sentences, such as the following closing to a letter requesting a favor.

Thank you for your help in this matter.

If your reader is a client or colleague, you may choose to be polite and businesslike or, if appropriate, you may choose a friendly tone.

Please call if you have any further questions.

or

I am looking forward to our next tennis match.

If your reader is your client's opponent or a client who has not paid you for three months, you may sometimes choose a tough, businesslike tone.

Please pay this bill promptly.

or

I trust this settles the matter.

2. Creating the appropriate tone through word choice and sentence structure.

Choosing your words carefully is one effective way to establish your tone. For example, if you want to create an informal and friendly tone, use less formal words, such as *talk* and *meeting*. If you want to create a more formal tone, use more formal words, such as *confer* and *discussion*.

Avoid, however, using formal words to the point that your letter becomes hard to read or stuffy.

Regarding this question, I have conferred with Ms. Jamison's attorney, who explained that . . . .

rather than

In pursuit of this query, I have held consultations with counsel for Ms. Jamison, who elucidated the point by stating that . . . .

Another way to avoid a stuffy tone is to avoid inappropriately using the third person, such as *this attorney*, when the first person, *I*, is accurate. In general, letters are addressed from one person to another, and so the use of *I* is appropriate, or *we* if you are speaking officially for a group of people, such as a whole law firm.

You may also establish your tone by using appropriate SENTENCE STRUCTURE. For example, if you want to create a friendly, informal tone, use longer sentences rather than terse ones.

Thank you for your kind invitation to speak at your annual banquet honoring outstanding alumni from the law school.

rather than

Thank you for the invitation to speak at the law school alumni banquet.

Conversely, if you want to create a tough, no-nonsense tone, use short, rather choppy sentences.

My client, Ms. Ambrose, does not intend to pay this bill. She has no reason to pay you. She did not receive any software from your company. She did not order any software from your company. Until receiving your bill, she did not know your company existed.

rather than

My client, Ms. Ambrose, does not intend to pay this bill because she has no reason to do so. She did not receive or order any software from your company, and in fact did not know your company existed until receiving your bill.

3. Keeping the tone consistent.

Inconsistent tone occurs most often when a letter includes words that are noticeably more formal or informal than the rest of a letter. For example, a writer may use a formal phrase, such as *please be advised that*, in an otherwise informal letter. Or a writer may use a colloquialism, such as *ripped off*, in an otherwise businesslike letter.

Uneven tone also sometimes occurs when sentence structure changes markedly. For example, a reader might be taken aback by a series of three SHORT SENTENCES near the end of an otherwise friendly letter. Similarly, a reader might be put off by a long, complex sentence in an otherwise informal letter. Therefore reread your letters just for consistent tone.

For more help in choosing the appropriate tone, see the following more specific entries: GENERAL CORRESPONDENCE LETTERS; REQUESTS FOR PAYMENT; or TOUGH, SOUNDING THAT WAY. For more help in keeping the tone consistent, see WORD CHOICE and SENTENCE STRUCTURE.

TOPICAL ORGANIZATION

Topical organization refers to organizing the facts or the analysis by legal topic. In a memo, topical organization can be used in the STATEMENT OF FACTS, the DISCUSSION SECTION, or both. In a brief, it can be used in the STATEMENT OF THE CASE, the ARGUMENT SECTION or both. For example, when an appellate brief contains both procedural and substantive issues, under topical organization the procedural and substantive facts would be presented separately. The Argument section would then follow the same large-scale organization.

Use topical organization when the chronology of events is not as important as the legal character of the events themselves. For example, when a memo discusses two issues, such as one on *the Family Car Doctrine* and another on the *definition of a minor child under the wrongful death statute*, following the chronology of events would not be as important as organizing the events into two groups: those to which the Family Car Doctrine applies and those to which the wrongful death statute applies. To make this topical organization clear to the reader, try separating the topics by paragraphs or, if each covers several paragraphs, by subheadings.

In contrast, see CHRONOLOGICAL ORGANIZATION. For related information, see MEMOS; BRIEFS; APPELLATE BRIEFS; ORGANIZATION, LARGE–SCALE; and REWRITING.

TOPIC SENTENCES

Topic sentences, or main sentences, deserve particular attention in legal writing because they convey the main points of PARAGRAPHS. Topic sentences are therefore most effective at POSITIONS OF EMPHASIS. For example, use a topic sentence at the beginning of a paragraph to state the conclusion the paragraph supports. Alternatively, use it to create a question in the reader's mind and then explain the answer in the body of the paragraph. Thus the topic sentence sets up an expectation that the body of the paragraph fulfills.

> **Although the 1969 Act eased the singles penalty, it did so at the expense of married couples.**

The questioning legal reader will ask, "Okay, so how exactly did the Act disadvantage married couples?" If this is the point the paragraph explains, the topic sentence has prepared the reader for the paragraph's content. Or use a topic sentence at the end of a paragraph to summarize or conclude; remember, however, that busy legal readers may skip the end or get impatient about any suspense created by waiting for the point.

For related information, see ORGANIZATION, SMALL–SCALE; POSITIONS OF EMPHASIS; PARAGRAPHS; and TRANSITIONS.

TOTALLY

See COMPLETELY.

TOUGH, SOUNDING THAT WAY

Try the following techniques to sound tough.

1. Use shorter sentences, perhaps several in a row. This creates a clipped, no-nonsense tone.

> **My client, Ms. Ambrose, does not intend to pay this bill. She has no reason to pay you. She did not receive any software from your company. She did not order any software from your company. Until receiving your bill, she did not know your company existed.**

2. Use objective language. If you use emotional words *(unabashedly, horrendous, outrageous)*, you will sound angry, but not tough. Tough people stay in control. Think of Joe Friday saying, "Just the facts, Ma'am, just the facts." Instead, persuade with careful use of POSITIONS OF EMPHASIS and SENTENCE STRUCTURE. See OBJECTIVE WRITING and PERSUASIVE LETTERS.

3. If appropriate, explain the options the reader has and the results of those options. This puts the responsibility clearly in the reader's lap. If the reader is at all inclined to feel guilty, this explanation makes that

reader squirm. If the reader has no sense of guilt, the explanation will still make your position clear, so you have lost nothing.

4. Never threaten idly. The people with whom you most likely need to get tough are often those people who have heard many threats in their lives and have learned to ignore them. They may be experienced enough, however, to recognize a genuine threat that is well-presented.

For related information, see LETTERS; GENERAL CORRESPONDENCE LETTERS; SETTLEMENT LETTERS; BAD NEWS, GIVING IT; TONE IN LETTERS; and TONE.

TRANSITIONS

One way to communicate the logical connection between two points is to use headings, sentences, phrases, or words. These devices signal the relationship between the content of one section, paragraph, or sentence to the next. To make these connections clear, choose accurate, exact transitions that reveal the nature of the connection. Use headings to convey the connection between the sections.

> **I. POLICE VIOLATED DEFENDANT'S FOURTH AMENDMENT RIGHTS FIRST WHEN THEY ENTERED HER HOME WITHOUT A WARRANT.**

and

> **II. POLICE VIOLATED DEFENDANT'S FOURTH AMENDMENT RIGHTS AGAIN WHEN THEY SEIZED EVIDENCE THAT WAS NOT IN PLAIN VIEW.**

Connect paragraphs within a section with strong TOPIC SENTENCES.

> **Plaintiff was a holder in due course because she took the check in good faith.**

and

> **As a holder in due course, Plaintiff is now entitled to the value of the check.**

When using transitional words between paragraphs or sentences, you may find that you use only one or two transition words most of the time, perhaps repeating one word three or four times on a page. This overuse can signal several problems. Sometimes, overuse of one transition signals ORGANIZATION problems. For example, if you use *however* frequently, check to see if you are combining points that could better be presented in separate paragraphs. Other times, overuse of one transition may mean that you are using the word out of habit rather than out of conscious choice. If so, some other word will probably be more precise. For example, *similarly* may be more precise for a comparison than *additionally*. To help you choose the most

T

accurate transition quickly, consult the following list of transitions grouped by their logical functions.

1. Signalling similarity: *similarly, analogously, as.*

2. Signalling contrast: *not ... but; but; conversely; however; in contrast; nevertheless; on the contrary; while; yet.*

3. Introducing conditions: *although, even if, if, only if, provided that, unless, when, whenever, whereas, while.*

4. Introducing results: *if ... , then; when ... , then; accordingly; as a result; consequently; hence; so; so that; therefore; thus.*

5. Introducing reasons for a result: *because, if, since.*

6. Introducing examples or explanations: *as if, as though, for example, namely, specifically.*

7. Signalling a list: *first, second, third, etc.; both ... and; either ... or; neither ... nor; additionally; also; and; furthermore; last; nor; or.*

8. Showing time relationships: *after, afterward, as, as long as, before, before this, during, earlier, later, meanwhile, now, once, since, simultaneously, then, until, when, whenever, while.*

9. Showing relationship of place: *where, wherever.*

10. Summarizing: *finally, in conclusion, in summary.*

For other ways to make transitions, see CONNECTIONS, MAKING THEM.

TRIAL BRIEFS

Trial briefs are usually filed with the court before the trial begins. They inform the trial court of counsel's theory of the case by presenting the applicable rules and the arguments constructed from the rules as they are applied to the facts. A trial brief should indicate what is to be proven, how it is to be proven, and what the outcome of the case should be.

Each side files a trial brief so that the court has an idea of the structure of the trial before it begins. Except under extraordinary circumstances, both sides exchange trial briefs.

Check your jurisdiction for the specific requirements for format of a trial brief; in particular, consider your AUDIENCE; if possible, check with someone who knows that judge. For the usual FORMAT for a trial brief, see BRIEFS.

For related information, see PERSUASIVE WRITING, POINT HEADINGS, ISSUE STATEMENTS, and STATEMENT OF THE CASE.

UNCLEAR MEANING

See MODIFIERS, DANGLING; PRECISION; AMBIGUITY, WAYS TO AVOID; or READABILITY.

UNDERLINING

Underlining has five specific uses in legal writing. To avoid confusion, underlining should not be used solely to recreate the emphasis a word would be given in speech.

1. Underline to add emphasis to important terms in quotes, such as in a rule or holding. When you underline part of a quote, add *(emphasis added)* after the citation following the quote.

> **As this court itself has stated, "[T]he court must intervene because the issue of mutuality, not to mention that of duress, requires that the court examine <u>the parol evidence surrounding the signing</u> of the contract." <u>Durant v. Colt</u>, 945 F. Supp. 641 (D.D.C. 1999) (emphasis added).**

2. Underline to add emphasis to the key phrase in QUOTATIONS long enough to be indented and single-spaced in the text. Underlining may encourage the legal reader to read the quote by making the single spacing more palatable. Again, when you underline add *(emphasis added)* after the citation on the first line of text following the indented quote, not within the indented quote itself. The phrase *(emphasis added)* within a quote would signal that that phrase was present in the original quote.

> **The court in this case addressed the issue of mutuality.**

> > **Despite the defendant's emotional plea regarding the centrality of upholding contracts to the free working of a democracy, we cannot ignore the plaintiff's complaint. In this case, the court must intervene because <u>the issue of mutuality</u>, not to mention that of duress, <u>requires that the court examine both the contract's wording and the parol evidence</u> surrounding the signing of that contract.**

> **<u>Holmes v. Cardozo</u>, 945 F. Supp. 498 (D.D.C. 1999) (emphasis added).**

3. Underline cases in citations in text.

> **<u>Peabody v. Hart</u>, 958 F.2d 391 (7th Cir. 1999).**

4. Underline references to the record, if your jurisdiction so requires.

> **Defendant failed to use his turn signal. <u>Tr. 17.</u>**

5. Underline phrases from other languages if they are not commonly incorporated into English. Often, however, the phrase you use

will have been incorporated, such as Latin phrases that are TERMS OF ART.

The court appointed a guardian ad litem.

6. Do not use underlining to replace the emphasis you would give a word when speaking. This use of underlining is acceptable in casual writing, such as in a letter to a friend or an informal memo to a coworker, but it is less effective in briefs or research memos for several reasons. First, the use of underlining can be confusing. Often the legal reader's first reaction to underlining is to assume you are highlighting a quote or indicating one of the other four specific uses of underlining in legal writing. Second, legal readers may think you are resorting to the obvious, which can make you seem less in control of the text. To avoid this problem, use POSITIONS OF EMPHASIS and SENTENCE STRUCTURE techniques instead of underlining. For ways to do this, see EMPHASIS. For related information, see QUOTATIONS, HOW TO PUNCTUATE and CITATIONS.

UNDERSTANDABILITY

See CLARITY and READABILITY.

UNDOUBTEDLY

Avoid the term. The point is probably not undoubted by all legal readers. If it is, you do not need to tell the reader this. If you must use *undoubtedly*, do not spell it *undoubtably*.

UNINTERESTED OR DISINTERESTED?

See DISINTERESTED OR UNINTERESTED?

UNIQUE

Unique means that the item or idea referred to is the only one of its kind, or without an equivalent. *Unique* is not preceded by qualifying adverbs. For example, do not say *the most unique* or *rather unique* or *somewhat unique*. If it is unique, it is *unique*.

UNITY

See COHERENCE.

UNLESS

Use *unless* with care because it is easily misread. *Unless* is actually a negative, like *not* or *no*, but often readers do not realize this.

As a result, readers may miss the negative and think the *unless* phrase means the opposite of what the writer intended. To avoid this ambiguity, substitute another word for *unless* when possible.

> **Come to the hearings only if you are subpoenaed.**

rather than

> Do not come to the hearings unless you are subpoenaed.

> **Signatures on absentee ballots must be notarized. The only exception to this is absentee ballots signed by members of the military.**

rather than

> All signatures on all absentee ballots must be notarized unless the absentee voter is a member of the military.

UNOBTRUSIVE DEFINITIONS

Unobtrusive definitions are short, conveniently placed explanations of technical terms that may not be completely familiar to the reader. These definitions are helpful to include when you are not sure whether or not you should include a definition. The reader who understands the term can skip over the definition easily, because the definition is structurally identifiable as a definition. The reader who needs the definition, however, will read it and thus understand your point. There are three ways to include unobtrusive definitions.

1. Include an appositive, or a few words in a phrase inserted right after the term being defined.

> **The tortfeasor, the person committing the tort,** . . . .

For related information, see APPOSITIVES.

2. When a longer definition is needed, insert an explanatory sentence right after the sentence using the phrase.

> **At least 80% of the net tax should be paid during the tax year. Net tax is the tax remaining after all deductions have been included.**

Sometimes these definitions are placed in parentheses. But be careful to avoid overusing PARENTHESES because they can become a visual distraction to the reader.

3. If you need to insert many definitions, you can include an alphabetical list of those definitions in a separate section, such as the definition sections in statutes, contracts, or trusts.

Sometimes writers are afraid they will offend sophisticated readers if they define legal terms, and occasionally readers are indeed irritated by excessive definitions. More often, however, readers are frustrated by undefined terms. For example, a judge may be frustrated by *exercise of purchase option* because the judge has to stop a minute and remember exactly what that contract term means. Similarly, a client may be frustrated by *tortfeasor* because the client is not sure exactly what the word means. When in doubt, give your AUDIENCE the definitions for any KEY TERMS or TERMS OF ART that may be unfamiliar. For related information, see READABILITY, LEGALESE, JARGON, and PRECISION.

UNTIL SUCH TIME AS

Substitute *until*; you will gain CONCISENESS with no loss in PRECISION.

UNTO

Just use *to*. *Unto* means *to*; it does not mean *onto*.

UPDATING THE LAW

There are four major ways of updating the law, all indispensible to thorough research.

1. Use *Shepard's Citations*.

This set of books provides specific updating service for all cases, statutes, rules, and constitutional provisions. For specific directions in using *Shepard's*, see SHEPARD'S.

2. Use pocket parts and supplements.

Pocket parts and supplements update volumes in the law, such as case digests, annotated statutes, treatises, legal encyclopedias, and the words and phrases book. Those volumes using pocket parts have them enclosed in a pocket within either the front or back cover. Those using supplements have the supplements stacked separately after the volumes on the library shelf. Whichever your volume uses, make sure to check both the main volume and the pocket part or supplement for the most current developments in that topic.

3. Use looseleaf reporters.

Looseleaf reporters cover specific areas of the law. These are useful for updating the law because they sometimes get cases and information on a specific area of law before that information appears in the reporter system, and sometimes before it appears in the computer. Each looseleaf has its own system for use, so check the how-to-use section in each looseleaf you use.

4. Use a computer system.

Each computer system has its own supplementary method of updating the law in addition to *Shepard's*, so use both *Shepard's* and the computer. For help here, see COMPUTERS FOR RESEARCH.

For related information, see RESEARCH STRATEGY CHART.

UTILIZE

Substitute *use,* which is precise, readable, and not suggestive of JARGON.

Please use this form to provide the information requested.

rather than

Please utilize this form to provide the information requested.

UTTERLY

Omit this word; in legal writing, it almost always strikes the reader as an overstatement that weakens the statement rather than strengthening it. To emphasize a point, try using a short, direct statement rather than adding *utterly.*

The plaintiff's statement is false.

rather than

The statement made by the plaintiff is utterly false.

For related information, see EMPHASIS, ACCURACY, and LITERAL MEANING.

VAGUE WORDS

See AMBIGUITY, WAYS TO AVOID; PRECISION; and WORD CHOICE.

VARIETY

The word *variety* is sometimes used as a noun meaning a *collection of various things.* As such, it is too general to be useful in legal writing. If there is a variety, that variety will usually have to be explained.

In legal writing, avoid varying NOUNS or VERBS solely for the sake of variety. Legal readers look for consistency, particularly in TERMS OF ART and KEY TERMS. For more on this, see REPETITION.

Do vary SENTENCE LENGTH and SENTENCE STRUCTURE, but let this variety arise naturally from the logical relations of your content. For ways to achieve this, see SENTENCE STRUCTURE and EMPHASIS. Also vary your choice of transition words by using those that reflect the precise relationship of ideas. For help with this, see TRANSITIONS. For related information, see CONNECTIONS, MAKING THEM.

VERBAL OR ORAL?

See ORAL OR VERBAL?

VERBOSITY

See CONCISENESS.

VERBS

Verbs, which are words expressing an action or a state of being, focus the legal reader more than any other part of speech. Legal readers want to know what was done, what can be done, what will be done. The following five guidelines can help you use verbs effectively.

1. Use active voice.

    Active voice describes an action done by the subject.

    The court decided that freedom of association was not an issue.

rather than

    It was decided that freedom of association was not an issue.

Active voice is easier to read and more concise. It also adds PRECISION because it makes clear who did what. Therefore, use active voice unless the writing requires passive voice for effect. For more help here, see ACTIVE VOICE, PASSIVE VOICE, and CONCISENESS.

2. Use specific verbs.

    Verbs move legal writing when they are specific, halt it when they are vague. Try to state important action in the verb, rather than wasting this part of the sentence on information less important to the reader.

    The show-up I.D. negated the effect of capturing the defendant one block from the crime.

rather than

    The court stated that the show-up I.D. negated the effect of capturing the defendant one block from the crime.

In this example, the legal point is more important than the fact that the court stated it. Use a cite to give that information.

Avoid abstract combinations like *it is*, *there is*, or *there were*. Use nouns instead of those pronouns, specific verbs instead of those verbs of being.

False imprisonment occurs when a person is restrained without his or her consent.

330

rather than

> There is false imprisonment when a person is restrained without his or her consent.

For related information, see CONCISENESS and THERE IS ... THAT.

3. Use the auxiliary verb that best expresses your shade of meaning.

> Careful use of auxiliary verbs can clarify the exact meaning of your verb. For example, if you wanted to communicate that the defendant had the capacity to do something but did not, use *could*.

> **The defendant could have set the emergency brake.**

Conversely, if you want to communicate that the defendant had good reason for not setting the brake, use *would have*.

> **The defendant would have set the emergency brake had he not been rushing to assist the people in the other car.**

> For specific information about this use of verbs, see VERBS, AUXILIARY.

4. Split infinitives only if it is necessary for ACCURACY. For a definition of infinitives, see VERBS, TENSES.

> The standard wisdom here has been to avoid splitting infinitives at all times.

> **to move afterwards**

rather than

> **to afterwards move**

Because many of your readers will be of that school, you should avoid splitting infinitives when possible.

> On rare occasions, however, a split infinitive will avoid ambiguities.

> **The mayor agreed to only suggest the alternative if the matter came up in committee meeting.**

In this case, putting *only* before *to* would communicate that this was the only thing to which the mayor agreed.

> **The mayor agreed only** ....

Putting *only* after *suggest* would communicate that this is the only alternative the mayor would suggest.

> **The mayor agreed to suggest only this alternative** ....

When forced to make a choice like this, choose the clarity of the split infinitive over the elegance of the ambiguous unsplit version. You may find, however, that you can avoid the problem by restructuring the sentence altogether.

The mayor agreed that she would only suggest the alternative if the matter came up in the committee meeting. She would refrain from requesting it.

This is the safest route; your revised version will offend no one and still avoid ambiguity. For related information see PRECISION; ONLY, WHERE TO PLACE; and MODIFIERS.

5. Make sure subjects and verbs agree.

Sometimes when the subject and verb are far apart in a sentence, the writer accidentally uses a plural verb with a singular subject, or a singular verb with a plural subject. One good way to avoid having this happen is to avoid putting more than seven words between your subject and verb. This will not only help you avoid agreement problems, but will also make your writing more readable.

Each of the therapists interviewed had become less willing to treat these patients after finding their practice restricted by these recent holdings.

rather than

In the interviews, *each* of the many therapists currently finding their practice restricted by these recent holdings *were* less willing to treat these patients.

For related information, see READABILITY.

For more detailed information about specific kinds of verbs, see SPLIT INFINITIVES; VERBS, LINKING; VERBS, PARTICIPLES; VERBS, IRREGULAR; VERBS, AUXILIARY; VERBS, MOODS; VERBS, PARTICIPLES; and VERBS, TENSES.

VERBS, AUXILIARY

Auxiliary verbs, or *helping verbs*, are added to the basic verb to change verb tenses and to add specific shades of meaning. Choosing the correct auxiliary verbs, therefore, can help you be more precise and persuasive. The following list explains how to use specific auxiliary verbs.

1. *Should.*

Should implies that some action was preferable, but was not in fact taken. For example, it can be useful for suggesting a breach of duty.

The defendant should have set the emergency brake.

2. *Could.*

Could implies the capacity to do something, but suggests that the action will not or has not been done.

The defendant could have set the emergency brake.

3. *Would.*

Would implies that an action would have been taken had conditions been different.

The defendant would have set the emergency brake had he not been rushing to assist the people in the other car.

4. *Can.*

Can implies capacity to do something, although the action has not yet been taken.

When weighing the evidence, the jury can take into account the witness's apparent intelligence and the clarity of the witness's memory of the event.

5. *Might.*

Might implies possibility.

The district attorney might prosecute.

Often *might* suggests if *facts were otherwise.*

6. *May.*

May implies permission to do something.

If the Seller fails to comply with the nondiscrimination clauses of this contract, the Seller may be declared ineligible for further government contracts ....

May also implies the possibility of something happening.

The grand jury may subpoena you.

Because it has two possible meanings, watch for potential ambiguities when using *may* in drafting. Sometimes, but not always, the meaning of *may* will be clear in context. When ambiguity is possible, use *might* for possibility and add some phrase like *if he or she chooses* for permission.

7. *Must.*

Must implies a requirement to do something or to refrain from doing something.

The Seller must not in any manner advertise the fact that the Seller has contracted to furnish goods to the Buyer without first obtaining the Buyer's written consent.

8. *Shall.*

Shall can imply a requirement, and is used to mean this in LEGISLATION.

All Petitioners shall file ....

But in general writing *shall* also implies the future tense.

The Williams opera shall premiere in December, if all goes as planned.

333

Therefore *shall* can be ambiguous to nonlegal readers. Whenever ambiguity is possible, use *must* for requirements and *will* for future tenses. For related information, see SHALL.

9. *Do.*

Do adds emphasis. It often indicates a positive answer when a negative one is expected.

On the contrary, I do plan to attend the hearings.

10. *Do not.*

Do not denies an action.

My client does not know of any such plans.

11. *Am, are, is, was, were, has, had, have,* and *been.*

These auxiliaries combine with the main verb to form other tenses.

I am meeting with the client today.

We are considering the matter.

The defendant is planning to testify.

We were considering the matter, but decided it was not worth further pursuit.

The defendant was planning to testify before this evidence came to light.

Ms. Wiley had considered settling out of court.

Both attorneys have filed pretrial motions.

They have been planning this banquet for months.

For more details, see VERBS, TENSES.

VERBS, IRREGULAR

Irregular verbs are verbs that do not form their past participles in quite the same way that regular verbs do.

Present

Regular verb: **I finish, you finish, it finishes.**

Past

Regular verb: **I finished, you finished, it finished.**

Present

Irregular verb: **I am, you are, it is.**

Past

Irregular verb: **I was, you were, it was.**

Common irregular verbs are *to be, to go,* and *to have.* For more information, see VERBS, PARTICIPLES and VERBS, TENSES.

VERBS, LINKING

Linking verbs, such as *to be* or *to seem*, link a subject and a predicate but show no action. They are roughly equivalent to equal signs. Avoid overusing linking verbs, because they are not as emphatic, interesting, or precise as active verbs.

The court reasoned that ....

rather than

The court's reasoning was that ....

VERBS, MOODS

Mood refers to changes made in the form of the verb to indicate whether or not the action described by the verb happened in fact. These changes in the form of the verb are called inflections, and create three moods. These moods are important conveyors of meaning in legal writing.

1. Indicative.

The indicative mood refers to actions that have in fact happened, are happening, or will in fact happen. This mood is used most often in legal writing, and can be used with any tense.

The defendant filed a motion for failure to state a claim.

The buyer is agreeing to assume this responsibility.

The legislature will consider the matter in the next session.

2. Subjunctive.

The subjunctive mood refers to actions that will not necessarily happen, but are being discussed hypothetically.

If I were you, I would file a claim.

The subjunctive mood can be used with any verb tense, as the following list illustrates.

   (a) Past Subjunctive.

   If the legislature intended for the law to exempt owner-operated bars, it should have stated so in the law itself.

   (b) Past Progressive Subjunctive.

   If the legislature had been planning to exempt owner-operated bars, documentation of that plan would surely have appeared somewhere in the legislative history of the law.

   (c) Past Perfect Subjunctive.

> If the legislature <u>had intended</u> for the law to exempt owner-operated bars, it surely would have stated so in the law itself.

(d) Future Subjunctive.

> If the legislature <u>were to exempt</u> owner-operated bars, it would create a suspect classification.

(e) Future Progressive Subjunctive.

> If the legislature <u>were planning</u> to exempt owner-operated bars, local bar owners' associations would surely be made aware of that plan.

(f) Future Perfect Subjunctive.

> If the legislature <u>were to have exempted</u> owner-operated bars, they certainly were not aware of that intention when they drafted the law.

For related information, see VERBS, TENSES.

3.   Imperative.

The imperative mood states commands directly to the reader.

> In preparation for this meeting, please <u>complete</u> this question-aire and <u>bring</u> it with you to the meeting.

Direct address creates a more personal tone, and so it must be used appropriately. For example, direct address is natural for a request in a letter.

> For our next meeting, please (1) bring all documents relating to the previous sale of your house and (2) collect all tax information for 1992.

You could also naturally use it in a written request to someone you supervise.

> When researching the DuBois case, check the statutes for any provisions relating to previous sales.

But it is not used in formal court documents, such as a pleading. There, use the third person.

> The plaintiff respectfully requests that this court overturn the trial court's ruling.

It may also be inappropriate in a note to a superior or colleague, for reasons of TONE. In that situation, use the question form if adding *please* is not sufficiently deferential.

> Could you please provide me a copy of the client's letters that address his preferences for the will?

VERBS, PARTICIPLES

Participles are the forms of verbs that combine with auxiliary verbs to form different verb tenses. This entry provides an overview of participles.

The present participle ends in *-ing*, such as *deciding, continuing, being, losing,* and *going.* It is used to form progressive tenses.

The trial is <u>continuing</u> to draw much attention from the media.

The children were <u>playing</u> near the pool when the accident happened.

The Court will be <u>deciding</u> this issue next month.

In contrast, this *-ing* form is called a GERUND when it is used as a NOUN.

<u>Seeing</u> is believing.

The past participle of regular verbs ends in *-ed,* such as *decided* and *continued.* The past participles of irregular verbs such as *been, lost,* and *gone,* do not end in *-ed.* Past participles are used to form past and perfect tenses.

The attorneys had already <u>decided</u> how to proceed when the settlement offer came.

The defendant has <u>lost</u> on appeal, but is going to pursue other possible actions.

Participles are also used to introduce phrases.

<u>Discouraged</u> by this lack of response, Allen decided to leave the organization.

The defendant tried to put out the flames with a blanket but was forced back, <u>coughing</u> and <u>gasping</u> for air.

VERBS, TENSES

Verb tenses must be used accurately to clarify the chronological relationship between events, but they can also be used to add shades of meaning. The following list shows you the various tenses available in English and suggests ways to use them to your advantage in legal writing. For related information, see VERBS, AUXILIARY.

1. Present Tense.

Use the present tense for a current or habitual action.

I <u>handle</u> all the estate planning in the firm.

Its main use in legal writing is for referring to statutes or other rules still in effect.

False imprisonment <u>occurs</u> when ....

This statute <u>requires</u> all nonresidents to ....

Do not use the present tense in situations where you do not want to imply that this is a habitual action. Instead, use the present progressive tense.

Our client <u>is complaining</u> that the Jones Corporation ....

rather than

Our client <u>complains</u> that the Jones Corporation ....

2. Present Progressive.

Use the present progressive tense for actions currently in progress.

The client <u>is suing</u> the Jones Corporation.

This tense is formed by *am*, *are*, or *is* and the *-ing* participle.

Also use the present progressive tense for actions going on during or in the context of some present action.

Even as we <u>are debating</u> the issue here, the courts face the same issue in <u>Colson v. Perry</u>.

3. Present Perfect.

Use the present perfect tense for actions now completed but related to a current action.

After the testator <u>has executed</u> the will, the will becomes valid.

The present perfect tense is formed by *have* or *has* plus the past participle. When used in context with another action, that action is usually stated in the present tense, as in the previous example.

The present perfect tense is useful for showing that a current action is logically subsequent to a previous recent action.

Once the offeree <u>has relied</u> to his detriment upon the offer, the contract is enforceable.

4. Past.

Use the past tense for actions completed before the current writing.

The court <u>decided</u> to review the case.

The past tense is useful for suggesting an action is finished and cannot be changed.

The Supreme Court <u>resolved</u> this issue in ....

5. Past Progressive.

Use the past progressive for actions completed before the current writing but going on over a period of time in relation to some other past action.

Mr. Jones <u>was changing</u> a flat tire when Mr. Smith's car struck him.

The past progressive tense is formed by *was* or *were* and the present participle, or the *-ing* form of the verb. When used with another action, that action is usually stated in the past tense, as in the previous example.

The past progressive tense is useful for showing the context in which some past action happened, and thus it can suggest mitigating circumstances.

So bad was Julia's health that, even though he was battling cancer at the time, Colonel Hart insisted that Julia never be left alone.

6. Past Perfect.

Use the past perfect tense for actions completed before some other past action took place.

Because Anderson <u>had accepted</u> the original offer, the contract was legally valid.

The past perfect is formed by *have*, *had*, or *has* and the past participle. When used in context of another action, that action is usually stated in the past tense, as in the previous example.

The past perfect is useful for expressing a previous past action that logically led to a subsequent past action.

Since the tenant <u>had given</u> the landlord permission to enter the apartment to repair the faucet in the kitchen, the landlord assumed he could also repair the broken latch on the bedroom closet door.

7. Future.

Use the future tense for actions not yet done.

We <u>will send</u> you a draft of your new will so that you can review it before our next conference.

The future tense is formed by *will* and the same form of the verb that would go after *to* in the infinitive verb, such as *send*, *finish*, or *be*.

The future tense suggests that the action will in fact happen, even though it has not yet happened. It is useful for suggesting a result is certain.

Judge Roland Hausler <u>will win</u> the election.

8. Future Progressive.

Use the future progressive tense for actions that will be going on over a period of time in the future.

This action <u>will be pending</u> for many years before the court reaches a decision.

The future progressive is formed by *will be* plus the present participle, or *-ing* form of the verb. When used in the context of another action, that action is usually stated in the present tense, as in the previous example.

9. Future Perfect.

Use the future perfect tense for actions that are not yet completed but will have been completed before some other action.

The company will have bound itself legally to the contract when it accepts the offer.

The future perfect tense is formed by *will have* and the *-ed* form of the verb. When used in the context of another action, that other action is usually stated in the present tense, as in the previous example.

This tense is useful for showing the logical consequence of future possible actions.

If the court accepts the plaintiff's reasoning, then it will have opened the door to unharmed plaintiffs seeking to recover damages.

10. Emphatic.

The emphatic tense is formed by adding *do* to the verb.

You may use the emphatic tense to underscore a positive or negative response.

He does plan to pursue the matter.

She does not consider this offer acceptable.

11. Past Future.

Use the past future tense for actions that may happen, depending on some other future action. The past future tense is formed by adding *would* to the verb.

He would settle if the conditions were right.

12. Past Future Perfect.

Use the past future perfect for actions that would have happened, but did not because of some other past action. The past future perfect is formed by adding *would have* to the verb.

He would have settled if his attorney had advised him fully of the difficulties of the case.

13. Infinitive Verbs.

Although the infinitive is not technically a tense, it can be used to clarify sequence and meaning, like a tense. The infinitive form is not tied to any person or time. It consists of *to* plus the verb.

To appeal may be too expensive.

It is useful when you want to suggest that the point you are making is always true, rather than focusing particularly on the present instance.

To say that one idea cannot be expressed in print is to say that all ideas are subject to potential censorship.

VERB TENSES, DIFFERENT ONES IN THE SAME TEXT

Keep the verb tense consistent throughout your text whenever you can without loss of ACCURACY. For example, use past tense in both of the following sentences.

The trial court found that the defendant had made a good faith effort to inform the plaintiff of the impending problems meeting deadlines. The court also stated that the plaintiff had ignored the defendant's requests.

rather than

The trial court found that the defendant had made a good faith effort to inform the plaintiff of the impending problems meeting deadlines. The court also states that the plaintiff had ignored the defendant's requests.

But two different tenses are often necessary to keep the time relationship of two actions clear.

past

Because the court has determined that state law applies

present

rather than federal, it now can address the question of jurisdiction.

past

Although the plaintiff argued his case under a theory of

present

restitution, he now requests what are in effect punitive damages.

In contrast, the following version, which uses a consistent tense, is inaccurate because the events did not occur at the same time.

past perfect

Although the plaintiff has argued his case under a theory of

past perfect

of restitution, he now has requested what are in effect punitive damages.

VERSATILITY

Because the legal AUDIENCE is varied in both background and needs, the legal writer must develop versatility for maximum effectiveness. To develop this versatility, first study examples of others' writing, particularly those who are your primary audience. Exchange ideas with others about strategy, theory, and practical recommendations; then practice varying your approach to ORGANIZATION and STYLE. If you are working for a supervisor who sees a different theory or structure to your document, try to compose the document that way, even if you disagree about why. Similarly, if you are working for a judge who prefers terse expression, or even a partner who demands FLOWERY LANGUAGE, try imitating those styles. Practice adapting to different audiences' needs. Your own writing will improve as you add to your repertoire the successful structures, approaches, writing PATTERNS, and STYLES of others. With these additions, you will become more adept and quick in your ability to choose the expression and approach you want.

VERY

Avoid overusing *very*. Often it adds little meaning, and often it detracts from the word it modifies, rather than emphasizing it.

This issue is crucial.

rather than

This issue is very important.

For related information, see MODIFIERS, EMPHASIS, and CONCISENESS.

VIRGULE

See SLASH.

VIRTUALLY

Virtually means *essential to all purposes* or *in effect*.
It contrasts with LITERALLY.

The exceptions have virtually swallowed the rule.

VIZ.

Viz., or *videlicet*, is unnecessary because there are clear English equivalents. Use *namely*, *that is*, or *that is to say* instead.

For related information, see LEGALESE and JARGON.

VOICE

Voice is the way you transmit the image you adopt when writing a particular document. Your image might be that of a bill collector asking a client to pay an overdue bill, an advocate trying to change a judge's mind, or an apologetic bearer of bad news.

Thus your voice in legal writing shifts in response to the situation, just as your voice shifts when you talk to your spouse or your judge. Nevertheless, this shift lies within a range that is smaller than all the possible voices, and this narrower range reflects elements of your personal legal writing style.

Many writers feel as if they lose their voices in legal writing because they are creating voices different from those they used previously. But this is not the case. Instead, you are simply expanding your repertoire to include the voices necessary for good legal writing. Experiment with them, observe others, and incorporate the subtle shifts in TONE, SENTENCE STRUCTURE, and WORD CHOICE that create each voice.

VOICE, ACTIVE OR PASSIVE?

Voice is a verb form that indicates the relation between the subject and the action expressed by the verb. In ACTIVE VOICE the subject does the action; in PASSIVE VOICE the subject receives the action.

The boy hit the ball. [Active voice]

The ball was hit. [Passive voice]

The defendant assaulted the victim. [Active voice]

The victim was assaulted. [Passive voice]

The court held the identification evidence admissible. [Active voice]

The identification evidence was held admissible. [Passive voice]

Using active voice instead of passive voice usually eliminates extra words. Using active voice also eliminates the ambiguity that might be caused by abstract verbs, such as *consists of* or *concerns* or *involves*.

Passive voice is useful, however, in four specific situations. In legal writing, use it consciously and for these reasons only; otherwise eliminate it.

1. Passive voice is useful for de-emphasizing unfavorable facts or law. For example, the attorney for the defense might want to write the following.

The plaintiff was assaulted by the defendant.

The attorney for the prosecution, however, might write the following.

343

The defendant assaulted the plaintiff.

2. Passive voice is useful for hiding the identity of the actor.

A decision was made to cut your salary.

Here, passive voice avoids telling who made the decision.

It can be argued that the defendant assumed the risk.

3. Passive voice is also useful when the subject is very long. In this situation, using passive voice creates a more readable sentence because the active voice would put the subject and verb so far apart that the sentence would be too hard to read.

This action is required by statutory law, by the common law principle of due care, and by a general sense of justice.

rather than

Statutory law, the common law principle of due care, and a general sense of justice require this action.

4. Finally, passive voice is useful when the subject is much less important than the object.

Freedom of speech cannot be encumbered by concerns of propriety.

rather than

Concerns of propriety cannot encumber freedom of speech.

WAS OR WERE?

See THERE IS OR THERE ARE?

WE

Use *we* as a plural subject. Be careful to use it precisely, so that you include only those people who should be included in *we*.

We [the members of the firm] suggest you try to settle the case.

rather than

We [I, but I don't want to admit it] think the merits of the case are too weak.

or

We [who?] now move on to the next issue.

For more on problems with *we*, see AMBIGUITY, WAYS TO AVOID, subsection 2.

We can also be used in constructions where a verb is implied. For example, *as well as we* implies *as well as we are*, and *such as we* implies *such as we are*.

I am sorry to inform you that the defendant's firm is unwilling to discuss a settlement with lawyers such as we.

WELL OR GOOD?

See GOOD OR WELL?

WHEN AM I DONE?

See WHEN TO STOP.

WHEN OR IF?

Use *when* to refer to a relationship of time; use *if* to refer to a logical relationship. See also WHEN OR WHERE?

WHEN OR WHERE?

When indicates a point in time; *where* indicates a physical place. In Questions Presented and ISSUE STATEMENTS, use *when* because it is more precise, describing events in time. Use *if*, however, when referring to a logical relationship rather than the relative timing of two different events.

WHEN TO STOP

The purpose of this section is to help you overcome any tendencies you may have to fiddle with a document forever, miss your deadlines, frustrate your coworkers and typists, or drive yourself crazy with uncertainty about your writing. Ideally, each document you produce would be perfect. Realistically, that is not possible. It is seldom possible to get even one document perfect, let alone all that you write. You therefore have to make some decisions about which documents are worth pushing closer to perfection and which must be turned in sooner.

The following guidelines can help you make these difficult decisions at each stage of the WRITING PROCESS. But also use your COMMON SENSE and revise the list as needed to suit your circumstances. For related information, see WRITING BLOCK.

1. When to stop researching.

Stop when you keep finding the same sources. Save time by following the RESEARCH STRATEGY CHART and by completing all updating. Do not waste time looking for the fictitious smoking gun, or the case exactly like yours; concentrate instead on the sources that turn up repeatedly.

2. When to stop PREWRITING.

345

If you tend to linger at this stage so long that you have inadequate time for the later stages of the WRITING PROCESS, stop when you have completed enough of an outline to give shape to your general ideas and when you have listed specific points under each general idea. In general, however, allow plenty of time for this stage; it will prevent time-consuming errors at later stages.

3. When to stop WRITING.

The critical factor here is to stop REWRITING during this first draft. Let your ideas flow, unedited. If you sense holes in your reasoning, let them pass for now; fill them in later in the rewriting stage. If you sense awkward phrases, let them pass also; you can revise them later.

4. When to stop REWRITING.

Stop when you have the large-scale ideas in place, the PARAGRAPHS in a logical order, the TOPIC SENTENCES in place, and all needed content and explanation in the text. Make sure the organization is clear enough to be followed by any legal reader. Also make sure any unneeded information is omitted. Then move on to revising.

5. When to stop REVISING.

The key here is to do first things first. Ask yourself the following critical questions before you move on to those concerns that are desirable but not critical.

(a) Does each topic sentence state the point clearly and unambiguously? For help here, see TOPIC SENTENCES.

(b) Is every supporting sentence accurate and logically connected to the paragraph in which it is included? For help here, see ACCURACY and ORGANIZATION, SMALL–SCALE.

(c) Is all unneeded information omitted?

(d) Is the POINT OF VIEW consistent and appropriate?

Then, as you have time, revise the text further, asking yourself each of the following questions.

(e) Are the sentences readable? For help here, see READABILITY.

(f) Are POSITIONS OF EMPHASIS used effectively?

(g) Are EMPHASIS techniques used effectively?

(h) Is TONE consistent and appropriate?

6. When to stop POLISHING.

When polishing, first ask yourself the following questions.

(a) Are all CITATIONS complete and written in accurate form?

(b) Does the document meet all FORMAT requirements?

(c) Are all quotes letter perfect? See QUOTATIONS, HOW TO PUNCTUATE.

(d) Are all numbers correct, including such details as numbers in citations and dollar amounts?

(e) Are all names spelled properly?

Then proofread the text for typographical, grammatical, and punctuation errors. Make sure to incorporate on the list your own frequent errors.

When this is done, if you have time left, you may go back and check any other concerns that you wish. If you have no time left, at least you can take comfort in the fact that you have avoided major writing errors.

WHERE OR WHEN?

See WHEN OR WHERE?

WHETHER

Whether is a subordinating conjunction that introduces a dependent clause.

Whether the court will address this question is unknown.

Therefore a *whether* clause by itself cannot be a complete sentence.

whether the court will address this issue

In legal writing, however, *whether* is often used to introduce questions presented and ISSUE STATEMENTS.

To avoid writing your issue or QUESTION PRESENTED as an incomplete sentence, you may simply reformulate it as a question, leaving out *whether*.

Did the trial court err in awarding custody of both children to the mother when ...?

rather than

Whether the trial court erred in awarding custody of both children to the mother when ....

If you use the *whether* form of a Question Presented or Issue Statement, end it with a period, not a question mark.

WHICH OR THAT?

See THAT OR WHICH?

WHO OR WHOM?

Use *who* as a subject, *whom* as an object. Thus, use *whom* whenever it is the object of a preposition.

To whom did you present the question about the gun?

Use *whom* as the object of a verb.

Whom did you see on the night of the incident?

Or use *whom* as the subject of a complementary infinitive.

Defendant is the person whom the plaintiff saw on the night of the crime.

Use *who* as a subject of a sentence.

Who took my shoes?

Also use *who* as the subject of a clause.

You are the person who called me yesterday.

WILLS, DRAFTING

The principles for writing wills are much the same as those for writing CONTRACTS. You might also want to use forms to help you get started. For help here, see FORMS, USE OF. In addition to the principles listed under CONTRACTS, DRAFTING, focus on these important tasks.

1. Thoroughly ascertain the client's needs and the jurisdiction's requirements.

Interview the client thoroughly, so that you are clear about his or her desires and concerns. Ascertain the many details you need about matters such as assets, legal domicile, and beneficiaries and other relatives. Ask the client to identify alternative beneficiaries and personal representatives. But while concentrating on getting all the needed information, pay attention also to the sensibilities of your client. Preparing a will is an emotional event; the client will appreciate and need a sensitive interviewer.

Next research, or make sure your knowledge is current on, your jurisdiction's statutory and procedural requirements for wills. If your jurisdiction's requirements are less stringent than other states, consider creating a will that conforms to even those higher standards. For example, even if your jurisdiction requires only two witnesses to the will, include three witnesses so that the will would also be recognized in other states.

In your research, consider also the tax and property ownership consequences. Anticipate possible problems in transferring ownership of various properties. Consider what happens to debts incurred by the testator. Prepare for possible challenges to the will. Allow sufficient time for this critical planning.

2. Choose and organize the document's content.

Generally, wills include at least the following parts: (a) an introductory clause naming the testator, (b) what to do with anything left over (the residuary clause), (c) general and specific bequests, (d) appointment of personal representatives, (e) a place for the testator's signature (the testimonium), and (f) a place for witnesses to sign, saying that the will was properly executed. Some wills also include trust arrangements, instructions to pay burial expenses, instructions to pay just debts, statements of disinheritance, naming of guardians for minors, and other special clauses. Adding these special clauses can create problems as well as prevent them, depending on the specific circumstances. Therefore, make sure you have researched the ramifications of each provision you decide to include. Check your jurisdiction, rather than relying on this list.

3. Revise the document for ACCURACY and CLARITY.

The will must stand up to legal scrutiny, but the client must also understand all the particulars of the will. Rewrite and revise with these two goals in mind. As when drafting a contract, plan to make many passes through the document, checking for consistent and unambiguous language, specific references, and absence of LEGALESE. Identify all needed TERMS OF ART and make sure that you have explained them to the client. Never include a single word or phrase that you yourself do not understand. You must be able to explain this document to the client, so you must be able to answer any questions about it. Even more important, the document must stand under the ultimate scrutiny of a wide legal and nonlegal AUDIENCE.

4. Adjust language for tone if needed.

Use FLOWERY LANGUAGE only if your client prefers this because of the seriousness of the situation. Never substitute flowery language for PRECISION.

5. POLISH with great care.

Revise painstakingly for grammatical accuracy and correct PUNCTUATION. Mistakes in these areas can translate into thousands of dollars, as the following phrases show.

my daughter's share of the estate

or

my daughters' share of the estate

divided equally among my nephew, my son, my daughter and my son-in-law

or

> **divided equally among my nephew, my son, my daughter, and my son-in-law**

6. At some stage near the end, look again at the will as a whole and make sure it accomplishes your client's wishes and is legally sound. The detail work necessary to drafting can temporarily blind you to the effectiveness of the whole. Before you review the will with the client, reread the document as a whole, so you can again check that the parts knit smoothly into the whole. For more detail about drafting wills, see Mary B. Ray & Barbara J. Cox, *Beyond the Basics, a Text for Advanced Legal Writing,* Chapter 16 (West 1991).

WOMAN, LADY, OR FEMALE?

Use *woman.*

WORD CHOICE

Choose words carefully because every word counts in legal writing. The following list provides an overview of the major concerns involved in effective word choice.

1. Use concrete nouns and specific verbs rather than ABSTRACT NOUNS and general verbs. This will help focus the reader on your main points.

> **The defendant moves to dismiss the case under Fed. R. Civ. P. 12(b)(6).**

rather than

> This concerns the defendant's motion to dismiss.

For related information, see PERSUASIVE WRITING and EMPHASIS.

2. Use TERMS OF ART or KEY TERMS, but avoid unneeded verbiage, such as LEGALESE.

For related information, see PRECISION and READABILITY.

3. Avoid unneeded MODIFIERS; use only modifiers that give the reader essential information.

> **An <u>alcoholic</u> father cannot serve the <u>best</u> interests of <u>his</u> children.**

rather than

> An <u>habitually</u> alcoholic father <u>clearly</u> cannot serve the best interests of his <u>unfortunate</u> children.

For related information, see CONCISENESS and EMPHASIS.

4. Use accurate TRANSITIONS to convey the precise LOGICAL LINKS between ideas.

> The litigation may cost more than the amount our client could recover if she wins the suit. **Nevertheless, she has chosen to pursue her claim.**

rather than

> The litigation may cost more than the amount our client could recover if she wins the suit, and she has chosen to pursue her claim.

5. Use consistent wording. Use the same term for the same concept throughout the document; do not change it just for VARIETY.

> **The defendant proposes that his repair of the water heater was adequate. This proposal, however, ...**

rather than

> The defendant proposes that his repair of the water heater was adequate. This suggestion, however, ...

For related information, see READABILITY and EMPHASIS.

6. Use the most specific term possible. For example, do not say *vehicle* when you mean *school bus*. Use more general terms only when you need to be ambiguous for some reason, or the context requires them.

For related information, see REPETITION and AMBIGUITY, WAYS TO AVOID. For a discussion of situations where you may need to be vague or ambiguous, see EMPHASIS, subsection 2.

7. Make sure all PRONOUNS are unambiguous. For example, if two or more women are mentioned in a text, then *she* is likely to be AMBIGUOUS. Therefore, check each pronoun.

> **Ms. Jones did not ask Ms. Wilson to double-check the amount because Ms. Wilson routinely checked all the amounts listed.**

rather than

> Ms. Jones did not ask Ms. Wilson to double-check the amount because she routinely checked all the amounts listed.

Also make sure each *this* is unambiguous. *This* is the pronoun most likely to cause inaccuracies. *This* can refer to an idea or a thing, one word or a whole sentence; as a result, you must make sure that the reader always knows what *this* means. If there is any question, add the appropriate noun after *this*.

> **The court reasoned that the difference in the age of the fetuses was not the factor determining this issue. This reasoning ....**

For more examples, see THIS and AMBIGUITY, WAYS TO AVOID.

WORDINESS

See CONCISENESS, READABILITY, and MODIFIERS.

WORDY PHRASES

For general information, see CONCISENESS. For a discussion of specific phrases, see AS A MATTER OF FACT; AT THIS POINT IN TIME; AT THE TIME THAT; CLEARLY; FACT THAT, THE; FACT OF THE MATTER, THE; FOR THE PERIOD OF; IN ABSENCE OF ; IN QUESTION; IT IS SAID THAT; IT IS ... THAT; OBVIOUSLY; OF COURSE; POSSIBILITY THAT; PRIOR TO; REALLY; THERE ARE ... THAT; TO ALL INTENTS AND PURPOSES; UNDOUBTEDLY; UNTIL SUCH TIME AS; UTTERLY; and VERY.

WOULD

Would implies that something should have been done but was not in fact done.

The defendant would have set the emergency brake had he not been rushing to assist the people in the other car.

It can be useful to express hypotheticals or dicta.

The assumption would be valid if the defendant had intended to purchase the property, thus showing some interest in its transfer. But he made no such purchase.

But do not use *would* if you mean to imply that something will be done or if you do not want to imply that it should have been done. For related information, see VERBS, AUXILIARY.

WRITER'S BLOCK

See WRITING BLOCK.

WRITING

Writing is a creative act, not a critical one. It is translating your ideas into a first draft. When you reach this stage of the WRITING PROCESS, try to write the whole paper without stopping to correct anything: don't get it right, get it written. At this stage, your ideas need to be translated unencumbered by revision concerns. The critical voice will have time to correct and revise later, in the REWRITING and REVISING stages.

One way to do this is to keep your words flowing onto the page. If you get stuck on a point because you are suffering from WRITING BLOCK, either skip that part or break it down into smaller pieces, but try not to stop. If necessary, even write nonsensical phrases to keep you writing. Keep the creative energy moving throughout the entire writing process. When you finish, leave the draft, even if only for a few minutes. Let it breathe before you begin rewriting. Then, after you finish this first draft, remember that rough drafts, although necessary, are not final drafts. Go on to rewriting and revising.

Other ways to keep writing creative, rather than critical, include changing the medium you use to write, writing before you outline rather than after, and writing a middle section first rather than starting at the beginning. For example, you might try dictating rather than typing the first draft. You might write a draft as a means of brainstorming before you outline. Or you might begin by writing about the point most familiar to you.

There is no one right method to use; the right method is the one that helps you get the job done.

WRITING BLOCK

Writers may suffer from writing blocks at any stage of the WRITING PROCESS, but usually the cause is that the writer (1) feels overwhelmed by the task, (2) believes the written product must be perfect, (3) feels he or she is inadequate to the task, or (4) experiences all of the above. Almost all writers suffer from writing blocks occasionally; some endure them on almost every project.

Fortunately, writing blocks can usually be overcome by using any or all of the following techniques.

1. Divide and conquer.

Break the writing task into littler steps, and keep breaking it down until you see a step that does not look overwhelming. Never mind if the list of steps is pages long; each of those steps may go rather quickly. These small tasks may be boring, but they will not be overwhelming. Then order the steps and start doing them. To gain a sense of progress, check each one off as you finish. For example, if the whole project seems overwhelming, start by listing all the tasks involved, such as *research*, *outline*, *write*, *rewrite*, and *revise*. Then break each one of those down. You might break *outlining* into *list all possible points*, *group those points somehow*, *summarize each group*, and *decide which group goes first, second, etc.* If this is still overwhelming, you can break *list all possible points* into *list all points that make sense to me*, *list all points mentioned in any analogous cases*, and *identify all points that occur on both lists*.

2. Start somewhere else.

If you are stuck on a particular writing task, set it aside and work on something else. For example, if you cannot decide how to organize the facts section of a memo, leave it and begin writing the issues. If you cannot write the issue, try writing the conclusion. You need to complete many tasks in any writing project, but you need not complete them in any particular order.

3.   Separate the essential from the desirable.

You do not have time as a legal writer to make everything perfect; you must focus on quality and adequacy, but not on perfection.   For example, when REVISING, focus on essentials, such as ACCURACY and clear ORGANIZATION, before you tackle desirables, such as EMPHASIS and TONE.   For help doing this, see WHEN TO STOP and WRITING PROCESS.

If you are finding it hard to get started, see GETTING STARTED. If you are having trouble finishing, see WHEN TO STOP.   For related information, see WRITING PROCESS and PERFECTIONISM.

WRITING PROCESS

The writing process is the entire creative, analytical, and critical experience that begins with an idea or assignment and ends with a finished document.   The process incorporates five stages: PREWRITING, WRITING, REWRITING, REVISING, and POLISHING.   You can save a great deal of time and become much more effective throughout the process by understanding each of these stages.   The key to success in streamlining your writing process is breaking it into pieces and fixing one piece at a time.   Over a period of time, your techniques will work themselves into a smooth process that is strictly yours.   The following suggestions can help you make your writing process both more efficient and more effective.

1.   Identify at which point in the process you are most comfortable. You might like research but hate revising, or you might feel comfortable correcting mechanics and citations but very uncomfortable in writing.   You are probably fastest at that point where you feel most comfortable, so you can allocate the least amount of time for that step when you establish your schedule.

2.   Identify where you are least comfortable.   For example, you may dislike revising because you are not sure of grammatical structures and how to fix them, so you get bogged down in miscellaneous questions. Or you may dislike writing because you feel each sentence has to be perfect before you go on to the next one.   Separate the creative from the critical and decide if you are trying to do too many things at once. Then allocate the greater amount of time for those least comfortable.

3.   Start with your deadline and work backwards toward the starting point, setting interim deadlines for each stage of the process.   By allocating the most time for the place that is the least comfortable and the least time for the place that is the most comfortable, you can set a more realistic schedule that you will be more likely to meet.

4.   Break each writing task into subtasks and give your full attention to each subtask.   For example, if you dislike revising, try not to revise all of every sentence all at once.   Instead, revise the whole text once

just for SENTENCE STRUCTURE. Then revise it again just for TRANSITIONS. Revise a third time for accurate WORD CHOICE. These small read-throughs can be done in between other tasks during the day. Additionally, by giving them your full concentration, you can complete them effectively in a minimal amount of time.

5. Concentrate on breaking bad habits by conquering one bad habit in each major writing assignment that you have. For example, if you are weak on TRANSITIONS, concentrate primarily on transitions in the revision process on one paper. Keep working on transitions on subsequent assignments until you feel comfortable with them; then move on to another bad habit. For example, you might concentrate next on better SENTENCE STRUCTURE.

The following example shows one way you might organize your writing process and interim deadlines for an appellate brief.

Notice of appeal filed	**April 16**
Read Record For Error	**April 18**
Preliminary Issues	**April 22**
Research Strategy for Each	**April 22**
Research	**April 22–May 2**
Select Arguments	**May 5**
Complete research	
OUTLINING	**May 6**
Draft POINT HEADINGS	
Fill in holes by doing more research	
WRITING (Dictating) First Draft	**May 8–9**
Issue I to sec'y	**May 12**
Issue II to sec'y	**May 13**
Issue III to sec'y & Conclusion	**May 14**
REWRITING	
Issue I	**May 19**
Issue II	**May 20**
Issue III	**May 21**
Pull Table of Cases, Contents	**May 21**
REVISING	
Issue I	**May 22**
Issue II	**May 23**
Issue III	**May 26**
POLISHING	**May 28**
Point Headings	
Cites	
Text	
Tables	
Conclusion	
Brief Due	**June 2**

WRITING PROCESS CHECKLIST

Your writing process is personal and so should be comfortably fitted to your own temperament and work habits. Yet your process must also be productive and effective, building on your strengths while compensating for your weaknesses. Thus you may want to evaluate your process and adapt changes that improve it. Re-evaluate it periodically; you will probably find yourself outgrowing your old process as your experience and skill increase. To implement changes, work through your process chronologically because improvement in the early stages of the process may change the later stages automatically. The following checklist follows this chronology, and offers some questions to ask yourself as you complete this evaluation.

1. PREWRITING

(a) Have I taken effective notes from the assigning attorney, supervisor, or other AUDIENCE?

(b) Have I written down the issues or thesis statement? Do I return to these periodically to keep my FOCUS, SCOPE, and PURPOSE clear?

(c) Have I written down a research strategy that is designed specifically for this project, my experience level, my client's budget, and my library's resources? See RESEARCH STRATEGY CHART.

(d) Have I scheduled and recorded interim and final deadlines?

(e) Have I researched effectively?

(1) Have I followed my strategy and adjusted where necessary?

(2) Have I allotted time for each step, each source?

(3) Have I avoided becoming overly rigid, instead adapting my research strategy when the sources dictate a change?

(f) Have I taken effective notes?

(1) Have I recorded the date of the source and of my notes?

(2) Have I written down the full citation, in whatever form required in the final version of this document?

(3) Have I related my source's information to my issues?

(4) Have I kept track of sources so I will not repeat any research?

(5) Have I updated my sources?

(g) Have I avoided tangential research?

(h) Have I organized effectively for the readers?

(1) Have I translated my research into an outline?

(2) Have I connected my research with my outline in my notes, with cross-references or other indicators?

(3) Have I tried other organizational approaches, so I know I chose the best approach for this project?

(4) Have I checked with my AUDIENCE about the overall organization, where appropriate?

2. WRITING

(a) Have I organized my materials for ready access?

(b) Have I focused on just getting it written, rather than editing while I write?

3. REWRITING

(a) Have I made final decisions about the theme or message?

(b) Does the organization match this message?

(1) Is this ORGANIZATION still working? Does it match PURPOSE, SCOPE, and the AUDIENCE's needs?

(2) Does the structure accurately reflect the substantive law's structure as it applies to my client's facts?

(c) Have I filled in all holes?

(1) Have I included all needed facts? For details, see BACK-GROUND FACTS, EMOTIONALLY SIGNIFICANT FACTS, LEGALLY SIGNIFICANT FACTS.

(2) Have I included all relevant issues?

(3) Is the law correct and complete? Have I included all relevant constitutional provisions, statutes, cases, regulations?

(4) Have I supported my arguments with appropriate authority?

(5) Have I included strengths and weaknesses of all arguments? Have I explained why some legal points are stronger than others?

(6) Have I included all steps in the reasoning?

(7) Have I connected the points in my analysis throughout the document so that the audience understands the reasons I reached my conclusions?

(d) Have I omitted tangents?

(e) Have I checked the order?

(1) Are threshold issues first?

(2) If writing persuasively, have I organized the issues in the most persuasive order?

(f) Have I conveyed the organization clearly?

(1) Have I used POSITIONS OF EMPHASIS well?

(2) Have I kept my VOICE consistent throughout the text?

(g) Have I included prediction, remedy, result, practical steps, where appropriate?

4. REVISING

(a) Have I mercilessly critiqued my own writing?

(b) Have I incorporated all criticisms systematically throughout the paper, changing PARAGRAPH STRUCTURE, SENTENCE STRUCTURE, WORD CHOICE, TONE, and overall STYLE appropriately?

(c) Have I ensured ACCURACY?

(1) Is the content accurately stated? Could any points be misinterpreted because of ambiguity? See AMBIGUITY, WAYS TO AVOID.

(2) Are TERMS OF ART and KEY TERMS used correctly? See SUBJECT–VERB COMBINATIONS.

(3) Is each PARAPHRASE used accurately?

(4) Is the name and status of each party correct?

(d) Is small-scale organization working well?

(1) Are PARAGRAPHS internally logical?

(2) Do TOPIC SENTENCES give the overall message of each paragraph, usually appearing at the beginning of the paragraph?

(3) Are sentences ordered logically?

(4) Do clear and precise TRANSITIONS connect paragraphs and sentences?

(5) If used, do headings, when read apart from the text, present the skeleton of the document?

(e) Is the document readable for any prospective AUDIENCE?

(1) Are subjects and verbs close together?

(2) Is there more ACTIVE VOICE than PASSIVE VOICE?

(3) Are sentences free of unnecessary NOMINALIZATIONS?

(4) Are unnecessary MODIFIERS eliminated, such as *clearly* and *obviously?*

(5) Is SENTENCE LENGTH appropriate throughout? Is it varied for interest?

(6) Are lists clearly structured? See LISTS, STRUCTURE OF.

(7) Are sentences free of unnecessary PREPOSITIONS and prepositional phrases?

(8) Is the text generally concise? See CONCISENESS.

(9) Is the text free of excessive quotations, string citations, and JARGON?

(f) Is the POINT OF VIEW unified throughout the document?

(g) Is VOICE unified throughout the document?

(h) Is the TONE and level of formality appropriate and consistent?

5. POLISHING

(a) Have I divided the paper into sections to be polished one at a time?

(b) Have I checked all cites according to the BLUEBOOK, or the assigned source for citations?

(1) Are CITATIONS complete, accurately ordered, and accurately punctuated?

(2) Are PINPOINT CITES used for specific propositions, rules, holdings, quotes?

(3) Are case names spelled accurately?

(4) Are page numbers and years accurate?

(c) Have I run a computer check for spelling, or checked spelling myself?

(d) If I ran a computer check for spelling, have I also read each section separately for wrong words and words left out? For techniques, see POLISHING.

WRITING TO OTHER ATTORNEYS

You can often relax your correspondence style when writing to these readers, because they share your profession and may be personal friends. You might include more legal terms and fewer definitions. Or you might dwell on analysis and interpretation more than description. Just do not relax so much that you lose ACCURACY or CLARITY.

The first subsection below outlines how writing for legal readers differs from writing for nonlegal readers in WORD CHOICE. The second and third subsections discuss how your TONE and level of detail may vary when writing to different legal readers.

1. Word choice.

You may use technical legal vocabulary and TERMS OF ART more frequently with legal readers, as a shorthand way of expressing a point. But use a term only when you are sure the reader will understand it readily. For example, you might write the following sentence to another attorney in your firm.

Our client was probably a holder in due course because he took the check in good faith without any notice.

In contrast, the following sentence, written for your client, would use fewer legal terms.

> **You are probably entitled to keep the check because you had no idea that Mr. Hobbs had forged it.**

2. Tone.

Tone conveys your relationship to the reader and the situation, apart from the literal content of the document. As that relationship varies, your tone will vary. For example, when writing an informational memo to a close colleague, you may use more personal phrases or more informal, direct language.

> **Jane, I'll be writing my first brief for Judge Chang next week. I know you have a lot of experience in his court—got any helpful hints about writing for him?**

In contrast, you may use a more formal tone to a colleague you do not know.

> **Dear Mr. Morton:**
>
> **You and I will be representing the plaintiffs in Carolet v. McCartney. To coordinate our strategies, I would like to meet with all the plaintiffs' attorneys. I suggest that the meeting be during the second week in February. Please call my office this week to confirm a mutually convenient time.**

3. Level of detail.

Include as much detail as your reader needs to understand your point. Beyond that, adjust the level of detail to make your reader comfortable. Some attorneys prefer that all memos be kept as brief as possible, while others feel uneasy if not fully informed of the thought or research behind a point. If possible, ask the reader whether he or she wants copies of cases, short summaries of legal conclusions, or the middle route of the standard memo. Ask if he or she has good examples you can review. The more you learn about your reader, the more effective, efficient, and comfortable writing will be for you. For related information, see AUDIENCE.

YET

Yet, a conjunction, can be used in legal writing to indicate *nevertheless* or *despite this*. Like *but*, *yet* can be an effective transition to show contrast and opposing ideas.

> **Plaintiff still claims my client is guilty, yet he has failed to meet his burden to prove that guilt.**

> **Most commentators rely on this reasoning. Yet none has provided adequate authority on which to base that reasoning.**

For related information, see CONJUNCTIONS; TRANSITIONS; and CONNECTIONS, MAKING THEM.

YOU

Use the second person, *you*, to address the audience directly, when appropriate. For example, you may use *you* in GENERAL CORRESPONDENCE LETTERS where you want to sound like you are talking to a person face to face.

You asked that I write to you about the legal consequences of your automobile accident.

You may also use *you* in consumer contracts or other situations when you need to tell someone clearly what he or she can or cannot do.

If you choose to change attorneys, you must notify . . . .

Do not, however, use *you* in BRIEFS to the court or in other situations when you are not addressing a person directly. In those situations you are focusing on the argument itself, rather than on a one-to-one conversation.

Equity requires consideration of this issue.

rather than

You must consider this issue.

†

Notes

Notes

Notes

Notes

Notes